Transforming the Internal World and Attachment

Transforming the Internal World and Attachment

Volume I: Theoretical and Empirical Perspectives

Geoff Goodman

JASON ARONSON
Lanham • Boulder • New York • Toronto • Plymouth, UK

Published by Jason Aronson
An imprint of Rowman & Littlefield Publishers, Inc.
A wholly owned subsidiary of The Rowman & Littlefield Publishing Group, Inc.
4501 Forbes Boulevard, Suite 200, Lanham, Maryland 20706
http://www.rowmanlittlefield.com

Estover Road, Plymouth PL6 7PY, United Kingdom

British Library Cataloguing in Publication Information Available

Library of Congress Cataloging-in-Publication Data

Goodman, Geoff.
Transforming the internal world and attachment / Geoff Goodman.
p. cm.
Includes bibliographical references and index.
ISBN 978-0-7657-0538-9 (cloth : alk. paper) — ISBN 978-0-7657-0748-2 (electronic)
1. Psychotherapy. 2. Attachment behavior. I. Title.
RC480.G659 2010
616.89'14—dc22 2009034588

∞™ The paper used in this publication meets the minimum requirements of American National Standard for Information Sciences—Permanence of Paper for Printed Library Materials, ANSI/NISO Z39.48-1992..

Printed in the United States of America

To Valeda Frances Dent

I found a bond of love
That takes away the fear
A bond that spans the differences
Between me and you
—excerpted from our wedding vows

Even though I walk through the darkest valley, I will fear no evil, for you are with me. . . . Therefore my heart is glad and my tongue rejoices; my body also will rest secure, because you will not abandon me to the grave. . . . You will fill me with joy in your presence.
—Psalms 23:4; 16:9–11

Contents

Figures and Tables

FIGURES

TABLES

Acknowledgments

No one ever told me the second book would be immeasurably harder to write. I never imagined that the entire process would actually yield three books (see also Goodman, *Therapeutic Attachment Relationships*). That was not my intention. Part of the difficulty had to do with the fact that I chose a topic that fell just outside my zone of proximal development. I have established a career writing about the intergenerational transmission and development of psychopathology from an attachment perspective, so turning my attention to the implications of attachment theory for psychotherapy process proved challenging. I overcompensated for my lack of expertise by reading everything I could on the subject matter, reflecting on this accumulated body of knowledge, and writing about it from an outsider's point of view. What helped me most was the treatment of two adult control cases to fulfill the training requirement for my psychoanalytic certificate. I have received outstanding supervision on these two cases from three persons—Phyllis Sloate, John Rosegrant, and William Greenstadt. The learning curve was steep, and the lessons I learned at their feet will stay with me for a lifetime.

The other part of the difficulty had to do with all the other things simultaneously going on in my life: preparing to graduate from my psychoanalytic training program, applying for grants from the International Psychoanalytical Association and the American Psychoanalytic Association, applying for board certification from the American Board of Professional Psychology (ABPP), preparing from scratch a new doctoral-level course on object relations theories, leaving my group practice to fly solo, and planning my wedding. I have two pieces of advice to those of you planning to write a book: (1) be sure you have time to write it, and (2) be sure to check the word count in your book contract *before* you start writing.

I need to make several additional general acknowledgments related to the realization of this book. Valeda Dent, associate university librarian for research and instructional services at Rutgers University, reproduced in Microsoft Word and PowerPoint all the tables and figures presented in this book (unless otherwise noted); read the entire manuscript for comprehension as well as grammar, spelling, and punctuation; located and obtained reference materials; and obtained the copyright for the painting she selected for the book cover (which she also designed). Other than me, no one was more dedicated to the realization of this book than she was. Valeda's fingerprints are all over this document. Now we can turn our attention to writing our wedding vows! I hope that process will not take quite as long. Marcia Miller, chief librarian at Weill Cornell Medical College, is simply the best librarian in psychiatry and psychology I have ever worked with. Long ago, I lost count how many times Marcia went out of her way to locate a reference, suggest other references that she thought might be helpful to me, or simply show an interest in what I was writing about. I wish all of you had a librarian of this caliber at your disposal, because you would understand the depth of my gratitude if you did. Dustin Kahoud, my faithful research assistant, alphabetized the entire reference section, a massive undertaking that he accomplished with a smile. Ian Rugg undertook the arduous task of creating two separate reference sections for volumes I and II and checking the text citations against the reference sections. Sushma Meka alphabetized all the journal articles and book chapters I cited and neatly placed them into folders. The Psychodynamic Research Listserve cofounded by Mark Hilsenroth and Andrew Gerber has educated me about many of the issues tackled in this book. I thank Mark and Andrew for inviting me to join. Darryl Vorhees produced the high-resolution digital image of the painting for the book cover. Cristin O'Keefe Aptowicz of the Artists Rights Society assisted with the use of copyrighted art. Julie Kirsch and Jessica Bradfield provided steady editorial leadership at Jason Aronson. Patricia Stevenson, production editor, does Jason Aronson proud with her meticulous work, which makes me sound almost like a professional writer. Leonard Rosenbaum, who also worked with me on my first book in 2002, provided the skill and precision necessary to compile the author and subject indexes.

I will acknowledge the other persons to whom I am indebted chapter by chapter. For chapter 3, my colleague at Yeshiva University, Louise Silverstein, generously provided me with her expertise on qualitative research methods. She and her Yeshiva collaborator, Carl Auerbach, first enlightened me about the benefits of conducting qualitative research in two workshops they conducted at Long Island University in April 2007 and July 2008.

For chapter 4, I want to acknowledge my mentor and friend Jim Hull (and the Weill Cornell Medical College Institutional Review Board) for granting me access to the transcribed psychotherapy sessions of five patients diagnosed with borderline personality disorder. I also need to acknowledge Jim's role as one of my highly esteemed clinical supervisors in transference focused psychotherapy (TFP) during my two-year postdoctoral psychology fellowship on Otto Kernberg's inpatient unit dedicated to the treatment of patients diagnosed with borderline personality disorder. These data were collected with a grant from the Fund for Psychoanalytic Research of the American Psychoanalytic Association awarded to James W. Hull (principal investigator) and to John F. Clarkin and Frank E. Yeomans (co-investigators). I secured additional funding for the completion of this study from the International Psychoanalytical Association Research Advisory Board (Celeste Schneider, co-investigator) and the Long Island University Research Fund. Stuart Ablon, Raymond Levy, and Tai Katzenstein provided timely consultation on the use of the psychotherapy process Q-set (PQS). Stuart Ablon graciously shared with me his PQS prototype data. I appreciate the assistance of the two groups of expert raters who supplied me with their PQS ratings of the prototypical psychotherapy sessions characterizing TFP and dialectical behavior therapy (DBT). Giacomo Buscaino, Keiha Edwards, Silvia Fiammenghi, Anna Marantidis, and Alana Tappin provided expert coding assistance. Mary Beth Brady faithfully transcribed all 127 session audiotapes. Joyce McFadden, Jennifer Neill, and Freddy Aguero took time out of their hectic work schedules to assist with the retrieval of hospital records. Finally, I want to thank the four therapists and five patients for their participation in this study.

In preparation for writing chapter 6, I attended two workshops—the first on coding for reflective functioning (RF) taught by my colleague and friend Howard Steele, and the second on conducting mentalization-based treatment (MBT) taught by Anthony W. Bateman and Peter Fonagy. These two workshops together provided me with a feel for mentalization not captured by their writing on the subject. I appreciate their willingness to mentalize this construct for me in person. Figure 6.2 was reproduced in Microsoft PowerPoint by whiz kid Heather Carpenter-Sarmiento and modified for chapter 6 by Valeda Dent. Figures 7.1 and 7.2 were reproduced in Microsoft PowerPoint by the creative and clever Natasha Bhagwanani, who is currently attending Stony Brook University. Various patients served as incidental clinical illustrations, for which I am grateful.

On a personal note, I wish to thank Marshall Silverstein, my esteemed colleague and friend at Long Island University, for offering constant encouragement and support in all my academic endeavors. Marshall is a true friend. Celeste Schneider has recently become a collaborator on various research projects. I am grateful to have her in my corner as an astute researcher, therapist, and friend. Dr. Marvin Markowitz, my psychoanalyst for the past thirteen years, has helped me to transform my own internal world and attachment. A simple "thank you" is not enough for showing me how to carry my emotional burden. My dear Uncle Ed and Aunt Fran urged me to include them in my acknowledgments, and why not? Throughout the entire process, they supported me with regular e-mail messages asking me about the book's progress. Finally, I want to acknowledge my mother, Carol Steele Goodman, and my late father, George David Goodman, for making me who I am. Everything begins and ends with them.

Chapter One

Introduction

> Come to me, all you who are weary and burdened, and I will give you rest.
>
> Matthew 11:28

> Carry each other's burdens.
>
> Galatians 6:2

The year was 1987, and I was a twenty-six-year-old doctoral student at Northwestern University. I wanted to find out for myself what psychoanalysis was all about. I had read about it and studied it in school, and found it gently pulling me toward it, like the moon's gravitational pull on the ocean tides. I had heard that psychoanalytic institutes offered low-fee psychoanalysis to persons who agreed to work with their candidates, and thought this might be the most economical way of experiencing psychoanalysis for myself.

I contacted an institute near my university dormitory on Chicago's North Lake Shore Drive and scheduled an appointment with one of their candidates. I have no memory of this call. I do remember the initial appointment. The analyst's office was located in a red brick office building just a couple of blocks away. I took the elevator to the office and took a seat in the waiting area. A short, slender, white-haired, middle-aged woman with an accent I could not place opened the office door at the appointed time. I tentatively walked into her office as she motioned that I take a seat on the black leather couch. She sat down in a chair across from where I was seated and asked me why I was coming for treatment. I explained that I was a doctoral student in clinical psychology and had an interest in learning more about psychoanalysis. I then launched into some pervasive family problems that were making me feel depressed at the time. The analyst listened intently as I shared with this stranger some hidden details of my life—details I had never shared with anyone else before. I began to share with her some childhood experiences that bore directly on the family problems and noticed that the theme of feeling depressed kept emerging in my narrative.

At some point, the analyst stopped me and asked, “Are you in pain?” No one had ever asked me that question before. I thought, what a strange yet compassionate question to ask! This person actually cared about whether I was in pain. I had never thought that I was in pain—only that I felt sad about some things in my life that I had always kept to myself. That question has haunted me ever since. It has helped me to frame what it is that patients come to see me for: relief from pain. Of course, patients come to see me for many reasons, but I believe that this is the chief reason. Why else would people spend all that time and money and risk the shame of exposure to talk to someone they have never met?

Thus began my first four-times-per-week psychoanalysis, my experiential introduction to the world of Freud. More important, though, it was my experiential introduction to the world of caring—the experience of someone listening to my emotional burdens and, during a forty-five-minute session, taking them on herself. For me, psychotherapy is the daily carrying of another person’s burdens. Only when the person is ready to carry his or her own load do we give them back. This idea about psychotherapy resonates with the work of Bion (1962, 1967), who compared the therapist to a temporary container of the patient’s unbearable emotional states. The therapist is responsible for detoxifying these states—making them easier to carry—and then returning them to the patient, who is now ready to carry them with the help of loved ones in his or her daily life. This is how the therapist transforms the internal world and attachment.

The idea to write this book series coalesced in 2005. I had been invited to contribute a chapter to an edited book on attachment interventions for children. Simultaneously, a colleague of mine invited me to consult with her on an early intervention project in which she was giving videotaped feedback to biological mothers of children in foster care. In June of 2005, I attended a presentation by Tai Katzenstein (2005) at the ninety-fourth annual meeting of the American Psychoanalytic Association in Seattle titled, “Validating Change: Empirical Methods and Clinical Work.” Tai presented her work with Stuart Ablon at Harvard Medial School. She had used the Psychotherapy Process Q-Set (PQS; Jones, 2000) to examine therapist adherence to cognitive-behavioral, interpersonal, and psychodynamic process in seventeen treatments of patients diagnosed with panic disorder. She found that cognitive-behavioral process was most characteristic of these treatments, but psychodynamic and interpersonal process was significantly correlated with outcome.

The PQS grabbed hold of my fascination. I had been aware of Q-sort methodology since the publication of Waters and Deane's (1985) attachment Q-set. I loved its idiographic properties—the fact that Q-sort methodology could yield a profile of a single person independent of normative data. It seemed ideally suited for characterizing the uniqueness of the therapeutic relationship. I had also had my own personal experience with Q-sort methodology, having developed my own Q-sort to measure the quality of the caregiver's mental representations of his or her child (Goodman, 2005). Thus, I was familiar with this clever methodology and wanted to learn more about how Enrico Jones had applied it to the assessment of psychotherapy process.

The fact that I had just begun work in the fall of 2004 on two control cases to fulfill the training requirement for my psychoanalytic certificate also stimulated my interest in psychotherapy process. Both patients fell in the spectrum of borderline psychopathology but had different personality features. I chose two supervisors who advocated different approaches to these patients' treatment but who both helped me navigate an effective psychoanalytic process with both patients (see volume II, chapters 2 and 3). All these experiences coalesced into a decision to write about psychotherapy from the perspective of someone who has spent his entire professional career writing about the intergenerational transmission and development of psychopathology from an attachment perspective. Initially, I questioned mounting such an ambitious project because psychotherapy process and outcome research represented a shift away from the familiar area of psychopathology, my comfort zone. Did I want to risk writing a book series outside this comfort zone? When I stopped to think about it, however, I realized that I had entered the field of clinical psychology to help people. I studied psychopathology so that others could use this knowledge to help people. Thus, it made sense to apply my knowledge of psychopathology to psychotherapy.

This two-volume book, therefore, is a sequel to my first book, *The Internal World and Attachment*. Unfortunately, so little actual research has been conducted on psychotherapy process and outcome from an attachment perspective that this sparse literature has left me to speculate about what the application of attachment theory to psychotherapy research would look like. The theoretical treatise published several years ago by Peter Fonagy and his colleagues (Fonagy, Gergely, Jurist, and Target, 2002) represents a giant leap in this direction because it laid the foundation for a psychotherapeutic approach to psychopathology grounded in contemporary attachment research. Bateman and Fonagy's (2004b) treatment manual explicating an attachment-informed psychotherapy for patients diagnosed with borderline personality disorder represents one application of this theoretical work. Yet we still know so little about the mysteries of the consulting room.

In this two-volume work I offer some tentative ideas about these mysteries. Specifically, I review and discuss three theories about what makes psychotherapy effective across forms of treatment, treatment settings, and diagnostic categories: mindfulness, mentalization, and psychological mindedness. In a third book, *Therapeutic Attachment Relationships: Interaction Structures and the Processes of Therapeutic Change* (Goodman, in press), I review and discuss a fourth theory—the therapeutic attachment relationship.

In volume I of this two-volume work (*Transforming the Internal World and Attachment: Theoretical and Empirical Perspectives*), I offer some provisional hypotheses about therapeutic effectiveness and suggest some ways of testing these hypotheses empirically. In advocating an empirical approach to understanding the mysteries of psychotherapy, I share Seligman's (1991) concern that "the quantification of complex theoretical systems [in empirical research] here threatens to confine a critical topic that has emerged from a very rich clinical and theoretical soil to a relatively narrow arena" (p. 128). I believe, however, that this empirical work is a risk worth taking. With sophisticated assessment instruments such as the PQS that measures psychotherapy process, the Social Cognition and Object Relations Scale–Global (SCORS-G; Westen, 1995) that measures quality of object relations, the Adult Attachment Interview (AAI; George, Kaplan, and Main, 1996) that measures attachment organization, and the Reflective Functioning Scale (RFS; Fonagy, Target, Steele, and Steele, 1998) that measures reflective functioning, researchers can approach psychotherapy process and outcome research with a level of complexity and nuance not available to psychotherapy researchers of previous generations.

Without this research, the entire field of psychotherapy is in crisis. Managed-care companies are withholding reimbursements for treatments not considered "empirically supported." From 1995 to 2005, psychiatric hospital referrals to outpatient treatment after discharge dropped from 90 percent to 80 percent. In that same period, referrals from primary care physicians to psychotherapy dropped between 40 percent and 50 percent as physicians increasingly prefer the putative benefits of psychopharmacotherapy. This diminishing demand for the services of mental health professionals has produced a 15 percent decrease in reimbursement fees from managed-care companies and the federal government, while inflation has exceeded 15 percent in the same period (Cummings, 2008). Those of us who care about the survival of all forms of psychotherapy, and particularly those treatments with a smaller evidence base such as psychodynamic therapy, need to support efforts to test the therapeutic effectiveness of these treatments. Otherwise, to paraphrase Rosenzweig (1936), we might all go the way of the dodo bird, even as we fight among ourselves about which form of treatment is superior. It reminds me of the black-on-black violence of apartheid-era South Africa: we end up displacing our frustrations onto each other as the pharmaceutical companies and managed-care companies laugh all the way to the bank.

Instead of engaging in horse races with randomized controlled trials (RCTs), we need to establish an empirical basis for the therapeutic effectiveness of all forms of treatment. I am suggesting moving beyond examining common factors such as the therapeutic alliance (Wampold, 2001) and turning our collective attention to common factors that psychotherapy researchers often erroneously promote as specific factors. Perhaps these so-called specific factors produce therapeutic change regardless of the brand-name treatment packages through which they are typically delivered. These specific factors might also work better for particular groups of patients with specific problem areas such as affect dysregulation and impulsivity. Clinical practice guidelines need to promote empirically informed change processes rather than horse-race winning treatment packages. If we as a community of therapists want our craft to survive, we must submit it to empirical scrutiny before the pharmaceutical drug lords strip it away from us.

Volume I is divided into two broad sections. In part I, "Processes of Therapeutic Change in the Context of Psychoanalytic and Attachment Theories," I discuss the need to turn away from brand-name treatments and a treatment outcome mentality and turn our collective attention instead to the processes of therapeutic change that promote both symptomatic and structural change. In part II, "Specific Factors Related to Common Processes of Therapeutic Change," I discuss three specific factors that might be effective across forms of treatment: mindfulness, mentalization, and psychological mindedness. I consider part II to contain the central message of volume I: to direct the reader to the effective ingredients in therapeutic processes rather than to treatment outcomes such as symptom reduction, which often proves fleeting in follow-up studies (Westen, Novotny, and Thompson-Brenner, 2004a).

In volume II (*Transforming the Internal World and Attachment: Clinical Applications*), I discuss the application of processes of therapeutic change from both psychodynamic and attachment perspectives. I close volume II with a most unusual application of therapeutic processes to four clinical interviews I conducted with two political refugees.

I will now provide an overview of the chapters contained in volume I. Chapters 2–4 form part I. In chapter 2, I discuss empirically derived processes of therapeutic change in the context of two-person psychoanalytic and attachment theories. While many transformations have taken place within psychoanalysis since Freud, the two most profound transformations have taken place within clinical theory and clinical epistemology. The writings of Sandor Ferenczi (1932/1988), Melanie Klein (1946), and Theodor Reik (1948) heralded a paradigm shift from a one-person psychology—with the analyst acting as a blank screen for the patient's fantasies and projections—to a two-person psychology—with the patient's transference and therapist's countertransference mutually influencing each other to create a co-constructed, dyadic experience. This shift to a two-person psychology was accompanied by theoretical challenges to the time-honored status of interpretation as the uniquely effective ingredient of therapeutic change. For example, Alexander and French (1946) reasoned that it was not the interpretation of unconscious conflict but rather a corrective emotional experience that produced such change. Attachment research has been instrumental in establishing an empirical foundation for a two-person psychology with its emphasis on the quality of the therapeutic relationship—conceptualized as an attachment relationship—as a uniquely effective ingredient of therapeutic change (see also Goodman, in press).

Simultaneously with these developments, the case study method, used since Freud as evidence to support hypotheses formulated within clinical theory and practice, gradually yielded to empirical assessments of clinical evidence such as RCTs and, more recently, naturalistic single-case and multiple-case research designs. One fallacy associated with retrospective accounts of clinical data, underscored by Eagle (1995, 1996, 1997), is that causality cannot be inferred; however, psychoanalysts use these data to support their preferred hypotheses of therapeutic change but never exclude them from further consideration. As a result, the case study method has produced a proliferation of clinical theories in psychoanalysis that sounds more like a cacophony of voices than the Mormon Tabernacle Choir. The case study has also become a vehicle for showing off the therapist's brilliance rather than a laboratory for understanding his or her failures. The public humiliation of presenting a failed treatment to one's colleagues appears to have outweighed the benefits of learning about what does *not* work in treatment. Thus, the case study upstages the patient as the hero in the psychotherapy drama (Duncan, 2002).

Moreover, as some attachment theorists (e.g., Lyons-Ruth, 1991) have suggested, psychoanalysts have mislabeled certain forms of psychopathology (e.g., autism, schizophrenia, depression) as fixations at or regressions to early stages of normal development rather than as complex transactions between genetic endowment and factors of psychosocial risk and resilience that influence systems as diverse as neuroendocrine functioning and affect regulation. In his seminal article that challenged six assumptions that undergird most object relations theories, Westen (1990) signaled a new era of psychoanalytic inquiry that would no longer rely exclusively or even peripherally on case-report methodology: "Future developments in object relations theory . . . are not likely to come exclusively or even primarily from the consulting room. That era has passed" (p. 689).

In chapter 2, I argue that just as the flaws of case study methodology have been exposed, so too have the flaws of RCTs—the empirical evidence of clinical efficacy preferred by managed-care companies. Manualized treatment packages, which RCTs are designed to test and support, are particularly attractive to managed-care companies because they both reflect an interest in the bottom line—outcomes at the expense of knowledge about the processes by which these outcomes are achieved. Unfortunately, RCTs so narrowly define the patient population under study, the therapist competence and adherence to the treatment manual, the range of clinical interventions prescribed by this manual, and symptomatic improvement that the resulting treatment bears no resemblance to what therapists in the real world actually do with real, comorbidly diagnosed patients (see Westen et al., 2004a). Others (e.g., Ablon and Jones, 1998) have demonstrated the failure of the medical RCT model to identify the uniquely effective ingredients of these treatment packages. I argue that RCTs represent a regression to a zero-person psychology in which the therapist's state of mind with respect to the patient and the patient's state of mind with respect to the therapist are unceremoniously taken out of the equation—which refutes the latest findings from attachment and psychotherapy process research that support a two-person psychology.

New methods for assessing processes of therapeutic change based on empirical observation have been recently developed (e.g., Jones, 2000). Psychotherapy researchers have begun to apply these new empirical methods of observation to assess both time-honored and new theories of therapeutic change to determine if and how psychotherapy process and outcome are related to each other. Based on this new information, I present the most discriminating features of psychodynamic and cognitive-behavioral therapy and discuss how these processes occur across different forms of treatment. For example, a psychodynamic therapist sometimes discusses cognitive themes, while a cognitive-behavioral therapist sometimes makes a transference interpretation (Ablon and Jones, 1998). Interestingly, in this study, the psychodynamic processes identified in cognitive-behavioral therapy were significantly correlated with symptom improvement, while in my study of transference focused psychotherapy with patients diagnosed with borderline personality disorder (chapter 4), psychotherapy process in which the therapist exerts control in the session was significantly correlated with symptom improvement. Based on these studies, we can draw the tentative conclusion that therapists—even those whose adherence to a particular form of treatment is being closely monitored—apply a combination of techniques that produce an array of psychotherapy processes that reflect influences from several different forms of treatment. I argue that just as a football team needs to adjust its offensive plays to the specific team it is playing against, so too do therapists need to adjust their techniques to the patient's needs rather than conform to the standard plays laid down in the treatment manual playbook.

In chapter 2, I also introduce the concept of interaction structure (Jones, 2000)—the observable manifestation of the repetitive transference-countertransference matrices between the therapist and the patient. Interaction structures are enactments that originate in the interaction between both participants, not just one. Therapist and patient reciprocally influence each other at every moment in every session. The PQS is specifically designed to assess these interaction structures in psychotherapy sessions. What seems to be largely missing from the psychotherapy literature is the application of attachment theory to the concept of interaction structures that form in therapeutic relationships. I propose that interaction structures are determined in part by the attachment histories of the two participants. If attachment organization is viewed on a continuum between deactivating and hyperactivating strategies for regulating affects (Goodman, 2002; Kobak, Cole, Ferenz-Gillies, Fleming, and Gamble, 1993), then the therapeutic relationship can be conceptualized as a finite set of interaction structures defined by each member's pattern of affect regulation and dysregulation. Psychotherapy-process researchers could conduct studies in which the attachment organizations of both therapist and patient are assessed prior to the onset of treatment to determine which combinations of patterns of affect regulation are responsible for the finite number of interaction structures that form over time in the therapeutic relationship. These interaction structures are also determined by the phase of treatment, the diagnostic features of the patient (and therapist), and the treatment setting (e.g., inpatient or outpatient). Knowledge about which therapist-patient pairs produce the most desirable therapeutic processes and outcomes will ultimately serve to make psychotherapy more effective.

In chapter 3, I discuss the reasons why it is critical that rank-and-file therapists become involved in the research enterprise of discovering what works for whom. The field of psychotherapy research is just beginning to shift away from RCTs of manualized treatment packages to naturalistic studies specifically designed to identify the uniquely effective ingredients of therapeutic change within specific therapeutic dyads, recently made possible by powerful and easy-to-use observational techniques such as the PQS used in single-case or multiple-case research designs. Psychoanalytically informed therapists as well as therapists who practice other forms of treatment can begin to assess processes of therapeutic change in their own and others' clinical work using the new observational tools now available. These change processes can then be empirically associated with assessments of structural as well as symptomatic outcome to determine not which treatment packages work for which patients, but rather which processes of therapeutic change work for which therapeutic dyads interacting in the real world. Empirical instruments that assess change processes such as the PQS or the RFS could be applied to session transcripts of rank-and-file therapists in quantitative or qualitative single-case or multiple-case research designs.

Chapter 3 enables psychoanalysts, psychoanalytic institutes and outpatient clinics, attachment and psychotherapy process and outcome researchers, clinical and developmental psychologists, and graduate students to catch this new *Zeitgeist*—to begin to observe their own clinical work more systematically in a discipline-wide effort to identify the developmental and contemporaneous processes of therapeutic change within specific therapeutic dyads and across diagnostic and attachment categories of patients. I envision a grassroots movement of therapists that could empirically ground the uniquely effective ingredients of psychoanalysis and its related therapies, and rekindle a more widespread interest in psychodynamic approaches to treatment.

There are obstacles to this grand movement, however. I present the results of a study I conducted with 101 members of 2 well-known psychoanalytic institutes in the New York area. In this study, I asked these study participants to disclose whether they audio- or video-record their sessions and how they would feel about doing so. I also asked them to identify their reasons for not wanting to record their sessions. Assessing therapists' attitudes toward session recording is important because only a verbatim rendering of sessions can provide accurate information about psychotherapy process. I learned that psychoanalysts feared that recording sessions would influence the psychotherapy process in general and the patient's self-disclosures in particular. I argue that if psychodynamic therapy and its derivatives are to enter the twenty-first century, they must be ready to put their preferred change processes to the test. The task will require rank-and-file therapists to record their psychotherapy sessions to preserve an accurate and objective series of observations of the interactions between the therapist and the patient. Therapists' attitudes about the recording of psychotherapy sessions must change before we put ourselves in the position of being able to call psychodynamic therapy "empirically informed" (Westen et al., 2004a, p. 658).

In chapter 4, I apply the ideas presented in the previous two chapters to a naturalistic, quantitative single-case research study with five cases. These five cases were psychiatrically hospitalized patients diagnosed with borderline personality disorder receiving three-times-per-week transference-focused psychotherapy (TFP; Clarkin, Yeomans, and Kernberg, 2006). I sought to answer two broadly defined questions: (1) what goes on in a prototypical TFP session, and (2) what goes on in an actual TFP session? To answer these two questions, I used the PQS to assess psychotherapy process. A group of three expert raters in TFP process arranged the one hundred PQS items to characterize an ideally conducted session of psychotherapy that adheres to the therapeutic principles of TFP. As a point of comparison, a group of three expert raters in dialectical behavior therapy (DBT; Linehan, 1993a) process also arranged these same items to characterize an ideally conducted session of DBT. Stuart Ablon at Harvard Medical School had also provided me with psychodynamic, cognitive-behavioral therapy (CBT), and interpersonal therapy (IPT) prototypes for comparison. I found that, as expected, TFP process was positively correlated with psychodynamic process, while DBT was positively correlated with both CBT process and psychodynamic process. I concluded that the psychodynamic process identified as overlapping with DBT process could partially account for the effectiveness of DBT with BPD patients (Linehan, 1993a).

I also led a team of doctoral students to code the 127 psychotherapy sessions of the 5 BPD patients. I learned that four interaction structures characterized the therapeutic relationships of these five treatments. Interestingly, each therapist-patient dyad presented a different combination of interaction structures, illustrating that the psychotherapy process of each of these five treatments was unique. Just as methane, propane, methanol, propanol, ethanol, glucose, carbon dioxide, carbon monoxide, and water are all unique substances that share the same three elements—hydrogen, oxygen, and carbon—so too did these five therapist-patient pairs develop unique relationships that shared the same interaction structures. I also discovered that the TFP-trained therapists in this study adhered more to CBT process than to TFP process and that CBT process was correlated with symptom improvement, particularly the therapist's exertion of control in session. It appears that these therapists adjusted their technical approaches "on the fly" to facilitate symptom improvement rather than rely on the received "wisdom" of a treatment manual. In spite of TFP proponents' recent emphasis on TFP's enhancement of mentalization (Clarkin et al., 2006), I found no evidence that TFP actually enhances mentalization properties. I argue that additional naturalistic studies on therapeutic relationships treating patients grouped by problem area (e.g., affect dysregulation, impulsivity) and attachment organization are needed to determine which interaction structures and adherence to which change processes touted by brand-name treatment packages (i.e., psychodynamic, CBT, IPT, TFP, DBT) are most highly correlated with treatment outcome among these groups. Clinical practice guidelines could then be written around empirically informed change processes rather than treatment packages that claim to do one thing but actually do another (e.g., Ablon and Jones, 1998).

Chapters 5–7 form part II. In chapter 5, I discuss mindfulness as an effective ingredient of therapeutic change. Mindfulness is paying attention to one's immediate internal and external experience in the here and now. It is as simple—and as difficult—as that. As a thirteen-year veteran of the practice of free association in my personal psychoanalysis, I can tell you that the practice of mindfulness is extraordinarily difficult. Mindfulness treats all mental phenomena as symbols that easily move into conscious awareness and back out again. One does not identify with one's feelings but rather observes them as they pass by like parade marchers. Although originating in Buddhist philosophy 2,500 years ago, mindfulness has become integrated into the so-called third wave (S. C. Hayes, 2002, 2004) of behavior therapies such as DBT. I argue that mindfulness is conceptually similar to the psychoanalytic construct of free association—the fundamental rule of psychoanalysis to say whatever comes into one's mind (Freud, 1912a). I also compare mindfulness to the construct of mentalization, popularized in the psychoanalytic literature by Fonagy (e.g., 1991). I suggest that mindfulness and mentalization are conceptually similar but that mindfulness lacks an interpersonal component necessary for an effective therapeutic process. I argue that mindfulness is nevertheless therapeutically effective because patients are exposing themselves to unbearable feelings during the practice of mindfulness in the presence of a nonjudgmental therapist who metabolizes these feelings and returns them to the patient in a tolerable form (Bion, 1962, 1967). Mindfulness might be helpful to those patients who identify with their feelings but perhaps unhelpful to those patients who experience detachment from their feelings.

In chapter 6, I discuss a relatively new construct in the psychoanalytic literature: mentalization. Mentalization and reflective functioning (RF), defined as the operationalization of mentalization processes, refer to understanding the mental states of oneself and others and the connections between them and the behaviors of oneself and others. Mental states include all mental phenomena such as thoughts, feelings, beliefs, wishes, fears, fantasies, and attitudes. These mental states both influence and are influenced by the mental states of others and their related behaviors. The origin of mentalization is derived from mother-infant and father-infant attachment research (Fonagy, 1991; Fonagy, Gergely, et al., 2002; Fonagy, Steele, Steele, Moran, and Higgitt, 1991; Fonagy and Target, 1997) and has inspired a new treatment model for BPD that has been subjected to preliminary empirical testing (Bateman and Fonagy, 2004a, 2004b).

A child spends the earliest years of his or her life experiencing three modes of mentalizing: psychic equivalence, pretend, and reflective. In psychic equivalence mode, internal reality and external reality are confused. In pretend mode, internal reality is dissociated from external reality. In reflective mode, the child understands that internal reality and external reality are symbolically linked, neither identical nor unrelated to each other. Relying on my own ideas regarding attachment quality and personality organization developed in my first book (Goodman, 2002), I develop a model of mentalization that contextualizes this construct within a theory of personality organization and attachment. This model contains three elements: (1) the psychic equivalence mode shares conceptual overlap with Klein's (1946, 1952) paranoid-schizoid position and with a hyperactivating attachment strategy (Kobak et al., 1993); (2) the pretend mode shares conceptual overlap with Kernberg's (1970, 1975, 1984, 1986a, 1986b) pathological grandiose self and with a deactivating attachment strategy (Kobak et al., 1993); and (3) the reflective mode shares conceptual overlap with Klein's (1933, 1937, 1952) depressive position and with a secure attachment strategy (Kobak et al., 1993). I then apply the construct of mentalization to the traditional stages of psychosexual development as conceptualized by Freud (1905b, 1940). Specifically, I argue that excessive libidinal arousal in any of these three stages can interfere with mentalization and disrupt the parent-child attachment relationship. Parent-child interventions need to focus on improving the mentalization capacity of both parties (see also volume II, chapter 7).

In chapter 7, I discuss a third effective ingredient of therapeutic change, psychological mindedness. I trace the evolving definition of psychological mindedness from its inception at the Menninger Clinic in 1956 (Wallerstein and Robbins, 1956) to a contemporary definition from the cognitive-behaviorist Grant (2001). Most psychodynamic therapists use some variation of Farber's (1985) definition that psychological mindedness is the disposition to reflect on the meaning and motivation of the mental states and behaviors of oneself and others. Over time, psychological mindedness has increasingly encroached on mentalization's conceptual territory. I compare three constructs—mindfulness, mentalization, and psychological mindedness—and propose that mentalization encompasses the conceptual components of both mindfulness and psychological mindedness and adds another component—understanding the mutual influence of the mental states of oneself and others and the likely behavior following from these mental states. I conclude that the construct of mentalization has probably rendered the construct of psychological mindedness outdated. Nevertheless, I suggest how to reconceptualize psychological mindedness as a two-dimensional construct that includes both patterns of affect dysregulation from attachment theory—hyperactivating and deactivating. I offer two illustrations of low psychological mindedness from the AAI.

Transforming the Internal World and Attachment: Theoretical and Empirical Perspectives (volume I) comes at a time when psychodynamically oriented therapists are becoming acquainted with attachment theory and the ambitious project to ground psychoanalytic theory and practice in empirical research and neuroscience findings. These ideas are just beginning to find publication in the psychoanalytic journals. No book has formally introduced the psychoanalytic audience to empirically derived processes of therapeutic change (e.g., interaction structures, mentalization) within a theoretical framework grounded in psychoanalytic and attachment theories. The twofold shift to a two-person psychology and an empirical assessment of clinical evidence has created fertile ground for the psychoanalytic community to examine the compelling evidence provided by attachment research to support key aspects not only of its theories of development and psychopathology (Goodman, 2002) but also of its processes of therapeutic change.

It has been twenty-one years since I walked into my first psychoanalyst's office for the first time and heard the words, "Are you in pain?" To understand the pain of another person, we must be open to experiencing that pain—in all its sadness, rage, desperation, and ultimately helplessness. This book attempts to understand the process of bearing the burden of pain in our patients and in ourselves in the therapeutic encounter.

Part One

PROCESSES OF THERAPEUTIC CHANGE IN THE CONTEXT OF PSYCHOANALYTIC AND ATTACHMENT THEORIES

Chapter Two

Empirically Derived Processes of Therapeutic Change in the Context of Two-Person Psychoanalytic and Attachment Theories

> Future developments in object relations theory . . . are not likely to come exclusively or even primarily from the consulting room. That era has passed.
>
> D. Westen, "Towards a Revised Theory of Borderline Object Relations: Contributions of Empirical Research"

> Many, if not most, of the major clinical innovations in the history of our field have come from clinical practice. . . . We should take advantage of one of the greatest resources at our disposal, clinical practice, which can and should serve as a natural laboratory for both generating and testing hypotheses.
>
> D. Westen, C. M. Novotny, and H. Thompson-Brenner, "The Empirical Status of Empirically Supported Psychotherapies: Assumptions, Findings, and Reporting in Controlled Clinical Trials"

As therapists, we say and do things to get our patients to change how they think, how they feel, and how they behave toward themselves and others. What we say and do to produce this change depends on many variables, including our theoretical understanding, our clinical training, and our own experience of the world and our encounters with others over the course of our lives. As researchers, we say and do things to get our therapists to change how they think, how they feel, and how they behave toward themselves and their patients. What we say and do to produce this change also depends on many variables, including our theoretical understanding, our clinical training (occasionally), and our own experience of the world and our encounters with others over the course of our lives.

From this perspective, researchers are intervening in the psychotherapy practices of therapists and, as I will show, are wielding enormous influence on how therapists intervene in the lives of their patients. One might even say that therapist intervention mediates the relation between researcher intervention

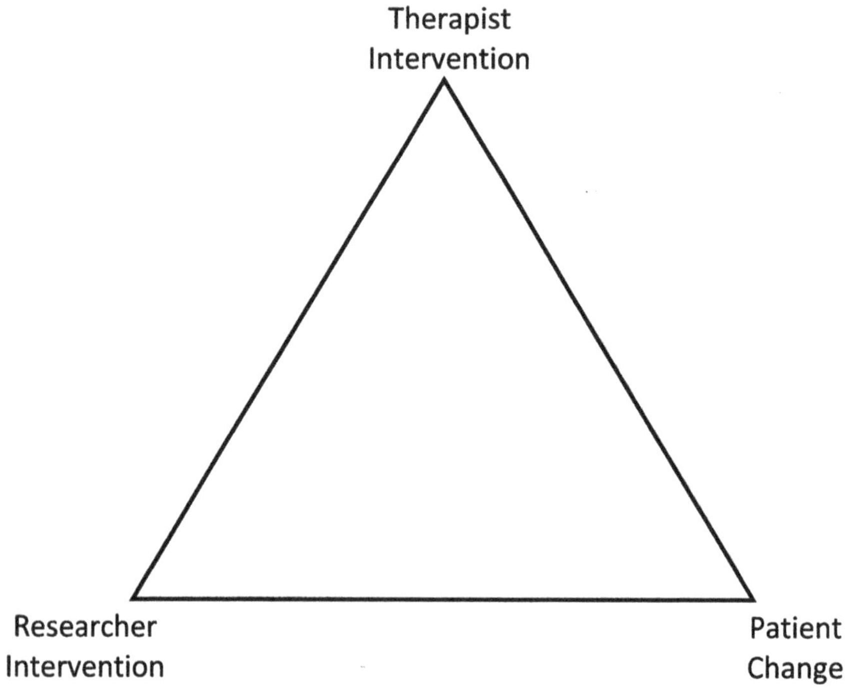

Figure 2.1. Mediational Model of Therapeutic Intervention

and patient change (see figure 2.1). Researchers, therefore, from this perspective, have a profound indirect impact on the state of therapeutic change.

Drew Westen and his colleagues (Westen, 1990; Westen et al., 2004a) have drawn our attention to the paradox of the therapist's reliance on the researcher to provide new theoretical insights into human nature and its capacity to change, and the researcher's reliance on the therapist to provide clinical insights that can be suitably tested against the reality of the consulting room. On the surface, this mutual relationship would not seem paradoxical at all. Therapists and researchers, each with their own specialized knowledge base and skill set, would work together to implement "what works for whom" (Fonagy, Target, Cottrell, Phillips, and Kurtz, 2002; Roth and Fonagy, 2005).

Unfortunately, this sentiment is indeed paradoxical because therapists and researchers have marked their own distinctive professional territories. And it appears that researchers, coveting their neighbors' land, are trying to subjugate its inhabitants—the therapists—for their own purposes. Researchers are instructing therapists to follow their manuals, which spell out for the therapist *how* to say and do things to get their patients to change. The therapist then becomes a technician, or a research assistant, carrying out the researcher's procedural protocol. Or the researcher is like a "master chef" (typically a franchise restaurateur with some prior culinary experience) who creates the recipe for a new dish that everyone wants to try. What makes the recipe so delicious, he or she would have us believe, is the secret sauce—the ingredient that sets this new dish apart from all the others. The master chef then tests the new dish in focus groups to verify that, indeed, this new recipe appeals to a certain demographic, and trains chefs in franchise restaurants all over the country to follow the recipe and make this new dish. Of course, this new dish was specifically created to appeal to a particular demographic, so it can be served only to people who meet these stringent demographic criteria. These local chefs quickly become bored serving dishes following recipes created by others. They find that the patrons of their local restaurants do not meet the demographic criteria to be served the new dish, nor does it particularly appeal to them. After a time, the local chefs forget how to create their own recipes, so they are stuck serving only the dishes created from the master chef's recipes. Eventually, everyone develops gastrointestinal cramps.

There was a time when the roles were reversed. Researchers were the second-class citizens, and therapists were the kings of the land. In discussing the introduction of psychology into the medical school curriculum, Freud (1919b) lamented the fact that psychology lectures "were based on academic psychology or on experimental psychology (which deals only with questions of detail), [and] were unable to . . . bring [the student] any nearer to the problems of life in general or to those of his profession" (p. 172). Later in his career, Freud responded negatively to any attempts to explore psychoanalytic theory by laboratory methods (Rosenzweig, 1997). For example, Freud (1933a) commented on a colleague's initial attempts to publish treatment effectiveness data on psychoanalysis: "Statistics of that kind are in general uninstructive; the material worked upon is so heterogeneous that only very large numbers would show anything. It is wiser to examine one's individual experiences" (p. 152). Freud led by example, publishing a number of case studies in his career. His most famous case studies included Katharina (Freud, 1893), Dora (Freud, 1905a), Little Hans (1909a), the Rat Man (1909b), and the Wolf Man (Freud, 1918). Psychoanalysts began to use case studies to illustrate an intervention or series of interventions, make theoretical observations, or underscore particular diagnostic features of the patient.

THE CASE STUDY METHOD

The method of using case studies to illustrate and elaborate on the theoretical, diagnostic, and clinical knowledge base of psychoanalysis remained in vogue for a number of years. As the experimental psychology of Edward Thorndike and John Watson and others gained ascendancy in academic circles, with their operational definition of independent and dependent variables, assessment instruments, and procedural protocols, the publication of case studies declined. By 1971, Anna Freud (1971) remarked that case studies had mostly disappeared from the psychoanalytic landscape. From 1969 to 1982, no case studies appeared among the most frequently cited articles in the psychoanalytic journals of that era (Klumpner and Frank, 1991). Concurrent with this disappearance, research methodologists (Campbell and Stanley, 1963; Kiesler, 1971) were busy broadcasting the shortcomings of the case study method—specifically, its lack of validity and reliability. While acknowledging the case study method's ability to generate hypotheses, Kiesler (1971) nonetheless proclaimed that the case study method "has little place in the confirmatory aspect of scientific activity" (p. 66).

These shortcomings are indeed manifold. As traditionally conceptualized, the case study method can never be used to test hypotheses, only to generate them. According to its opponents, the experimental method—with its techniques of random selection and random assignment of subjects to experimental and control groups and its measurement of operationalized constructs administered to subjects in a standardized manner—is necessary to test hypotheses. With the case study method, the reliability of the therapist/reporter's observations could be subject to distortion. Retrospective accounts of clinical data contain not only distortions of memory (on the parts of both the patient and therapist) but also sampling biases (Eagle, 1995, 1996, 1997). Therapists listen to the narratives of patients who have traversed deviant developmental pathways and then extrapolate backward in time to a "normal" developmental phase without any evidence that others who exhibit similar psychopathology would have had similar childhood experiences, or that others who have had similar childhood experiences would one day exhibit similar psychopathology (Goodman, 2002).

A case study report or model of psychopathology seldom qualifies its conclusions by acknowledging these assumptions. For example, the rapprochement subphase of separation-individuation is presumed to be a universal phenomenon (Mahler, Pine, and Bergman, 1975), yet the observations on which this developmental theory are based have been challenged on the grounds of sampling biases (Lyons-Ruth, 1991). This error led some theoreticians (e.g., Kernberg, Selzer, Koenigsberg, Carr, and Appelbaum, 1989; Mahler et al., 1975) to assume that borderline psychopathology—often characterized by profound ambivalence resembling infantile rapprochement conflicts with the caregiver—represents the inevitable outcome of a fixation at or regression to this early period (Westen, 1990).

The clinical data presented in a case study, even if factually accurate and contextualized within a normative population, could be open to multiple interpretations. The patient could be responding to many variables acting upon him or her both within and outside the therapist-patient relationship—variables not directly under the therapist's control. The fact that a single case is presented preempts comparison with another case or cases. Replication of the results, a hallmark of the experimental method, is impossible with the case study method because the therapeutic dyad never steps into the same river twice. The case study has also become a vehicle for showing off the therapist's brilliance rather than a laboratory for understanding his or her failures. The public humiliation of presenting a failed treatment to one's colleagues appears to have outweighed the benefits of learning about what does *not* work in treatment. Thus, the case study upstages the patient as the hero in the psychotherapy drama (Duncan, 2002). These are just a few of the shortcomings of the case study method underscored by its critics.

The case study method seems simple enough: the therapist reports what happened, how he or she helped this happen, and how he or she understood how this occurred (Bernstein, 1992). Ideally, anyone who closely follows the therapist's narrative would be equipped to try out the same intervention with the same kind of patient under similar circumstances. The case study narrative, however, contains much more than a report of the facts of a case. The narrative also unavoidably contains unconscious aspects of the transference and countertransference that other methodologies would be unlikely to yield. The case study method, therefore, offers a unique glimpse into the psychotherapy process—in spite of the aforementioned limitations. For this reason, Tuckett (1993) declared, "Rather than a weakness . . . the analyst's narrative [could] be considered the quintessential aspect of a psychoanalytic clinical presentation. . . . The analyst says more than he knows. . . . The presentation, including the selection [of clinical process], is part of the material offered to the audience" (p. 1184). In this sense, a case study contains valuable clinical information available in no other form.

Michels (2000) has suggested that the case study "reflect[s] something . . . different from what is captured by a verbatim transcript, much as a painting reflects a landscape in a way other than does a map or an aerial photograph" (p. 363). If you want to experience the emotional impact of a starry night, would you turn to a photograph or to van Gogh's 1889 painting? The painting captures the emotional essence of an evening under the stars in Saint-Rémy-de-Provence in a way a photograph never could because the painting bends external reality to conform to an internal emotional compass that tells us what *feels* real instead of what *is* real. In this sense, the painting is a more accurate rendering of a starry night than any photograph could ever be. Similarly, one could argue that the narrative canvass of the case study method depicts psychotherapy process more accurately than any historically accurate information yielded by the experimental method.

Some theoreticians within the psychoanalytic community champion the view that only a hermeneutical approach to psychotherapy process can yield truly meaningful information (e.g., Green, 1996; Schafer, 1996). Under this view, any quantification of clinically meaningful constructs results in their distortion. Heisenberg's uncertainty principle—that the measurement of the location of an electron changes its momentum by an uncertain amount—illustrates this view at the subatomic level. The mere act of observing the psychotherapy process changes that process in unpredictable ways. The only persons who can "know" anything about the psychotherapy process are the two participants. According to Schafer (1996):

> [The idea of historical truth] assumes an ideal observer who adheres to no point of view at all, has no shaping and selective preconceptions, values, and methods of observation, and so is in a position of total disinterestedness and is invulnerable to critique from any other point of view. . . . There are ongoing objectivist research projects producing statistically reliable results [to which] the narrativist could reply that not every analyst accepts the relevance of this research to the clinical process. These clinicians are particularly attentive to the necessary artificialities of method, the simplification of variables, the probabilistic nature of the findings as regards reliability and validity, and often the banality of the findings themselves. . . . There do seem to be good grounds to question whether such research is essential to clinical work and its betterment. (pp. 249, 251)

Even as Schafer questioned scientific authority, one might also question where Schafer gets his own narrative authority. Nevertheless, the relational school of the psychoanalytic community has largely embraced this point of view. Its proponents have advocated "throwing away the book" (Hoffman, 1994, p. 187) and have compared the therapeutic relationship to "a snowflake. . . . No two are alike. Nor are any two patient-analyst pairs" (Kantrowitz, 2001, p. 403). This narrative point of view—that systematic, "objective" observation of the psychotherapy process is severely limited in its ability to teach us anything new or confirm what we already know about the psychotherapy process—itself seems severely limiting.

Over the past thirty years, quasi-experimental research paradigms in infant research such as the strange situation (Ainsworth, 1979; Ainsworth et al., 1978) and the face-to-face still-face paradigm (Tronick, Als, Adamson, Wise, and Brazelton, 1978) have helped to shape contemporary ideas of affect regulation and interactional mental representations critical to contemporary theories about the therapeutic relationship (e.g., Fonagy, Gergely, et al.,

2002; Goodman, 2002; Tronick et al., 1998). The crippling methodological limitations inherent in the case study method cast doubt on its ability to tell us anything beyond the psychotherapy process of the two people in the consulting room. The case study method establishes what is possible between the two participants, not what is common (Hilliard, 1993). Given the advantages and disadvantages associated with the use of case study methodology, I am proposing a moderate position in which neither narrative truth, encapsulated in the case study method, nor historical truth, encapsulated in the experimental method, can be elevated to a privileged status in the discovery or confirmation of truth. Both methodologies can provide distinct, yet overlapping, areas of knowledge about the psychotherapy process.

RANDOMIZED CONTROLLED TRIALS (RCTS): A ZERO-PERSON PSYCHOLOGY

As psychoanalysis gradually moved from a one-person psychology (almost exclusive focus on the patient's mental state) to a two-person psychology (focus on the mental states of both therapist and patient; Aron, 1990), the privileged status of interpretation as the "secret sauce" of therapeutic change in psychoanalysis came under suspicion. The relationship between the therapist—now viewed as a subjective agent in the psychotherapy process—and the patient began to draw the attention of a number of writers (e.g., Alexander and French, 1946; Racker, 1968; Reik, 1948) as a uniquely effective ingredient of therapeutic change in its own right. This paradigm shift from a one-person to a two-person psychology, and the related shift from interpretation as the *sine qua non* of therapeutic change to alternative modes of therapeutic change such as a corrective emotional experience (Alexander and French, 1946), significantly complicated our understanding of the therapeutic relationship and the processes of change that emerge from this relationship.

In the post-Sputnik era, American society became obsessed with the ability of science to improve our lives. Laundry detergents were "scientifically proven" to remove stains. Intelligence quotient (IQ) tests could reliably identify mental defectives and make the workforce more efficient (J. M. Blum, 1978). With the advent of powerful psychotropic medications in the 1950s, society could deinstitutionalize the chronically mentally ill and return them to society as productive members (Borus, 1981). These medications were empirically tested for their effectiveness using randomized controlled trials (RCTs). Subjects would be randomly assigned to two groups. One group—the active or experimental condition—would receive the medication being tested, while the other group—the control condition—would receive a placebo such as a sugar pill. A baseline measurement of the symptoms that the medication was designed to treat would be taken. In a stringent variation on this research design, both the physician and patient would be blind to whether the pill being administered is the medication or the placebo (double-blind procedure). After an appropriate length of time that would allow the active medication to take effect, a second measure of the symptoms would be taken. If no significant differences between the experimental and control groups on the symptoms measured were found at baseline (virtually guaranteed by random assignment), but significant differences between the two groups existed on the symptoms measured at the end of the trial, then one would naturally conclude that the drug was effective for treating the symptoms under study.

This medical model of testing the effectiveness of medications for the treatment of psychiatric symptoms was eventually applied to psychotherapy treatment. Subjects are randomly assigned to two groups: an experimental group designated to receive the psychotherapy treatment under study, and a control group designated to a waiting list for treatment at some later time or a "treatment as usual" (TAU) condition—the treatment usually available to a patient with similar symptoms. Baseline and endpoint measures are again taken to determine symptom levels, and significant differences are tested. If significant differences between the two groups exist on the symptoms measured at the end of the psychotherapy trial, then one would naturally conclude that this brand of psychotherapy is effective for treating the symptoms under study.

It does not take a Sputnik scientist to notice the differences between applying the RCT model to testing medication efficacy and applying the RCT model to testing psychotherapy efficacy. I will elaborate on these differences later. For now, I want to focus on the administration of the treatment in these two applications of the medical RCT model. In the first application, a physician dispenses a pill to the patient to ingest. The physician does not know whether this pill is the medication or a placebo. Presumably, the mode of therapeutic action is the interaction between the active chemical compound contained within the pill and certain neuroreceptors in the brain. In the second application, a therapist dispenses a psychotherapy treatment to the patient. The therapist (and perhaps the patient) knows whether this treatment is active or TAU. Presumably, the mode of therapeutic action is the interaction between the therapist and the patient. In the first application, it does not really matter how the physician dispenses the pill as long as the patient takes the proper dosage. The physician can hand the pill to the patient in the palm of her hand or make a fade-away jump shot into the patient's mouth. Meanwhile, the patient can take the pill with water, swish it around her mouth before swallowing, or do a little jig in celebration of the physician's successful jump shot. The method of dispensing the pill has no impact on its effectiveness. In the second application, however, how the therapist dispenses the psychotherapy treatment constitutes the mode of therapeutic action as well as how the patient receives the treatment.

In the first application of the medical RCT model, only one variable actually varies between the experimental and control groups: the pill (active medication or placebo). In the second application, three variables actually vary between the two groups: the treatment (active or TAU), the therapist's behavior (infinite variability), and the patient's behavior (infinite variability). The scientific method dictates that if more than one variable is varying between the experimental and control groups, then one cannot conclude that a significant difference exists between them because of the variable of interest (i.e., the treatment). Furthermore, because these three variables are inextricably intertwined, experimental control becomes hopelessly compromised.

To solve this problem, researchers who use RCTs to test psychotherapy efficacy have decided to turn the therapist and patient variables into constants so that only the treatment varies between the experimental and control groups. Thus, how the therapist dispenses the treatment must be strictly regulated and controlled. Intricately detailed treatment manuals that spell out for the therapist exactly what to do with the patient in every session have become the norm (Westen et al., 2004a).

Similarly, patients randomly assigned to the RCT experimental and control conditions are carefully selected, again to regulate and control any variation. The thinking seems to be that if we can limit the therapist's behaviors to those directly related to the treatment intervention, and simultaneously limit the patient's symptoms to those that the active treatment was designed to target, then we can hold the therapists and patients constant and vary only the treatment between the experimental and control groups. The unfortunate outcome, however, is a homogenized treatment, an unrecognizable caricature of psychotherapy. The field has moved from the one-person psychology of Freud to a two-person psychology with its complexity, subjectivity, and messiness, and, finally, to a zero-person psychology disemboweled of any semblance of humanity.

The obsession with boosting the internal validity of RCTs extends to additional requirements for the therapists and patients who participate (see Chambless and Ollendick, 2000; Goldfried and Wolfe, 1998; Jones, 2000; Kendall, Marrs-Garcia, Nath, and Sheldrick, 1999; Nathan, Stuart, and Dolan, 2000; Seligman, 1995; Westen et al., 2004a). Patients must not have comorbid *DSM-IV* (American Psychiatric Association [APA], 2000) diagnoses, not have been treated effectively in previous studies, be willing to be audio- or video-recorded and complete self-report questionnaires, and accept the therapist who has been randomly matched to them. Therapists must have specialized training in the active treatment to be dispensed (i.e., competence), endure a rigorous supervision process to verify that the active treatment is being dispensed properly (i.e., adherence), conduct the treatment using a manual with a specified length (typically, ten to twenty sessions), and restrict their interventions to only the symptoms the active treatment is designed to target.

In empirical psychology, changes in internal validity do not necessarily imply changes in external validity and vice versa. For example, self-report measures of children's depression seem to have high external and internal validity (Goodman, Bass, Geenens, and Popper, 2006; Kovacs, 1992), yet self-report measures of children's hyperactive/inattentive and oppositional behaviors have high external validity but questionable internal validity (Chi and Hinshaw, 2002; Hart, Lahey, Loeber, and Hanson, 1994; Loeber, Green, Lahey, and Stouthamer-Loeber, 1989, 1991). When it comes to the application of the medical model in the form of RCTs to psychotherapy research, however, the consequences of boosting internal validity in the service of external validity are catastrophic (Duncan, 2002). A manualized, RCT-tested psychotherapy treatment is unrecognizable as an interaction between two persons. Even therapists who use manualized, RCT-tested treatments in private practice make critical modifications to the prescribed intervention strategies and treatment length (Westen et al., 2004a). Researchers conducting an RCT of medication efficacy expect physicians in the community to prescribe the brand-name medication at the prescribed dosage; however, psychotherapists in the community routinely dispense off-label modifications of the prescribed "medication" and "dosage." Because two-person interaction *is* the treatment, the therapist and patient variables must vary from the manualized script. Thus, the application of the medical RCT model to test psychotherapy efficacy is profoundly flawed. I am suggesting that those members of the psychoanalytic community who have bought into the RCT hype (e.g., RCTs for transference-focused psychotherapy [TFP; Clarkin, Yeomans, and Kernberg, 1999, 2006] and mentalization-based treatment [MBT; Bateman and Fonagy, 2004b]) have taken the first steps away from a two-person psychology toward a brave new zero-person psychology.

Kazdin (2006) has compiled a list of criteria for a psychotherapy treatment to achieve brand-name status: (1) comparison with waiting list or TAU control group, (2) statistical significance between the active treatment and the control group, (3) two or more RCTs documenting these effects, (4) replication of findings from outside the originator's research group, (5) well specified patient sample (inclusion and exclusion criteria and psychiatric diagnosis), and (6) the use of a treatment manual. This list reveals additional problems with the application of the medical RCT model to psychotherapy efficacy research. Briefly, I want to highlight the additional problems inherent in using this research method. My discussion of these flaws will overlap with some of my earlier points.

Although RCTs follow a rigorous scientific methodology for testing psychotherapy efficacy that renders the psychotherapy process unrecognizable, the treatment manuals are based more on alchemy than on science. As Westen and his colleagues (Westen et al., 2004a) revealed, these recipe books represent the researchers' best guess about what works for whom. The manuals themselves are created prescientifically and often do not elaborate on the psychotherapy process. Thus, when an RCT supposedly demonstrates the efficacy of a particular brand-name treatment, no one knows precisely how the treatment actually worked. Was it the witch's wart or the eye of toad? To paraphrase Otto von Bismarck, treatment manuals are like sausages; it is better not to see them being made.

Even when therapists are trained to adhere to these mysteriously concocted treatment manuals, adherence checks do not necessarily guarantee that the RCT therapists are adhering to the specified treatment. For example, psychodynamic process quantitatively assessed in manualized cognitive-behavioral therapy for unipolar depression was significantly correlated with positive outcome on four different measures, while cognitive-behavioral process was significantly correlated with positive outcome on only one measure (Ablon and Jones, 1998; see also Jones and Pulos, 1993). According to Ablon and Jones (2002), "The use of [psychodynamic] techniques not prescribed by the cognitive behavior therapy manual probably escaped the detection of adherence checks; nevertheless, they proved to be significant correlates of patient change" (p. 776). Recently, Ablon and Marci (2004) have explained this escape in detection as a flaw in the procedures for checking treatment adherence. While adherence checks focus on the content of the therapist's interventions (e.g., targeting irrational beliefs), the actual psychotherapy process (e.g., authoritative, didactic therapist providing cognitive strategies to compliant, submissive patient) is overlooked.

In these two studies (Ablon and Jones, 1998; Jones and Pulos, 1993), some of the trained, supervised RCT therapists were properly dispensing the content of the active treatment (cognitive-behavioral therapy) but simultaneously engaging in a psychodynamic process (neutral therapist drawing attention to feelings of active patient). Some researchers (Castonguay, Goldfried, Wiser, Raue, and Hayes, 1996) have even shown that adherence to cognitive therapy for depression is inversely proportional to treatment outcome: the therapists attempted to correct problems in the therapeutic alliance by increasing treatment adherence, further straining the therapeutic alliance and thereby dooming the outcome. This phenomenon led Ablon and Jones (2002) to this conclusion:

> It may in fact not be possible to control, to a sufficient degree, how treatments are actually conducted. . . . It is not possible to draw conclusions about what promotes patient change, let alone establish the validity of a treatment's underlying theory of therapy. . . . The usefulness of the clinical trials [RCT] model for validating particular psychological therapies must be questioned. (p. 782)

Freud (1913b) compared psychoanalytic process to a chess match in which "the infinite variety of moves which develop after the opening defy any such description" (p. 123). Adherence checks make sense for RCT patients taking a pill; they do not make sense for two persons interacting with each other.

This rigid need of researchers to control the chess moves to guarantee a favorable outcome can compromise the therapist's clinical judgment. The treatment manual of cognitive-behavioral therapy (CBT) for bulimia nervosa places limited emphasis on interpersonal problems to minimize treatment overlap with interpersonal psychotherapy (IPT; Westen et al., 2004a). Thus, a CBT therapist participating in an RCT must focus the patient on his or her bulimic symptoms even if the patient discloses current suicidal ideation because his or her partner just left the relationship. Any deviation from the treatment manual compromises not only treatment adherence but also clinical judgment and clinical safety—a phenomenon described as "the methodological tail wag[ging] the clinical dog" (Westen et al., 2004a, p. 642).

I am making the case that RCT-tested psychotherapy treatments—far from representing the *sine qua non* of clinical practice—can actually pose safety risks to patients due to their rigid, dogmatic devotion to treatment purity. In an RCT testing medication efficacy, the physician might discontinue a patient experiencing side effects while taking a medication and perhaps offer a different one. Philosophical differences, however, might interfere with a researcher's referral of a refractory patient to a treatment of a different theoretical orientation. I cannot imagine Marsha Linehan, the founder of dialectical behavior therapy (DBT), referring a refractory borderline patient to Otto Kernberg for a trial of TFP. Such is the political climate in scientific circles these days.

Empirically supported or evidence-based treatments (ESTs) have acquired brand names (e.g., TFP, MBT, DBT) in part because they were successfully tested using the medical RCT model and shown to produce more positive outcomes than a control group of patients on a waiting list or in TAU (Kazdin, 2006). Researchers tend to use a TAU instead of a waiting list because TAU supposedly controls for placebo effects. These scientific horse races, however, resemble a contest between Secretariat and Mr. Ed rather than the

Kentucky Derby, or a basketball game between the Harlem Globetrotters and the Washington Generals rather than the Boston Celtics and Los Angeles Lakers. These TAUs have been described elsewhere as "intent-to-fail conditions" (Westen et al., 2004a, p. 651) because their intended failure makes the active treatment appear that much more effective. A significant difference between the two treatments is more likely if one of the treatments is severely handicapped.

IPT was initially conceptualized as a psychodynamically informed complement to psychopharmacological intervention for depression (Frank and Spanier, 1995) and later used as a TAU for an RCT testing the efficacy of CBT for bulimia because it came in manualized form (Westen et al., 2004a). The RCT researchers prohibited the IPT therapists from talking with the patients about their bulimic symptoms, eating habits, and even their weight to maximize the content differences between the CBT experimental condition and the IPT control condition (Fairburn et al., 1991). But a funny thing happened on the way to the consulting room: the bulimic patients treated with IPT had comparable outcomes to the bulimic patients treated with CBT at follow-up assessments (Agras et al., 2000; Fairburn, 1997; Fairburn et al., 1991; Fairburn, Marcus, and Wilson, 1993). Following these unexpected findings, the IPT manual was then published as an empirically supported treatment for bulimia (Klerman and Weissman, 1993) "despite the lack of any empirical evidence for one of its key components (or noncomponents), the counterintuitive injunction against discussing one of the main things the patient came in to talk about" (Westen et al., 2004a, p. 643). In this case, the Washington Generals actually beat the Harlem Globetrotters. It was not supposed to happen. Who knew that *not* discussing bulimic symptoms would reduce them as much as discussing them?

Elsewhere in their outstanding article, Westen and his colleagues (Westen et al., 2004a) discussed the substandard TAUs routinely pitted against the putative brand names of psychotherapy. For example, the quality and availability of DBT therapists cannot be compared to the quality and availability of TAU therapists used in RCTs testing the efficacy of DBT because these two groups of therapists "differ on so many variables that it is difficult to draw causal conclusions from such comparisons" (p. 651). Overworked, poorly paid community mental health practitioners with no supervision are not going to perform as well as available, adequately compensated, highly trained, and well supervised psychologists—regardless of the treatment package offered (for a critique of the empirical basis of DBT, see Scheel, 2000). When pitted against such lowly competition, "Any 10- to 20-session intervention will produce an initial response in most patients if carried out by a clinician who expects it to be effective (Luborsky, McLellan, Diguer, Woody, and Seligman, 1997). . . .

Doing something is better than doing nothing" (Westen et al., 2004a, p. 651). Even TAUs outperform waitlisted control groups equally well to active treatments (Lambert and Bergin, 1994; Wampold, 2005).

Follow-up studies of RCTs are seldom conducted (Westen et al., 2004a); thus, enduring change is seldom demonstrated. Given the fact that brand-name treatments are generally ten to twenty sessions in length, it appears unlikely that they would in fact produce lasting changes in psychiatric symptoms, global adaptive functioning, or personality organization. We know from the attachment literature that as humans develop, their internal working models become increasingly resistant to change (Bowlby, 1980). Insecure and, in particular, unresolved internal working models have been associated with a variety of psychopathologies in children and adults (Goodman, 2002). One point of entry for intervention would logically be a person's internal working model (see volume II, chapter 7). If the internal working model produces a general vulnerability to psychopathology (Goodman, 2002), and if internal working models become increasingly resistant to change, then it follows that treatments targeting internal working models would be slow to manifest measurable change. The clinical work would take a long time, perhaps even years, to produce changes at this fundamental level of personality organization. No one would suggest that ten to twenty psychotherapy sessions would be sufficient to modify an internal working model that has taken an entire childhood to develop. If we make the twin assumptions (1) that the insecure internal working model creates a diathesis for psychopathology and (2) that symptom remission in the absence of modifications to the internal working model is transitory, then twenty-session treatments would not likely produce enduring changes. It is not surprising, then, that follow-up studies of these RCT treatments are seldom conducted.

Another reason why follow-up studies are seldom conducted is that patients on a waiting list or TAU control group are unwilling to endure their symptoms with no treatment or substandard treatment. The problem of maintaining a control group over the course of a long-term treatment such as psychoanalysis reduces the likelihood that the medical RCT model could even be applied to psychoanalysis (Jones, 2000).

In an effort to enhance their findings even further, RCT researchers tend to measure treatment outcomes in diagnostic and symptomatic domains rather than in global domains of functioning such as general adaptation, well being, or personality organization. Categorical approaches to psychiatric diagnosis have been seriously questioned (e.g., Clarkin, 2008; Depue and Lenzenweger, 2005; Kernberg, 1996), yet RCT researchers continue to emphasize putative changes in psychiatric diagnosis. Diagnostic comorbidity complicates the diagnostic picture of many patients with personality disorders (Clarkin, 2008), not only disqualifying them from RCTs (Westen et al., 2004a) but also depriving them of "officially approved" treatments. Common sense would suggest that treatments should be designed to address a constellation of interrelated problems such as affect dysregulation, mentalization deficits, and core conflictual themes (Clarkin, 2008) rather than psychiatric diagnosis, the internal validity of which has itself been called into question. For example, 256 different combinations of symptoms can qualify a person for the diagnosis of borderline personality disorder (APA, 2000). A treatment focus on general vulnerabilities (Jones, 2000) rather than psychiatric diagnosis would result in treatments that produce structural as well as symptomatic changes that endure. I briefly discuss seven instruments that measure general vulnerabilities in chapter 3. For example, using the Adult Attachment Interview (AAI; George et al., 1996) as a measure of structural change (Levy, Meehan, et al., 2006) represents a first of many steps that RCT researchers need to take in assessing genuine clinical efficacy.

The problem of clinical efficacy has haunted RCT researchers from the beginning (Jacobson and Truax, 1991). In spite of efforts to encourage RCT researchers to use indices of clinically significant change such as shifts from clinically significant symptom levels to normal symptom levels, only the significant differences between the active treatment and the TAU are typically reported (Kazdin, 2006). Even if an active treatment outperforms a TAU, it is still possible that neither treatment produces patients within a normal range of symptoms. Thus, such a treatment could be designated "empirically supported" while offering no clinically meaningful relief to the patient. Such treatments might be empirically supported but clinically inert.

Small sample sizes used in RCT conditions also pose problems for understanding the change processes responsible for positive outcomes (Craighead, Sheets, Bjornsson, and Arnarson, 2005). Thase (2002) has argued that a sample size of three hundred in each condition would be required to detect genuine treatment effects. Approximately two-thirds of the treatment variance in RCTs can be accounted for by placebo effects—that patients presenting themselves for treatment are expecting to get better and actually do get better based solely on their expectations. Any significant differences between active and TAU conditions are therefore spurious. As of 2005, only one RCT—CBT for chronic depression—had a sufficiently large sample size to draw conclusions about treatment efficacy (Craighead et al., 2005; Keller et al., 2000). Three decades of meta-analyses of treatment efficacy (e.g., Ahn and Wampold, 2001; Bergin, 1971; Bergin and Lambert, 1978; Horvath and Symonds, 1991; Lambert, 2004; Lambert and Bergin, 1994; Lambert and Ogles, 2004; Lipsey and Wilson, 1993; Luborsky, Singer, and Luborsky, 1975; Martin, Garske, and Davis, 2000; Meltzoff and Kornreich, 1970; Shapiro and Shapiro, 1982;

Smith and Glass, 1977; Smith, Glass, and Miller, 1980; Stevens, Hynan, and Allen, 2000; Stiles, Shapiro, and Elliot, 1986; Wampold, 2001; Wampold et al., 1997; Weinberger, 1995) have yielded (1) significant findings that support the efficacy of psychotherapy and (2) nonsignificant findings that support the superiority of one active treatment over another. Aggregating many studies of short duration (i.e., ten to twenty sessions) and small sample size (i.e., fewer than three hundred patients per condition) still does not permit researchers to examine the incremental effects of specific over common factors (those factors common to all treatments that account for their equivalent efficacy; Westen et al., 2004a).

Aggregating treatment outcome data, whether in RCTs or in meta-analytic studies of RCTs, can also eliminate significant treatment effects of a particular subgroup of patients in the active condition (type II error) or produce significant treatment effects when only a subgroup of patients in the active condition benefited from the treatment (type I error). For example, Levy and his colleagues (Levy, Meehan, et al., 2006) found that after one year of TFP, borderline patients in this condition were rated higher on Fonagy, Target, Steele, and Steele's (1998) Reflective Functioning Scale (RFS) than borderline patients in the other two conditions—DBT and modified psychodynamic-supportive psychotherapy (SPT). It is possible that a subgroup of borderline patients with narcissistic or antisocial features in the TFP condition demonstrated a (falsely) high level of RF improvement (see Bateman and Fonagy, 2004b, p. 75) and therefore pulled up the overall RF mean among all the borderline patients in the TFP condition. This subgroup effect could produce an artifactual significant difference between TFP and the other two treatment conditions on the RF outcome measure (type I error).

Conversely, aggregating individual outcome scores into homogenized group means can obscure genuine treatment effects and cause the frequent lack of significant findings between active treatment conditions and TAUs or waitlisted control conditions reported by many meta-analytic studies (type II error). Interaction effects between treatment condition and patient characteristics are seldom tested in RCTs (Westen et al., 2004a) but need to be systematically investigated because patient characteristics "are far more robust predictors of outcome than are treatment techniques" (Ablon and Jones, 2002, p. 782). Two groups of psychotherapy outcome researchers (Beutler, 1979; Beutler and Harwood, 2000; Blatt and Felsen, 1993; Blatt and Ford, 1994; Blatt and Shahar, 2005) have produced evidence that matching particular patients to particular treatment conditions produce effective treatment outcomes. In chapter 6 of Goodman (in press), I discuss the idea of matching the patient's attachment pattern with the therapist's attachment pattern in a noncomplementary manner to produce a "gentle challenge" (Dozier and Bates,

2004, p. 174) in the therapist-patient interaction (see figure 6.1). In such a treatment, the therapist maintains mentalizing functioning while behaving at odds with the implicit expectations of the patient's internal working model. These therapist-patient matches, and the interaction structures derived from them (see Goodman, in press, figure 3.1), could be more predictive of effective treatment outcomes than the treatment condition to which the patient is assigned.

Indeed, the idea that rank-and-file therapists should apply boilerplate techniques packaged in RCT-tested brand-name treatments to individual cases "violates the logic of inference" (Jones, 2000, p. 268). The syllogism operating in the minds of RCT researchers testing the efficacy of their preferred treatment package (illustrated below with brand-name treatments for borderline personality disorder) seems to be the following:

1. According to the significant findings of RCTs, patients diagnosed with borderline personality disorder benefit from a trial of DBT [fill in your preferred empirically supported treatment here].
2. Mary is a patient diagnosed with borderline personality disorder.
3. Therefore, Mary will benefit from a trial of DBT.

Unfortunately, Mary might not benefit from a trial of DBT. She might have a comorbid Axis I diagnosis or comorbid Axis II features that would reduce the effectiveness of DBT or make this treatment package altogether ineffective for her. Mary might instead benefit from a treatment that permits her to explore the meaning of her impulsive borderline behaviors within the context of the therapeutic relationship (i.e., TFP). Mary might have an adverse reaction to the therapist's rigid adherence to the DBT manual and consequently experience difficulty establishing a therapeutic alliance, thereby dooming the outcome. The truth is that we do not know why a trial of DBT would work or not work for Mary, even though DBT has acquired an official status as a so-called empirically supported treatment.

An alternative method of testing treatment efficacy that does not violate the logic of inference is to examine what interventions do work for individual patients at the level of a single case and gradually aggregate these data (Ablon and Jones, 1999, 2005; Jones, 1993, 2000; Jones, Ghannam, Nigg, and Dyer, 1993). According to Jones (2000):

> A single-case research model . . . attempts to establish the generality of its findings through replication on a case-by-case basis rather than through group averages. . . . Establishing the presence of certain patterns or configurations of variability across a series of cases would begin to form the basis for generalizability.

> The scientific base for clinical psychoanalysis would be greatly strengthened by a programmatic research effort that attempts to replicate findings over a succession of studies of individual cases. (pp. 268, 269)

The syllogism operating in the single-case research model seems to be the following:

1. Mary is a patient diagnosed with borderline personality disorder, with specific symptoms clustered around impulsivity (Clarkin, Hull, and Hurt, 1993) in the context of a dismissing attachment strategy (Main et al., 1985). She benefited from an interaction with a warm, empathic, securely attached therapist who contained Mary's impulsive borderline behaviors by showing her that intimacy within the therapeutic relationship terrified her and made her seek emotional relief in these impulsive behaviors.
2. John is another patient diagnosed with borderline personality disorder, with specific symptoms clustered around impulsivity (Clarkin et al., 1993) in the context of a dismissing attachment strategy (Main et al., 1985). He also benefited from an interaction with a warm, empathic, securely attached therapist who contained John's impulsive borderline behaviors by showing him that intimacy within the therapeutic relationship terrified him and made him seek emotional relief in these impulsive behaviors.
3. Therefore, patients diagnosed with borderline personality disorder with specific symptoms clustered around impulsivity (Clarkin et al., 1993) in the context of a dismissing attachment strategy (Main et al., 1985) will benefit from an interaction with a warm, empathic, securely attached therapist who contains the patient's impulsive borderline behaviors by showing him or her that intimacy within the therapeutic relationship terrifies him or her and makes him or her seek emotional relief in these impulsive behaviors.

Clear specification of the therapist's characteristics, patient's characteristics, and interaction structures between them—for a specific therapist-patient dyad—can uncover conditions under which the treatment for this individual patient worked. The same treatment strategies could then be applied to similarly specified patients under similar treatment conditions. If the treatment proves to be effective under similar treatment conditions for a succession of patients, then one could claim that this particular treatment is effective for this particular patient under these particular conditions. As a profession, we need to test our theories of therapeutic change, not with the medical RCT model but with a model that can identify "what kinds of treatments are effective, for what kinds of patients, in what kinds of ways, and through what kinds of mechanisms or processes of therapeutic change (Blatt and Shahar, 2004;

Blatt, Shahar, and Zuroff, 2002)" (Blatt and Zuroff, 2005, p. 480). I would add to this statement the need to specify what therapist characteristics work for what patients: "One may need to expand 'what works for whom' to 'who doing what works for whom'" (Eagle, 2006, p. 1092).

RCTs test active treatment conditions using therapists and patients who do not resemble therapists and patients in the real world. RCT therapists who participate in the active condition are highly trained, well supervised, and adequately compensated. Perhaps most important, these therapists have a palpable allegiance to the active treatment condition. Expectancies of researchers have been shown to influence their findings (Harris and Rosenthal, 1985; Rosenthal and Rubin, 1978). The therapist's allegiance to the treatment accounts for over 69 percent of the variance in outcome across many psychotherapy efficacy studies (Luborsky et al., 1999) and, if accurate, "would have tremendous consequences for the enterprise of testing psychotherapies" (Westen et al., 2004a, p. 640). It is unknown how the therapist's allegiance actually boosts treatment outcome (Weinberger, 2002; Weinberger and Eig, 1999), but it is likely that the therapist conveys to the patient (consciously or unconsciously) an abiding faith that the treatment being dispensed will work. Ironically, under such circumstances, the placebo effect derived from the therapist's allegiance could differentially boost outcome in the active condition over and above the TAU "placebo" condition. If therapist allegiance effects were controlled for, perhaps significant differences between brand-name treatments and TAUs would disappear altogether.

The patients selected for RCTs also do not adequately represent typical patients in the real world. As mentioned previously, RCT researchers exclude patients with comorbid psychiatric diagnoses and previous treatment failures (Jones, 2000). According to Westen and his colleagues (Westen et al., 2004a), comorbidity of Axis I diagnoses ranges from 50 percent to 90 percent (e.g., Kessler et al., 1996; Kessler, Stang, Wittchen, Stein, and Walters, 1999; Newman, Moffitt, Caspi, and Silva, 1998; Oldham et al., 1995; Shea, Widiger, and Klein, 1992; Zimmerman, McDermut, and Mattia, 2000). These percentages therefore suggest that RCT patients represent an atypical diagnostic population. RCT-tested treatments, however, are expected to be applied to the entire diagnostic population for which the particular RCT-tested treatment was designed. Journals published by the American Psychological Association inform us that untested treatments are "less essential and outdated" (Calhoun, Moras, Pilkonis, and Rehm, 1998, p. 151) even though the patients on which these preferred treatments were empirically validated are unrepresentative of the diagnostic population from which they are selected.

Moreover, patients who submit to audio- or video-recording and multiple self-assessments over time might themselves possess certain characteristics that make them atypical. Blatt and Zuroff (2005) have questioned whether the evaluative procedures inherent in RCTs adversely affect the treatment outcomes for certain patients (e.g., paranoid patients or perfectionistic patients whose anxieties are exacerbated by the evaluative procedures). Josephs and his colleagues (Josephs, Anderson, Bernard, Fatzer, and Streich, 2004) have suggested that the therapist and patient can experience a recording device as "a prying superego" (p. 1193). Without examining the patient's characteristics more closely at the beginning of treatment, one might draw erroneous conclusions about the ineffectiveness of a treatment (type II error). Patients who feel dissatisfied and perhaps even resentful about the externally imposed, arbitrary termination of an RCT at the sixteenth or twentieth session might disengage from the psychotherapy process near the end, and thus stop making progress or even lose the gains they had previously made (Blatt and Zuroff, 2005). Contrary to the perception that RCTs do a great job of controlling for experimental artifacts, the medical RCT model could actually "induce other experimental artifacts as a consequence of the meaning to the patients of participating in a design in which they feel controlled, observed, and evaluated beyond what would occur in a more natural treatment relationship" (Blatt and Zuroff, 2005, p. 480).

Just how many patients are negatively (or positively) affected by the evaluative procedures of RCTs is unknown because these iatrogenic effects are never considered by RCT researchers and therefore never measured. How a researcher would even go about making patient observations without the patient's awareness is unclear. Heisenberg's uncertainty principle lives on: the mere act of observing the psychotherapy process changes that process in unpredictable ways (for additional information on therapists' attitudes about recording sessions, see chapter 3).

Before leaving this discussion of the profound conceptual and methodological flaws inherent in the medical RCT model of testing psychotherapy efficacy, I want to underscore what I believe to be the even more profound ethical flaws inherent in this model. Imagine that you are about to enter a world in which you must choose the parents who will be raising you. You would probably spend a considerable amount of time and energy constructing a list of qualities that you would want your parents to have—kindness, altruism, empathy, protectiveness, firmness, gentleness, emotional availability, nonjudgmentalness, compassion, expertise, a sense of humor, and love. You want parents whom you can get along with, feel comfortable and secure with. Now imagine that as you enter this world, you find out to your dismay that your parents have already been chosen for you. You have no control over who your parents are or how they will relate to you. You might feel an overwhelming sense of helplessness and resentment. In the real world, we are born into a particular family without any choice, but we do not mind because most parents are "fulfilling [their] task in teaching the child to love" (Freud, 1905b, p. 223). We start needing our parents almost from birth—a primitive form of loving. Psychotherapy could be considered a form of reparenting that takes place in the patient's transference of wishes, thoughts, and feelings from the parental mental representations of childhood onto the mental representation of the therapist.

Although we could never choose our parents, it is certainly true that we can choose our therapist. Most of us who have been in our own psychotherapy took great care in selecting a therapist. Indeed, we encourage prospective patients to shop around for the therapist who possesses the emotional availability, expertise, and other parenting qualities (see above) that will help us to become emotionally mature adults. In an RCT, the researchers take this entire selection process out of our hands. They assign us a therapist and a treatment without any consideration for what our needs or wishes might be. If we have been assigned a man when we wanted to work with a woman, that is too bad. If we wanted DBT but have instead been assigned to a TAU condition (or worse, a wait-listed condition), that is too bad. Of course, no one is forcing these patients to enroll in the RCT; however, the promise of free psychotherapy to someone with a low-income job and no healthcare insurance constitutes a form of coercion in which grant-funded RCT researchers are exploiting emotionally vulnerable people seeking help with no other choices available to them. These people agree to receive help sometimes at the cost of feeling comfortable and secure with the therapist and treatment that have been chosen for them. The fact that these prospective patients are emotionally vulnerable (why else would they present for treatment?) makes the coercion all the more egregious. Who among us, if given a true choice, would participate as a patient in an RCT?

Patients who have other means to pay for treatment shop around for a therapist who suits them, but there might be patients who welcome participation in an RCT. I am guessing that in a restaurant, these persons will eat anything set before them without making a fuss. They will never complain about the quality of food or service, even if it is substandard. Part of their psychopathology consists of their passivity and utter lack of assertiveness. Yet these kinds of patients are not being treated for this psychopathology in an RCT because they would leave. In fact, any psychopathology not targeted by the treatment manual in an RCT goes untreated. For example, Westen and his colleagues (Westen et al., 2004a) noted that CBT for bulimia places limited emphasis on interpersonal problems. For a patient who walks into session and says that she is feeling suicidal because her partner just ended their relationship, however, this "distraction" from the binging and purging symptoms would probably result in the end of treatment and possibly a referral for an EST for depression. What is ethical about that?

The medical RCT model of testing psychotherapy efficacy privileges the treatment manual over the relationship between the therapist and the patient. When the primary motivation of the therapist becomes adherence to the treatment manual instead of treatment of the patient's needs, one must question the ethics of this situation. When boilerplate techniques that comprise a treatment manual do not fit every patient's needs, some patients are forced into the strictures of the treatment model like a tight-fitting shoe. Thus, the therapeutic alliance becomes compromised (Hubble, Duncan, and Miller, 1999), and increased adherence further strains the therapeutic alliance and produces a negative outcome (Castonguay et al., 1996). "The methodological tail wag[ging] the clinical dog" (Westen et al., 2004a, p. 642) means that some patients who do not conform to the strictures of the treatment model are receiving substandard care. Ablon and Marci (2004) sarcastically pointed out that "a treatment manual for prescribing patient behavior has yet to be written" (p. 666). In our general linear model, we have two constants—the therapist and patient—participating in a scientific experiment in which the only aspect permitted to vary is the treatment condition. The assumption of a zero-person psychology underlies the medical RCT model. The two participants are robbed of their subjectivity—depersonalized and controlled—because subjectivity represents a confound in the experimental design. The human relationship, therefore, becomes mechanized for the sake of science. For all the reasons I have mentioned, that is both bad psychotherapy and bad science.

In developmental psychology, where I have spent most of my research career studying the predictors of child psychopathology from an attachment perspective, the experimental method is seldom if ever used. For obvious reasons, we cannot randomly assign children to caregivers to control for genetic and other nonrandom effects on childrearing. We conduct cross-sectional and longitudinal correlational research, using multiple regression equations and structural equation modeling to test mediational and moderational pathways of influence on child psychopathology (e.g., Goodman, Hans, and Bernstein, 2005; Goodman, Sapp, Stroh, and Valdez, 2007). Experimental research is not available to us on ethical grounds, yet the field has survived and thrived on the use of sophisticated statistical techniques that control for "extraneous" variables whose variance can be measured and understood in the context of the hypotheses under study. Few would question the validity of the foundations of attachment research, yet many question the validity of psychodynamic psychotherapy because it has not been rigorously RCT-tested. A behaviorist colleague of mine actually laughed at me when I referred to naturalistic research studies (Fonagy and Target, 1996b; Target and Fonagy, 1994a, 1994b) that support the effectiveness of child psychoanalysis. He cited these studies' lack of a control group and random assignment as the chief reasons for his dismissal of their relevance to our conversation about the effectiveness of psychodynamic psychotherapy.

Like Freud (1910, 1915), who believed that countertransference is a phenomenon to be controlled, not used to understand the patient as a tool for change, RCT researchers believe that human subjectivity is a phenomenon to be controlled, not used to understand the therapeutic relationship as a tool for change. I am urging scientific organizations and research groups that support the use of RCTs to validate treatment packages to consider the ethical as well as methodological and conceptual problems with their misapplied medical model and move instead toward an alternative model used in other disciplines such as developmental psychology that permits testing mediational and moderational pathways of influence on treatment outcome. One alternative method is to study treatment effectiveness using a naturalistic research design. As I have argued, the choice that lies before us is whether to study psychotherapy or a sanitized facsimile that bears no resemblance to the original.

NATURALISTIC STUDIES: THE REINTRODUCTION OF A TWO-PERSON PSYCHOLOGY

In the latter part of the nineteenth century and early part of the twentieth century, women began to organize themselves in what became known as the Mothers' Movement—a product of the new science of child development and feminism (Ehrenreich and English, 1978). The Mothers' Movement consisted of mothers organizing themselves into clubs all over the United States, the purpose of which was to share their observations of their children's behaviors, attitudes, emotions, cognitions, and development. The Society for the Study of Child Nature, formed in New York City in 1888, "set out to explore every facet of child 'nature'—from music appreciation to the concept of private property" (p. 173). Referring to this movement, one historian (Wishy, 1968) has cynically observed, "The child was no longer merely a beloved offspring or the nation's future in microcosm but a home-laboratory experiment as well" (p. 119). Although the motives of these women might be questioned, their desire to transform society through their efforts to understand their children's development suggested that they understood the importance of childrearing to children's development and their pivotal role in this process.

Soon after this movement began, however, "child-raising experts" entered the scene "to tell the mothers what to do" (Ehrenreich and English, 1978, p.

177). The mother's career as a domestic scientist was thus short-lived because these experts were "not interested in the amateurish contributions of mothers" (p. 181). Only scientists could collect data and formulate best-practice guidelines from these data. According to Ehrenreich and English (1978), "All that was left for mothers was to follow the instructions" (p. 181). Thus began the industrial approach to child-raising—scientists instructing mothers how to fit their children into the socially stratified positions awaiting them in the regimented world of the factory.

George Santayana (1905) wrote, "Those who cannot remember the past are condemned to repeat it" (p. 284). The field of psychology has forgotten about its tendency to strangle an area of inquiry and suffocate the life right out of it. What the child-raising "experts" did to scientifically curious mothers in the latter part of the nineteenth century and early part of the twentieth century, the RCT "experts" are doing to scientifically curious therapists in the latter part of the twentieth century and early part of the twenty-first century. A colleague informed me just today that Great Britain is gradually moving toward the criminalization of therapists who practice treatments considered not empirically supported by the scientific establishment. Therapists need to take back control of their practice domain rather than appease the scientific organizations and research groups that seek to direct what therapists do in the privacy of their own consulting rooms.

Just as mothers organized themselves to study their own children one hundred years ago, therapists need to organize themselves to study their own psychotherapy cases today. Best-practice guidelines are only as helpful as the people who write them and the data on which they are based. I have demonstrated that the application of the medical RCT model to psychotherapy research cannot yield ethically or methodologically sound treatment-outcome data to guide best practice. A grassroots movement of rank-and-file therapists—including psychoanalysts—could stem the tide of the well-financed medical RCT model by turning their consulting rooms into their own personal laboratories to study what works and does not work with specific patients. Psychodynamic and cognitive-behavioral therapists alike could conduct naturalistic studies yielding process and outcome data that could lend empirical support to their therapeutic interventions. These process and outcome data—based on the patient's and therapist's own observations and verbatim session recordings—could be collected in more ethically valid ways, and the findings from such studies could be used to develop more ecologically valid best-practice guidelines. Data collection is as simple as recording one's own treatment sessions and both completing and handing out a questionnaire or two (see chapter 3).

In contrast to RCTs, which rely on the experimental method of random assignment to active treatment and control conditions, naturalistic studies rely on the quasi-experimental correlational method of longitudinal research that can identify mediating and moderating variables related to treatment outcome—even with a single case. The "noise" inherent in naturalistic studies can be measured and tested for its association with treatment outcome rather than artificially removed as in RCTs, which fatally tampers with the very process it purports to study. Naturalistic studies maximize the ecological validity of the findings because they occur in the treatment settings of rank-and-file therapists, not in a laboratory. In naturalistic settings, there is typically no treatment manual, no special supervision, no adherence checks, no specified treatment length, no rigorous screening of patients—no artificial additives. This method of conducting research has a logic of its own that could prove to be a more powerful force for the EST movement than the sum total of RCTs conducted in the service of brand-name treatments.

What do therapists do when they actually adjust their interventions to meet the needs of their patients? This question cannot be answered using the medical RCT model. How do changes made by the patient act upon the therapist's interventions? According to Westen, Novotny, and Thompson-Brenner (2004b), "Therapist responsiveness or attunement [to the patient's needs] should be a measured variable in its own right, which is likely to predict outcome" (p. 681). Interaction structures—the patterns of interaction that go on between the therapist and patient (Jones, 2000)—are not examined in RCTs because interaction structures imply a two-person psychology, while RCTs imply a zero-person psychology. When two persons are interacting with each other without a script, what happens? Can the mutual experience, recognition, and understanding inherent in these interaction structures be harnessed for the benefit of therapeutic change? RCTs cannot answer this question because both parties are following a script that the researchers have written for them—typically the roles of an authoritative therapist teaching manualized activities to a compliant, submissive patient (see Ablon and Marci, 2004).

What I and others (e.g., Westen et al., 2004a) are envisioning is the empirical observation of psychotherapy process and outcome without the screenwriters, actors, or script. In other words, is ad-libbed psychotherapy effective? Naturalistic studies can help us answer that question. Westen and his colleagues (Westen et al., 2004a) perhaps said it best: "[Our field] need[s] to reconsider the top-down, unidirectional model of science and practice that has become increasingly prevalent in recent years, which assumes that knowledge flows primarily from researchers to clinicians" (p. 656). We need to reverse the flow of knowledge and create a grassroots, bottom-up movement by involving rank-and-file therapists in naturalistic studies of the psychotherapy cases culled from their own practices.

It is quite possible that the scientific "impurities" unceremoniously filtered out of RCT treatments might actually have therapeutic properties. For example, cycles of rupture and repair in the therapeutic alliance have been associated with advances in treatment (e.g., Safran and Muran, 1996, 2000). Naturalistically collected data could be used to demonstrate (1) how these ruptures occur under "battlefield" conditions, (2) how the therapist and patient work together to repair them, and (3) where the repair process goes awry. This information could in turn educate the entire mental health community about what works and does not work in the repair process and what kinds of repair processes lead to what kinds of therapeutic change and stagnation.

Jones (2000) was perhaps the most vocal proponent of the use of naturalistic studies conducted by therapists in the community to build up empirical support for therapeutic intervention from the ground up. Before his untimely death in 2003, Jones envisioned "an organized, systematic attempt to replicate findings over a number of individual cases" (p. 270) gradually aggregated "to form the basis for generalizability" (p. 269). This bottom-up method of research relies on the study of the single psychotherapy case in the consulting room. Jones (2000) was aware that this focus on single-case research design conducted in a naturalistic setting represented a call to come full circle for the therapeutic community: "Single-case research models are closer to traditional models of psychoanalytic investigation, and are likely to have more direct relevance to theoretical questions as well as to clinical practice [than experimental research designs]" (p. 269). Other authors (e.g., Ablon and Marci, 2004; Westen et al., 2004a) have echoed this position. A contemporary quantitatively based method for studying individual cases could legitimize and update yesterday's qualitatively based case study method.

Because naturalistic studies reflect a two-person psychology with the two participants—the therapist and patient—behaving as variables rather than as constants, variation also occurs in the process that emerges between them. Psychotherapy process is nothing more than the infinite variety of interactions that occur within the therapeutic dyad. Jones (2000) studied the repetitions that occurred within this process—the interaction structures that he observed with the assistance of the Psychotherapy Process Q-Set (see chapter 3 and volume II, chapter 5). He argued that only psychotherapy process research could identify those specific interaction structures that produce therapeutic change. The medical RCT model reveals only the main effects of a treatment—that is to say, whether the active treatment condition is significantly different from the control condition on the measures of outcome selected by the researchers. Exactly how the therapeutic dyads in the two groups differ in their interaction structures is not a concern because the medical RCT model intentionally attempts to remove the variation in the behaviors of both participants.

As discussed earlier in this chapter, Jones and his colleagues (Ablon and Jones, 1998, 1999, 2002; Jones and Pulos, 1993) learned, however, that variations in this process nevertheless do exist unintentionally, even in RCTs. In a review of this work, Ablon and Marci (2004) noted that while the therapeutic content between treatment conditions in RCTs might systematically vary (e.g., between CBT and IPT treatment conditions), the therapeutic process within these conditions contains considerable unsystematic variation. In the National Institute of Mental Health (NIMH)–sponsored Treatment of Depression Collaborative Research Program (TDCRP), the CBT and IPT treatment conditions systematically differed in the content of the therapist interventions but shared one process—CBT process. In both treatment conditions, active, authoritative therapists were coaching compliant, deferential patients to behave differently. A possible reason why RCTs seldom demonstrate impressive effect sizes for active treatments in comparison with TAUs is that although therapeutic content differs, the underlying therapeutic process inherent in all brief (i.e., ten to twenty sessions) psychotherapies promotes therapeutic change in similar ways (Ablon and Marci, 2004; Goldfried and Wolfe, 1998). In fact, significant *unintentional* variation was found in the therapeutic process of different brand-name treatments (Ablon and Jones, 1998, 1999, 2002; Jones and Pulos, 1993). This unintentional variation was then used to predict treatment outcomes in the RCTs of these brand-name treatments. The authors found that psychodynamic process such as a neutral therapist making a transference interpretation to an active patient was predictive of positive treatment outcome in both psychodynamic and cognitive-behavioral treatments. As mentioned earlier, cognitive-behavioral process such as an authoritative therapist providing encouragement to a compliant patient characterized both CBT and IPT treatment conditions. An examination of the therapeutic process within these treatments yields valuable data overlooked by most RCT researchers regarding how therapeutic change takes place in these superficially different treatments.

Naturalistic studies provide an ideal context in which to study psychotherapy process because, in contrast to RCTs, where researchers are attempting to remove all human variation, the consulting room accentuates the variation that naturally exists when two individuals interact freely with each other. Such studies can teach us therapists which interventions work across the board with all our patients (common factors) as well as which interventions work with certain kinds of patients (specific factors). Therapist interventions that might have previously been considered specific factors (e.g., transference interpretations) might actually represent common factors tacitly used by all therapists in their work with patients: "What are often referred to as *nonspecific effects* [common factors] in the literature may actually represent the specific effects of shared processes" (Ablon and Marci, 2004, p. 666, italics in original; see also Ablon and Jones, 2002, p. 780). Thus, perhaps transference interpretations should be promoted as an effective ingredient of therapeutic change regardless of one's allegiance to a brand-name treatment that otherwise discourages such interventions.

In the borderline personality disorder (BPD) treatment literature, Bateman and Fonagy (2004a) have suggested, "The potential effectiveness of all treatments depends not so much on their frame but on their ability to increase a patient's capacity to mentalize" (p. 46). In this book, I discuss three effective ingredients of therapeutic change—mindfulness (chapter 5), mentalization (chapter 6), and psychological mindedness (chapter 7). Specifically, I evaluate their fitness as common factors even though most therapists would consider them as specific factors unique to particular theoretical orientations. In another book (Goodman, in press), I discuss a fourth effective ingredient of therapeutic change—the attachment relationship. For example, mindfulness is widely considered a specific factor of so-called third-wave cognitive-behavioral treatments (see chapter 5), but I consider whether mindfulness might be present in all effective treatments—even in those treatments for which mindfulness is not intentionally promoted.

How does the idea that shared common processes function across a wide range of patients and treatments affect our training and supervision of students? Instead of teaching an infinitely expanding series of narrowly focused, boilerplate, manualized techniques designed specifically to treat a specific disorder, clinical supervisors need to teach a series of broadly focused techniques that can be tailor-made to the unique person of the patient and the uniqueness of the therapist-patient dyad. Consistent with this idea, Blatt and Zuroff (2005) suggested that training be focused

> not on learning particular manual-directed treatments for specific disorders, but on the development of fundamental clinical skills that will enable students to become competent clinicians capable of establishing effective therapeutic relationship with their patients as well as being able to identify personality characteristics of their patients that are likely to facilitate or impede their patients' response to various forms of treatment. (pp. 479, 480)

Attachment researchers have begun to report on the effects of a patient's quality of attachment organization in relation to treatment outcome (see Goodman, in press, chapter 3). In fact, patients whose attachment strategy differs from his or her therapist's tend to have more positive treatment outcomes than patients paired with therapists who share the same attachment strategy (principle of noncomplementarity). Rather than focusing on manualized techniques, therapists need to focus instead on using themselves as instruments of change. In particular, therapists need to adapt themselves to the secure-base needs of their patients, depending on their patients' quality of attachment organization. In chapter 3 of Goodman (in press), I argue that therapist-patient matching according to quality of attachment organization necessarily constrains the range of transference-countertransference paradigms (i.e., interaction structures) available to the therapist-patient dyad. It is the mutual experience, recognition, and understanding of these transference-countertransference paradigms that produce therapeutic change, not the mastery of a dizzying array of bags of tricks. Transference interpretations (Ablon and Jones, 1998, p. 81; Jones and Pulos, 1993) and mentalization (Bateman and Fonagy, 2004a) have been suggested as methods of helping the patient understand these interaction structures manifested from the patient's implicit procedural memory (e.g., Allen, 2003; Bateman and Fonagy, 2004a, 2004b; Fonagy and Target, 1997; Lyons-Ruth, 1999).

Of course, as Blatt and Felsen (1993) have already pointed out, different kinds of folks may need different kinds of strokes. For example, patients who have an unresolved attachment organization related to abuse, unresolved loss, or other traumatic events might need therapist interventions that suppress anxiety and provide support, structure, and reassurance rather than technical neutrality and transference interpretations (see Jones, Cumming, and Horowitz, 1988). Thus, even common factors defined as "the specific effects of shared processes" (Ablon and Jones, 2002, p. 780; Ablon and Marci, 2004, p. 666) are not always appropriate. Patient characteristics always need to be considered when formulating a treatment plan, whether they be symptom-based (e.g., posttraumatic stress disorder), attachment-based (e.g., unresolved attachment organization), or problem-focused (e.g., mentalization deficits, affect dysregulation).

Contrary to what some RCT researchers would like to believe, patient characteristics account for approximately 40 percent of improvement in psychotherapy (Assay and Lambert, 1999). According to some researchers (e.g., Ablon and Jones, 1999, 2002; Ablon and Marci, 2004; Blatt, Quinlan, Pilkonis, and Shea, 1995; Duncan, 2002; Garfield, 1978; see also chapter 3), the ability of patient characteristics to predict treatment outcome far exceeds that of treatment techniques. Even the therapeutic alliance, considered by many researchers as an effective ingredient of all psychotherapies (e.g., Wampold, 2005), is largely determined by patient characteristics (e.g., DeRubeis, Brotman, and Gibbons, 2005; Kazdin, 2005). Therapists must therefore adjust their interactions to facilitate the therapeutic properties of those patient characteristics most predictive of treatment outcome. These patient characteristics include feeling helped or understood, achieving a new understanding, introspection, organized self-expression, animation, commitment to work in therapy, and positive expectations about therapy (Ablon and Jones, 1999, p. 72). To the extent that we teach our students how to facilitate their patients' unique paths of growth, we will be training them to be effective therapists.

Clinical theory has come full circle. The reporting of anecdotal case studies eventually gave way to the medical RCT model, which in turn is gradually giving way to naturalistic studies featuring single-case quantitative research designs. I have outlined a program of research that features the discovery of effective change processes rather than the confirmation of brand-name psychotherapies. The field of discovery needs to be open to all sources of variation in the psychotherapy process, including the therapist, the patient, and the process generated between them in addition to the specific techniques employed. We need to maintain an attitude of humility toward our efforts to help our patients. As Duncan (2002) has noted, the patient is the hero in the psychotherapy drama, not the therapist. Specific techniques might be necessary features of the psychotherapy process, but only insofar as they provide a rationale for the patient (Wampold, 2005; Weinberger, 2002). Specific techniques in and of themselves might turn out to be therapeutically inert. An attitude adjustment oriented toward the patient just might be the most helpful thing we can do to facilitate our patient's progress.

Chapter Three

The Return of the Repressed: Single-Case and Multiple-Case Research Designs to Assess Processes of Therapeutic Change

It is left to the patient in all essentials to determine the course of the analysis and the arrangement of the material; any systematic handling of particular symptoms or complexes thus becomes impossible. In complete contrast to what happened with hypnotism and with the urging method, interrelated material makes its appearance at different times and at different points in the treatment. To a spectator . . . an analytic treatment would seem completely obscure.

Sigmund Freud, "An Autobiographical Study"

Psychotherapy outcome researchers may have overreacted and moved the field in the wrong direction. . . . It has become overly dependent on the 'clinical trials' method to determine how to best treat 'disorders' . . . condoning the medicalization of psychotherapy . . . [and] placing unwarranted emphasis on the putative fixed efficacy of specific interventions.

Mr. Goldfried et al., "Psychotherapy Practice and Research: Repairing a Strained Alliance"

The possibilities of single-case research for providing evidence of . . . causal relations have not been sufficiently recognized, despite the fact that intensive single-case designs would seem to be a natural domain for the study of psychotherapy process.

E. E. Jones, J. Ghannam, J. T. Nigg, and J. F. P. Dyer, "A Paradigm for Single-Case Research: The Time-Series Study of a Long-Term Psychotherapy for Depression"

In 1896, Freud (1896) was formulating his theory of repression: symptoms are compromises between the repressed and repressing forces. The repressing forces (e.g., ego defenses and superego pressures) can hold the repressed forces (e.g., aggressive and libidinal wishes and impulses) in check but can never extinguish them. In fact, Freud's theory suggests that the repressed forces demand a hearing and end up getting one (albeit in distorted form) through the manifestation of symptoms. The repressed forces are a part of our biological identity, a part of the fabric of what is most true about us. Locking up the repressed forces and throwing away the key is not an option.

According to the Task Force on Psychological Intervention Guidelines of the American Psychological Association (1995), messy psychotherapy approaches need to be sanitized by applying the medical RCT model (see also chapter 2). Just as the repressing forces act on the repressed forces, which then seek covert expression through symptom formation, the medical RCT model succeeded in cleaning up the study of messy human interactions—but at a tremendous price. The resulting manualized treatments are mechanized caricatures of human interaction; they are seldom systematically applied to real, comorbidly diagnosed patients in real communities (see chapter 2; Seligman, 1995; Westen et al., 2004a, pp. 648–50). In fact, in the community, it appears that therapists on both sides of the theoretical orientation aisle (psychodynamic/interpersonal and cognitive-behavioral) mix and match approaches according to the perceived needs of the patient (Ablon et al., 2006; Westen et al., 2004a)—even when they are participating in research studies (Ablon and Jones, 1998, 1999, 2002; Jones and Pulos, 1993)! Messy human interactions ultimately cannot be controlled, no matter how hard the American Psychological Association (APA) tries to legislate sanctioned techniques for specific disorders. The APA instead needs to suggest broadly defined clinical skills used to establish an effective therapeutic relationship with the human being who comes through the office door, accepting all the messiness that that encounter inevitably entails. In the absence of such broadly defined guidelines of clinical practice, rank-and-file therapists are going to continue doing whatever they have been doing all along.

Considering the massive chasm in transporting RCT-tested treatments to widespread distribution at the community level, some researchers are seeking to study messy human interactions without this useless sanitization process that destroys the very object of study. These researchers study the phenomena of therapeutic relationships in naturalistic settings with rank-and-file therapists and rank-and-file patients. Atypical patient exclusion criteria are not used beyond the criteria that therapists normally use (e.g., imminent suicide or homicide risk). Therapists are not trained or supervised beyond the training and supervision they would normally receive. Regardless of theoretical orientation, therapists treat patients for longer than the RCT-sanctioned ten to twenty sessions (Westen et al., 2004a). Yet therapists continue to practice effectively in the community (Ablon et al., 2006; Westen et al., 2004a) in spite of (or perhaps because of) the uncontrolled conditions in which they work. Interestingly, a meta-analysis of treatment outcomes for RCT versus nonrandomized studies demonstrated that the mean effect size for RCTs (Cohen's $d = .46$) was not significantly different from the mean effect size for nonrandomized studies (Cohen's $d = .41$; Lipsey and Wilson, 1993, p. 1192). Thus, random assignment seems quite unnecessary in the pursuit of documenting treatment efficacy/effectiveness.

How do these treatments work without controlling the treatment conditions and without applying brand-name treatments? To study this question, some researchers have turned to quantitative single-case research designs to assess the processes of therapeutic change. The premise of this research is that rank-and-file therapists must be doing something right, so let us understand the processes that produce therapeutic changes in these naturalistic settings. These change processes can then be easily transported to similar treatment settings where patients with similar personality organization or similar diagnostic problem areas are presenting for treatment. The purpose of this chapter is to acquaint the therapist with the use of research designs that he or she can easily apply to naturalistic settings. Collectively, we can discover which change processes work with which patients and therapists in the real world, not in a sterile research laboratory.

In an impressive body of work (Ablon and Jones, 2005; Jones, 1993, 2000; Jones et al., 1993; Jones and Price, 1998; Jones and Windholz, 1990; Pole and Jones, 1998), Jones and his colleagues articulated the advantages of quantitative single-case research designs. In 2000, for example, Jones (2000) noted the routine criticism psychoanalytic case studies received for not controlling for the passage of time—that is to say, the phenomenon of spontaneous remission. In response, he drew attention to quantitative methods of assessing the temporal unfolding of variables within the therapeutic dyad. Hilliard (1993) identified three quantitative techniques for analyzing this temporal unfolding without the direct manipulation of variables (characteristic of the medical RCT model): time-series analysis, sequential analysis, and growth-curve analysis. Growth-curve analysis can be used in single-case or aggregated research designs (e.g., Goodman, Hull, Clarkin, and Yeomans, 1998). Time-series analysis, however, is typically used with single-case studies to determine how one set of variables (set A) occurring at a certain point in time (time 1) influences another set of variables (set B) occurring at a later point in time (time 2), over and above the influence of the set B variables at time 1. For a technical discussion of this statistical method, I refer the reader elsewhere (Bakeman and Gottman, 1986; Borckardt et al., 2008; Gorman and Allison, 1996; Gottman, 1981; Gottman and Ringland, 1981; Gottman and Roy, 1990).

Time-series analysis permits the therapist to test theories of causation regarding the relationships between interaction structures (measured by instruments such as the Psychotherapy Process Q-Set [PQS; Jones, 2000]) and changes in symptoms and other indices of change. One can also determine how interaction structures mutually influence each other (Jones et al., 1993). With the assistance of a computer software statistics package such as Statistical Package for the Social Sciences (SPSS® for Windows, 2006), a therapist can examine gradually evolving interactional processes in their own psychotherapy cases. Therapists can document these change processes identified in their individual cases, and researchers can aggregate them across diagnostically or structurally similar cases. Eventually, researchers and therapists can collaborate on compiling these change processes for various patients and disseminating them to the wider therapeutic community. This method of collecting psychotherapy process and outcome data directly challenges the hegemony of the brand-name treatments (e.g., DBT, TFP, MBT, IPT, CBT) and seeks to "reach across the aisle" to forge new alliances based on a bottom-up empiricism that the entire therapeutic community can embrace.

Qualitative single-case and multiple-case research designs represent yet another path to identifying and understanding change processes in effective psychotherapy treatments (Auerbach and Silverstein, 2003; Silverstein, Auerbach, and Levant, 2006). According to these researchers, qualitative research is particularly well suited to the study of clinical phenomena because "it uses words rather than numbers to describe psychological phenomena" (Silverstein et al., 2006, p. 351). Furthermore, qualitative research is hypothesis generating rather than hypothesis testing. In other words, qualitative research does not set out to confirm the answers to questions the researcher feels he or she already knows. Rather, qualitative research uncovers new information that can help answer a particular question about psychotherapy process or raise new questions altogether that blaze a trail of perpetual discovery. Researchers can then submit these unanticipated hypotheses to quantitative research methods such as those described earlier to confirm or disconfirm their veracity for a particular sample.

Using what is known as grounded theory (Fassinger, 2005; Glaser and Strauss, 1967; Strauss and Corbin, 1998), Silverstein and her colleagues (Silverstein et al., 2006) used this theory "to allow the participants' voices to structure the interpretation of the data" (p. 352). Briefly, the therapist or researcher formulates an open-ended question (e.g., how did you experience your divorce and its aftermath?), then sifts through the data source (e.g., psychotherapy session transcripts or even process notes) to identify relevant text that bears on this question. Then actual segments of relevant text are classified into repeating ideas (the authors suggested that approximately thirty-five repeating ideas are sufficient to represent most samples). These repeating ideas are then grouped into themes (approximately half the number of repeating ideas), which are then organized into theoretical constructs used to create a theoretical narrative directly related to the original question. Session transcripts or process notes taken from treatments with other patients are then studied using the same method to refine the open-ended question and the theoretical constructs that emerged from the first case. Like quantitative single-case research designs, qualitative single-case and multiple-case research designs represent an alternative method of studying psychotherapy process based on a bottom-up empiricism that the entire therapeutic community can embrace.

An interesting feature of this method of research is that process notes can be used (Silverstein et al., 2006), although verbatim session transcripts are recommended (Silverstein, personal communication, July 29, 2008). Process notes inevitably introduce therapist bias into the data source, which can interfere with an accurate rendering of the relevant text and, ultimately, the creation of the hypothesis-generating theoretical narrative. In spite of this caveat, Silverstein and her colleagues (Silverstein et al., 2006) used grounded theory to code the process notes of five psychotherapy sessions over the course of ten weeks of individual psychotherapy—developing theory from the bottom up to answer the open-ended question, how does family-of-origin work help patients? The organization of the data into progressively higher levels of abstraction yielded a psychotherapy process in which the patient shifted back and forth between doing family-of-origin work and resisting it. These shifts coincided with increased self-other differentiation and subsequent improvements in his pervasive pessimism, used in the service of resistance, and in his relationships with his wife and members of his family of origin. Although the question chosen by the authors did not lead to an identification of interaction structures involved in therapeutic change, a therapist or researcher could easily apply grounded theory toward this end.

A comprehensive model of single-case or multiple-case research that mixes both quantitative and qualitative methods could be used to triangulate findings and increase our confidence in the conclusions we draw from the data source or sources. For example, the identification of three or four interaction structures operating over the course of a long-term psychotherapy using grounded theory could illustrate how interaction structures mutually influence each other and evolve over time as the psychotherapy process moves through successive phases (Howard et al., 1996; Howard, Kopta, Krause, and Orlinsky, 1986; Howard, Lueger, Maling, and Martinovich, 1993). Grounded theory could also demonstrate how these interaction structures and the shifts among them coincide with changes in the patient's symptom patterns. This hypothesis-generating qualitative phase (phase 1) of the research study would organically prepare the way for a hypothesis-confirming phase (phase 2) in which an instrument such as the PQS (Jones, 2000) could be used to confirm these same interaction structures initially identified by the qualitative method outlined by Silverstein and her colleagues (Auerbach and Silverstein, 2003; Silverstein et al., 2006). Time-series analysis could be used to confirm the causal connections suggested by the theoretical narrative regarding the relationships between the interaction structures and changes in symptom patterns. Alternatively, this hypothesis-generating qualitative phase could yield new instruments better suited to assessing interaction structures because the items would have suggested themselves directly from the data. This bottom-up approach to pattern discovery and confirmation partially guards against the potentially subtle but powerful influence of existing theories reified in the psychotherapy literature—theories we have grown up with and use to structure our perceptions of how psychotherapy works.

In the absence of this model of research, we are left with a top-down psychotherapy literature that was not constructed in the organic, bottom-up manner that I have described here. This literature contains a number of internal inconsistencies with regard to the effective ingredients of psychotherapy, perhaps because the foundations of this literature were laid down with the cinder blocks of aggregated treatment outcome studies that have no direct relation to the individual patient (see chapter 2). As Jones (2000) pointed out, only from the replication of single cases can theories about common and specific factors across cases be constructed. In spite of this shortcoming, the psychotherapy literature has produced several interesting hypotheses about change processes and patient characteristics, the enhancement of which produces therapeutic change. In this book, I review some of the change processes most compelling to me: mindfulness (chapter 5), mentalization (chapter 6), and psychological mindedness (chapter 7). In another book (Goodman, in press), I also review the attachment relationship. I suggest that these change processes might be responsible for successful outcomes in a wide variety of treatments (common factors) even though most therapists might consider them specific to their preferred treatment approach (specific factors).

Specific factors (Butler and Strupp, 1986) consist of patient or therapist characteristics that specific treatment approaches claim to enhance through the intentional application of specialized therapist techniques. Common factors (Rosenzweig, 1936; see also Castonguay, 1993; Castonguay and Holtforth, 2005), on the other hand, consist of patient or therapist characteristics that most or all treatment approaches enhance regardless of any specialized therapist techniques used. I will briefly review this literature, and then illustrate how single-case and multiple-case research designs can effectively assess these processes of therapeutic change.

DODO BIRD VERDICT

In his classic 1936 paper on the processes of therapeutic change, Saul Rosenzweig quoted Lewis Carroll's (1865) Dodo Bird, who said, "*Everybody* has won, and *all* must have prizes" (p. 412). He was referring to the observation, later demonstrated by many researchers (e.g., Luborsky et al., 1975; Smith, Glass, and Miller, 1980; Stiles et al., 1986), that psychotherapy outcomes are essentially equivalent across approaches and across levels of therapist expertise (Christensen and Jacobson, 1994; Strupp and Hadley, 1979). Rosenzweig (1936) accounted for this outcome equivalence by postulating the implicit activity of common factors—effective ingredients of therapeutic change that exist in all forms of psychotherapy. While all forms of psychotherapy apply externally different methods of therapy, these common factors are allegedly responsible for the outcomes. The common factors proposed by Rosenzweig included (1) the therapeutic relationship, (2) a therapeutic rationale, (3) the interdependence of aspects of the patient's personality, and (4) the therapist's personality. Let us briefly examine each of Rosenzweig's original common factors.

The contemporary psychotherapy outcome literature refers to the therapeutic relationship as the therapeutic alliance (see Goodman, in press, chapter 3). To champions of common factors (e.g., Duncan, 2002; Wampold, 2001), relationships that develop between two persons are inherently therapeutic, regardless of the techniques practiced or the credentials held by the therapist. The therapeutic alliance has been shown to be predictive of outcome across many forms of treatment (Horvath and Bedi, 2002; Horvath and Symonds, 1991; Martin, Garske, and Davis, 2000; Shirk and Karver, 2003). To detractors of common factors (e.g., DeRubeis et al., 2005), however, the therapeutic alliance as a common factor is highly overrated. The correlations between therapeutic alliance and symptom improvement in two meta-analytic studies—.22 (Horvath and Symonds, 1991) and .26 (Martin et al., 2000)—are not sufficiently large to conclude that a strong association exists between these two variables (DeRubeis et al., 2005). In addition, the causal direction of these two variables is not clear; symptom improvement might influence the quality of the therapeutic alliance, which would disqualify therapeutic alliance as a common factor or catalyst of therapeutic change. Finally, therapeutic alliance might serve as a proxy for therapist or patient variables that drive treatment progress, although some evidence refutes this suggestion (Horvath and Bedi, 2002; Klein et al., 2003). This confusion about the contribution of therapeutic alliance to treatment outcome has led one observer to conclude, "We still do not know how or why the therapeutic relationship is ameliorative" (Weinberger, 2002, p. 70).

A therapeutic rationale for the treatment—whether it is psychotherapy, medication, or Santeria—is a necessary condition of all forms of cure. The therapist instills belief in the patient that he or she will get well through an engagement with the process, according to a common factors model. Howard and his colleagues (Howard et al., 1986; Howard et al., 1993; Howard et al., 1996) have proposed a three-phase dose-response model of psychotherapy in which the patient initially experiences remoralization—the belief that help is imminent. This is the essential definition of a placebo effect. Thus, according to this view, specific explanations for treatment effectiveness are common to all treatments intended to be therapeutic because they provide a rationale for the patient to hold onto in faith that they will recover. Frank (1973) added the observation that, regardless of their content, specialized techniques or rituals also enhance the patient's belief in the viability of the treatment, which in turn enhances the treatment's effectiveness. Typically, researchers want to exclude placebo effects from their treatments because they want to show that effectiveness is attributable to their specialized techniques and the preferred clinical theory on which they are based. Weinberger (2002) has identified the irony in the attempts of psychotherapy outcome research to control a psychological phenomenon rather than study it and harness it to enhance treatment effectiveness.

The interdependence of aspects of the patient's personality is a little studied phenomenon. Essentially, Rosenzweig (1936) is referring to the idea that all roads lead to Rome. For example, a behaviorist might shape a troublesome symptom like panic attacks into extinction, but the absence of this symptom might also improve the patient's self-esteem and agoraphobia. An interpersonal therapist might focus on improving the patient's agoraphobia, but an improvement in this symptom might also improve the patient's self-esteem and panic attacks. In chapter 7 of volume II, I discuss attachment-based intervention in relation to various points of entry in the family system. According to Rosenzweig (1936), the interconnected quality of the human personality allows the therapist to use a number of points of entry into a problem area to effect therapeutic change. Thus, brand-name treatments that promote specialized techniques designed for specific diagnoses do not appreciate this interconnected quality and instead approach their therapeutic goals in a needlessly inflexible manner (Blatt and Zuroff, 2005).

The therapist's personality also might contribute to the processes of therapeutic change as a common factor. In chapter 6 of Goodman (in press), I discuss the idea of matching the therapist's attachment organization with the patient's attachment organization in a noncomplementary manner to produce a "gentle challenge" (Dozier and Bates, 2004, p. 174) to the patient's patterns of interaction. In this model, the therapist's personality per se would not be a common factor, but rather his or her personality, in combination with the patient's personality, might represent a common factor of effective psychotherapy.

Another common factor of the therapist's personality is the allegiance the therapist feels toward the treatment and its curative properties. This aspect of the therapist's personality parallels the patient's own faith in the ability of the treatment to cure. One of the many problems with the application of the medical RCT model to psychotherapy outcome research is that the therapists conducting the TAU are not blind to this condition and therefore lack the allegiance to it that the therapists conducting the active condition automatically have. The therapists conducting the brand-name treatment are true believers in their craft, whereas the therapists conducting the sham treatment are doubters in their craft. Patients sense this lack of allegiance and adjust their own allegiance to the treatment accordingly (Baskin, Tierney, Minami, and Wampold, 2003; Luborsky et al., 1999; Wampold, 2001).

Therapist variance in treatment outcome has been shown to be greater than the treatment delivered (Crits-Christoph et al., 1991; Crits-Christoph and Mintz, 1991; Huppert et al., 2001; Kim, Wampold, and Bolt, 2006; Wampold and Brown, 2005), and even greater than adherence to the treatment manual (Wampold, 2001). Freud's (1912a) theory of transference cure derives partly from the therapist's nonjudgmental, accepting attitude toward the patient. Consistent with this idea, Duncan (2002) has suggested that the necessary and sufficient conditions of therapeutic change espoused by Carl Rogers (1957)—empathy, genuineness, and unconditional positive regard—are all provided by the therapist. These therapist characteristics are consistently mentioned in patients' reports of successful therapy (Lambert, 1992).

Patient characteristics belong to a category of common factors not previously identified by Rosenzweig (1936) but widely considered one of the most critical components of treatment outcome. In addition to the effects of the patient's attachment organization on therapeutic change (described earlier and in Goodman, in press, chapter 3), the patient's personality, allegiance to treatment, ability to form a therapeutic alliance, symptom severity, and unconscious motivational factors comprise this category. Bohart (2000) has suggested that equivalence in effective treatment outcomes across all forms of psychotherapy reflects patients' averaged regenerative powers.

The literature has neglected the contribution of patient characteristics because it has elevated the status of the therapist to heroic proportions (Tallman and Bohart, 1999). A skeptic could argue that patient characteristics in RCTs are controlled for by random assignment into active and control conditions; however, even in this ideal situation, patients could experience these conditions differently, thus yielding different treatment outcomes mistakenly attributed to the effects of specific factors. Patients in the control group usually know that they are not receiving the active treatment and therefore lack faith that they can benefit from the TAU, which activates a self-fulfilling prophecy. Ablon and his colleagues (Ablon and Jones, 1999; Ablon and Marci, 2004) noted that in their studies, the patient's contributions to psychotherapy process predicted treatment outcome more robustly than the therapist's contributions or the contributions of their interactions. Summarizing this view, Duncan (2002) declared, "Clients are the main characters, the heroes and heroines of [the] therapeutic stage . . . the most potent contributor to psychotherapeutic change" (p. 38). Until a brand-name treatment is specifically designed to enhance those patient characteristics that influence treatment outcome, the therapist's explanation of therapeutic change will be a tale told by an idiot, full of sound and fury, signifying nothing (Shakespeare, 2004).

Other researchers believe that Rosenzweig (1936) is wrong about the universal influence of common factors. Specific factors—those factors that distinguish one brand-name treatment from another—promote therapeutic change. For example, T. A. Brown and Barlow (1995) concluded that CBT for panic disorder, which uses the specific technique of exposure to the source of the panic, is superior to other forms of psychotherapy for this diagnosis. The medical RCT model assumes that specific factors produce treatment outcomes over and above any other factors shared between the active condition and the TAU. The fact that all forms of psychotherapy appear roughly equivalent in producing therapeutic change (Rosenzweig, 1936) does not suggest that specific factors are ineffective. Perhaps the instruments used to assess treatment outcomes are not sufficiently sensitive to detect differences (Kazdin and Bass, 1989). Equivalence in treatment outcomes across all forms of psychotherapy also could mean that factors specific to each treatment are equally effective via specific means in producing therapeutic change. This explanation, however, resembles Rosenzweig's (1936) common factor of the interdependence of aspects of the patient's personality. Specialized techniques act on specific aspects of the patient's personality; however, these specific aspects are interdependent with other aspects. The interdependence of neural associational networks (Gabbard and Westen, 2003) makes this theory plausible as a process of therapeutic change.

The question whether common or specific factors are responsible for therapeutic change is difficult to answer because findings that presumably demonstrate the superior effectiveness of one treatment over another are open to multiple interpretations. Active and TAU conditions might differ according to the quantity of specific factors as well as the quantity of common factors, which makes it difficult to attribute therapeutic properties to the specific factors. For example, therapist allegiance to the treatment (see earlier discussion) might vary by treatment condition, which could produce differential findings (Kazdin, 2005).

Nilsson and his colleagues (Nilsson et al., 2007) have suggested that quantitative equivalence in treatment outcome disguises qualitative differences that can be detected only through qualitative means. Using grounded theory (Strauss and Corbin, 1998) to detect such differences in patients interviewed retrospectively about their subjective experiences of therapeutic change, these authors found similar numbers of dissatisfied patients in both psychodynamic therapy and CBT but different reasons for the dissatisfaction. Patients treated with psychodynamic therapy wished they had received more structure, support, and guidance, while patients treated with CBT wished they had received a more nondirective, collaborative experience. The findings were used to argue in favor of treatment-patient matching. Specific factors were responsible for patients' subjectively different perceptions of their treatment experiences, originally concealed by the quantitative finding of similar numbers of dissatisfied patients in both treatment conditions. If common experiences reflect common factors, then different experiences might reflect specific factors over and above common factors (Nilsson et al., 2007). According to the authors, "Directiveness versus nondirectiveness may be a concept that best summarizes these [qualitative] differences" (p. 564).

Given the current state of the psychotherapy outcome literature, it is difficult to determine the relative contributions of common and specific factors to therapeutic change. For example, Wampold (2001, 2005) has suggested that common factors account for all the variance in treatment outcome. On the other hand, Craighead and his colleagues (Craighead et al., 2005) have suggested that common factors such as the therapeutic alliance are necessary but not sufficient conditions of treatment outcome. A CBT therapist "well trained in exposure and response prevention, but who fails to develop a strong therapeutic relationship, will find it essentially impossible to get a patient with severe OCD [obsessive compulsive disorder] or PTSD [posttraumatic stress disorder] to engage in the exposure procedures" (p. 191). These authors advocated for an investigation of the relative contributions of each of these categories of factors as well as their interaction. A meta-analysis conducted by Stevens and his colleagues (Stevens, Hynan, and Allen, 2000) confirmed that the contribution of specific factors exceeds that of common factors, but only for severely disturbed patients.

Assay and Lambert (1999) examined the relative contributions of common factors across treatment outcome studies and estimated that 40 percent of treatment outcome variance could be attributed to patient factors, 30 percent to relationship-mediated variables (e.g., therapeutic alliance), 15 percent to placebo factors, and only 15 percent to specific model/technique factors. Specialized techniques, the "secret sauce" of therapeutic change in brand-name treatments, account for a small portion of the variance in treatment outcome, yet most treatment manuals focus almost exclusively on the specific factors delivered rather than on the common factors that comprise most of the arsenal of interventions in any given treatment. Craighead and his colleagues (Craighead et al., 2005) estimated that therapist adherence to CBT is rated on scales for which under 50 percent of the items are related to common factors. When therapist adherence to a brand-name treatment is primarily focused on only 15 percent of the total variance accounting for treatment outcome (i.e., specific factors), we have a problem. Brand-name treatments appear to be shooting themselves in the foot by not doing all they can to facilitate their therapists' proper use of common factors.

One way of looking at the value of specific model/technique factors is to consider how they might "enhanc[e] the potency of the other common factors: client, relationship, and placebo" (Duncan, 2002, p. 42). Specific factors could be viewed as therapist healing rituals—"technically inert, but nonetheless powerful, organized methods for enhancing the effects of placebo factors" (p. 41). In other words, actually doing something to the patient increases the patient's belief in the healing power of the therapist and contributes to the patient's remoralization (Howard et al., 1986; Howard et al., 1993; Howard et al., 1996).

In some Pentecostal churches, the pastor lays his hands on the sick when he performs the healing miracle. In tenth-grade biology class, I learned about placebo effects. Always the empiricist, I decided to try out this idea. In our backyard (while my parents were not available), my nine-year-old brother complained of a headache. I told him that I knew of a fail-safe cure for headaches. (My brother's belief in this cure was virtually guaranteed as he idolized me as a child—an allegiance factor.) I hit him on the head. More like a tap. Then I told him to rub his stomach three times. I announced that I had completed the procedure. I asked him how he felt. He said that the headache miraculously went away! I think that my cure might have failed without the "specific factors" of the head-tapping and stomach-rubbing.

To what extent are the specific factors of our preferred psychotherapy approaches merely rituals that enhance placebo effects or other common factors that promote cure? I never asked my brother whether his headache returned. I wonder whether common factors facilitate the patient's remoralization phase of treatment, while specific factors take the patient through the subsequent phases of treatment—remediation and rehabilitation. Of course, this idea assumes that specific factors have active as well as inert properties.

Perhaps specific factors can be active or inert or some combination of the two, depending on the patient, the therapist, the interaction between them, the treatment approach, and the treatment phase.

The research methods used to determine the commonness or specialness of the essential ingredients of therapeutic change can hinder us in our search for their properties. As I discussed in chapter 2, RCTs and meta-analyses of RCTs identify only the main effects rather than the psychotherapy processes responsible for the main effects. Even detecting the main effects in these studies is difficult because treatment conditions typically have insufficient sample size (Craighead et al., 2005). The aggregation of patients in RCTs also eliminates any chance of discovering which patients experienced improved outcomes in both conditions, and which psychotherapy processes accounted for these improved outcomes. Conversely, we cannot discover which patients experienced stagnant or worsened outcomes in both conditions, and which psychotherapy processes accounted for these stagnant or worsened outcomes. Collectively as a discipline, we must turn to psychotherapy process research and alternative research designs to solve the riddle of common and specific factors.

PSYCHOTHERAPY PROCESS RESEARCH USING SINGLE-CASE AND MULTIPLE-CASE RESEARCH DESIGNS

It is my belief that the National Institute of Mental Health (NIMH) is not funding the most exciting psychotherapy research currently being conducted. This research is not taking place at multiple laboratory sites but rather in the therapist's own consulting room. Researchers are studying the key elements of psychotherapy process one patient at a time using single-case research designs. Earlier in this chapter, I discussed the work of Jones and his colleagues (Ablon and Jones, 2005; Jones, 1993, 2000; Jones et al., 1993; Jones and Price, 1998; Pole and Jones, 1998), who articulated the advantages of quantitative single-case research designs. These researchers demonstrated that the influence between the therapist and patient is not unidirectional but rather mutual; the patient influences the therapist as much as the therapist influences the patient. In addition, symptom changes can influence as well as be influenced by therapist interventions.

In other work (Ablon and Jones, 1998, 1999, 2002; Jones and Pulos, 1993), Jones, Ablon, and their colleagues conducted secondary analyses of four samples of archival psychotherapy data, focusing on psychotherapy processes and their relation to outcome rather than on main effects, and developed an interesting hypothesis that bears directly on the controversy surrounding common and specific factors. These researchers made two important contributions to this literature. First, they suggested that specific factors that distinguish different brand-name treatments sometimes reflect underlying commonalities in psychotherapy process (Ablon and Jones, 1999, 2002; see also Ablon and Marci, 2004). In their words, "what are often referred to as nonspecific effects [common factors] in the literature may actually represent the specific effects of shared processes" (Ablon and Jones, 2002, p. 780; Ablon and Marci, 2004, p. 666). Second, these researchers suggested that the specific factors promoted by certain brand-name treatments might be inert, while the specific factors promoted by other brand-name treatments might be active across brand-name treatments (Ablon and Jones, 1998; Ablon et al., 2006; Jones and Pulos, 1993). In other words, some specific factors might actually function as common factors because therapists promote them unintentionally. These brand-name treatments advertise their efficacy, and, by implication, their preferred specific factors, when in reality, the specific factors claimed by another form of treatment actually functioned as common factors in boosting their efficacy. In subsequent chapters, I review three such specific factors claimed by brand-name treatments that might actually function as common factors across a wide variety of psychotherapy approaches.

The authors of some of these brand-name treatments sometimes explicitly promote the secret sauce of their psychotherapy as a common factor. For example, Bateman and Fonagy (2004a), the originators of MBT, have suggested, "The potential effectiveness of all treatments depends not so much on their frame but on their ability to increase a patient's capacity to mentalize" (p. 46). Other researchers, however, emphasize the superiority of certain brand-name treatments—and the specific factors they promote—over others (e.g., DeRubeis et al., 2005). The research conducted by Jones, Ablon, and his colleagues, however, has demonstrated that specific factors might in fact be inert (see below). Thus, given these findings, the twin goals of psychotherapy process research, therefore, should be (1) to identify these effective ingredients of therapeutic change operating across a variety of psychotherapy approaches and (2) to link them to treatment outcome. For example, do all therapists who conduct effective treatments foster a process of mentalization in their patients, and can this mentalization process be causally linked to successful outcome?

As these so-called specific factors become identified as common factors, treatment packages can be designed around the enhancement of these factors rather than around an empirically untested theoretical foundation (e.g., breaking stimulus-response links, removing the repression barrier). Rather than running the same old horse race, perhaps we can focus our attention on the factors that can make all the horses in the field run faster and smarter. What training regimens and nutritional supplements work best for which horses? What kinds of horseshoes give the best traction in different kinds of weather? What do winning jockeys do differently from losing jockeys? Can most or all jockeys be trained to be winners? If all the horses won, however, then there would be no race. Academic and professional careers might be lost. But why can't the Dodo Bird be right? Why can't the APA one day announce, "*Everybody* has won, and *all* must have prizes?" The treatment package (horse) should matter less than the change processes that could make nearly every horse a winner. After all, we are trying to help *all* people lead loving and productive lives, not help only those people who bet on the winning horse.

I want to elaborate on the contributions of Jones, Ablon, and his colleagues because their research should serve as a beacon to the rest of us groping in the dark for answers to the question, "What works for whom?" For both their quantitative single-case and multiple-case research studies, these researchers relied on an instrument developed by Jones (2000) called the Psychotherapy Process Q-Set (PQS; see also volume II, chapter 5). The PQS is a set of one hundred items covering an exhaustive array of psychotherapy processes used to rate an entire audiotaped or videotaped psychotherapy session, which is the unit of analysis. Items were selected from the psychotherapy literature and from leading experts to cover psychotherapy processes found in a wide variety of treatment approaches, including cognitive-behavioral, psychodynamic, gestalt, humanistic/existential, and interpersonal (Ablon and Jones, 1999, 2002; Jones, Hall, and Parke, 1991; Jones and Pulos, 1993). Every item was constructed to cover a unique aspect of psychotherapy process not duplicated by any other item and to guarantee maximum variability across sessions and across patients. These items are rated on a scale from 1 (most uncharacteristic of the session being rated) to 5 (neither uncharacteristic nor characteristic of the session being rated) to 9 (most characteristic of the session being rated). A specified number of items are assigned to each rating: five items assigned to ratings 1 and 9, eight items assigned to ratings 2 and 8, twelve items assigned to ratings 3 and 7, sixteen items assigned to ratings 4 and 6, and eighteen items assigned to rating 5. This item arrangement forms a normal distribution suitable for parametric statistical analysis.

Because the one hundred items are ranked ordinally (i.e., in relation to each other) rather than rated independently of each other (as in Likert-type ratings), the overall arrangement of these items uniquely characterizes the session under study. This forced-choice method is referred to as ipsative or idiographic in contrast to the normative or nomothetic method typically used to characterize group data. Item comparisons are made within a single subject rather than among subjects; thus, the PQS is ideally suited to characterizing the psychotherapy process of a single session.

The PQS, along with its companion, the Child Psychotherapy Process Q-Set (CPQ; Schneider, 2004; Schneider and Jones, 2004; Schneider, Pruetzel-Thomas, and Midgley, in press), descriptively captures three elements of psychotherapy process: (1) the patient's attitude and behavior or experience; (2) the therapist's actions and attitudes; and (3) the therapist-patient interaction, or the climate or atmosphere of the encounter (Jones, 2000; Schneider and Jones, 2004). (Schneider [personal communication, October 30, 2007] is currently developing an adolescent version of the CPQ.) Approximately one-third of the items for both instruments were designed to assess each of these three elements. For example, item 64 of the CPQ assesses the child's behavior: "Child draws therapist into play." If this item is highly characteristic of the psychotherapy session being rated, *relative to the other ninety-nine Q-sort items*, it would be assigned one of the highest ratings (8 or 9). Item 100 of the PQS assesses the therapist's intervention: "Therapist draws connections between the therapeutic relationship and other relationships." If this item is highly uncharacteristic of the psychotherapy session being rated, *relative to the other ninety-nine Q-sort items*, it would be assigned one of the lowest ratings (1 or 2). Item 11 of the PQS assesses the therapist-patient interaction: "Sexual feelings and experiences are discussed." Again, this item is placed along the continuum from 1 to 9, *relative to the other ninety-nine Q-sort items* (for a complete list of the PQS and CPQ Q-sort items, see Jones, 2000, and Schneider and Jones, 2004).

Perhaps the most exciting aspect of these instruments is their unique ability to capture "the context-determined meaning of events" (Jones et al., 1993, p. 381) in the psychotherapy session being rated. Because each item is rated in relation to all the others, we know what the patient is saying and doing in relation to what the therapist is saying and doing and in relation to how the interaction between them is unfolding. Other psychotherapy process instruments (e.g., the Collaborative Study Psychotherapy Rating Scale [CSPRS] [Hill, O'Grady, and Elkin, 1992], the Comparative Psychotherapy Process Scale [CPPS] [Hilsenroth, Blagys, Ackerman, Bonge, and Blais, 2005], the Psychotherapy Process Rating Scale for Borderline Personality Disorder [PPRS-BPD] [Levy, Wasserman, et al., 2006]) capture only the application of therapist techniques without the simultaneous assessment of the patient behaviors or therapist-patient interactions that preceded or followed the emergence of these techniques. According to Jones and his colleagues (Jones et al., 1993), technique-focused instruments such as these yield a "'decontextualized' conception of process . . . because it assumes that an isomorphism exists between outcome and the relative frequency of a particular therapist intervention" (p. 382). While these other instruments are designed to capture therapist adherence, the PQS and CPQ are more comprehensive in scope as they are designed to capture reciprocal causal processes between the therapist's words and behaviors and the patient's words and behaviors.

Interaction structures—the driving force behind therapeutic change—can be captured only with an instrument like the PQS or CPQ that uniquely characterizes the therapist and patient in interaction with each other. Sessions coded over time using the PQS or CPQ can identify causal relationships between interaction structures and changes in symptom levels or personality structures or between therapist techniques and patient affects and behaviors. For example, a time-series analysis (see earlier discussion) revealed that over a course of treatment, transference interpretations were bidirectionally related to the patient's dysphoric affect. In other words, transference interpretations increased dysphoric affect, while increased dysphoric affect increased transference interpretations. In addition, the patient's dysphoric affect increased defense interpretations (Jones, 2000; Jones et al., 1993). Therapist technique checklists such as the CSPRS, CPPS, and PPRS-BPD could never yield process data of this depth and complexity. Only instruments such as the PQS and CPQ have the ability to capture true psychotherapy process—the dynamic interplay between therapist and patient and the interaction structures that inevitably form between them.

Single-Case Research Studies Using the PQS

I want to review some of the other findings from the single-case research studies that used the PQS to give the reader a flavor of the range of possibilities available to him or her in the collective search for effective change processes. In the case of Ms. M (Jones, 2000; Jones et al., 1993; Pole and Jones, 1998), fifty-three PQS ratings of every fourth session over the course of a twice weekly, two-and-a-half-year psychodynamic psychotherapy were subjected to a P-technique (Luborsky, 1953, 1995) principal components factor analysis with varimax rotation that yielded four factors: (1) therapist neutral acceptance; (2) therapist suppresses patient's negative self-representions; (3) psychodynamic technique; and (4) patient's dysphoric affect. Factors 1 and 3 can be considered therapist factors, while factor 4 can be considered a patient factor. Factor 2, however, can be considered an interaction structure that captures a therapist intervention (i.e., suppression) in the context of the patient's negative self-representations. Plotting these four factors over time, one can easily see that as the therapist became more suppressing of the patient's negative self-representations, her dysphoric affect diminished. A time-series analysis revealed that lower therapist neutral acceptance over time caused lower general symptom levels. Greater patient dysphoric affect caused greater therapist neutral acceptance, which in turn activated greater use of psychodynamic technique. Both supportive and reassuring interventions caused greater dysphoric affect. These findings provide a general sense of the valuable process information that the PQS can yield.

In the case of Ms. A (Jones, 2000; Jones and Price, 1998), sixty-three PQS ratings of every second session over the course of a twice weekly, two-year psychodynamic psychotherapy were subjected to a principal components factor analysis with varimax rotation that yielded three factors: (1) collaborative exploration; (2) ambivalence/compliance; and (3) provoking rescue. While factor 2 can be considered a patient factor, factors 1 and 3 can be considered interaction structures that capture a therapeutic alliance as well as the patient's tendency to act helpless and self-denigrating and to demand interventions from the therapist. Factor 3 was shown to diminish over time as the therapist interpreted this interaction structure and its defensive and transference functions. A time-series analysis also demonstrated that decreases in this interaction structure caused decreases in symptom levels but that decreases in symptom levels did not cause decreases in this interaction structure.

In the case of Mr. B (Jones, 2000; Jones and Price, 1998), 104 PQS ratings of every second session over the course of a twice weekly, two-and-a-half-year psychodynamic psychotherapy were subjected to a principal components factor analysis with varimax rotation that yielded three factors: (1) collaborative exploration; (2) resistant and withdrawn; and (3) angry interaction. While factor 2 can be considered a patient factor, factors 1 and 3 can be considered interaction structures that capture a therapeutic alliance as well as angry exchanges between the therapist and patient. A time-series analysis revealed that, unlike the two previous examples, increases in symptom levels actually caused increases in angry interaction and decreases in collaborative exploration. Conversely, decreases in symptom levels actually caused increases in collaborative exploration. The pattern of results represents a situation in which the symptomatic tail is wagging the psychotherapy process dog. Not surprisingly, Jones (2000) concluded, "This unanalyzed, and relatively unchanging interaction pattern [i.e., angry interaction] was associated with the fact that the patient reported only little improvement at termination. It is an illustration of a largely unconscious pattern of interaction that may have led to a stalemate in the treatment" (p. 297). In this example, the PQS was used to analyze what was going wrong in this treatment. Ruptures in the therapeutic alliance that are not repaired can derail an entire treatment (Safran and Muran, 1996, 2000).

In the case of Mrs. C (Ablon and Jones, 2005; Jones and Windholz, 1990), sixty PQS ratings of ten consecutive sessions from each of six years of four-times-weekly psychoanalysis were subjected to a principal components factor analysis with varimax rotation that yielded three factors: (1) patient self-exploration/analyst acceptance; (2) analyst activity; and (3) playing stupid. While factor 2 can be considered a therapist factor, factors 1 and 3 can be considered interaction structures that capture a therapeutic alliance as well as the patient's becoming muddled and confused in her thoughts in the context of talking about sexual feelings with a therapist who becomes more talkative than usual. Factors 1 and 3 diminished over the course of the analysis, while factor 2 increased over time. As the analysis unfolded, the therapist became more active, while the patient "played stupid" less often when discussing sexual feelings. The PQS demonstrated how the psychotherapy process unfolded over time in what the authors considered a successful analysis. Unfortunately, no symptom data were reported. A time-series analysis was not conducted on these data.

In the case of Mrs. G (Ablon and Jones, 2005), sixty PQS ratings of randomly selected sessions over the course of a four-times-weekly, three-year psychoanalysis were subjected to a principal components factor analysis with varimax rotation that yielded three factors: (1) positive transference/countertransference; (2) analyst's authoritative responsiveness; and (3) erotized transference. While factor 2 can be considered a therapist factor and factor 3 a patient factor, factor 1 can be considered an interaction structure that captures a therapeutic alliance with aspects of patient compliance and idealization and therapist validation. Factors 1 and 3 diminished over the course of the analysis, while factor 2 remained constant over time. PQS items that loaded onto factor 2 suggested a problematic interaction. For example, "analyst's own emotional conflicts intrude into relationship" (item 24) and "analyst is not sensitive to patient's feelings, not attuned to patient, not empathic" (item 6) reflect some of the items from factor 2. The authors suggested that the patient ended the analysis prematurely because "it is quite likely that the meaning of the interaction was not fully recognized, interpreted, or comprehended by the dyad" (p. 563). Unfortunately, no symptom data were reported. A time-series analysis was not conducted on these data.

One other group of researchers (Josephs et al., 2004; Josephs and Fatzer, 2006) used a quantitative single-case research design to study the psychotherapy process of Ms. Q (see also volume II, chapter 5). First, thirty-six PQS ratings of the final four years of a three-times-weekly, nine-year psychoanalysis were subjected to a principal components factor analysis with varimax rotation. (In years 6 and 7, a week of three sessions was rated every six months [twelve sessions]. In years 8 and 9, a week of three sessions was rated every three months [twenty-four sessions].) The factor analysis yielded five factors: (1) supportive defense analysis of an insightful but passive patient; (2) supportive environment; (3) exploring feelings; (4) supporting while presenting a different perspective to a committed but provocative, angry, self-accusatory, and sad patient; and (5) angry patient, rejecting analyst (Josephs and Fatzer, 2006). The authors characterized factors 1–3 as different ways of working with the patient's positive transference. Factor 1 suggests working analytically while being supportive, factor 2 suggests being supportive while not working analytically, and factor 3 suggests working analytically in a general exploratory manner. Factors 4 and 5 demonstrate two different ways of working with the patient's negative transference. Factor 4 suggests working analytically while the patient is experiencing dysphoric affect, while factor 5 suggests a mutually antagonistic therapist-patient interaction structure. Factor 4 increased over the course of the analysis, while the other factors remained constant over time. Josephs and Fatzer (2006) concluded, "Fortunately, the more constructive form of engaging the negative transference [factor 4] is increasing over the course of treatment while the less constructive form [factor 5] is not" (p. 26).

A time-series analysis revealed that increases in factor 4 (constructively engaging the negative transference) caused increases in levels of reflective functioning (see chapter 6) but that increases in levels of reflective functioning did not cause significant increases in factor 4. In other words, constructively engaging the negative transference was the only interaction structure of the five identified by the PQS that caused increases in the patient's reflective functioning. Helping the provocative patient to reflect on his or her own and others' mental states without becoming mutually antagonistic seems to be the most productive way of boosting reflective functioning. This finding demonstrates the depth of insight into the psychotherapy process that the PQS can provide. This hypothesis now awaits testing on other therapist-patient dyads to begin to approach generalizability.

How can a therapist conduct a quantitative single-case research study in his or her own backyard? The first step is to purchase audio-recording equipment that works well so that therapy sessions could be recorded with some regularity (weekly or biweekly intervals). Computer software programs such as Audacity® for PC-based computers (free download at audacity.sourceforge.net) and Garage Band® for Apple®-based computers (download at store.apple.com/us/product/MB615Z/A) can enable your computer to record directly into an MP3 file that can be easily saved. Later in this chapter, I will discuss the obstacles to recording psychotherapy sessions, which is necessary to apply the PQS accurately. A therapist must also collect data that could reasonably be expected to measure progress over time. Brief questionnaires that assess psychiatric symptoms include the Symptom Checklist-90-Revised (SCL-90-R; Derogatis, 1983); the Brief Symptom Inventory (BSI; Derogatis, 1993; Derogatis and Melisaratos, 1983), which is a brief version of the SCL-90-R; the Brief Psychiatric Rating Scale (BPRS; Overall and Gorham, 1962); and, for children and adolescents, the Child Behavior Checklist—Parent Version (CBCL-P; Achenbach, 1991; Achenbach and Edelbrock, 1981). These instruments could be administered to the patient at weekly or monthly intervals, depending on the anticipated length of treatment. A therapist could administer such an instrument only at the beginning and at the end of treatment, but a time-series analysis requires repeated measures of the outcome variable over the entire course of treatment, or at least a significant portion of it.

If symptom change is too superficial a measure of therapeutic progress (which many therapists believe), then other measures that assess structural or personality variables can also be administered. These instruments do not rely on the patient to provide the outcome data but rather on the therapist (or coder of psychotherapy transcript data). The Social Cognition and Object Relations Scale—Global (SCORS-G; Westen, 1995; see also Hilsenroth, Stein, and Pinsker, 2004; Peters, Hilsenroth, Eudell, Blagys, and Handler, 2006) measures interpersonal representations applied to narrative data such as psychotherapy transcriptions. The Shedler-Westen Assessment Procedure–200 (SWAP-200; Shedler, 2002; Shedler and Westen, 1998; Westen and Shedler, 1999a, 1999b, 2000) is a two-hundred-item Q-sort that measures pathological and health aspects of personality applied to narrative data such as psychotherapy transcriptions. The Reflective Functioning Scale (RFS; Fonagy, Gergely, et al., 2002; Fonagy, Target, Steele, and Steele, 1998; see also chapter 6) is an eleven-point rating scale that measures "the psychological processes underlying the capacity to mentalize" (Fonagy, Gergely, et al., 2002, p. 24). This scale was designed for use specifically with the Adult Attachment Interview (AAI; George et al., 1996; Main, Kaplan, and Cassidy, 1985) but has been successfully applied to psychotherapy transcriptions (Josephs et al., 2004; Josephs and Fatzer, 2006; Karlsson and Kermott, 2006).

Lesser-known instruments could also be used in quantitative single-case research studies conducted by a therapist. The Differentiation-Relatedness Scale (Auerbach and Blatt, 2002; Diamond, Blatt, Stayner, and Kaslow, 1992; see also chapter 6) is a ten-point rating scale that measures differentiation and relatedness among the patient's self- and object representations based on the subject's oral or written descriptions of mother, father, self, and therapist. Although this method would require the therapist to engage the patient in an extra-therapeutic procedure (viz., requesting an oral or written open-ended description of each of the significant persons listed above), it might be possible to apply this rating scale to psychotherapy transcriptions. The Structural Analysis of Social Behavior (SASB; Benjamin, 1993) measures two aspects of patient-reported personality: control and affiliation. The Adolescent Attachment Prototype Questionnaire and Adolescent Attachment Questionnaire (Westen, Nakash, Thomas, and Bradley, 2006) are two different measures of "both interpersonal and narrative indicators of attachment status" (p. 1069) completed by the therapist. The authors applied these instruments to both adolescent and adult samples. Although these questionnaires were not specifically designed for use as repeated measures, it would be possible to complete them at regular intervals over the course of treatment. All these instruments yield rich, clinically meaningful data that a therapist could use to measure therapeutic progress over the course of treatment in place of or in addition to symptom data.

With the assistance of SPSS® for Windows (2006), a therapist can calculate a Pearson correlation between the session number and the outcome data to determine whether changes in the outcome data occurred over time. A significant correlation would indicate that as treatment progressed, the outcome changed. For example, one would expect symptoms to decrease (negative correlation) or reflective functioning (RF) to increase (positive correlation) over the course of treatment. Each of the recorded sessions could be Q-sorted using the PQS. These PQS Q-sorts could be correlated with a PQS Q-sort prototype—a composited Q-sort derived from the PQS Q-sorts of experts who were asked to sort the PQS items to reflect the ideal psychotherapy process from their particular theoretical orientation (Ablon and Jones, 1998, 2002). Prototypical PQS Q-sorts are currently available for psychodynamic psychotherapy, cognitive-behavioral therapy (CBT), and interpersonal therapy (IPT; Ablon and Jones, 1998, 2002) as well as dialectical behavior therapy (DBT) and transference-focused psychotherapy (TFP; see chapter 4). Correlations between the PQS Q-sorts of each psychotherapy session and the prototypical Q-sort comprised of the experts reflect the extent to which a particular session adheres to the ideal principles of a particular theoretical orientation. These adherence correlations can then be treated as scores. Changes in adherence scores over time can be calculated by correlating the adherence scores with the session number. Did the therapist become more adherent or less adherent as the treatment progressed? Adherence scores can also be used to predict the outcome data. Did the therapist's adherence to a particular theoretical orientation correlate with positive or negative outcome changes?

A therapist could also calculate the means of each of the PQS items over the course of the treatment to determine which aspects of the psychotherapy process were most prominent. Each PQS item could also be correlated with the outcome data (after applying a Bonferroni correction, $p < .001$, to decrease the probability of type I errors) to determine which aspects of psychotherapy process are associated with changes in outcome. For example, the PQS item, "therapist draws connections between the therapeutic relationship and other relationships" (item 100), might be significantly negatively correlated with depression and anxiety (e.g., Jones et al., 1993). This information tells us that transference interpretations reduced this patient's depression and anxiety.

For the more adventurous therapist with over fifty PQS-rated sessions (Jones, 2000, p. 266), the PQS Q-sorts could be subjected to a principal components factor analysis with varimax rotation (thus minimizing the number of items that have high loadings on multiple factors) that yields conceptually different facets of psychotherapy process. Each of these factors can then be correlated with session number (to determine the waxing and waning of these different facets over the course of treatment), outcome data (to determine which factors are associated with changes in outcome), and adherence scores (to determine which factors are more closely aligned with the theoretical orientation being practiced). Finally, as mentioned earlier in this chapter, a time-series analysis can be conducted to determine how one set of variables (e.g., process factors) occurring at a certain point in time (time 1) influences another set of variables (e.g., outcome data) occurring at a later point in time (time 2), over and above the influence of the outcome data at time 1. As I have illustrated from the literature, a time-series analysis can identify (1) causal relationships between each of the process factors and the outcome data and (2) causal relationships among the process factors themselves (Jones et al., 1993). In chapter 4, I illustrate some of these statistical methods using a sample of five patients diagnosed with BPD who received six months of three-times-per-week TFP.

The goal is to identify the reciprocal influences between interaction structures (i.e., process factors) and the outcomes measured, whether they are symptoms or structural features of personality. Interaction structures favorable to outcome would be replicated (if possible) in other treatments to determine whether such change processes generalize to other therapeutic dyads working on other problem areas. These empirically derived change processes can then be recommended to others. All of this is possible right in the therapist's own backyard.

Multiple-Case Research Studies Using the PQS

Researchers have also used the PQS in multiple-case research studies to investigate important questions about both common and specific factors associated with treatment outcome. I want to review some of the findings from the multiple-case research studies that used the PQS. Earlier in this chapter, I referred to the work of Jones, Ablon, and their colleagues (Ablon and Jones, 1998, 1999, 2002; Jones and Pulos, 1993), who made two important contributions to the literature. First, these researchers suggested that specific factors that distinguish different brand-name treatments sometimes reflect underlying commonalities in psychotherapy process (Ablon and Jones, 1999, 2002; see also Ablon and Marci, 2004). Specifically, CBT and IPT manualize different technical procedures (i.e., the secret sauce) but share essentially the same underlying psychotherapy process.

In the earlier study (Ablon and Jones, 1999), session 4 and session 12 of twenty-session treatments of thirty-five patients randomly assigned to IPT and twenty-nine patients randomly assigned to CBT were Q-sorted using the PQS, totaling 128 ($2 \times [35 + 29]$) PQS ratings. A *t*-test with a Bonferroni correction tested which of the one hundred PQS items could distinguish between the two treatments—IPT and CBT. Fifty-two of the one hundred items did not significantly distinguish the two treatments. Furthermore, ten of the twenty most and least characteristic items of each treatment overlapped. Of these ten overlapping items, seven of them were related specifically to the patient. The one hundred PQS items were then correlated with two different depression measures across both treatments after controlling for pretreatment depression scores. Of the twenty-three PQS items significantly correlated with outcome, twenty-two of them described patient characteristics, experiences, or qualities in session. Of these twenty-two PQS items, eighteen of them were equally characteristic of both IPT and CBT. In examining these common items, the authors concluded, "In both treatment modalities, therapists were very supportive, and patients were highly accepting, compliant, and agreeable. Patients in the two samples were similar across many dimensions of therapy process" (p. 72).

Reviewing these findings a year later, Jones (2000) characterized both IPT and CBT as "predominantly supportive in nature" in which "differences [in therapy content] were rather superficial" (p. 215). In supportive treatments like IPT and CBT, "the patient may risk different, more assertive behavior to maintain a passive, dependent relationship with a therapist who takes the role of a benevolent parental figure" (Ablon and Jones, 1999, p. 73), as indicated by the overlapping PQS items that reflect shared psychotherapy process. Because the effectiveness of such treatments depends on the benevolent presence of the therapist/parent, enduring symptomatic change is seldom observed, as the follow-up data indicated (Shea, Elkin, et al., 1992).

In the later study (Ablon and Jones, 2002), eleven experts in IPT and ten experts in CBT were asked to rate the PQS items to reflect the ideal psychotherapy process from their particular theoretical orientation. The Q-sorts of each group of experts were composited, yielding two prototypical Q-sorts of IPT and CBT. Six of the twenty most characteristic items of each treatment overlapped. These prototypical Q-sorts were then correlated with the 128 PQS ratings of actual sessions. Surprisingly, both forms of treatment adhered more closely to prototypical CBT than to prototypical IPT. Adherence scores derived from correlations between the 128 actual sessions and both prototypical Q-sorts were positively correlated with symptom outcomes in both treatments. My own calculation of the Spearman-Brown correlation between the IPT and CBT prototypical Q-sorts (obtained from Stuart Ablon) is $r = .51, p < .001$, a very significant positive correlation. Thus, each brand-name treatment accounted for a whopping 26 percent of the psychotherapy process variance in the other treatment ($r^2 = .51 \times .51 = .26$).

Again, the authors concluded that these two forms of psychotherapy share underlying process despite their superficial differences in technique. Despite the fact that both forms of treatment were considered adherent to their respective treatment manuals, the underlying process significantly overlapped. Thus, RCT researchers believe that the specific factors (i.e., therapist techniques) associated with a brand-name treatment are responsible for treatment efficacy when the secret sauce might actually be the supportive processes that underlie both forms of treatment. According to Ablon and Jones (2002), "A narrow focus on the different content of these manualized treatments makes it easy to overlook the high degree of correspondence in process" (p. 781). These findings therefore offer an explanation for the treatment outcome equivalence usually reported between different brand-name treatments: "What are often referred to as nonspecific [common] effects in the literature may actually represent the specific effects of shared processes" (Ablon and Jones, 2002, p. 780). Again, the authors emphasized the undervalued contribution of the patient as the common thread between IPT and CBT. Submissive, idealizing patients got better, while resistant, devaluing patients did not. The image of the therapist as the slayer of psychopathology with his mighty technique has vanished. Freud's (1912b) own metaphor of the analyst as surgeon implies an active therapist and passive (anesthetized) patient, whereas this research suggests that the patient's attitude and behavior profoundly affect treatment outcome—even if these characteristics consist of submissiveness and idealization prompted by didactic, short-term treatments.

The second important contribution to the literature made by Jones and his colleagues (Ablon and Jones, 1998; Jones and Pulos, 1993) was to demonstrate that some specific factors identified with a particular brand-name treatment do not actually predict outcome, while other specific factors not so identified do predict outcome. In their examination of three archival psychotherapy data sets, Jones and his colleagues demonstrated that CBT process does not predict positive treatment outcome, while psychodynamic process does predict positive treatment outcome, in *both* psychodynamic *and* CBT treatments.

In the earlier study (Jones and Pulos, 1993), session 1, session 5, and session 14 of fifteen-session treatments of thirty patients in psychodynamic therapy and thirty-two patients in CBT were Q-sorted using the PQS, totaling 186 (3 × [30 + 32]) PQS ratings. A *t*-test with a Bonferroni correction tested which of the one hundred PQS items could distinguish between the two treatments—psychodynamic and CBT. Unlike the findings of the previously reported studies (Ablon and Jones, 1999, 2002) that found strong similarities between IPT and CBT process, this study found strong differences between psychodynamic process and CBT process. Fifty-seven of the one hundred items significantly distinguished the two treatments. Rather than conducting one hundred *t*-tests to determine which aspects of psychotherapy process were correlated with symptom outcomes, the authors subjected the 186 PQS ratings to a principal components factor analysis with varimax rotation and then associated these factors with symptom outcomes. The factor analysis yielded four factors: (1) psychodynamic technique; (2) cognitive-behavioral technique; (3) patient resistance; and (4) negative patient affect. Factors 1 and 2 can be considered therapist factors, while factors 3 and 4 can be considered patient factors. All the items that loaded onto psychodynamic technique and cognitive-behavioral technique were significantly different from each other. In other words, the items that comprised these two factors did not overlap. These four factors were then correlated with symptom outcomes after controlling for pretreatment symptom scores. Surprisingly, psychodynamic technique was significantly positively correlated with patient improvement on four of the five outcome measures in CBT, while cognitive-behavioral technique was not correlated with patient improvement in this same treatment. Patient resistance was significantly negatively correlated with five of the nine outcome measures in both treatments.

The authors (Jones and Pulos, 1993) concluded, "The common core of therapeutic process across different approaches may well be located in this domain [psychodynamic technique]" (p. 316). This domain consists of "the evocation of affect, bringing troublesome feelings into awareness . . . and using the therapist-patient relationship" (p. 315) as an instrument of change, while cognitive-behavioral technique, according to the findings, consists of "the cognitive control of negative affect through the use of intellect and rationality, combined with vigorous encouragement, support, and reassurance on the part of the therapist" (p. 315). This study found that patient improvement was associated with the evocation of affect, not its suppression.

In the later study (Ablon and Jones, 1998), eleven experts in psychodynamic therapy and ten experts in CBT were asked to rate the PQS items to reflect the ideal psychotherapy process from their particular theoretical orientation, yielding two prototypical Q-sorts of psychodynamic therapy and CBT (as in the Ablon and Jones, 2002, study). None of the twenty most characteristic items of each theoretical orientation overlapped. The items most characteristic of each theoretical orientation in this study resembled the items identified in the earlier study (Jones and Pulos, 1993). My own calculation of the Spearman-Brown correlation between the psychodynamic and CBT prototypical Q-sorts (obtained from Stuart Ablon) is $r = .01$, *ns*. Thus, each brand-name treatment accounted for 0 percent of the psychotherapy process variance in the other treatment ($r^2 = .01 \times .01 = .00$). These prototypical Q-sorts were then correlated with one hundred PQS ratings of actual sessions (a psychodynamic sample of thirty-eight patients was added to the psychodynamic sample of thirty patients and CBT sample of thirty-two patients previously reported in Jones and Pulos, 1993; the three PQS ratings per patient in that study were composited). While the thirty-two CBT sessions adhered closely only to prototypical CBT, the sixty-eight psychodynamic sessions reflected an even mixture of adherence to prototypical psychodynamic therapy and prototypical CBT. Psychodynamic adherence scores derived from correlations between the prototypical psychodynamic Q-sort and the thirty original psychodynamic sessions and thirty-eight new psychodynamic sessions were then correlated with symptom outcomes after controlling for pretreatment symptom scores. Confirming the findings of Jones and Pulos (1993), the psychodynamic adherence scores were significantly positively correlated with patient improvement on three of the six outcome measures in the thirty-patient psychodynamic sample and four of the six outcome measures in the thirty-two-patient CBT sample. Cognitive-behavioral adherence scores similarly derived from correlations between the prototypical CBT Q-sort and the thirty-two CBT sessions were then correlated with symptom outcomes after controlling for pretreatment symptom scores. Again confirming the findings of Jones and Pulos (1993), the cognitive-behavioral adherence scores were significantly positively correlated with patient improvement on only one of the six outcome measures in each of the thirty-patient psychodynamic sample and thirty-two-patient CBT sample. Finally, adherence scores were not correlated with patient improvement on any of the outcome measures in the thirty-eight-patient psychodynamic sample, perhaps because neither psychodynamic nor cognitive-behavioral techniques were helpful to this sample of PTSD patients.

The authors (Ablon and Jones, 1998) concluded that, despite the fact that the CBT therapists adhered closely to a treatment manual, aspects of psychodynamic process infiltrated those CBT treatments and were correlated with patient improvement, not aspects of CBT process. This finding suggests that psychodynamic technique can be found in a wide array of treatments, including CBT. The authors combed through some of the CBT sessions and identified a transference interpretation to illustrate their point that CBT therapists closely adhering to cognitive-behavioral technique nevertheless use psychodynamic technique at times. The fact that the CBT therapists adhered to the treatment manual so closely might account for the nonsignificant correlations between cognitive-behavioral process and treatment outcome: responding to problems in the therapeutic alliance with increasing adherence to the treatment model further strains the therapeutic alliance and can jeopardize outcome (Castonguay et al., 1996). Thus, the findings do not necessarily suggest that CBT techniques do not work but rather that slavish devotion to a treatment manual does not work. Taken together, the findings suggest that equivalence in treatment outcomes across studies might result from the implementation of psychodynamic techniques in all forms of treatment—a common factor that masquerades as a specific factor. Second, therapist adherence to the techniques prescribed by a treatment manual is virtually impossible: "Unlike medication, psychotherapy cannot be administered in such pure form" (Ablon and Jones, 2002, p. 782). Other techniques inevitably creep in. Third, rigid adherence to any form of treatment strains the therapeutic alliance, a necessary ingredient for all effective treatments (Craighead et al., 2005).

I want to review two recent multiple-case research studies that used the PQS to assess psychotherapy process. Ablon and his colleagues (Ablon et al., 2006) conducted a small naturalistic study consisting of seventeen patients presenting for treatment of panic disorder. The majority of the sample had comorbid psychiatric diagnoses and had previously pursued psychotherapy. Therapists treated these seventeen patients as they normally would. No treatment manuals were used. Treatment length averaged twenty-one sessions. Session 12 of these seventeen treatments was Q-sorted using the PQS. These seventeen PQS ratings were correlated with each of the three prototypical Q-sorts—psychodynamic, IPT, and CBT. The therapists, who had identified themselves as psychodynamic, conducted treatments that adhered primarily to CBT and secondarily to IPT and psychodynamic. Only the psychodynamic process and IPT process, however, were correlated with treatment outcomes. The PQS items most highly positively correlated with treatment outcome consisted of the evocation of affect, particularly negative affect, while the PQS items most highly negatively correlated with treatment outcome consisted of focusing on cognitive themes and the therapist's suggestive influence and prescriptive stance.

These findings are particularly interesting in the context of impressive results for CBT for panic disorder conducted in a community mental health setting (Stuart, Treat, and Wade, 2000). In addition to the fact that the CBT researchers who conducted the follow-up assessments introduced experimenter bias by not keeping themselves blind to the patients' treatment condition (Westen et al., 2004a, p. 649), psychotherapy process was not studied at all. The findings of Ablon and his colleagues (Ablon et al., 2006) suggest that the success of this treatment could be attributed to the unintended psychodynamic techniques practiced by the CBT therapists. Empirically supported treatments (ESTs) might work, but for the wrong reasons. The RCT medical model cannot inform the academic community or the public why ESTs work (see chapter 2). It is indeed ironic that CBT—perhaps the most highly touted EST—works because its practitioners inadvertently use psychodynamic techniques, which we are informed are "less essential and outdated" (Calhoun et al., 1998, p. 151) than EST techniques (see also Task Force on Psychological Intervention Guidelines of the American Psychological Association, 1995). Perhaps psychodynamic techniques now need to be considered "*empirically informed*" (Westen et al., 2004a, p. 658) and CBT techniques less essential and outdated.

In the other recent multiple-case research study using the PQS, Karlsson and Kermott (2006) conducted a secondary analysis of archival data using the 128 PQS ratings of thirty-five patients randomly assigned to IPT and twenty-nine patients randomly assigned to CBT previously used by Ablon and Jones (1999, 2002). RF was assessed in each of these 128 sessions (for details on RF, see chapter 6) and was correlated with each of the one hundred PQS items with a Bonferroni correction. Six items were significantly positively correlated with RF, while five items were significantly negatively correlated with RF. Collectively, these items suggest that RF in patients is facilitated by "a therapeutic style characterized by working with unacceptable feelings in an empathic manner" in which patients "show signs of insight or new understanding" (p. 74). Conversely, RF in patients is hindered by patients' passivity and resistance and therapists who actively exert control over the interaction (e.g., by structuring or introducing new topics). The authors then correlated these eleven PQS items with symptom outcomes after controlling for pretreatment symptom scores and found that four of the six process items shown to facilitate RF were significantly correlated with positive outcomes, while four of the five process items shown to hinder RF were significantly correlated with negative outcomes.

In the authors' second study (Karlsson and Kermott, 2006), the ninety PQS ratings of thirty patients in psychodynamic therapy previously used by Jones and his colleagues (Ablon and Jones, 1998; Jones and Pulos, 1993) were correlated with RF as in the first study. Three items were significantly positively correlated with RF, while two items were significantly negatively correlated with RF. Collectively, these items suggest that RF in patients is facilitated by the expression of angry feelings in the context of exploration of mental states of self and others. Conversely, RF in patients is hindered by patients' passivity and resistance as in the first study. The authors then correlated these five PQS items with symptom outcomes after controlling for pretreatment symptom scores and found that two of the three process items shown to facilitate RF were significantly correlated with positive outcomes, while both process items shown to hinder RF were significantly correlated with negative outcomes.

In both these studies, Karlsson and Kermott (2006) demonstrated that specific aspects of psychotherapy process, irrespective of brand-name treatments, are correlated with RF as well as treatment outcome. A next step for someone to take with these data would be to conduct a multiple-case time-series analysis to determine whether RF influenced these aspects of psychotherapy process or whether these aspects of psychotherapy process influenced RF (see earlier review of Josephs and Fatzer, 2006; see also chapter 6). Someone could also test a mediational model of therapeutic change in which RF mediates the relation between psychotherapy process and treatment outcome. Perhaps specific aspects of psychotherapy process facilitate patient RF, which in turn helps these patients to understand the mental states of self and others and restores affect regulation, thus obviating the need for symptom formation. Only single-case and multiple-case research studies that examine psychotherapy process will illuminate the most effective change processes in psychotherapy conducted by rank-and-file therapists like you and me.

CONCEPTUAL DIFFERENCES BETWEEN PSYCHODYNAMIC AND COGNITIVE-BEHAVIORAL TECHNIQUE

I want to underscore the conceptual differences between psychodynamic and cognitive-behavioral technique found in the literature—the uniquely effective ingredients of therapeutic change promoted by each theoretical orientation. I have already mentioned that the Spearman-Brown correlation between the prototypical PQS Q-sorts of a group of psychodynamic experts and a group of cognitive-behavioral experts was $r = .01$, *ns*. Thus, we would expect little or no conceptual overlap between the techniques used by therapists in these two groups. The naturalistic study conducted by Ablon and his colleagues (Ablon et al., 2006) suggested that most psychodynamic therapists adhere to various therapeutic modalities in spite of their stated preference for one particular modality (see volume II, chapter 5). If psychodynamic and CBT techniques contradict each other, however, the rank-and-file therapist must decide when to intervene psychodynamically and when to intervene cognitive-behaviorally and what the consequences might be for the therapist-patient relationship as a result of such a decision. As you will see below, the choice between making a psychodynamic intervention and making a CBT intervention can be stark; thus, one might expect the psychological effects on the patient to be equally stark. The current focus on empirically validating treatment packages using the medical RCT model should be immediately replaced with a focus on empirically validating change processes such as the techniques listed below to assist therapists with the decision-making processes required to make the therapeutic interventions needed for that particular patient.

Jones and Pulos (1993) used the PQS to rate ninety sessions of thirty patients participating in psychodynamic therapy for psychotherapy process. The ten most characteristic and ten least characteristic items of these ninety PQS-rated sessions were listed in table 2 (p. 310). These authors duplicated this procedure with ninety-six PQS-rated sessions of thirty-two patients participating in CBT with the ten most characteristic and ten least characteristic items listed in table 3 (p. 311). Five years later, Ablon and Jones (1998) used a different method for identifying psychodynamic psychotherapy process: eleven psychodynamic experts provided prototypical PQS Q-sorts that reflect the ideal psychotherapy process from their particular theoretical orientation. The twenty most characteristic items of these eleven experts were listed in table 1 (p. 75). These authors duplicated this procedure with prototypical PQS Q-sorts from ten cognitive-behavioral experts with the twenty most characteristic items listed in table 2 (p. 76).

I want to compare these PQS-derived process variables with the exhaustive literature review conducted by Blagys and Hilsenroth (2000), who sought to identify the most important techniques and processes of psychodynamic therapy that distinguish it from CBT. The seven distinctive features of psychodynamic therapy are listed in table 8 (p. 185). Two years later, Blagys and Hilsenroth (2002) conducted a second exhaustive literature review to identify the most important techniques and processes of CBT that distinguish it from psychodynamic therapy. The six distinctive features of CBT are listed in table 7 (p. 701). For the sake of comparison, I have included the psychodynamic process items of Jones and Pulos (1993) and Ablon and Jones (1998) and the seven distinctive features of psychodynamic therapy of Blagys and Hilsenroth (2000) in figure 3.1. I have also included the CBT process items of Jones and Pulos (1993) and Ablon and Jones (1998) and the six distinctive features of CBT of Blagys and Hilsenroth (2002) in figure 3.2. In each figure, I have drawn lines among the three lists (Jones and Pulos, Ablon and Jones, Blagys and Hilsenroth) to illustrate the conceptual commonalities of psychodynamic process (see figure 3.1) and CBT process (see figure 3.2) in spite of the methodological differences used in these different studies.

Perhaps the most glaring difference between the techniques and processes of psychodynamic therapy and CBT is the therapist's response to

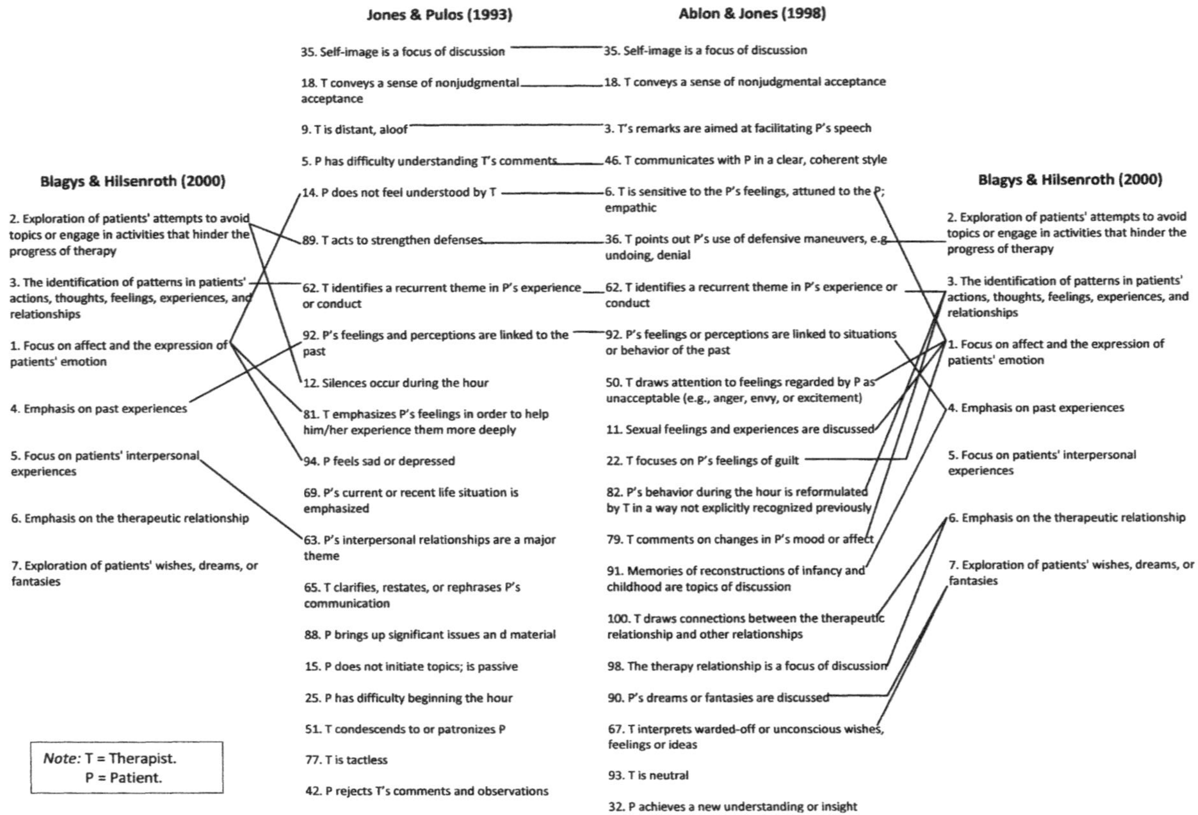

Figure 3.1. Psychodynamic Therapy

Figure 3.2. Cognitive-Behavioral Therapy

the patient's affect. In psychodynamic therapy, the therapist facilitates the patient's expression of affect and identifies patterns of affect and experience, particularly within the therapeutic relationship. In CBT, by contrast, the therapist didactically directs the patient by focusing on the patient's cognitive experience (specifically, illogical or irrational thoughts and beliefs), providing information, teaching skills, and assigning homework. In figure 3.1, only four of the twenty psychodynamic PQS items from Jones and Pulos (1993) perfectly correspond to the twenty psychodynamic PQS items from Ablon and Jones (1998), whereas in figure 3.2, eight of the twenty CBT PQS items from Jones and Pulos (1993) perfectly correspond. The reason is that the most and least characteristic psychodynamic PQS items from Jones and Pulos (1993) were derived from actual PQS ratings of ninety psychodynamic sessions that contained an admixture of CBT process (see Ablon and Jones, 1998, p. 78). For example, item 69—"patient's current or recent life situation is emphasized"—was one of the most characteristic items of the ninety PQS-rated psychodynamic sessions even though this item characterizes CBT according to the ten CBT experts (see figure 3.2).

On the other hand, twice as many CBT PQS items from Jones and Pulos (1993) perfectly correspond to the twenty CBT PQS items from Ablon and Jones (1998) because the Jones and Pulos (1993) CBT items were derived from actual PQS ratings of ninety-six CBT sessions that contained only a small (but active) admixture of psychodynamic process (see Ablon and Jones, 1998, p. 78). Thus, a greater conceptual overlap exists between these items and the twenty items that characterize CBT according to the ten CBT experts. Notably, a focus on self-image (item 35) made the list of most characteristic CBT PQS items from Jones and Pulos (1993) even though this item characterizes psychodynamic therapy according to the eleven psychodynamic experts (see figure 3.1). Perhaps a focus on self-image is one of the aspects of psychodynamic process that contributed to significant positive correlations between psychodynamic process and four of the six outcome measures in the CBT sessions.

It is interesting to note that six of the ten least characteristic items in the two Jones and Pulos (1993) lists—psychodynamic and CBT—overlap. Five of these six items reflect patient characteristics. Effective psychotherapy process—regardless of theoretical orientation—requires a patient who feels understood by the therapist and is open to taking in the therapist's comments and observations.

Finally, it is notable that Blagys and Hilsenroth's (2000, 2002) exhaustive reviews of the literature do not perfectly correspond to the PQS item lists from Jones and Pulos (1993) and Ablon and Jones (1998). Specifically, Blagys and Hilsenroth's (2000) psychodynamic category 5—a focus on the patient's interpersonal experiences—is covered in the Jones and Pulos (1993) list of psychodynamic items derived from PQS-rated sessions (item 63) but not covered in the Ablon and Jones (1998) list of psychodynamic items derived from expert PQS ratings (see figure 3.1). The reason is that Blagys and Hilsenroth (2000) curiously combined psychodynamic and interpersonal techniques and processes. According to eleven psychodynamic experts, a focus on interpersonal relationships is not most characteristic of psychodynamic therapy (see column 2, figure 3.1), although psychodynamic therapists do focus on interpersonal relationships in actual practice (see column 1, figure 3.1). My own calculation of the Spearman-Brown correlation between the psychodynamic and IPT prototypical Q-sorts (obtained from Stuart Ablon) is $r = .11$, *ns*, while the Spearman-Brown correlation between the IPT and CBT prototypical Q-sorts is $r = .51$, $p < .001$, a very significant positive correlation. Thus, according to the experts, IPT has more in common with CBT than it does with psychodynamic therapy. If Blagys and Hilsenroth (2000) had removed IPT from their exhaustive review, therefore, the resultant list of psychodynamic techniques and processes would have been more conceptually cohesive. A later meta-analysis (Diener, Hilsenroth, and Weinberger, 2007) confirmed that the therapist's facilitation of the patient's expression of affect is an effective ingredient of therapeutic change in psychodynamic therapy.

Blagys and Hilsenroth's (2002) cognitive-behavioral category 4—a focus on the patient's future experiences—is not directly covered in either of the lists compiled by Jones and Pulos (1993) and Ablon and Jones (1998). I drew lines to PQS item 4—"the patient's treatment goals are discussed"—and PQS item 85—"the therapist encourages the patient to try new ways of behaving with others"—because treatment goals and behaving in new ways imply a vision of the patient's future functioning (see figure 3.2). It might be more correct to say that CBT focuses on current life situations (PQS item 69), while psychodynamic therapy focuses on memories from childhood (PQS item 91) and their links to current feelings or perceptions (PQS item 92).

Some PQS items do not correspond with either of Blagys and Hilsenroth's (2000, 2002) categories because the authors constructed the categories to capture psychodynamic and CBT therapist techniques that distinguish these two forms of treatment from each other. The PQS items, on the other hand, were designed to capture a wide array of psychotherapy processes that encompass therapist techniques as well as patient attitudes and behaviors or experiences and interactions between the therapist and the patient. The PQS items also capture the psychotherapy process of other theoretical orientations, such as client-centered, gestalt, and rational-emotive behavior therapy (Jones and Pulos, 1993). Thus, items that reflect a therapeutic alliance (e.g., the therapist communicates with the patient in a clear, coherent style [PQS item 46]) would not correspond with distinctive features of psychodynamic therapy or CBT, according to Blagys and Hilsenroth (2000, 2002).

At the risk of oversimplifying these findings, I want to propose that psychodynamic therapy facilitates the patient's expression of affect, while CBT facilitates the patient's suppression of it. I am not referring here to dialectical behavior therapy (DBT) or other so-called third-wave therapies (see chapter 5) in which mindfulness practice encourages patients to acknowledge their feelings. Even mindfulness therapists, however, instruct patients to let go of their feelings once they experience them, like watching a parade from the reviewing stand rather than joining the parade (S. C. Hayes, 2004). Experiencing and expressing affect is conceptually different from observing or suppressing it. We need rank-and-file therapists to conduct single-case and multiple-case research studies using psychotherapy process instruments such as the PQS and CPQ to discover which change processes—experience and expression of affect or observation and suppression of affect—work best for which patients, under which conditions, paired with which therapists—regardless of theoretical orientation. For example, Jones and his colleagues (Jones et al., 1988) found that among patients suffering from severe PTSD, a psychotherapy process that facilitated anxiety suppression predicted positive outcome. Ablon and Jones (1998) later suggested, "Modified prototypes with greater specificity may be needed for variations of therapy technique used to treat specific patient populations" (p. 80). In chapter 4, I report on two such modified PQS prototypes—one for DBT and the other for TFP used to treat patients suffering from BPD. Only by empirically testing change processes one case at a time and then aggregating these cases can we arrive at a consensus about the effectiveness of these change processes. This research program looks decidedly different from the multimillion-dollar, multisite RCTs currently the rage in psychotherapy research.

VERBATIM RECORDING: OBSTACLE TO THE COLLECTION OF SINGLE-CASE AND MULTIPLE-CASE RESEARCH DATA

The use of powerful instruments such as the PQS and CPQ requires the therapist to audio-record or video-record the psychotherapy session to preserve an accurate and objective series of observations of the interactions between the therapist and the patient. These audio-recorded or video-recorded sessions of rank-and-file therapists and their patients could be used to identify empirically derived processes of therapeutic change in naturalistic settings in lieu of conducting expensive, time-consuming, and externally invalid RCTs (see chapter 2).

One barrier to this new era of establishing empirically supported change processes based on what rank-and-file therapists do with their patients in their private offices at a grassroots level is the ambivalence toward audio-recording or video-recording of psychotherapy sessions experienced among some therapists. Anecdotally, therapists sometimes feel that patients who agree to audio-recording or video-recording would become inhibited or suspicious of the therapist's motives for the recording of sessions. For example, Josephs and his colleagues (Josephs et al., 2004) suggested that a recording device could become a "prying superego" (p. 1193) for both the therapist and patient. Would a recorded patient "unconsciously try to generate a certain outcome to seductively gratify or perversely frustrate the analyst's wish to look good to a wider analytic community" (p. 1193)? Alternatively, the therapist might experience performance anxiety related to the evaluation of his or her work by his or her peers, and, particularly, anxiety over the inevitable countertransference enactments caught on tape.

Although a recording device could introduce iatrogenic effects, there is only limited evidence for this belief. Surprisingly few researchers have even explored the issue. In the only study I could find, both audio-recording and video-recording inhibited self-exploration of patients with educational-vocational problems (Gelso, 1973). On the other hand, process notes, the traditional method of recording psychotherapy process, introduce a variety of distortions into the process data (Wolfson and Sampson, 1976). No study has been conducted to explore the reasons behind therapists' decision to record or not to record psychotherapy sessions. Understanding these reasons could lead to formulating strategies for convincing rank-and-file therapists of the benefits of recording their sessions for uncovering the therapeutic processes that work best to effect symptomatic and structural change in their patients. Although the following study is primarily descriptive, one hypothesis was formulated: therapists who do not record their sessions are primarily concerned about a recording's inhibiting effects on patient self-disclosures (based on Gelso's [1973] findings).

I developed a research questionnaire (see appendix at the end of this chapter) that contains forty-seven items rated on a Likert-type scale with anchor points ranging from 1 ("not important at all") to 7 ("extremely important"). These items assess therapists' attitudes about the recording of psychotherapy sessions and are divided into four sections: (1) attitudes about audio-recording; (2) attitudes about video-recording; (3) circumstances that might change the therapist's mind about recording sessions; and (4) a brief demographic section that assesses areas such as age and theoretical orientation that could be associated with these attitudes. The questionnaire takes about ten minutes to complete. I mailed this questionnaire to all members (not candidates) of two prestigious nonmedical psychoanalytic institutes in a large metropolitan area along with a stamped, self-addressed envelope in which respondents could return it. Respondents were instructed not to place their names or any other identifying information on the questionnaire. Because no names were collected, I informed the respondents that I would consider the returned questionnaire an indication of informed consent to participate in the study. The Long Island University Institutional Review Board approved this research study.

I mailed questionnaires to the 240 members that comprise Institute A and the 179 members that comprise Institute B. I received seventy-three questionnaires from members of Institute A (30.4 percent response rate) and twenty-eight questionnaires from members of Institute B (15.6 percent response rate). A combined total of 101 psychoanalysts returned questionnaires (combined 24.1 percent response rate). Nine respondents indicated that they were no longer in private or group practice and were thus excluded from the study. Thus, ninety-two respondents completed the entire questionnaire. Because the members of Institutes A and B did not significantly differ on any of the demographic, private practice, or theoretical orientation questions, these two groups were combined for all subsequent data analyses. The respondents were almost exclusively Caucasian (98.9 percent), middle-aged ($M = 61.8$ years, $SD = 9.0$, range = 40–86), and mostly female (70.7 percent). Regarding highest advanced professional degree earned, 67 percent held a doctoral degree (MD, PhD, PsyD), while 33 percent held a master's degree (MSW, MA, MSN). The respondents averaged 27.7 years in private practice ($SD = 8.8$, range = 11–50). Regarding populations served, 69 percent worked with geriatrics, adults, or adolescents, while 31 percent worked with children and at least one of the other populations listed. Regarding theoretical orientation, 85 percent identified as "psychoanalytic" and another 12 percent identified as "psychodynamic."

Surprisingly, not one of the ninety-two respondents audio-recorded or video-recorded their psychotherapy sessions. I then conducted a series of paired-samples *t*-tests on the audio-recording data (items 7–21) and video-recording data (items 28–42) to determine whether any significant differences existed between these two sets of items regarding therapists' attitudes. On only two item-pairs, 19/40 and 20/41, were significant differences found. Therapists were more likely to endorse video-recording as too cumbersome (questions 19 and 40; $t(88) = -3.28$, $p < .01$) and too expensive (questions 20 and 41; $t(88) = -5.34$, $p < .001$) than audio-recording. Otherwise, the two sets of items were answered in approximately the same way. Thus, I will report on only the results for the set of items pertaining to audio-recording (questions 7–21). The two most important reasons cited by this sample of ninety-two psychoanalysts for not audio-recording sessions were (1) "recording would modify the patient's self-disclosures" (item 8; $M = 5.5$, $SD = 1.9$) and (2) "recording would change the therapeutic process" (item 11; $M = 5.5$, $SD = 1.9$). Thus, my hypothesis was confirmed: the most important reason endorsed by this sample of psychoanalysts for not audio-recording sessions is related to modifications in the patient's self-disclosures. Items 7–21, with means and standard deviations, are listed in table 3.1.

Table 3.1. Correlations between Psychoanalysts' Age and Their Attitudes about the Recording of Psychotherapy Sessions with Descriptive Statistics

Questions	*Mean*	*Standard Deviation*	*Age*
Q7 Would inhibit patient's self-disclosures	5.4	2.0	−.25*
Q8 Would modify patient's interventions	5.5	1.9	−.22*
Q9 Would inhibit therapist's interventions	4.7	2.0	−.04
Q10 Would modify therapist's interventions	4.8	2.0	−.06
Q11 Would change the therapeutic process	5.5	1.9	−.27*
Q12 Would change the goal of treatment from serving patient interests to serving the research/therapist interests	4.7	2.0	−.15
Q13 Would cause patient to treat session as a performance	4.8	1.7	−.14
Q14 Would cause therapist to treat session as a performance	4.6	1.7	−.01
Q15 Might allow patient to confer private meaning onto recording of sessions, which could affect experience of treatment	5.2	2.0	−.25*
Q16 Patient might feel coerced into consenting to recording	5.2	2.1	−.15
Q17 Patient could request access to recordings in the future, potentially impeding treatment	4.1	2.0	−.06
Q18 Patient could request access to recordings in the future, increasing therapist's liability	3.9	2.1	−.11
Q19 Would be too cumbersome to undertake	3.7	2.1	−.07
Q20 Would be too expensive to undertake	2.8	2.0	−.20
Q21 Have not thought much about recording sessions	4.5	2.5	−.12
Q45 Evidence that process notes produce a distorted record of the therapeutic process	3.4	2.1	.21*
Q46 Patient's signed consent that prohibits patient access to the recording	3.3	2.2	.25*

Note. Questions rated on a scale from 1 to 7.
*$p \leq .05$.

To test this hypothesis formally, patients could be randomly assigned to two conditions: a recording and a nonrecording condition. The null hypothesis would be that treatment outcomes do not significantly differ between the two conditions. Although I sharply criticized RCTs in chapter 2, this proposed study uses random assignment not to validate a brand-name treatment package but rather to test the effects of recording on treatment outcome. The recordings made in the experimental condition could then be used to assess for qualitative signs of a recording influence on psychotherapy process in general and on the patient's self-disclosures in particular.

Regarding the third section—circumstances that might change the therapist's mind about recording sessions—the mean scores of all five items were below the midpoint of 4, which means that none of the circumstances listed was likely to change the psychoanalysts' minds about session recording. The most important circumstance—"education about naturalistic single-case research designs that use recording of sessions to identify which therapeutic processes work best to effect change in the patient" (item 43)—garnered a mean of only 3.8 ($SD = 2.1$).

Finally, I analyzed the demographic data in the fourth section in relation to the first three sections. A series of independent-samples *t*-tests revealed that adult and child analysts significantly differed on only item 12—"audio-recording would change the goal of treatment from serving the interests of the patient to serving the interests of research or other interests of the therapist"—with adult psychoanalysts endorsing this item as a more important reason for not recording sessions than child psychoanalysts ($t(88) = 2.90$, $p < .01$). Men and women significantly differed on only item 42—"I have not thought much about video-recording sessions"—with women endorsing this item as a more important reason for not recording sessions than men ($t(88) = 2.48$, $p < .05$). Pearson correlations revealed that age was significantly correlated with four items pertaining to audio-recording (see table 3.3). Surprisingly, older psychoanalysts were less likely to perceive audio-recording as problematic for patient self-disclosures or the therapeutic process than younger psychoanalysts. Older psychoanalysts were also more likely to consider education about the flaws of process notes (item 45) and a patient's signed consent form to record sessions (item 46) as circumstances that might change their minds about recording sessions than younger psychoanalysts were. It appears that as psychoanalysts become older, they become less concerned about potential perturbations in the psychotherapy process and more open to changing their minds about recording sessions. I doubt that a cohort effect would account for these findings because younger psychoanalysts would be more familiar with the increasing prevalence of recording sessions for research and supervision purposes than older psychoanalysts would.

In a sample of Caucasian, middle-aged, mostly female psychoanalysts, therapists did not make session recordings because they feared that recordings would influence the psychotherapy process in general and the patient's self-disclosures in particular. Perhaps familiarizing psychoanalytic candidates with recording sessions would remove this stigma from psychoanalytic institutes. I suspect that therapists who adhere to other theoretical orientations such as cognitive-behavioral might feel less ambivalent about recording sessions because patient self-disclosures are perhaps less important in psychotherapies such as CBT, where the therapist's direction of session activities and provision of information and instruction are emphasized (Blagys and Hilsenroth, 2002). Perhaps one of the reasons why CBT has been conferred EST status is that its practitioners do not feel conflicted about doing what it takes to verify its effectiveness, including administering questionnaires to patients and audio- or video-recording sessions to assess therapist competence and adherence to the treatment manual. If psychodynamic therapy and its derivatives are to enter the twenty-first century, they must be ready to put their preferred change processes to the test. The task will require rank-and-file therapists to record their psychotherapy sessions to preserve an accurate and objective series of observations of the interactions between the therapist and the patient. As we have seen, however, therapists' attitudes about the recording of psychotherapy sessions must change before we put ourselves in the position of being able to call psychodynamic therapy "empirically informed" (Westen et al., 2004a, p. 658).

ATTACHMENT AND CHANGE PROCESSES: RECIPROCAL INFLUENCE

Over the past twenty years, psychoanalytic theoreticians (e.g., Eagle, 2003; Jones, 2000; Treurniet, 1993) have increasingly drawn our attention to the fact that effective psychotherapy consists of more than just "the pure gold of analysis" (Freud, 1919a, p. 168). In addition to interpretation, the quality of the relationship between the therapist and the patient has emerged as an effective instrument of therapeutic change in its own right. Of course, this idea has been around for the past eighty years, first given a voice by Ferenczi and Rank (1924) and Alexander and French (1946) and popularized outside the psychoanalytic community by Fritz Perls (1969). In chapters 3 and 6 of Goodman (in press), I discuss the attachment relationship as an effective ingredient of therapeutic change. Briefly, I want to foreshadow some of the ideas discussed in these chapters as they relate to the links between psychotherapy process and outcome. One of the most exciting areas of contemporary attachment theory is the theoretical and empirical establishment of the primary influence of the caregiver-infant relationship on the simultaneous formation of a system of affect regulation and a primitive organization of mental representations of self and others (e.g., Fonagy, Gergely, et al., 2002; Goodman, 2002; Kobak et al., 1993; Kobak and Sceery, 1988). In a reciprocal process, increased affect regulation facilitates the formation of self- and object representations, while the formation of self- and object representations facilitates increased affect regulation. The caregiver-infant attachment relationship mediates the organization of both developmental processes.

Given the call for therapists to treat "problem areas"—dimensions of patient functioning such as "emotion dysregulation" (Clarkin, 2008, p. 225)—rather than categorically determined *DSM-IV* (APA, 2000) diagnoses, we must therefore look to cues from the caregiver-infant attachment relationship to understand how psychotherapy can facilitate the restoration of affect regulation. It is a plausible hypothesis that the therapist-patient relationship, over and above the therapist technique of interpretation, is needed to restore a patient's dysregulated affects.

In chapters 3 and 6 of Goodman (in press), I argue that both a therapist's attachment organization, based on their childhood relationships with their caregivers, and a patient's attachment organization, based on their childhood relationships with their caregivers, codetermine the range of possible interaction structures that can develop in the psychotherapy process of the therapeutic dyad. These attachment organizations govern the extent to which a person's emotional expression is undercontrolled (overstimulated or unfiltered) or overcontrolled (repressed or suppressed). Because the quality of a person's attachment organization can vary continuously between deactivating/dismissing and hyperactivating/preoccupied (see Goodman, in press, chapter 6; Kobak et al., 1993; Main et al., 1985), both therapist and patient can enter into the therapeutic relationship with a range of similar or dissimilar attachment organizations. The extent of dissimilarity between the therapist and patient's attachment organizations—what Dozier and her colleagues (Bernier and Dozier, 2002; Bernier, Larose, and Soucy, 2005; Dozier, 2003; Dozier and Bates, 2004; Dozier, Cue, and Barnett, 1994; Dozier and Tyrrell, 1998; Tyrrell, Dozier, Teague, and Fallot, 1999) have referred to as noncomplementarity—has been shown to predict treatment outcome. The missing link in these studies, however, is the nature of the psychotherapy process—the interaction structures formed by the therapist and patient—that mediates the relation between the therapist-patient matching of attachment organizations and the symptom or structural outcomes.

I am proposing that rank-and-file therapists conduct naturalistic, quantitative single-case research studies in their own backyards in which they assess

(1) their own and their patient's attachment organizations at the outset; (2) the interaction structures that form between them by applying the PQS or CPQ to periodically recorded sessions; and (3) the patient's treatment outcome throughout the treatment using the symptom and structural measures described earlier. In chapters 2 and 3 of volume II, I report on two psychoanalyses I conducted in which I assessed my own attachment organization with the AAI and my patients' attachment organizations with the Adolescent Attachment Prototype Questionnaire and Adolescent Attachment Questionnaire (Westen et al., 2006). Because both patients were control cases in my psychoanalytic training, I had weekly supervision. Both my supervisors forbade me from recording my sessions or administering any outcome measures to these patients (see my study on therapists' attitudes about recording sessions above); thus, the clinical material I report in that chapter comes directly from my process notes taken during sessions. In spite of this inconsistency, I am recommending that therapists do as I say and not as I do. We need to learn about the links among (1) the matching of therapist-patient attachment organizations; (2) the nature of interaction structures derived from this matching; and (3) the outcomes expected from these interaction structures.

A collection of these quantitative single-case research studies could be categorized in various ways. One such system would yield four categories of cases: (1) deactivating/dismissing therapists matched with deactivating/dismissing patients; (2) deactivating/dismissing therapists matched with hyperactivating/preoccupied patients; (3) hyperactivating/preoccupied therapists matched with deactivating/dismissing patients; and (4) hyperactivating/preoccupied therapists matched with hyperactivating/preoccupied patients (see Goodman, in press, chapter 6). Another system would also yield four categories of cases: (1) patients judged to have a positive outcome by both therapist and patient; (2) patients judged to have a negative outcome by both therapist and patient; (3) patients judged to have a positive outcome by the patient but a negative outcome by the therapist; and (4) patients judged to have a negative outcome by the patient but a positive outcome by the therapist (for a similar procedure, see Nilsson et al., 2007). With a sufficient number of cases, sixteen cells (4 × 4 typology) could be created that could represent at least sixteen different categories of process. These two systems of categorization, of course, would not be orthogonal because, as Dozier and her colleagues (Bernier and Dozier, 2002; Bernier, Larose, and Soucy, 2005; Dozier, 2003; Dozier and Bates, 2004; Dozier, Cue, and Barnett, 1994; Dozier and Tyrrell, 1998; Tyrrell et al., 1999) have shown, noncomplementary matching of therapist-patient attachment organizations tends to yield a more positive treatment outcome than complementary matching. Nevertheless, 1,600 completed psychotherapy cases conducted in naturalistic settings and compiled at a central data bank might provide sufficient cell size to test hypotheses linking therapist-patient attachment-organization matching with psychotherapy process characterized by interaction structures and treatment outcome characterized by symptom or structural changes.

I would hypothesize that CBT treatments—with their focus on structure and the suppression of affects (see above discussion)—might be particularly effective with affective containment, while psychodynamic treatments—with their focus on nondirective exploration and affective expression (see above discussion)—might be particularly effective with affective discharge. I have always wondered whether CBT therapists tend to occupy the deactivating/dismissing end of the continuum of attachment organization, while psychodynamic therapists tend to occupy the hyperactivating/preoccupied end of this continuum. In other words, therapists select a theoretical orientation to practice based on their own attachment organization and, by extension, their own pattern of affect regulation.

With a large sample of single-case psychotherapy process and outcome data, one could properly test this hypothesis. That most psychodynamic therapists in naturalistic settings appear to practice an ecumenical mixture of treatment modalities (e.g., Ablon et al., 2006) might reflect these therapists' flexibility with a range of affect-regulation strategies judiciously applied according to the patient's emotional needs. The application of different kinds of interventions (e.g., psychodynamic, CBT) might depend on the patient's attachment organization, situational events (e.g., therapist or patient vacation), or the phase of treatment (Howard et al., 1996; Howard et al., 1986; Howard et al., 1993). These moderating variables could be tested within a larger mediational model that demonstrates how interaction structures mediate the relation between the therapist and patient's attachment organizations and the patient's treatment outcome. This program of research could ultimately identify empirically derived change processes that future therapists could consider using, depending on their own and their patient's pattern of affect regulation. You and I could usher in a new era of best practices based on naturalistic single-case research rather than on the outdated medical RCT model.

In conclusion, I paraphrase Marx and Engels (1848): I am calling on the therapists of the world to unite—you have nothing to lose but your treatment manuals! Therapeutic processes can be studied without the rigid controls imposed on them by grant-funded entrepreneurs peddling brand-name treatments to wide-eyed therapists willing to spend thousands of dollars to become "certified" in these treatments so that they can carve out a niche in the therapeutic marketplace as a DBT therapist or TFP therapist or MBT therapist. Perhaps these words are unsettling to some of you. I understand that people's livelihoods are at stake. I am advocating an alternative pathway to empirically informed treatment—one that everyone can participate in. When rank-and-file therapists are excluded from the process of empirical validation, empirically validated treatments become politically validated treatments (Duncan, 2002). I am calling on the international community of therapists to band together to study "what works for whom" in their own consulting rooms, using the quantitative and qualitative single-case research designs I have reviewed in this chapter.

APPENDIX: THERAPISTS' ATTITUDES ABOUT THE RECORDING OF PSYCHOTHERAPY SESSIONS

You are being asked to volunteer in a research study titled "Therapists' Attitudes About the Recording of Psychotherapy Sessions," conducted by Geoff Goodman, PhD, associate professor of psychology, Clinical Psychology Doctoral Program, Long Island University. This research questionnaire is designed to survey therapists' attitudes about the audiotaping and videotaping of psychotherapy sessions. It should take about ten minutes to complete. While there is no direct benefit to you for participation in the study, it is reasonable to expect that the results may provide information of value for naturalistic research studies of psychotherapy process.

Please answer all questions as truthfully as possible. A self-addressed, stamped envelope is included for your convenience. Please mail back the questionnaire when you have completed it. The return of your questionnaire automatically indicates your informed consent to participate in this study. The results of the data will be reported only in the aggregate. To maintain your confidentiality, please do not include your name or any other identifying information on this questionnaire. If you have questions about the research, you may contact the investigator, Geoff Goodman, PhD, at (516) 299-4277 (ggoodman@liu.edu), or the psychology department chair, Gerald Lachter, PhD, at (516) 299-2184. If you have questions concerning your rights as a subject, you may contact the executive secretary of the Institutional Review Board, Ms. Kathryn Rockett, at (516) 299-2523. If you are interested in a summary of the results of this questionnaire, you may contact Dr. Goodman at the e-mail address listed above. Thank you in advance for your participation.

Do you currently maintain a private practice or participate in a group practice?

Yes______ No______

If you answered "no" to this question, please place your questionnaire in the envelope provided and mail it back.

If you answered "yes" to this question, please answer the following questions regarding your patients in private practice or group practice.

1. Do you audiotape psychotherapy sessions?

   Yes________ No________

If you answered "no" to audiotaping, please skip to question 7. If you answered "yes" to audiotaping, what are the reasons? Please rate your responses on a seven-point scale, where 1 = not important at all, 2 = very unimportant, 3 = somewhat unimportant, 4 = neither important nor unimportant, 5 = somewhat important, 6 = very important, and 7 = extremely important. Check the line next to your answer.

2. Recording was conducted for purposes of research.

   1_____ 2_____ 3_____ 4_____ 5_____ 6_____ 7_____

3. Recording was conducted for purposes of clinical supervision.

   1_____ 2_____ 3_____ 4_____ 5_____ 6_____ 7_____

4. Recording was conducted to maintain an accurate record of the session.

   1_____ 2_____ 3_____ 4_____ 5_____ 6_____ 7_____

5. Recording was conducted because the patient requested it.

   1_____ 2_____ 3_____ 4_____ 5_____ 6_____ 7_____

6. Recording was conducted because it is a routine part of the treatment (e.g., audiotaped feedback).

   1_____ 2_____ 3_____ 4_____ 5_____ 6_____ 7_____

If you answered "yes" to audiotaping, please skip to question 22. If you answered "no" to audiotaping, what are the reasons? Please rate your responses on the same seven-point scale. Check the line next to your answer.

7. Recording would inhibit the patient's self-disclosures.

   1_____ 2_____ 3_____ 4_____ 5_____ 6_____ 7_____

8. Recording would modify the patient's self-disclosures.

   1_____ 2_____ 3_____ 4_____ 5_____ 6_____ 7_____

9. Recording would inhibit the therapist's interventions.

   1_____ 2_____ 3_____ 4_____ 5_____ 6_____ 7_____

10. Recording would modify the therapist's interventions.

    1_____ 2_____ 3_____ 4_____ 5_____ 6_____ 7_____

11. Recording would change the therapeutic process.

    1_____ 2_____ 3_____ 4_____ 5_____ 6_____ 7_____

12. Recording would change the goal of treatment from serving the interests of the patient to serving the interests of research or other interests of the therapist.

    1_____ 2_____ 3_____ 4_____ 5_____ 6_____ 7_____

13. Recording would cause the patient to treat the session as a performance for unknown others.

    1_____ 2_____ 3_____ 4_____ 5_____ 6_____ 7_____

14. Recording would cause the therapist to treat the session as a performance for unknown others.

    1_____ 2_____ 3_____ 4_____ 5_____ 6_____ 7_____

15. The patient could confer a private meaning onto the recording of sessions, which could affect his or her experience of the treatment.

    1_____ 2_____ 3_____ 4_____ 5_____ 6_____ 7_____

16. The patient might feel coerced into consenting to recording.

    1_____ 2_____ 3_____ 4_____ 5_____ 6_____ 7_____

17. The patient could request access to the recordings in the future, which could impede the progress of treatment or be detrimental to the patient's emotional health.

    1_____ 2_____ 3_____ 4_____ 5_____ 6_____ 7_____

18. The patient could request access to the recordings in the future, which could increase the therapist's liability exposure.

    1_____ 2_____ 3_____ 4_____ 5_____ 6_____ 7_____

19. Recording would be too cumbersome to undertake.

    1_____ 2_____ 3_____ 4_____ 5_____ 6_____ 7_____

20. Recording would be too expensive to undertake.

1_____ 2_____ 3_____ 4_____ 5_____ 6_____ 7_____

21. I have not thought much about recording sessions.

1_____ 2_____ 3_____ 4_____ 5_____ 6_____ 7_____

22. Do you videotape psychotherapy sessions?

Yes________ No_________

If you answered "no" to videotaping, please skip to question 28. If you answered "yes" to videotaping, what are the reasons? Please rate your responses on the same seven-point scale. Check the line next to your answer.

23. Recording was conducted for purposes of research.

1_____ 2_____ 3_____ 4_____ 5_____ 6_____ 7_____

24. Recording was conducted for purposes of clinical supervision.

1_____ 2_____ 3_____ 4_____ 5_____ 6_____ 7_____

25. Recording was conducted to maintain an accurate record of the session.

1_____ 2_____ 3_____ 4_____ 5_____ 6_____ 7_____

26. Recording was conducted because the patient requested it.

1_____ 2_____ 3_____ 4_____ 5_____ 6_____ 7_____

27. Recording was conducted because it is a routine part of the treatment (e.g., videotaped feedback).

1_____ 2_____ 3_____ 4_____ 5_____ 6_____ 7_____

If you answered "yes" to videotaping, please skip to the demographic questions at the end of the questionnaire. If you answered "no" to videotaping, what are the reasons? Please rate your responses on the same seven-point scale. Check the line next to your answer.

28. Recording would inhibit the patient's self-disclosures.

1_____ 2_____ 3_____ 4_____ 5_____ 6_____ 7_____

29. Recording would modify the patient's self-disclosures.

1_____ 2_____ 3_____ 4_____ 5_____ 6_____ 7_____

30. Recording would inhibit the therapist's interventions.

    1_____ 2_____ 3_____ 4_____ 5_____ 6_____ 7_____

31. Recording would modify the therapist's interventions.

    1_____ 2_____ 3_____ 4_____ 5_____ 6_____ 7_____

32. Recording would change the therapeutic process.

    1_____ 2_____ 3_____ 4_____ 5_____ 6_____ 7_____

33. Recording would change the goal of treatment from serving the interests of the patient to serving the interests of research or other interests of the therapist.

    1_____ 2_____ 3_____ 4_____ 5_____ 6_____ 7_____

34. Recording would cause the patient to treat the session as a performance for unknown others.

    1_____ 2_____ 3_____ 4_____ 5_____ 6_____ 7_____

35. Recording would cause the therapist to treat the session as a performance for unknown others.

    1_____ 2_____ 3_____ 4_____ 5_____ 6_____ 7_____

36. The patient could confer a private meaning onto the recording of sessions, which could affect his or her experience of the treatment.

    1_____ 2_____ 3_____ 4_____ 5_____ 6_____ 7_____

37. The patient might feel coerced into consenting to recording.

    1_____ 2_____ 3_____ 4_____ 5_____ 6_____ 7_____

38. The patient could request access to the recordings in the future, which could impede the progress of treatment or be detrimental to the patient's emotional health.

    1_____ 2_____ 3_____ 4_____ 5_____ 6_____ 7_____

39. The patient could request access to the recordings in the future, which could increase the therapist's liability exposure.

    1_____ 2_____ 3_____ 4_____ 5_____ 6_____ 7_____

40. Recording would be too cumbersome to undertake.

    1_____ 2_____ 3_____ 4_____ 5_____ 6_____ 7_____

41. Recording would be too expensive to undertake.

1_____ 2_____ 3_____ 4_____ 5_____ 6_____ 7_____

42. I have not thought much about recording sessions.

1_____ 2_____ 3_____ 4_____ 5_____ 6_____ 7_____

If you answered "no" to audiotaping or videotaping, what circumstances might change your mind? Please rate your responses on the same seven-point scale. Check the line next to your answer.

43. Education about naturalistic single-case research designs that use recording of sessions to identify which therapeutic processes work best to effect change in the patient.

1_____ 2_____ 3_____ 4_____ 5_____ 6_____ 7_____

44. Education about research that suggests neutral or positive benefits of recording sessions on the patient's well-being and outcome.

1_____ 2_____ 3_____ 4_____ 5_____ 6_____ 7_____

45. Education about research that suggests that process notes produce a distorted record of the psychotherapy process.

1_____ 2_____ 3_____ 4_____ 5_____ 6_____ 7_____

46. The patient's signed informed consent that protects his or her confidentiality and prohibits patient access to the recording.

1_____ 2_____ 3_____ 4_____ 5_____ 6_____ 7_____

47. A free supply of audio or video equipment and instructions on how to use it.

1_____ 2_____ 3_____ 4_____ 5_____ 6_____ 7_____

Please answer the following demographic questions.

Age_____
Gender: Female_______Male________
Ethnicity (check one): Caucasian_______ African American________
Asian________ Latin American_______ Mixed________
Other________
Degree: MD_____ PhD______ PsyD______ MSW_______
MA_______ RN_____
Number of years in private practice or group practice_______

Populations treated (check all that apply): children______
adolescents______ adults______ geriatrics______
Theoretical orientation (check one): behavioral______
cognitive-behavioral______ eclectic______ family systems______
humanistic/experiential/existential______ interpersonal______
psychoanalytic______ psychodynamic______

Chapter Four

Processes of Therapeutic Change in Transference-Focused Psychotherapy

> A surgeon of earlier times took as his motto the words: "I dressed his wounds, God cured him." The analyst should be content with something similar.
>
> Sigmund Freud, "Recommendations to Physicians Practising Psycho-Analysis"

Transference-focused psychotherapy (TFP) is a psychoanalytic form of treatment specifically designed for patients diagnosed with borderline personality disorder. Four published TFP treatment manuals describe the etiology of borderline personality disorder, the nature of the underlying mental representations that cause borderline psychopathology, and the intervention strategies that follow from these ideas (Clarkin et al., 1999, 2006; Kernberg et al., 1989; Yeomans, Clarkin, and Kernberg, 2002). Two other published books address special topics related to TFP: contract setting (Yeomans, Selzer, and Clarkin, 1992) and the application of TFP to other severe personality disorders (Koenigsberg et al., 2000). Empirical evidence to support TFP's effectiveness in treating BPD patients has begun to accumulate (Clarkin et al., 2001; Clarkin, Levy, Lenzenweger, and Kernberg, 2007; Giesen-Bloo et al., 2006; Levy, Meehan, et al., 2006). In this short space, I will provide a brief account of the theory behind TFP, its principles of intervention, and the change processes it purports to facilitate.

Over forty years ago, Kernberg (1966, 1967, 1975, 1986a) described a diagnostically diverse group of patients who nevertheless putatively shared a specific and remarkably stable form of pathological ego structure—borderline personality organization. Kernberg believed that this ego structure or organization was marked by identity diffusion and primitive defensive processes in the presence of generally intact reality testing. Although Kernberg noted some lack of differentiation of self- and object representations, the intrapsychic boundaries between them are stable, preventing lasting psychotic episodes. These persons are plagued by ego weaknesses such as lack of anxiety tolerance, lack of impulse control, and lack of developed sublimatory channels, and often experience shifts toward primary-process thinking, which can appear as primitive fantasies or behaviors.

The essential element of all these borderline manifestations is the lack of integration of good and bad self- and object representations in the presence of stable, clearly differentiated self-other boundaries. Initially, self- and object representations gradually develop in relation to each other because of affectively charged experiences. The components of the internal world "always include a self representation, an object representation, and an affective disposition that links them" (Kernberg et al., 1989, p. 9). Thus, the infant introjects mental representations of affectively connected interactions rather than isolated images. The division of mental representations into good and bad initially occurs "simply because of the lack of integrative capacity of the early ego" (Kernberg, 1986a, p. 299). Later, however, the good and bad self- and object representations are actively kept apart through the defense mechanism known as *splitting*. Splitting protects the infant's ego core from annihilation anxiety brought about by the danger that the bad self- and object representations will overpower and destroy this ego core, which consists of good self- and object representations with which the ego has become identified.

Kernberg argued that splitting continues to wreak havoc on the development of a stable ego identity for some persons who never succeed in establishing affectively modulated, integrated self- and object representations. These persons either (1) lack a constitutionally based capacity for anxiety tolerance, which naturally interferes with the integration of good and bad self- and object representations; (2) have constitutionally excessive and intense aggressive impulses, which naturally arouse annihilation anxiety; or (3) experience intense aggressive impulses secondary to extreme early frustrations. For these persons, all good self- and object representations are in danger of being destroyed by the bad self- and object representations, whose threatening qualities in the face of integration would be intensified by the magnitude of the aggressive impulses. These persons are typically diagnosed with borderline personality disorder (BPD). Kernberg and his colleagues (Kernberg et al., 1972) were among the first therapist/researchers to argue that under the appropriate circumstances, BPD patients can actually be effectively treated.

Kernberg and his colleagues (Kernberg et al., 1989) have presented case material that illustrates these characteristics of the personality organization that underlies BPD:

> Early in her treatment Miss A had great difficulty speaking about sex, feeling that sex was dirty. Clarifications of her perception of the therapist over time gradually revealed that she had come to view the therapist as a strict parent (one part object representation), profoundly disgusted by her body, seeing it as a dirty mess; she, in turn, experienced herself as a filthy, humiliated, depreciated being (one part self representation), who responded with fear and self-loathing to this attitude (the affective link). This view alternated with her view of her therapist as a warm, tolerant, caring person (a different part object representation), while she saw herself as loved and secure in the possibility of freely expressing her wishes to exhibit herself sexually bathing, urinating, and defecating (a different part self representation). In this frame of mind her dominant affective experience was that of being caressed and loved (a different affective link). (Kernberg et al., 1989, p. 93)

In this clinical example, we see the splitting of both self- and object representations into affectively charged fragments. Each split-off object representation is affectively linked with a split-off self-representation, which represents the affective context in which these two split-off mental representations are relating to each other. Split-off self- and object representations, dominated by unmodulated affects and splitting processes, represent the essence of BPD. The TFP therapist communicates to the patient the presence and function of these self-object representational pairings (see below).

According to Kernberg and his colleagues (Kernberg et al., 1989), TFP is designed to

> enhance the borderline patient's ability to experience self and others as coherent, integrated, realistically perceived individuals, and to reduce the need to use defenses that weaken the ego structure by reducing the repertoire of available responses. . . . The central treatment goal of integrating part self and object representations . . . is facilitated by the analysis of the defensive operations that actively maintain these split-off states. (pp. 8, 9)

Seventeen years later (Levy, Clarkin, et al., 2006), Kernberg and his colleagues' conceptualization of TFP's central treatment goal remains essentially the same: "The integration of these polarized affect states and representations of self and other into a more coherent whole" (p. 486).

In spite of its psychodynamic lineage, TFP is a highly structured treatment that includes an initial assessment phase, which consists of contract setting with the patient (Yeomans et al., 1992), and a treatment phase (Clarkin et al., 2006). In contrast to the fundamental rule for patients in psychodynamic therapy to say whatever comes to mind, the therapist actively addresses obstacles to such exploration by following a "hierarchy of priorities" (p. 130) in which threats to the patient's safety or to the integrity of the treatment are immediately addressed. Beyond the structured context provided by TFP, the therapist uses specific techniques to achieve the aims of treatment: clarification, confrontation, and interpretation. Clarification is the therapist's exploration of the patient's verbal and nonverbal communications. Confrontation is the therapist's observation of affectively discrepant (i.e., split-off) mental representations in the here-and-now relationship with the therapist (see illustration above). Interpretation is the linking of these discrepant mental representations.

In making an interpretation, the therapist uses clarification and confrontation to integrate preconsciously experienced material with the underlying unconscious functions and motivations that produce it. The aim of interpretation is to resolve these discrepant self- and object representations by communicating to the patient the unconscious motivations and defensive processes that facilitate an understanding of the logic behind these discrepancies. Kernberg and his colleagues (Clarkin et al., 2006) have defined interpretation as occurring at three levels: (1) interpreting how defensive processes are serving the patient's avoidance of perceived unacceptable or unbearable affects or mental representations; (2) interpreting an active self-object representational pairing in the transference (see illustration above); and (3) interpreting how an active, conscious self-object representational pairing is defending against a discrepant, unconscious self-object representational pairing in the transference. Interpretation provides the patient with a cognitive explanation for his or her feelings, thoughts, and behaviors related to his or her mental representations. In the briefest terms, this is the essence of TFP technique.

Here is an example of a transference interpretation: "I think you have been trying to provoke me into an argument—someone you now perceive to be a sadistic buzz kill—to avoid other feelings you have toward me—feelings of dependency on me and the accompanying fear that I might leave you in this vulnerable state." According to the theory, the effective ingredient of therapeutic change in TFP is the intensive focus on the interactions between the therapist and patient in the here and now and their expression of the patient's split-off object relations being activated in the affectively charged atmosphere of the therapy session. Transference interpretations are also linked with extra-transference material and long-term treatment goals (e.g., behavioral control).

Empirical evidence in support of the effectiveness and efficacy of TFP for the treatment of BPD has been gradually accumulating. In a sample that served as its own control, twenty-three BPD outpatients treated in twice-weekly TFP over the course of one year demonstrated fewer suicide attempts, lower medical risk for self-destructive behavior, fewer psychiatric hospitalizations, and shorter lengths of hospital stay (Clarkin et al., 2001). In a one-year RCT comparing thirty-one BPD outpatients randomly assigned to twice-weekly TFP with twenty-nine BPD outpatients in once-weekly dialectical behavior therapy (DBT; Linehan, 1993a) and thirty BPD outpatients in once-weekly supportive psychotherapy (SPT; Appelbaum, 2005; Rockland, 1992), TFP was associated with significant increases from insecure to secure attachment and significant increases in mentalization compared to DBT and SPT (Levy, Meehan, et al., 2006). Finally, in the same RCT, the BPD outpatients in TFP significantly improved in ten of twelve symptom domains, while the BPD outpatients in SPT significantly improved in only six domains and the BPD outpatients in DBT significantly improved in only five domains (Clarkin et al., 2007). Interestingly, no quantitative data on therapist adherence to TFP were reported in any of these three studies.

One study that tested the efficacy of TFP for the treatment of BPD was conducted outside Kernberg's research group. In a three-year RCT conducted by a Dutch research group, forty-two BPD outpatients randomly assigned to twice-weekly TFP were compared to forty-four BPD outpatients randomly assigned to twice-weekly schema-focused therapy (SFT; Young, 1994; Young, Klosko, and Weishaar, 2003). Both treatments were found to be effective in improving BPD symptoms, but the BPD outpatients in SFT demonstrated significantly greater improvement in all four broad domains of functioning than the BPD outpatients in TFP, including quality of life. In addition, the TFP condition posed a higher dropout risk than the SFT condition (Giesen-Bloo et al., 2006). In spite of the fact that the Dutch research group reported the statistical results of eight different competence and adherence measures that suggested adequate therapist adherence to TFP and SFT, Yeomans (2007), in a letter to the editor of the *Archives of General Psychiatry*, suggested that some TFP therapists were practicing not TFP but "psychodynamic treatment as usual" (p. 610). Two of the study's authors (Giesen-Bloo and Arntz, 2007) replied that TFP therapists were more than adequately trained, as their data indicated, and that therapist adherence to TFP was not associated with outcome (p. 611). Thus, all the evidence suggests that TFP is an effective and efficacious treatment for BPD but "not as efficacious as SFT" (p. 611).

Although the therapist's interpretation of split-off self- and object representations in the here and now of the transference has traditionally been the specific process of therapeutic change advertised by Kernberg and his colleagues, another change process—enhancement of reflective functioning (RF) or mentalization—has made a recent appearance in the TFP literature. Of the six books written by Kernberg and his colleagues about TFP (see above), only two even mention RF or mentalization. In 2000, Kernberg and his colleagues (Koenigsberg et al., 2000) spent a few pages reporting a previously published finding that two BPD outpatients showed improvement in RF over one year of TFP (Diamond et al., 1999). Curiously, the authors never explicated the relevance of this finding to a theory of effective TFP process. Similarly, the significance of the conversion of these two patients from an insecure to a secure attachment organization is not clear. In 2006, Kernberg and his colleagues (Clarkin et al., 2006) offered a couple of sentences to explain the relevance of mentalization to a theory of effective TFP process: "In our view, identity diffusion is the central pathology in borderline patients, and therefore successful treatment would enhance the patient's ability to conceptualize self and others. Thus one would expect that successful TFP treatment would result in an increase in reflective functioning" (p. 361).

In spite of the conceptual connection provided by these authors between TFP's goal of integrating split-off mental representations and the enhancement of mentalization (i.e., understanding the mental states of self and others and their interrelations), TFP was not designed with this explicit purpose in mind. The attachment theorist Fonagy and his colleagues (Fonagy, Steele, Steele, Moran, and Higgitt, 1991) introduced the concept of RF in the context of attachment theory as a developmental process in which the primary caregiver communicates both an empathic understanding of the child's mental states and a separateness from them that facilitate the symbolization of emotional phenomena as mental states to be observed as well as experienced. These communications take place within a secure attachment relationship in which the child feels secure in exploring his or her own mind as well as the mind of his or her primary caregiver (see chapter 6).

Given the fact that as recently as 1995, Kernberg (1976, 1995) has taken opportunities to make pointed criticisms of attachment theory (particularly with respect to its neglect of the motivational aspects of aggression), this recent (i.e., post-2000) marriage between TFP and attachment theory strikes me as puzzling. The theoretical framework that supports RF is alien to Kernberg's (1975, 1984) conflict theory of borderline personality organization as a synthesis of American ego psychology (Jacobson, 1964; Mahler, 1972; Mahler et al., 1975) and British Kleinian theory (Klein, 1946). It seems as if Kernberg and his colleagues were trying to pour new wine into old wineskins.

Following Fonagy and his colleagues' (Fonagy, Steele, Steele, Moran, and Higgitt, 1991) attachment-informed theoretical work on mentalization, Bateman and Fonagy (2004a, 2004b) developed mentalization-based treatment (MBT), a therapeutic approach to BPD in which RF is the cornerstone of therapeutic change. Referring to BPD patients' significant improvement in RF in the TFP condition but not the DBT or SPT condition, Levy and his colleagues (Levy, Clarkin, et al., 2006) concluded, "These changes are specific to TFP" (p. 496), as if they had shown that MBT does not improve RF—the central goal of this treatment. Elsewhere, Levy and his colleagues

(Levy, Meehan, et al., 2006) stated that they had conceptualized RF and attachment organization as change processes in TFP "on the basis of prior theorizing" (p. 1035), yet the only prior theorizing I could find were the two sentences quoted earlier and a brief passage in a 2006 paper (Levy, Clarkin, et al., 2006). TFP was formally conceptualized in 1989 (Kernberg et al., 1989), before Fonagy began publishing work on mentalization and RF. If the facilitation of mentalization processes is truly at the heart of TFP as the authors of TFP are suggesting, then this facilitation should be readily identifiable in the psychotherapy process of TFP session transcriptions (see below).

I also want to point out what appears to be confusion over whether RF is a process of therapeutic change or the outcome of such a process. In their 2006 RCT (Levy, Meehan, et al., 2006), the authors used RF as an outcome variable and reported significant changes in the TFP condition. Elsewhere, this research group referred to RF as an "essential mechanism of change" (Levy, Clarkin, et al., 2006, p. 490; see also Levy, Meehan, et al., 2006, p. 1035). This confusion between change and the processes that produce change is evident in Levy (2008): "Patients in Kernberg's transference-focused psychotherapy showed significant changes in reflective function, a hypothesized mechanism of change in transference-focused psychotherapy" (p. 558). Psychotherapy process is defined as the interaction between therapist and patient that produces change, measured as outcome. Psychotherapy process does not equal outcome.

As I understand MBT (Bateman and Fonagy, 2004a, 2004b), mentalization is the outcome of a confluence of therapist techniques and patient responses. In other words, these techniques and responses enhance mentalization in BPD patients. Alternatively, mentalization could be defined as the act of helping a patient understand the mental states of self and others and their interrelations—a process of therapeutic change. To avoid confusion, it is important to clarify the definition of mentalization that one is using—as a process of therapeutic change or as an outcome of that change. Mentalization, however, cannot be both the cause of change and its effect because this statement is tautological.

This confusion is important because it serves to obscure the fact that TFP processes were not originally conceptualized to change RF. The fact that TFP changes RF does not illuminate the processes that produce this particular outcome. As Bateman and Fonagy (2004a, p. 46) have suggested, mentalization could be a common factor of therapeutic change masquerading as a specific factor. In other words, the therapist techniques that facilitate mentalization are responsible for the effectiveness of all treatments. The therapeutic ingredients responsible for enhancing mentalization include empathic attunement, clarification of the mental states of self and others and their interrelations in the here and now, an emphasis on recovering mentalizing processes with a resultant deemphasis on achieving insight through complicated explanations of behavior such as transference interpretations, and an elaboration of the affects that immediately precede enactments (Bateman and Fonagy, 2004a, 2004b; Fonagy and Bateman, 2006).

Considering this list of therapeutic ingredients, the TFP authors also advocate the use of clarification but view it as insufficient to produce therapeutic change because "clarification alone does not address the conflicts that keep the partial representations separated" (Levy, Clarkin, et al., 2006, p. 488). These authors view confrontation and interpretation (i.e., cognitive explanation) as additional necessary steps taken to integrate split-off self- and object representations. "Evidence of insight" (Clarkin et al., 2006, p. 54) is considered an important outcome of a correctly formulated interpretation. Bateman and Fonagy (2004a, 2004b) eschew cognitive explanations and acquisition of insight in facilitating mentalization processes. From their point of view, these therapist techniques enhance intellectualization and an activation of the pretend mode of experience, not mentalization and an activation of the reflective mode of experience. In contrast to TFP, the MBT therapist does not make transference interpretations because

> the patient either angrily and contemptuously drops out of therapy feeling that their problems have not been understood, or mentally withdraws from treatment, or establishes a false treatment which looks like therapy but is in fact two individuals talking to themselves. (Bateman and Fonagy, 2004b, p. 208)

Thus, the authors of MBT do not view transference interpretations—the hallmark TFP intervention strategy—as conducive to mentalization.

Clearly, however, the enhancement of mentalization processes in TFP does occur: TFP was associated with significant increases in RF compared to DBT (Levy, Meehan, et al., 2006). The questions that arise from this discussion are (1) how this enhancement is occurring in actual TFP sessions and (2) whether the theoretical foundation on which TFP was built can support a major shift in what is considered effective change processes—from the integration of mental representations to the enhancement of RF on mental states (see chapter 6).

Dialectical behavior therapy (DBT) is a cognitive-behavioral form of treatment, which, like TFP, is specifically designed for patients diagnosed with BPD. Two published DBT treatment manuals describe the etiology of BPD, the nature of the emotions, cognitions, and behaviors that plague BPD patients, and the intervention strategies that follow from these ideas (Linehan, 1993a, 1993b). Other published books apply DBT to specific populations such as suicidal adolescents (Miller, Rathus, and Linehan, 2007). Empirical evidence to support DBT's effectiveness in treating BPD patients has begun to accumulate (Linehan, 1993a; Linehan, Armstrong, Suarez, Allmon, and Heard, 1991; Linehan et al., 2006; Linehan, Heard, and Armstrong, 1993; Linehan, Turek, Heard, and Armstrong, 1994).

DBT is based on the theory that BPD patients suffer chiefly from emotion dysregulation (Linehan, 1993a, 1993b). The etiology of this dysregulation is most likely a combination of genetic and other biological risk factors on the one hand and an emotionally unstable childhood environment on the other. DBT focuses on helping the patient to learn and apply adaptive skills that will improve emotion regulation and facilitate attempts to cope with intense emotions.

According to Linehan (1993a, 1993b), DBT consists of four parts: individual therapy, telephone contact, group skills training, and therapist consultation between the individual therapist and group therapist. The focus of individual therapy and group skills training is on learning and practicing adaptive skills that will facilitate optimal emotion regulation.

DBT teaches patients adaptive skills in four domains: mindfulness meditation skills, interpersonal effectiveness skills, distress tolerance skills, and emotion regulation skills. Mindfulness meditation skills are designed to help patients observe, describe, and pay attention to all internal and external experiences without judging them as "good" or "bad." These core skills are considered prerequisites for learning and applying the skills in the other three domains. Interpersonal effectiveness skills help patients to assert their needs and manage their conflicts in relationships. Distress tolerance skills promote learning strategies to tolerate and accept distress without engaging in self-destructive behaviors. Emotion regulation skills are designed to help patients learn to identify and manage their emotional reactions. Notably, DBT was one of the first cognitive-behavioral treatments to incorporate into its therapeutic technique a practice of mindfulness skills, which have their origins in Buddhist philosophy (Epstein, 1996). Since the advent of DBT, many other mindfulness-based treatments have been developed (see chapter 5).

Martin (1997) and Goodman (in press) have compared the concept of mindfulness to Freud's (1913b) definition of free association, which implies permission granted to the patient to follow his or her own train of thought in a general climate of therapist neutrality. Mindfulness psychotherapy process therefore seems to represent a departure from standard CBT process that emphasizes therapist control and a didactic approach to the patient's cognitions. Mindfulness-based treatments like DBT instead shift the emphasis to a nonjudgmental acceptance of the patient's experience and a more comprehensive focus on his or her emotions, cognitions, and behaviors. Thus, these mindfulness features would make DBT process more closely aligned with psychodynamic process than standard CBT process would be (see chapter 5).

The current study (see below) seeks to answer two broadly defined questions: (1) What goes on in the process of a prototypical TFP session and a prototypical dialectical behavior therapy (DBT) session, and (2) what goes on in an actual TFP session? To answer the first question, I present prototypical process data from two groups of three expert raters of prototypical TFP and DBT sessions. I then compare the process in prototypical TFP and DBT sessions with that in prototypical psychodynamic, CBT, and interpersonal therapy (IPT) sessions.

To answer the second question, I present process and outcome data from the treatments of five psychiatrically hospitalized BPD patients who participated in approximately six months of three-times-per-week TFP. Although TFP is currently designed as a twice-weekly treatment for BPD outpatients, its authors have found that "the principles of TFP can be applied in inpatient settings" (Clarkin et al., 2006, p. 366). Thus, TFP process might appear different in inpatient settings than it does in outpatient settings.

Related to this second question, I also identify the interaction structures most characteristic of TFP, calculate therapist adherence levels to the five treatment prototypes (see above), and correlate these variables with weekly symptom levels over the course of treatment. How conceptually similar or dissimilar in process are these five treatments from each other? How adherent were these TFP therapists to prototypical TFP process? How adherent were these TFP therapists to the processes characteristic of other forms of psychotherapy? To what extent is therapist adherence to TFP correlated with outcome? Finally, which aspects of psychotherapy process are most significantly correlated with outcome in these BPD inpatients, regardless of TFP adherence? I attempt to answer these exploratory questions in the following naturalistic, quantitative single-case research study with five cases. I offer ten tentative conclusions about TFP process at the end of the chapter.

METHOD

Participants

Experts

The experts who provided prototypical Q-sorts for this study were selected because of their extensive training and recognized expertise in their respective treatments. Regarding the credentials of the three TFP experts, two experts had completed a two-year, full-time postdoctoral fellowship program trained in the application of TFP by Otto Kernberg and his colleagues and have continued to treat patients with borderline personality disorder (BPD) using TFP. The third expert was a full-time clinical supervisor and coordinator of this postdoctoral fellowship program and participated in personal clinical supervision with Kernberg for many years. Regarding the credentials of the three DBT experts, all three experts are certified DBT trainers, personally trained and clinically supervised by Linehan and now training other DBT practitioners. Each expert was contacted by e-mail and was requested to sort the one hundred PQS items relevant to psychotherapy process—*as they see this process occurring within a prototypical psychotherapy session from their theoretical perspective*. Each expert was paid an honorarium for their participation in this IRB-approved study.

The credentials of the experts selected to represent the other three theoretical orientations used in this study—psychodynamic, CBT, and IPT—can be found elsewhere (Ablon and Jones, 1998, 2002). Stuart Ablon provided the composited prototypical Q-sorts of these three theoretical orientations.

Therapists

The four therapists who treated the five patients in this study were trained to practice TFP by Otto Kernberg or one of the clinical supervisors whom he personally trained. Three of the therapists (for Patients 1–3) were completing postdoctoral fellowship or residency training programs and were receiving weekly clinical supervision on their psychotherapy cases admitted to Kernberg's inpatient unit dedicated to the TFP treatment of patients diagnosed with borderline personality disorder. The fourth therapist treated Patients 4 and 5. He was one of the clinical supervisors of trainees on this inpatient unit (although he did not supervise the other three therapists). All four therapists had an allegiance to TFP and were motivated to participate in the treatment of these patients. The therapists of patients 1 and 3 were women, while the therapists of Patients 2, 4, and 5 were men.

Patients

The five patients who participated in this study were formally diagnosed with borderline personality disorder upon admission to Kernberg's inpatient unit. All five patients were women who had been admitted to this unit because they posed a danger to their own safety. All five women experienced horrendous childhoods with neglectful, unprotective, or abusive caregivers. I will now provide a brief description of each patient with modifications in historical details to protect patients' confidentiality.

Patient 1 Patient 1 was a twenty-six-year-old, single, college-educated Caucasian woman with no prior psychiatric hospitalizations. She was diagnosed with major depressive disorder on Axis I and borderline personality disorder on Axis II, according to her hospital records. She was taking medication for depression. She worked in the marketing department of a large insurance company but was on disability at the time of admission. Patient 1 had made three suicide attempts, including one that precipitated her hospitalization. Notably, Patient 1's mother shot herself in the head when Patient 1 was age four, but Patient 1 was not told the truth about the circumstances surrounding her mother's death until age twelve.

Patient 2 Patient 2 was a thirty-one-year-old, divorced, college-educated Caucasian woman with six prior psychiatric hospitalizations. She was diagnosed with bipolar disorder, anorexia nervosa, and bulimia nervosa on Axis I and borderline personality disorder on Axis II, according to her hospital records. She was taking medication for bipolar disorder. She was unemployed at the time of admission. Patient 2 had made six suicide attempts, including one that precipitated her current hospitalization. Notably, she had experienced the abrupt termination of her treatment by several previous therapists. She had a history of swallowing dangerous objects such as thumb tacks and complained of "inner deadness." She engaged in sexual promiscuity, self-mutilation, and drug and alcohol use. Patient 2 also was reportedly sexually abused by her father, mother, and a neighbor.

Patient 3 Patient 3 was a twenty-nine-year-old, single, college-educated Caucasian woman with five prior psychiatric hospitalizations. She was diagnosed with dysthymic disorder, obsessive compulsive disorder, alcohol dependence, and cocaine dependence on Axis I and borderline personality disorder on Axis II, according to hospital records. She was taking medication for depression. She was unemployed at the time of admission but had worked at a large shipping company. Patient 3 had made numerous suicide attempts and gestures, which precipitated her current hospitalization. Notably, she forged $3,000 of her grandmother's checks to support her cocaine addiction, which at its zenith was estimated at $500 per week. She also engaged in self-mutilation. Patient 3 reportedly had her stomach pumped at ages two and three for having ingested a bottle of aspirin and a bottle of furniture polish, respectively. Patient 3 was also reportedly sexually abused by her brother, beginning at age thirteen and continuing throughout adolescence.

Patient 4 Patient 4 was a thirty-five-year-old, single, Caucasian woman who had completed two years of college. She had five prior psychiatric hospitalizations. She was diagnosed with bipolar disorder on Axis I and borderline personality disorder on Axis II, according to hospital records. She was taking medication for bipolar disorder. She was unemployed at the time of admission but had worked as a registered nurse. Patient 4 had made numerous suicide attempts, including one that precipitated her current hospitalization. Notably, she had undergone twelve electroconvulsive shock treatments (ECTs). She reportedly physically attacked family members, including two disabled adult siblings in her care. Patient 4 engaged in drug and alcohol use as well as self-mutilation. In seventh grade, Patient 4 reportedly attempted to break her own arm with a skillet. She reported brief psychotic experiences—namely, auditory and visual hallucinations—and occasional panic attacks. Patient 4 terminated her hospital treatment against medical advice (AMA) because, according to hospital records, "she became aware that her family was adapting to life without her." She was permitted to leave the hospital because she no longer posed an acute suicide risk.

Patient 5 Patient 5 was a forty-one-year-old, married, college-educated Caucasian woman with seventeen prior psychiatric hospitalizations. She was diagnosed with major depressive disorder on Axis I and borderline personality disorder on Axis II, according to hospital records. She was taking medication for depression. She was a teaching assistant at the time of admission. Patient 5 had made numerous suicide attempts, including one that precipitated her current hospitalization. Notably, Patient 5 repeatedly eloped from the psychiatric unit to cut herself in the woods, making the entire staff extremely worried about her. She sometimes cut herself inside her vagina to avoid being discovered during body checks conducted by the nursing staff. Patient 5 reportedly had a long history of sexual and physical abuse at the hands of her brother beginning at age nine, including the insertion of objects (e.g., table knives, rocks, sticks) into her vagina. A neighbor also reportedly sexually abused her while babysitting her. Beginning in junior high school, Patient 5 began to engage in sexual promiscuity and was reportedly raped three times in college by provoking the men into doing so. Patient 5 reported brief psychotic experiences, including visual and auditory hallucinations of trees moving and talking to her.

It is noteworthy that, with the possible exception of Patient 5, the patients enrolled in this study were not unusual from the other patients typically treated on this psychiatric unit. Having worked on Kernberg's borderline inpatient unit myself for two years, the narratives of these five patients sound too familiar, even though I was not personally involved in the treatments of any of these five patients. The enormous number of prior hospitalizations was well within the mean of 5.45 reported by Hull, Yeomans, Clarkin, Li, and Goodman (1996) as well as the presence and number of comorbid Axis I disorders reported by Goodman and his colleagues (Goodman et al., 1998). Unfortunately, these patients would not be receiving TFP on today's psychiatric units. As a colleague of mine who still works at this psychiatric hospital is fond of saying, the therapeutic goal today is to "treat 'em and street 'em."

Measures

Psychotherapy Process Q-Set (PQS)

The method of empirical observation used in this study was the Psychotherapy Process Q-Set (PQS; Jones, 2000), a one-hundred-item instrument that assesses the processes of therapeutic change within an entire audiotaped or videotaped forty-five-minute psychotherapy session (see chapter 3 and volume II, chapter 5). The PQS was used because of its ease of use and its forced-choice procedure, which forces raters to place items in a normal distribution that characterizes both the high and low ends of a construct. The PQS can be used to delineate the conceptual similarities and differences among different theoretical orientations used to treat patients diagnosed with borderline personality disorder by recruiting experts willing to use a common vocabulary of one hundred items to characterize the processes of therapeutic change in their particular theoretical orientation. Approximately one-third of the PQS items were designed to capture aspects of the therapist's actions and attitudes, one-third designed to capture aspects of the patient's attitude and behavior or experience, and one-third designed to capture aspects of the interaction of the therapist-patient dyad, or the climate or atmosphere of the encounter (Jones, 2000).

The PQS items were selected from the psychotherapy literature and from leading experts to cover psychotherapy processes found in a wide variety of theoretical orientations, including cognitive-behavioral, psychodynamic, gestalt, humanistic/existential, interpersonal, and rational-emotive (Ablon and Jones, 1998, 1999, 2002; Jones et al., 1988; Jones et al., 1991; Jones and Pulos, 1993). Every item was constructed to cover a unique aspect of psychotherapy process not duplicated by any other item and to guarantee maximum variability across sessions and across patients. The reliability and validity of the PQS have been demonstrated across a variety of archived treatment samples (Ablon and Jones, 1998, 1999, 2002; Jones et al., 1988; Jones et al., 1991; Jones and Pulos, 1993). The interrater reliability across all 100 PQS items has yielded mean alpha coefficients in the range of .73 to .89 per rater pair across samples (Ablon, Levy, and Katzenstein, 2006; see below). Reliability analyses for individual PQS items have also yielded acceptable values in the range of .50 to .95 across samples (Ablon et al., 2006). Construct and discriminant validity has also been demonstrated across samples (Jones et al., 1988; Jones et al, 1991; Jones, Krupnick, and Kerig, 1987; Jones and Pulos, 1993).

The one hundred PQS items are placed into nine piles that range from "most uncharacteristic" to "most characteristic" of psychotherapy process (Block, 1978). Following a forced-choice distribution, the five most uncharacteristic items are placed in pile 1, and the five most characteristic items are placed in pile 9. Eight items are placed in piles 2 and 8, twelve items in piles 3 and 7, sixteen items in piles 4 and 6, and eighteen items in pile 5, thus forming a normal distribution (see Block, 1978, for additional information regarding Q-sort methodology and procedures). Expert raters' prototypical Q-sorts that represent each empirically supported treatment (i.e., TFP or DBT) were totaled and then divided by the total number of experts that represent that treatment (i.e., three) to form one composite prototypical Q-sort for each treatment (Block, 1978; J. Block, personal communication, April 30, 1997). These two composite prototypical Q-sorts, which reflect the psychotherapy processes that characterize TFP and DBT according to the two groups of experts, were used to test study 2's hypotheses.

Two teams of two clinical psychology doctoral students coded verbatim transcriptions of all 127 sessions of the 5 patients enrolled in this study using the PQS. Doctoral students were given extensive training on coding practice sessions using the PQS until their interrater reliability was sufficiently high to begin coding the current sample. Doctoral students were aware of the five patients' primary diagnosis of BPD but were blind to all other information about the patients and therapists. Doctoral students ranged in their own preferred theoretical orientations from cognitive-behavioral to psychodynamic; they were trained to code the transcripts in front of them based on the verbal exchanges recorded in each transcription, not on any prior theoretical ideas or clinical or personal experiences.

Throughout the duration of the coding process, weekly coding team meetings were held to go over discrepant PQS items to improve coding accuracy and to prevent interrater drift. As coding team leader, I also consulted with Stuart Ablon on a regular basis during this process whenever questions arose within the teams regarding specific items. Sessions from all five patients were randomly assigned to these two coding teams in random order. Thus, session 19 from Patient 5 might be coded one week, and then session 6 from Patient 2 might be coded the following week. The mean interrater reliability over all 127 sessions was .73 (range: .52–.87). This mean reliability score exceeds that of Karlsson and Kermott (2006), who reported a mean reliability score over 128 sessions using the PQS of .50 (p. 71). Our score of .73 also surpasses the generally acceptable criterion of .70 used to determine acceptable reliability in psychotherapy process and outcome research (Orlinsky and Howard, 1986).

Symptom Checklist-90-Revised (SCL-90-R)

The measure of weekly symptoms used in this study was the Symptom Checklist-90-Revised (SCL-90-R; Derogatis, 1983). The SCL-90-R is a self-report symptom checklist in which patients are asked to rate the severity of ninety symptoms over the previous week, using a five-point Likert-type scale (0 = not at all; 1 = a little bit; 2 = moderately; 3 = quite a bit; 4 = extremely). This assessment takes twelve to fifteen minutes to administer and is organized into ten scales: somatization, obsessive-compulsive, interpersonal sensitivity, depression, anxiety, hostility, phobic anxiety, paranoid ideation, psychotic thinking, and the global severity index (GSI). Because the GSI was designed to assess overall psychological distress, it was the only symptom measure used in this study. Patients 1, 3, and 5 completed the SCL-90-R on a weekly basis throughout their hospitalization (the other two patients refused). Test-retest reliability coefficients range from .80 to .90 (Derogatis, 1983). Internal consistency of GSI in this sample was .67.

Procedure

Patients whose therapists had previously agreed to participate in the study were approached consecutively to participate in a study of the effectiveness of psychotherapy for patients diagnosed with borderline personality disorder. Patients were contacted one to two weeks after admission, after having adjusted to the unit (for additional details, see Goodman et al., 1998). All patients signed informed consent forms that had been previously approved by the Weill Cornell Medical College Institutional Review Board. Patient 2 and Patient 4 refused to complete the SCL-90-R questionnaires. All five patients consented to have their sessions audiotaped.

All five patients were treated in three-times-per-week individual TFP. Every session was audiotaped, but only every third session was transcribed verbatim—typically the final session of each week. The treatment regimen consisted of TFP in combination with an intensive milieu program that included frequent therapy groups and a highly structured schedule of daily therapeutic activities. These treatment components were designed to help patients examine their interpersonal relationships. This process took place in two ways: (1) patients compared their own perceptions of self and others against the perceptions of the other patients for the purpose of clarifying the nature of each patient's internal distortions and interpersonal difficulties, and (2) intense and repeated confrontation of aggressive and maladaptive behaviors as they are manifested in the inpatient milieu served the purposes of ego integration and affect tolerance.

It is noteworthy that TFP as currently practiced (Clarkin et al., 2006) is conceptualized primarily as an outpatient treatment. Because managed care companies refuse to pay for lengthy hospital stays, in all likelihood patients with BPD no longer receive TFP in inpatient psychiatric units. Thus, the patients in this study are considered more severely disturbed than the patients for whom the current TFP manual is designed to treat (Clarkin et al., 2006). The patients in this study were actively self-destructive at admission—a condition that would effectively end an outpatient TFP treatment as the therapist would need to arrange for hospitalization. The findings of this study are therefore not necessarily generalizable to TFP as currently practiced in outpatient settings even though "the principles of TFP can be applied in inpatient settings" (Clarkin et al., 2006, p. 366).

The length of stay for these five patients varied according to their rate of symptom remission and the ability of the social worker to make adequate discharge plans. Patient 1 was audiotaped for twenty-three sessions (which represents sixty-nine sessions of TFP), Patient 2 for 31 sessions (representing ninety-three sessions of TFP), Patient 3 for twenty-one sessions (representing sixty-three sessions of TFP), Patient 4 for thirty-two sessions (representing ninety-six sessions of TFP), and Patient 5 for twenty sessions (representing sixty sessions of TFP). Overall, these five treatments lasted approximately six months. As mentioned previously, Patients 1, 3, and 5 completed SCL-90-R questionnaires, typically on the day of the final session of each week.

RESULTS: STUDY 1

I tested three hypotheses. First, the process in a prototypical TFP session is significantly correlated with the process in both a prototypical psychodynamic session and a prototypical CBT session. Second, the process in a prototypical DBT session is significantly correlated with the process in both a prototypical CBT session and a prototypical psychodynamic session. Third, psychotherapy process that would be expected to enhance RF is not correlated with the process in a prototypical TFP session. To test these hypotheses, I compare the prototypical process data from two groups of three expert raters of prototypical TFP and DBT sessions. I then compare the process in prototypical TFP and DBT sessions with that in prototypical psychodynamic, CBT, and interpersonal (IPT) sessions.

In study 1, I created two prototypical PQS Q-sort distributions that uniquely characterize or define the psychotherapy processes typically associated with two empirically supported treatments for patients with borderline personality disorder: transference-focused psychotherapy (TFP; Clarkin et al., 1999, 2006; Kernberg et al., 1989) and dialectical behavior therapy (DBT; Linehan, 1993a, 1993b). First, I tested the internal consistency of each group of experts. Cronbach's alpha, a statistic used to test the level of agreement on what constitutes a prototypical psychotherapy session among the expert raters of each treatment approach, was high: .84 for the three TFP expert raters and .87 for the three DBT expert raters. Second, I conducted a Q-factor analysis with varimax rotation to confirm that the six expert raters' PQS distributions loaded onto two distinct factors (Block, 1978; Goodman, 2005). In this statistical procedure, expert raters' prototypical Q-sorts were treated as separate variables, while the one hundred PQS items were treated as "subjects," to determine how expert raters' prototypical Q-sorts clustered. Only eigenvalues (a measure of commonality among expert raters) greater than 1.00 were considered. A two-factor solution accounted for 78.50 percent of the total variance. The three DBT expert raters loaded onto factor 1 (range of factor loadings: .87–.90), while the three TFP expert raters loaded onto factor 2 (range of factor loadings: .81–.90). These results provide a further indication that the PQS ratings of each expert rater were consistent with the ratings of the other expert raters from the same theoretical orientation. It also confirms that the TFP and DBT expert raters have two, and only two, distinct conceptualizations of ideal psychotherapy process.

Third, I constructed a correlation matrix of Spearman-Brown correlations, which measure the degree of association between two theoretical constructs derived from two composite prototypical Q-sorts provided by two groups of expert raters. (The Spearman-Brown correlation was used instead of the more common Pearson product-moment correlation because the mathematical formula used in its calculation takes into account the fact that the item distributions were composited.) Table 4.1 indicates that the TFP prototype was highly correlated with the psychodynamic prototype, $r = .72$, $p < .001$, and not significantly correlated with the DBT prototype, or with the CBT or IPT prototypes. The DBT prototype, on the other hand, was highly correlated with the CBT prototype, $r = .83$, $p < .001$, and also significantly correlated with the IPT prototype, $r = .58$, $p < .001$, and the psychodynamic prototype, r

Table 4.1. Spearman-Brown Correlations among Five Prototypical Q-Sorts of Psychotherapy Process

	TFP	*DBT*
TFP	—	.12
DBT	.12	—
Psychodynamic	.72***	.20*
CBT	−.04	.83***
IPT	.09	.58***

*$p < .05$. ***$p < .001$.

= .20, $p < .05$. The DBT prototype, however, was not significantly correlated with the TFP prototype.

A list of the most characteristic and most uncharacteristic PQS items of both TFP and DBT are displayed in table 4.2. Based on my reading of Bateman and Fonagy's (2004a, 2004b) definition, mentalization is the outcome of an empathically attuned, sensitive therapist (item 6) accurately perceiving the therapeutic process (item 28) and using this emotional knowledge to emphasize the patient's feelings in order to help him or her experience them more

Table 4.2. Most and Least Characteristic PQS Items for TFP Prototype, DBT Prototype, and 127-Session Sample

PQS #	*PQS Item*	*Mean Pile #*
Most Characteristic TFP Prototype		
98	The therapy relationship is a focus of discussion	8.67
63	P's interpersonal relationships are a major theme	8.33
67	T interprets warded-off or unconscious wishes, feelings, or ideas	8.33
2	T draws attention to P's nonverbal behavior	8.00
36	T points out P's use of defensive maneuvers (e.g. undoing, denial)	8.00
100	T draws connections between the therapeutic relationship and other relationships	8.00
50	T draws attention to feelings regarded by P as unacceptable (e.g., anger, envy, or excitement)	7.67
79	T comments on changes in P's mood or affect	7.67
93	T is neutral	7.67
Least Characteristic TFP Prototype		
77	T is tactless	1.00
51	T condescends to or patronizes P	1.00
38	There is a discussion of specific activities or tasks for P to attempt outside of session	1.33
27	T gives explicit advice and guidance	1.67
89	T acts to strengthen defenses	2.00
66	T is directly reassuring	2.00
47	T accommodates P to improve relations when interaction is difficult	2.00
45	T adopts supportive stance	2.00
37	T behaves in a teacher-like (didactic) manner	2.00
24	T's emotional conflicts intrude into relationship	2.00
21	T self-discloses	2.00
9	T is distant, aloof	2.00
Most Characteristic DBT Prototype		
69	P's current or recent life situation is emphasized	8.67
4	P's treatment goals are discussed	8.67
6	T is sensitive to P's feelings, attuned to P; empathic	8.33

(*continued*)

Table 4.2. (*continued*)

PQS #	*PQS Item*	*Mean Pile #*
18	T conveys a sense of nonjudgmental acceptance	8.33
2	T draws attention to P's nonverbal behavior	8.00
31	T asks for more information or elaboration	8.00
72	P understands the nature of therapy and what is expected	8.00
85	T encourages P to try new ways of behaving with others	8.00
38	There is a discussion of specific activities or tasks for P to attempt outside of session	8.00
28	T accurately perceives the therapeutic process	7.67
Least Characteristic DBT Prototype		
51	T condescends to or patronizes P	1.00
39	There is a competitive quality to the relationship	1.00
9	T is distant and aloof	1.33
77	T is tactless	2.00
36	T points out P's use of defensive maneuvers (e.g. undoing, denial)	2.00
67	T interprets warded-off or unconscious wishes, feelings or ideas	2.00
14	P does not feel understood by T	2.33
91	Memories of reconstructions of infancy and childhood are topics of discussion	2.33
93	T is neutral	2.33
Most Characteristic Items over 127 Sessions		
88	P brings up significant issues and material	7.37
69	P's current or recent life situation is emphasized	7.34
31[a]	T asks for more information or elaboration	7.24
46	T communicates with P in a clear, coherent style	6.97
23	Dialogue has a specific focus	6.91
86	T is confident or self-assured (vs. uncertain or defensive)	6.89
35	Self-image is a focus of discussion	6.87
63	P's interpersonal relationships are a major theme	6.87
12	Silences occur during the hour	6.74
26	P experiences discomforting or painful affect	6.73
Least Characteristic Items over 127 Sessions		
16	There is discussion of body functions, physical symptoms, health	3.76
2	T draws attention to P's nonverbal behavior	3.80
11	Sexual feelings and experiences are discussed	3.90
100	T draws connections between the therapeutic relationship and other relationships	3.91
87	P is controlling	3.95
24	T's emotional conflicts intrude into relationship	3.98
57	T explains rationale behind technique or approach to treatment	4.00
10	P seeks greater intimacy with T	4.04

Note. T=Therapist. P=Patient.

[a] PQS item 31 is also listed as one of the eight most significantly correlated items with the SCL-90-R (see table 4.5).

deeply (item 81) by getting the patient to elaborate (item 31) and by clarifying the patient's communications (item 65), which produces a feeling of being understood (item 14). Notably, none of these items were listed among the most characteristic of the TFP prototype (see table 4.2). Thus, contrary to recent claims that TFP produces therapeutic change through the enhancement of mentalization processes (Levy, Clarkin, et al., 2006; Levy, Meehan, et al., 2006), the data suggest that mentalization does not appear to be a central change process facilitated by prototypical TFP.

DISCUSSION: STUDY 1

As expected, the TFP and DBT prototypes were highly correlated with their parent prototypes, psychodynamic and CBT, respectively (see table 4.1). Although TFP has adopted what might be considered certain elements of CBT process such as structuring the treatment through contract setting (Yeomans et al., 1992), the general process is still psychodynamic in nature and uncorrelated with CBT process. Kernberg is still quite active in the psychoanalytic community and publishes in psychoanalytic journals; he would be the last person to say that he created a novel treatment independent of psychodynamic theory. The fact that the correlation between the TFP and psychodynamic prototypes is not perfect (i.e., 1.00), however, suggests that TFP does contain unique process features not completely accounted for by psychodynamic therapy (see table 4.2). For example, item 63—"patient's interpersonal relationships are a major theme"—is not listed among the twenty most characteristic items that comprise the psychodynamic prototype (Ablon and Jones, 1998, p. 75; see also chapter 3), yet this item is the second highest item listed in the TFP prototype. Similarly, item 2—"therapist draws attention to patient's nonverbal behavior"—is not listed among the twenty most characteristic psychodynamic items but is listed among the most characteristic TFP items. Interestingly, item 2 is listed as one of the *least* characteristic items conducted by the TFP therapists in the actual 127-session study (see table 4.2). Based on this item survey, it would be best to characterize TFP as a version of psychodynamic psychotherapy.

The data provided by TFP experts suggest that mentalization does not appear to be a central change process facilitated by prototypical TFP. Levy and his colleagues (Levy, Meehan, et al., 2006) reported that TFP was associated with significant increases in RF compared to DBT. On the surface, it would appear that TFP process produces changes in RF. Unfortunately, this study did not provide any quantitative information about therapist adherence to

TFP. Thus, these TFP therapists could have been practicing mentalization processes. Psychodynamic process was significantly correlated with more indices of outcome than CBT process in CBT with depressed patients (Ablon and Jones, 1998). The authors determined that the CBT therapists were inadvertently implementing psychodynamic techniques responsible for patient change. Similarly, the TFP therapists who increased RF (Levy, Meehan, et al., 2006) might have been inadvertently implementing mentalizing techniques in addition to prototypical TFP techniques such as transference interpretations.

As expected, the DBT prototype was correlated not only with the CBT prototype but also with the psychodynamic and IPT prototypes (see table 4.1). Because the correlation between the CBT and IPT prototypes is $r = .51$, $p < .001$ (see chapter 3), it makes sense that DBT, itself highly correlated with CBT, is also highly correlated with IPT. The correlation between the DBT prototype and the psychodynamic prototype, however, is interesting because the correlation between the CBT and psychodynamic prototypes is $r = .01$, *ns* (see chapter 3). Two items listed among the twenty most characteristic items that comprise the psychodynamic prototype (Ablon and Jones, 1998, p. 75; see also chapter 3) are also listed among the most characteristic items that comprise the DBT prototype: item 6—"therapist is sensitive to the patient's feelings, attuned to the patient; empathic"—and item 18—"therapist conveys a sense of nonjudgmental acceptance" (see table 4.2). These items no doubt reflect the influence of mindfulness practice on DBT process (see chapter 5). DBT and psychodynamic therapy thus share a nonjudgmental acceptance of and sensitivity to the patient's feelings not characteristic of standard CBT approaches (Ablon and Jones, 1998, p. 76; see also chapter 3). Based on this item survey, it would be best to characterize DBT as a version of CBT with an admixture of psychotherapy processes borrowed from psychodynamic therapy. It would be courteous of DBT originators to acknowledge their overlap with psychodynamic theory in the development of their own treatment model. Perhaps DBT's effectiveness in treating BPD patients can be partially attributed to its incorporation of psychodynamic process (see also Ablon and Jones, 1998).

RESULTS: STUDY 2

Construction of Factors

I wanted to discover whether an underlying factor structure existed across the TFP treatments of the five patients. The PQS ratings of these five patients' psychotherapy sessions ($N = 127$) were subjected to a principal-components analysis with varimax rotation. The factor analysis yielded four conceptually interpretable factors, which accounted for 34.02 percent of the total variance.

Interaction structure 1, labeled "Collaborative Relationship with a Supportive, Reassuring Therapist," reflects a therapeutic alliance with an unchallenging, accommodating therapist (see table 4.3). Interaction structure 2, "Therapist Attunement/Sensitivity/Affective Involvement," reflects the therapist's nonjudgmental acceptance and clarification of the patient's feelings. Interaction structure 3, "Erotized Transference," reflects the patient's sexual feelings in the therapeutic relationship. Interaction structure 4, "Controlling Therapist with Compliant Patient," reflects a therapist's provision of active,

Table 4.3. PQS Item Factor Loadings for the Four Interaction Structures

Item #	*PQS Item*	*Factor Loadings*
Interaction Structure 1: Collaborative Relationship with Supportive, Reassuring Therapist		
97	P is introspective, readily explores inner thoughts and feelings	.75
99	T challenges P's view	−.74
73	P is committed to work of therapy	.73
88	P brings up significant issues and material	.68
72	P understands the nature of therapy and what is expected	.65
17	T actively exerts control over the interaction	−.64
58	P resists examining thoughts, reactions, or motivations related to problems	−.64
36	T points out P's use of defensive maneuvers (e.g. undoing, denial)	−.63
89	T acts to strengthen defenses	.62
39	There is a competitive quality to the relationship	−.61
47	When the interaction with P is difficult, T accommodates in effort to improve relations	.58
37	T behaves in a teacher-like (didactic) manner	−.56
15	P does not initiate topics, is passive	−.55
45	T adopts supportive stance	.55
55	P conveys positive expectations about therapy	.53
14	P does not feel understood by T	−.53
32	P achieves a new understanding or insight	.52
3	T's remarks are aimed at facilitating P's speech	.50
42	P rejects T's comments and observations	−.50
93	T is neutral	.48
66	T is directly reassuring	.45
44	P feels wary or suspicious	−.44
91	Memories of reconstructions of infancy and childhood are topics of discussion	.44

(*continued*)

Table 4.3. (*continued*)

Item #	PQS Item	Factor Loadings
87	P is controlling	.44
76	T suggests P accept responsibility for his/her problems	−.43
68	Real vs. fantasized meanings of experiences are actively differentiated	−.43
13	P is animated or excited	.41
Interaction Structure 2: Therapist Attunement/Sensitivity/Affective Involvement		
9	T is distant, aloof	−.75
6	T is sensitive to P's feelings, attuned to P; empathic	.73
28	T accurately perceives the therapeutic process	.70
77	T is tactless	−.67
81	T emphasizes P's feelings in order to help him/her experience them more deeply	.66
51	T condescends to or patronizes P	−.66
18	T conveys a sense of nonjudgmental acceptance	.60
24	T's own emotional conflicts intrude into the relationship	−.59
50	T draws attention to feelings regarded by P as unacceptable	.50
20	P is provocative, tests limits of therapy relationship	−.49
65	T clarifies, restates, or rephrases P's communication	.43
Interaction Structure 3: Erotized Transference		
19	There is an erotic quality to the therapy relationship	.68
16	There is discussion of body functions, physical symptoms, health	.65
64	Love or romantic relationships are a topic of discussion	.61
11	Sexual feelings and experiences are discussed	.59
80	T presents an experience or event in a different perspective	−.51
33	P talks of feelings about being close to or needing someone	.42
63	P's interpersonal relationships are a major theme	.42
60	P has cathartic experience	.41
Interaction Structure 4: Controlling Therapist with Compliant Patient		
95	P feels helped	.65
49	P experiences ambivalent or conflicted feelings about T	−.56
84	P expresses angry or aggressive feelings	−.56
1	P verbalizes negative feelings	−.56
27	T gives explicit advice and guidance	.55
38	There is discussion of specific activities or tasks for P to attempt outside of session	.54
59	P feels inadequate and inferior	−.51
85	T encourages P to try new ways of behaving with others	.50
98	The therapy relationship is a focus of discussion	−.47
100	T draws connections between the therapeutic relationship and other relationships	−.42
94	P feels sad or depressed	−.40

Note. T=Therapist. P=Patient.

nonneutral assistance to an idealizing, submissive patient. Linear regressions were calculated to determine the contribution of each PQS item to the four factors. Factor scores represent the weighted sum of each PQS item. The items with the highest factor scores are most defining of the factor, and the items with the lowest factor scores are least defining of the factor. Table 4.3 contains the items of these four interaction structures with factor loadings greater than or equal to an absolute value of .40.

Symptom Improvement Over Time

Three of the five patients in this study completed weekly SCL-90-R questionnaires. The global severity index (GSI) from the SCL-90-R was used as the outcome measure in this study. The SCL-90-R scores were correlated with time measured in weeks. The results of these data are located in figure 4.1 and table 4.4. All three patients (designated Patient 1, Patient 3, and Patient 5) showed significant symptom improvement over time. Because of small cell

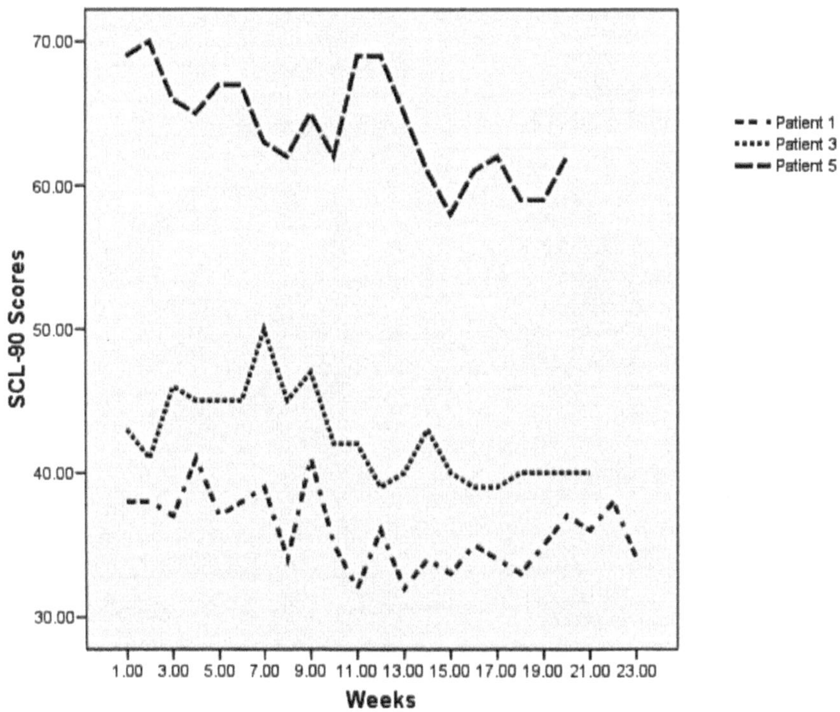

Figure 4.1. Plot of SCL-90-R Scores by Weeks in Treatment

Table 4.4. Effect Sizes of Interaction Structures and Adherence Factors on Weekly SCL-90-R Scores for Three Patients

	Weeks	*SCL-90-R*
PATIENT 1		
Weeks	—	−1.03**
Interaction Structure 1	−.81**	.14
Interaction Structure 2	.46	.06
Interaction Structure 3	−.50*	.10
Interaction Structure 4	.34	−.08
Psychodynamic Adherence	−1.11**	.43
CBT Adherence	.48	−.26
IPT Adherence	−.18	.63*
TFP Adherence	−-.76*	.22
DBT Adherence	−.39	.55*
PATIENT 3		
Weeks	—	−1.73**
Interaction Structure 1	−.22	.49
Interaction Structure 2	.75*	−.60*
Interaction Structure 3	−1.07**	1.22**
Interaction Structure 4	.12	−.68*
Psychodynamic Adherence	−.53*	.76*
CBT Adherence	.43	−.45
IPT Adherence	.49	−.20
TFP Adherence	−.23	.66*
DBT Adherence	−.73*	.03
PATIENT 5		
Weeks	—	−2.05**
Interaction Structure 1	.81**	−.50*
Interaction Structure 2	−1.52**	.68*
Interaction Structure 3	−.43	.33
Interaction Structure 4	−.75*	.19
Psychodynamic Adherence	−.53*	.49
CBT Adherence	−.60*	.23
IPT Adherence	.22	−.29
TFP Adherence	−.80**	.70*
DBT Adherence	.80**	−.38

sizes, Cohen's *d* effect sizes are reported in table 4.4. Effect sizes greater than or equal to an absolute value of .50 are notated with an asterisk to indicate a medium effect size (Cohen, 1992), while effect sizes greater than or equal to an absolute value of .80 are notated with a double asterisk to indicate a large effect size (Cohen, 1992). A negative effect size indicates that symptoms decreased as weeks increased. Patient 5, the most symptomatically disturbed of the three patients, showed the most dramatic improvement, followed by Patient 3 and Patient 1.

Interaction Structures and Symptom Improvement Over Time

Each of the four interaction structures was correlated with weeks and the SCL-90-R scores (see figure 4.2 and table 4.4). Figure 4.2 indicates that the four interaction structures did not always vary with symptom levels in a linear fashion. A pattern is not visually discernable. Figure 4.3 indicates the various contributions that each interaction structure made to the treatment of each of the five patients. Visual inspection of this figure should convince the reader that the constellation of interaction structures uniquely characterizes each of these five treatments. No two treatments were even remotely similar to each other. In other words, the four basic process ingredients varied quantitatively within these five therapist-patient relationships. The fact that the interaction structures of Patient 4 and Patient 5 appear so different supports the hypothesis that interaction structures are the product of the reciprocal interactions between the therapist and patient. When the therapist was held constant, the constellation of interaction structures across these two patients nevertheless varied.

Table 4.4 presents the visual data. Interaction structure 1, "Collaborative Relationship with a Supportive, Reassuring Therapist," dramatically decreased over time in Patient 1's treatment, but dramatically increased over time in Patient 5's treatment. When interaction structure 1 dramatically increased over time, as in the treatment of Patient 5, symptom levels decreased. Perhaps the therapist sensed that building a collaborative relationship resulted

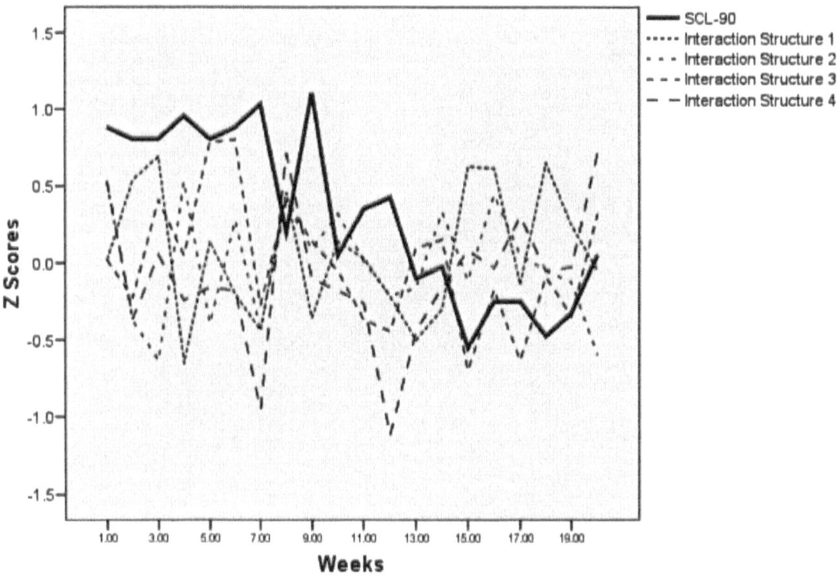

Figure 4.2. Plots of Mean SCL-90-R Scores and Intervention Structures by Weeks in Treatment

in symptom reduction and worked toward increasing this interaction structure over time. Interaction structure 2, "Therapist Attunement/Sensitivity/Affective Involvement," increased over time in Patient 3's treatment but dramatically decreased over time in Patient 5's treatment. The increase of this interaction structure was correlated with symptom reduction in Patient 3's treatment, while its decrease was correlated with symptom increase in Patient 5's treatment. Interaction structure 3, "Erotized Transference," significantly decreased over time in Patient 1's treatment and Patient 3's treatment. This interaction structure was correlated with a dramatic increase in symptom levels in Patient 3's treatment and a nonsignificant increase in the symptom levels of the other two treatments. Even though the means of interaction structure 3 were at or below 0 (see figure 4.3), its mere presence was positively correlated with increases in symptom levels. Although the mean of interaction structure 3 was higher in the treatment of Patient 5 than in the treatments of Patients 1 or 3, symptom levels were not significantly affected by its presence. It appears that the presence of interaction structure 3 is generally correlated with increases in symptom levels, but it is not known whether higher symptom levels cause increases in iteraction structure 3 or vice versa. It is probable that interaction structure 3 decreased over time when the therapist figured out that it was increasing symptom levels. Interaction structure 4, "Controlling Therapist with Compliant Patient," decreased over time in Patient 5's treatment. Its presence was correlated with a decrease

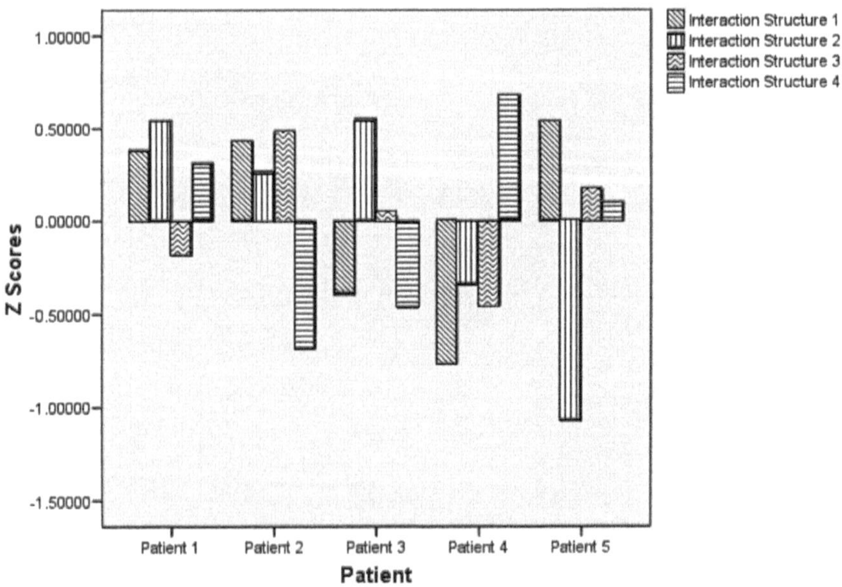

Figure 4.3. Four Mean Interaction Structures for Each Patient

in symptom levels in Patient 3's treatment. Perhaps a controlling, directive therapist provides the external structure needed to reduce symptoms in some patients—at least temporarily.

Adherence Factors (PQS Prototypes) and Symptom Improvement Over Time

Each of the five adherence factors (PQS prototypes) was correlated with weeks and the SCL-90-R scores (see figure 4.4 and table 4.4). Figure 4.4 indicates that the DBT adherence factor was the least favored psychotherapy process among these five treatments. The other four adherence factors seem to be bunched together over the course of these treatments. Figure 4.5 supports this idea. While the means of the first four adherence factors are in a positive range, the DBT adherence factor is in the negative range. Therapists tended to be conducting treatments at odds with DBT process. Interestingly, these five TFP-trained therapists were most adherent to CBT process and only second to TFP process. A series of ten paired-samples *t*-tests between every pair of adherence factors indicated significant mean differences between all of them, $p < .05$. In other words, CBT adherence was significantly greater than TFP adherence, which was in turn significantly greater than psychodynamic adherence, which was in turn significantly greater than IPT adherence, which was in turn significantly greater than DBT adherence.

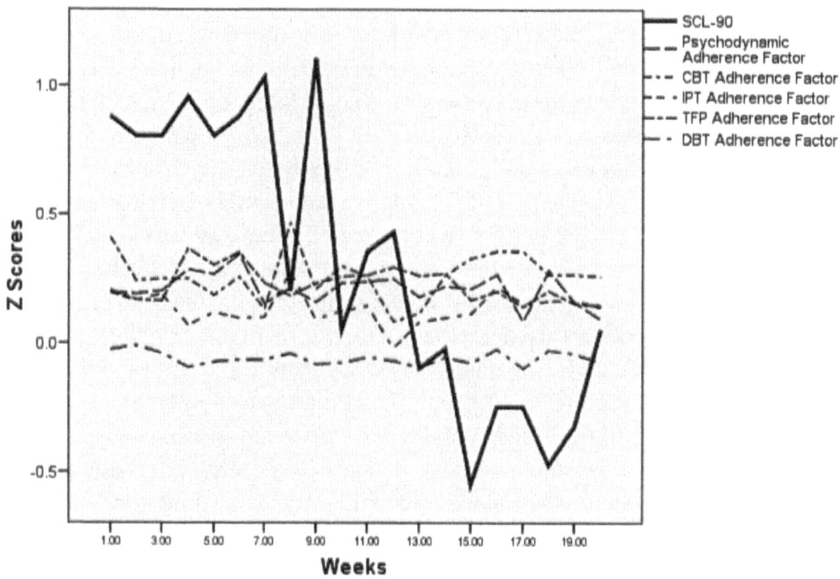

Figure 4.4. Plots of SCL-90-R Scores and Adherence Factors by Weeks in Treatment

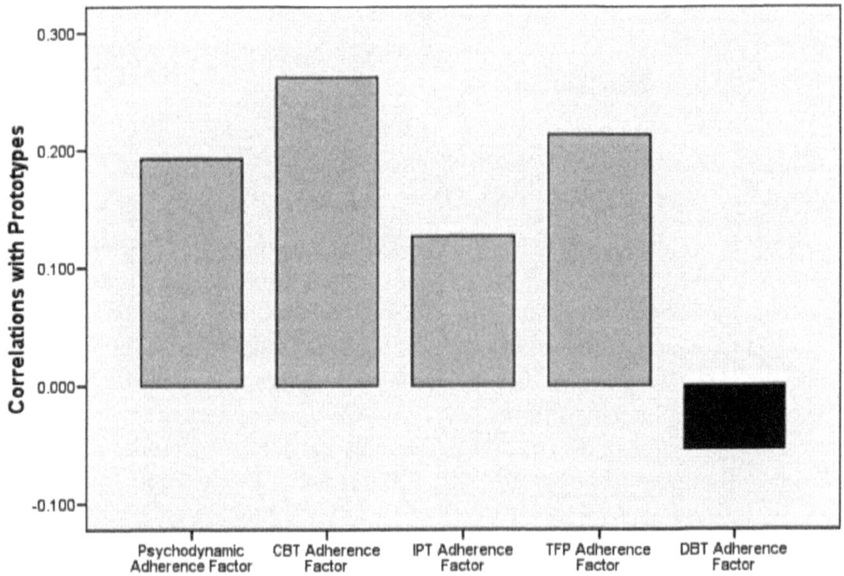

Figure 4.5. Five Mean Adherence Factors over Five Patients

Table 4.4 indicates some interesting patterns in these data. Psychodynamic adherence decreased over time in all three treatments for which I have SCL-90-R data. Psychodynamic adherence was correlated with an increase in symptom levels across all three treatments and a significant increase in Patient 3's treatment. Perhaps these therapists decided to ditch the psychodynamic psychotherapy process when they noticed their patients' symptom levels increasing. CBT adherence decreased over time in Patient 5's treatment. CBT adherence was correlated with nonsignificant decreases in symptom levels in the treatments of Patients 1 and 3 and a nonsignificant increase in symptom levels in Patient 5's treatment, which could account for this therapist's significant decrease in adherence to CBT over time. IPT adherence was significantly correlated with an increase in symptom levels in Patient 1's treatment, which could account for the nonsignificant decrease in IPT adherence over time in this treatment. TFP adherence decreased over time in all three treatments. This decrease was significant in the treatments of Patients 1 and 5. TFP adherence was also positively correlated with significant increases in symptom levels in the treatments of Patients 3 and 5 and a nonsignificant increase in symptom levels in Patient 1's treatment. Again, perhaps these therapists became less adherent to TFP process when they noticed their patients' symptom levels increasing. DBT adherence significantly decreased over time in Patient 3's treatment but significantly increased over time in Patient 5's treatment. In Patient 1's treatment, DBT adherence was significantly correlated with an increase in

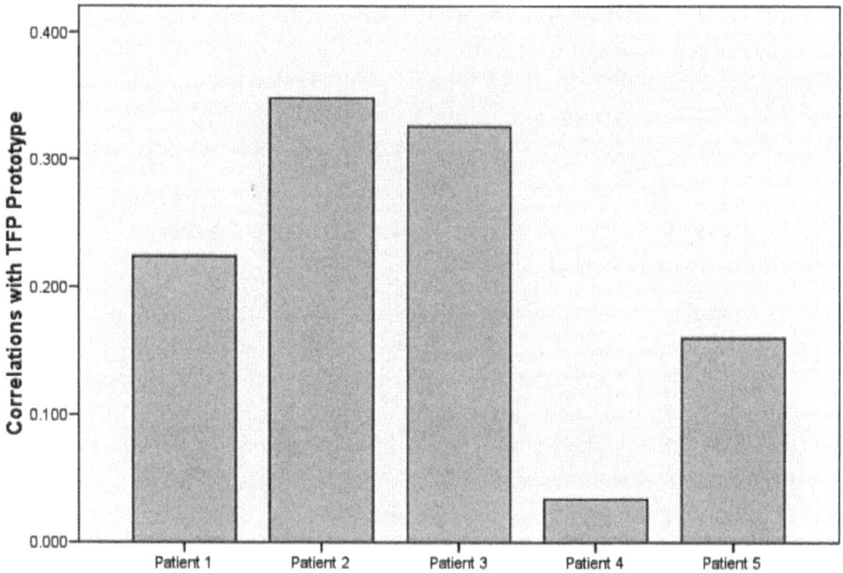

Figure 4.6. Mean TFP Adherence Factors

symptom levels, which could account for a nonsignificant decrease in DBT adherence in this treatment. Patient 5's symptom levels decreased nonsignificantly with DBT adherence, which is consistent with a significant increase in DBT adherence in this treatment.

Overall, it appears that these three therapists modified their adherence to a particular treatment approach to ameliorate their patients' symptom levels. Whether adherence levels cause changes in symptom levels or vice versa is not known. It is likely that these change processes are reciprocal: adherence to a psychotherapy prototype causes changes in patient symptom levels, which in turn cause changes in adherence levels, which in turn cause changes in symptom levels. Only time-series analysis of these data could confirm this hypothesis. Unfortunately, times-series analysis is beyond the scope of this chapter.

Figure 4.6 reflects the mean differences in adherence to TFP psychotherapy process among the five treatments. Visual inspection indicates that these five treatments were not uniformly adhered to TFP. A series of ten paired-samples t-tests between every pair of TFP adherence factors indicated significant mean differences between all of them except for pair 2 and 3 and pair 1 and 5, $p < .05$. Interestingly, the therapist of Patients 4 and 5 was the most highly experienced TFP practitioner of the four therapists, yet his TFP adherence in both treatments was the lowest among all five treatments. In spite of (or perhaps because of) this low TFP adherence, Patient 5 made the most dramatic symptom improvement of the three patients on whom I have

SCL-90-R data. Perhaps this therapist was adjusting his TFP adherence to the needs of the patient rather than adjusting the patient to the need for TFP adherence (see chapter 3). The fact that TFP adherence varied while the therapist remained constant in the treatments of Patients 4 and 5 further suggests that patient characteristics influence the application of TFP, not vice versa.

Psychotherapy Processes Significantly Correlated with Symptom Improvement

Finally, I wanted to identify the specific aspects of psychotherapy process regardless of PQS prototypes that correlated significantly with the SCL-90-R data. Table 4.5 lists the eight PQS items significantly correlated with symptom levels at $p < .001$ (a Bonferroni correction was applied to control for type I errors associated with conducting one hundred statistical tests). Interestingly, the process item most highly correlated with symptom reduction was emphasizing the patient's feelings, considered by Blagys and Hilsenroth (2000) as the most distinctive feature of psychodynamic therapy (see chapter 3, figure 3.1). Equally interesting, the second most highly correlated process item with symptom reduction was actively exerting control over the dyadic interaction, considered by Blagys and Hilsenroth (2002) as the second most distinctive feature of CBT (see chapter 3, figure 3.2). Therapist clarification was also highly correlated with symptom reduction. Both Kernberg and his colleagues (Clarkin et al., 1999, 2006) and Bateman and Fonagy (2004a, 2004b) have stressed the importance of the role of clarification in the treatment of patients with BPD. The therapist's empathy, emotional closeness, and interest all seem related to symptom reduction—characteristics that Fonagy and his colleagues (Fonagy, Gergely, et al., 2002) might identify as holding the patient in the therapist's mind. Two process items that seem to

Table 4.5. Significant Correlations between PQS Items and SCL-90-R

Item #	*PQS Item*	*r*
81	T emphasizes P's feelings in order to help him/her experience them more deeply	−.59
17	T actively exerts control over the interaction	−.57
6	T is sensitive to P's feelings, attuned to P; empathic	−.54
65	T clarifies, restates, or rephrases P's communication	−.49
28	T accurately perceives the therapeutic process	−.45
31	T asks for more information or elaboration	−.43
90	P's dreams or fantasies are discussed	.44
9	T is distant, aloof	.52

Note. $p < .001$. Bonferroni correction applied.

increase symptom levels are the therapist's aloofness and the discussion of dreams and fantasies. Patients with BPD need to feel that their therapist is emotionally accessible to them. Discussing dreams and fantasies not only blurs these patients' tenuous grip on reality but also interferes with their connection with the therapist. The only process item that appeared on both this list and the list of most characteristic items over the 127 sessions had to do with the therapist's show of interest in the patient (PQS item 31). Thus, these therapists could have done even more to reduce their patients' symptoms than they already did.

It is noteworthy that the PQS items that assess therapist confrontation, transference and defense interpretations, and patient insight—important psychodynamic and TFP interventions—were not significantly correlated with symptom reduction. On the other hand, therapist support and reassurance were significantly correlated with symptom reduction (r = -.32, r = -.28, respectively, $p < .05$). Perhaps in the short term, unstable patients with BPD benefit from the auxiliary ego offered by the therapist. Symptoms become less acute when the therapist allows the patient to rely on the therapist's approval, encouragement, and reassurance. In actively suicidal patients, this support might be critical to their stabilization. In the long term, however, it is not clear whether these therapist techniques would produce enduring structural change.

DISCUSSION: STUDY 2

This is the first research study to identify interaction structures in a sample of BPD patients. Four interaction structures characterized these five treatments of severely disturbed patients diagnosed with borderline personality disorder. In spite of the identification of these repetitive patterns of interaction across treatments, the constellation of these four repetitive patterns of interaction uniquely characterized each of the five treatments (see figure 4.3). In other words, each treatment differed in the quantity of these four ingredients, producing a unique therapeutic meal with its own unique flavors, smell, and consistency. This finding supports the view of Kantrowitz (2001), who compared a psychotherapy relationship to "a snowflake . . . no two are alike. Nor are any two patient-analyst pairs" (p. 403). Elaborating on this metaphor, psychotherapy relationships with BPD patients, like snowflakes, might present a limited number of interaction structures: snowflakes have six sides, while these BPD psychotherapy relationships in this small sample manifested four interaction structures. Yet the various quantities of these interaction structures, expressed at different phases of treatment in relation to the patient's symptomatic concerns, give each therapeutic dyad its own unique shape.

Who is responsible for the unique shape of these treatments—the therapist or the patient? While the hero of psychotherapy has traditionally been portrayed as the therapist by therapists, hero status has recently been conferred upon the patient (Duncan, 2002; see also Ablon and Jones, 2002; Ablon and Marci, 2004). While I would argue that both the therapist and patient equally contribute to the construction of the interaction structures through complex transference-countertransference matrices (see Jones, 2000), the evidence suggests that the therapist's personal characteristics do not alone determine the shape of these interaction structures. Because the same therapist treated both Patient 4 and Patient 5, any differences between the two patients in the constellation of interaction structures would implicate the patient's characteristics (or the unique interaction between the patient's characteristics and the therapist's characteristics) as the driving force behind these differences. Figure 4.3 again illustrates the two wildly different constellations of interaction structures of these two treatments. Similarly, this therapist's adherence to TFP also significantly differed between these two treatments (see figure 4.6).

Unexpectedly, the therapists relied primarily on CBT process to treat these patients (see figure 4.5) in spite of the fact that they were supposed to be adhering to TFP. The fact that TFP process was used less with arguably the two most severely disturbed patients, Patients 4 and 5, than with the other three patients in this small sample (see figure 4.6) suggests that CBT process, which consists of a therapist who exerts control over the session and provides support, might be necessary to provide immediate stabilization for BPD patients in crisis. This interpretation is supported by the fact that two characteristic CBT process items—the therapist exerting control over the session and providing support—were significantly correlated with symptom reduction. The most experienced TFP therapist was treating Patients 4 and 5 and probably deviated from TFP for good reason: he first wanted to stabilize the patients' symptoms and pave the foundation for later bread-and-butter TFP interventions (e.g., confrontation of the patients' views of herself and the therapist, transference interpretations) after discharge in an outpatient setting. The TFP experts rated these two PQS items among the fifteen least characteristic even though TFP is considered a more structured version of psychodynamic therapy (Yeomans et al., 1992). In addition, only one of the items listed as the most or least characteristic of the TFP prototype (see table 4.2) is simultaneously listed as one of the eight items most significantly correlated with symptom levels: therapist is distant or aloof (item 9; see table 4.5). Perhaps the application of TFP to more severely disturbed BPD patients requires the temporary use of more supportive, CBT-like processes that serve the treatment goal of stabilization before more ambitious interventions are attempted.

The fact that these five patients improved with adherence to CBT predominating these patients' sessions (see figure 4.5) suggests that the therapists were being sensitive to what seemed to be working to ameliorate their patients' symptoms. Bateman and Fonagy (2004b) have suggested that TFP expects too much agentive thinking from the patient, which the patient could perceive as blaming. In contrast, an MBT therapist "would not expect the patient to understand much of the discourse that the therapist might verbalize in relational terms" (p. 117). The reason is that BPD patients experience widespread "symbolic failure, particularly associated with incongruent mirroring" (p. 118). Thus, transference interpretations, particularly with the severely disturbed BPD patients in this small sample whose symbolic capacity has clearly failed, would be ineffective. Only after a primitive symbolic capacity has become activated should a therapist attempt transference interpretations with BPD patients.

Contrary to these findings, transference interpretations have been shown to be effective *only* with patients assessed as having poor object relations but not formally diagnosed with BPD (Høglend et al., 2008). Patients' quality of object relations (QOR) was calculated as the mean score on three eight-point scales. In Høglend et al.'s (2008) sample of one hundred patients, the mean QOR score was 5.1 out of a possible eight points (p. 765). The authors dichotomized the sample into high and low scorers, with low scorers averaging 4.4 points (p. 767). Clearly, the scores do not suggest object relations of extremely poor quality. The participants consisted of outpatients in once-weekly psychotherapy, while patients with "long-term inability to work" (p. 764) were excluded from the study. The five patients enrolled in my study, however, were highly emotionally disturbed persons diagnosed with BPD, four of whom with multiple prior psychiatric hospitalizations. In addition, four out of the five patients were unemployed and had experienced chronic employment problems. It is reasonable to conclude, therefore, that all five of these patients would have been excluded from Høglend et al.'s (2008) study.

I am therefore proposing a curvilinear relation between the quality of object relations (QOR) and treatment outcome in psychotherapy that uses a moderate quantity of transference interpretations, where treatment outcome is a curvilinear function of QOR. At the two extreme ends of the inverted U-shaped curve, both low and high scorers on QOR do not respond to transference interpretations, while moderate scorers in the middle of the curve (the low scorers in Høglend et al.'s [2008] sample) demonstrate significant functional improvement with this type of intervention. Perhaps low QOR scorers, such as the BPD inpatients in my study, would feel threatened by the therapist's focus on their relationship and arouse paranoia, thus undermining therapeutic gains. Piper and his colleagues (Piper, Joyce, McCallum, Azim, and Ogrodniczuk, 2002, p. 117) have suggested that low QOR scorers might be less able to tolerate the demands of the interpersonal situation, more fearful of losing the therapeutic relationship, and less receptive to the therapist's interventions than moderate or high scorers.

Perhaps high QOR scorers, on the other hand, would benefit from therapy regardless of the type of intervention used, thus diminishing the importance of transference interpretations as a specific factor in this group. In future research, the quality (e.g., tact, timing, accuracy), quantity, and type of transference interpretation (e.g., resistance to its awareness, genetic links) could also be assessed to determine whether these variables also interact with QOR to moderate treatment outcome.

In contrast to this theory, Bateman and Fonagy (2004b) have recommended only identifying the mental states in the patient and others and connecting these mental states to behaviors as the effective ingredients of BPD treatment—not transference interpretations. In fact, five of the eight most characteristic PQS items correlated with symptom reduction across all five patients support this recommendation (see table 4.5). Mentalization is the outcome of an empathically attuned, sensitive therapist (item 6) accurately perceiving the therapeutic process (item 28) and using this emotional knowledge to emphasize the patient's feelings in order to help him or her experience them more deeply (item 81) by getting the patient to elaborate (item 31) and clarifying the patient's communications (item 65). Combine this process with a highly structured therapy experience (item 17), and you have all the essential ingredients for an effective treatment for severely disturbed BPD patients. As previously mentioned, none of these items was listed among the most characteristic of the TFP prototype (see table 4.2).

Kernberg and other proponents of TFP might object that symptom reduction in the short term is not an accurate yardstick for measuring enduring structural change. A controlling, supportive therapist who empathizes with the patient's feelings might provide the auxiliary ego support necessary for stabilization of acute symptoms such as suicidality; however, the polarized state of the patient's self- and object representations would likely remain unchanged. Under these circumstances, therefore, symptom management would be short-lived without continued supportive therapy like CBT. Citing the follow-up data from a large RCT of IPT and CBT conducted by Shea and his colleagues (Shea, Elkin, et al., 1992), Jones (2000) concluded, "Changes in brief therapy brought about by supportive interventions under the rule of a positive transference are not enduring" (p. 220). Unfortunately, I do not have follow-up data on the five patients enrolled in this study. A more comprehensive conceptualization of weekly or monthly treatment outcome that had included both symptomatic and structural or personality change might have answered this question about the enduring quality of the changes experienced by these patients over the course of treatment (see chapter 3). Future quantitative single-case research designs need to adopt multiple methods of assessing outcome to determine the depth of change afforded by a highly structured, supportive psychotherapy process like CBT process.

Even though TFP has been shown to outperform DBT and SPT on a broad spectrum of outcome measures in an RCT (Clarkin et al., 2007; Levy, Meehan, et al., 2006), we do not know that the patients in the TFP condition received pure TFP and not an alloyed version. Clarkin and his colleagues (Clarkin et al., 2007) reported that twice-weekly outpatient TFP was associated with significant improvement in ten of twelve symptom domains, while once-weekly outpatient SPT was associated with significant improvement in only six domains and once-weekly outpatient DBT in only five domains. Levy and his colleagues (Levy, Meehan, et al., 2006) similarly reported that TFP was associated with significant increases from insecure to secure attachment and significant increases in RF compared to DBT and SPT. On the surface, it would appear that TFP produces both symptomatic and structural change. Unfortunately, neither of these studies provided any quantitative information about therapist adherence to TFP. Thus, these TFP therapists could have been practicing CBT process or mentalization process.

The Kernberg research group is similarly concerned about identifying the change processes associated with TFP and working on publishing psychotherapy process data collected from this RCT. It is possible that TFP process is better suited to BPD outpatients—the population targeted by the most recent TFP treatment manuals (Clarkin et al., 1999, 2006; Yeomans et al., 2002)—than it is to more severely disturbed BPD inpatients. As suggested in chapter 3, only TFP process studies conducted in community settings can address the question of "what works for whom." In this study, what worked for these BPD inpatients was a directive therapist facilitating a therapeutic climate in which mentalizing processes could take place. At the same time, each treatment required something different to achieve symptomatic change, as figure 4.3 dramatically illustrates. To paraphrase Blatt and Felsen (1993), different kinds of severely disturbed BPD patients may need different kinds of interaction structures (or at least in different quantities). I encourage other researchers to conduct additional studies on BPD patients' interaction structures so that we can determine whether symptom severity and treatment setting (outpatient vs. inpatient) determine their nature and quantity.

I want to make some additional observations about the four interaction structures identified in this study. The first two interaction structures appear to have something in common with a secure attachment relationship. A collaborative relationship with a supportive therapist (interaction structure 1) who is empathically attuned and sensitive to the patient's needs (interaction structure 2) resembles a secure base from which the patient can explore her feelings and thoughts and a safe haven to which the patient can return in times of distress (e.g., Bowlby, 1988). On the other hand, the second two interaction structures appear to represent the attachment relationship gone awry. An erotized transference (interaction structure 3) suggests that the patient is looking to an attachment figure, the therapist, for the fulfillment of sexual needs. Consistent with this idea, the treatments of Patients 1 and 4, the only two patients without reported childhood histories of sexual abuse, scored in the negative range on interaction structure 3, while the other three patients scored in the positive range. Perhaps Patients 2, 3, and 5 were enacting a childhood interaction structure by contributing to the creation of an erotized therapeutic atmosphere. A controlling therapist with a compliant patient (interaction structure 4) suggests a scripted, superficially happy relationship in which the patient is avoiding the therapist's imagined potential rejection by playing a submissive role.

Interestingly, this interaction structure predominated Patient 4's treatment (see figure 4.3). This patient left the hospital AMA because, according to hospital records, "she became aware that her family was adapting to life without her." In the context of the interaction structure data, however, another interpretation is available: Patient 4 no longer wanted to play the role of the compliant patient, keeping her angry and aggressive feelings to herself (see table 4.3). In the context of a collaborative relationship, a patient would feel secure expressing the hostile feelings that would inevitably emerge toward the therapist in any treatment of a BPD patient. The patient would know that the therapist would collaborate with her on understanding them. In a noncollaborative relationship, however, the role of compliant patient perhaps became too onerous for Patient 4, so she precipitously left treatment. In fact, figure 4.3 illustrates that, for Patient 4, interaction structure 1 was the lowest of the five patients, while interaction structure 4 was the highest of the five patients. This constellation of interaction structures would appear to be a recipe for termination. Treatment dropouts could be predicted and thus prevented using this method of assessing interaction structures early in treatment.

Attachment data on both the patients and the therapists could also illuminate the development of these interaction structures (see Goodman, in press, chapters 3 and 6). As I suggested earlier, the predominant interaction structure at any given phase of treatment might reflect the nature of the patient's attachment relationship to the therapist. The therapist's own attachment history might also contribute to his or her ability to provide a secure base for the patient, depending on what the patient needs from the therapist. The patient might recruit other motivational systems such as the sexual system into a unique profile of needs they are looking to the therapist to fulfill (Goodman, 2002). The erotized transference interaction structure illustrates this process. A therapist whose own attachment and sexual motivational systems are not clearly differentiated might experience countertransference reactions peculiar to the patient's transference. This therapist-patient complementary correspondence could exacerbate this interaction structure and inadvertently increase the patient's symptom levels. Data on therapist characteristics are seldom collected but sorely needed to help us understand the nature of psychotherapy process. As a field, we think nothing of recruiting research subjects for our RCTs, but we curiously back away from making ourselves the object of our own study. Freud (e.g., 1900) had the courage to share his own dreams with us. Where is our courage?

CONCLUSIONS

I offer ten tentative conclusions from the results of study 1 and study 2: (1) TFP process is similar but not identical to psychodynamic therapy process; (2) mentalization processes were not endorsed as belonging to the prototypical TFP technical arsenal; (3) DBT process is similar but not identical to CBT process and psychodynamic therapy process; (4) four interaction structures can be identified in a small sample of severely disturbed BPD patients; (5) each BPD treatment reflects a unique constellation of interaction structures; (6) TFP therapists were more adherent to CBT than to TFP; (7) TFP therapists differed in their adherence to TFP; (8) BPD patients improved under the predominance of CBT process; (9) the effective therapeutic ingredients of these five treatments were a directive therapist who facilitates a therapeutic atmosphere in which mentalization processes could take place; and (10) therapists adjusted their technical approaches "on the fly" to facilitate symptom reduction. Future researchers need to investigate adherence to prototypical TFP process with various types of BPD patients in various settings. Specifically, treatments of BPD patients with less severe disturbance or different constellations of symptoms (Clarkin et al., 1993), treatments in day treatment or outpatient settings, and treatments that systematically study pairings of therapist and patient attachment organizations could yield findings that enrich or even contradict the findings of this study. Future researchers also need to rectify the primary limitation of this study—that treatment outcome was limited to symptom data. Assessment of structural outcomes such as attachment organization, RF, and the complexity and quality of self- and object representations needs to be considered along with symptoms to create a more comprehensive picture of therapeutic change in patients suffering from borderline psychopathology.

Finally, I want to make a plea for a measure of flexibility in the treatment of BPD patients and, by extension, all patients. The data I presented in this chapter suggest that the therapists adjusted their technical approaches "on the fly" when they felt that their patients would benefit from a change in their intervention strategies. These technical modifications did not come from a treatment manual but from clinical intuition—the reflection on one's own countertransference reactions, or possibly a more broadly conceptualized empathic connection with the patient. Instead of training our students to be slaves to a treatment manual, we should be training them to be its master. Responding to criticism that his hungry disciples were picking grain on the Sabbath, Jesus said, "The Sabbath was made for man, not man for the Sabbath" (Mark 2:27). The training manual was made for us, not the other way around.

Treatment adherence is an important aspect of training students in a particular theoretical orientation (see volume II, chapter 5); however, inattention to "conditions on the ground," to borrow a currently popular political phrase, can spell disaster, as Castonguay and his colleagues (Castonguay et al., 1996) learned. We need to be empathically attuned to our patients so that we can become aware when our treatment approach becomes counterproductive. TFP and DBT are manualized treatments that nevertheless reflect a clinical reality: treatment purity (whether psychoanalysis or CBT) might not be most effective for certain types of patients. Training in global clinical skills such as empathy, countertransference awareness, and potential interaction structures (i.e., enactments) would more suitably position our students to become effective therapists than training them how to apply a treatment manual. Our field needs fewer technicians and more artists.

Part Two

SPECIFIC FACTORS RELATED TO COMMON PROCESSES OF THERAPEUTIC CHANGE

Chapter Five

It's Not Just for Yoga Anymore: Mindfulness as an Effective Ingredient of Therapeutic Change

> Do not dwell in the past, do not dream of the future, concentrate the mind on the present moment.
>
> Siddhartha Gautama (the historical Buddha)

> Do not worry about your life, what you will eat or drink. . . . Look at the birds of the air; they do not sow or reap or store away in barns. . . . Who of you can add a single hour to his life? . . . Therefore do not worry about tomorrow, for tomorrow will worry about itself.
>
> Jesus (Matthew 6:25–27, 34)

Over the years, psychotherapy process and outcome research has occupied itself with identifying the factor or factors common to all psychotherapy modalities responsible for therapeutic change. These researchers (e.g., Beitman, 2005; Binder and Strupp, 1997; Henry and Strupp, 1994; Lambert and Barley, 2001) have cited treatment outcome research that suggests the equivalent effectiveness of all psychotherapies (Luborsky, Singer, and Luborsky, 1975; Smith, Glass, and Miller, 1980; Wampold et al., 1997) to support their claim that so-called common factors cause therapeutic change to occur. Still others (e.g., Cutler, Goldyne, Markowitz, Devlin, and Glick, 2004, 2005; DeRubeis, Brotman, and Gibbons, 2005; Kazdin, 2005), however, have refuted this claim by arguing that equivalent effectiveness of all psychotherapies does not imply common processes operating across these therapies. Outcome evidence that a treatment helps patients get better does not explain *why* those patients got better. Thus, different processes of therapeutic change could nevertheless produce equivalent treatment outcomes. Further, the fact that empirical research has identified eighty-nine different common factors (Grencavage and Norcross, 1990) suggests that either all psychotherapies share many effective ingredients of therapeutic change, or the claims of "commonness" are exaggerated. It has been suggested that it is not common factors but rather common patient characteristics that account for this equivalent effectiveness. Given any treatment sample, certain patients are going to get better regardless of theoretical orientation. In fact, it is estimated that patient characteristics account for 55 percent of patient change (Cutler et al., 2004).

In spite of the controversy that surrounds the existence and identification of common factors of therapeutic change, theoreticians and researchers alike continue to search for the Holy Grail—that ingredient of therapeutic change common to all effective psychotherapies. Martin (1997) first proposed that the concept of mindfulness should be considered as a common factor. From his perspective, mindfulness helps "facilitate an *optimal* circumstance for psychotherapeutic change" (p. 292). He further suggested that mindfulness makes it possible to understand the operation of seemingly diverse treatment orientations. Interestingly, Martin (1997) has also conceptualized mindfulness as a state of mind to be cultivated in both the therapist and patient.

My thesis is that mindfulness and the psychoanalytic term "free association" are conceptually overlapping constructs that could function as effective ingredients of therapeutic change across a wide variety of treatment modalities, independent of other interventions typically associated with these modalities such as formal meditation or interpretation. Furthermore, mentalization is a neighboring construct whose strongly interpersonal dimension accounts for its conceptual distinctiveness from mindfulness. Finally, I argue that mindfulness in the absence of an interpersonal dimension reinforces a particular insecure attachment pattern characterized by defensive exclusion (Bowlby, 1973) of attachment needs.

MINDFULNESS IN CONTEXT

What are the origins of mindfulness? The origins of the construct can be traced to Siddhartha Gautama, a descendant of royalty, who was born in what is now the country of Nepal in 563 B.C. The Buddha ("Enlightened One"), as he came to be known, sought the relief of human suffering through meditation. The specific form of meditation originated by the Buddha was meant to cultivate a state of mindfulness that produces detachment from suffering ("Gautama Buddha," 2006).

What does Buddhism have to do with a proposed common factor of therapeutic change? Although William James predicted the absorption of Buddhism into Western psychology at the dawn of the last century (Epstein, 1996), it was not until 1982 that mindfulness was first introduced into the empirical literature of Western psychology (Kabat-Zinn, 1982). Kabat-Zinn and his colleagues (Kabat-Zinn, 1990; Kabat-Zinn et al., 1992) developed what they advertised as an empirically supported treatment package, mindfulness-based stress reduction (MBSR). MBSR placed mindfulness, achieved through the practice of meditation, at the heart of this treatment. Within the next several years, other so-called mindfulness-based technologies (S. C. Hayes and Wilson, 2003, p. 161) began to proliferate: mindfulness-based cognitive therapy (MBCT; Ma and Teasdale, 2004; Segal, Williams, and Teasdale, 2002; Teasdale et al., 2002; Teasdale et al., 2000; Teasdale, Segal, and Williams, 1995), acceptance and commitment therapy (ACT; S. C. Hayes, 2004; S. C. Hayes, Strosahl, and Wilson, 1999), relapse prevention (RP; Marlatt, 1994; Marlatt and Gordon, 1985), and the most visible of all, dialectical behavior therapy (DBT; Linehan, 1993a, 1993b; Linehan et al., 1991; Linehan et al., 2006; Linehan et al., 1993; Linehan et al., 1994). As of 1998 over 240 hospitals and clinics in the United States and abroad were using mindfulness-based treatment packages (Salmon, Santorelli, and Kabat-Zinn, 1998).

S. C. Hayes (2002, 2004) has called this proliferation of mindfulness-based treatments "the third wave" of behavior therapy. The first wave of behavior therapy was spearheaded by John B. Watson and B. F. Skinner and focused on stimulus and response—the transaction between perceptions and environmental stimuli. The second wave, spearheaded by the likes of Albert Ellis and Aaron Beck, was focused on faulty cognitions and not transactions with the environment. This second wave spawned cognitive-behavioral therapy (CBT). S. C. Hayes has argued that the mindfulness-based treatments represent a third wave because they do not share many of the assumptions of the first two waves of behavior therapy. Among these assumptions are the exclusive focus on outcome—the goals of treatment—and the inherent judgment of certain behaviors and cognitions as "irrational," "faulty," or "pathological" cognitive schemas. In contrast to these first two waves, the third wave of behavioral treatments encourages acceptance of one's problems in the here and now—a nonstriving to be "fixed" and a consequent focus on process rather than outcome.

S. C. Hayes (2002, 2004) and his colleagues (e.g., Dimidjian and Linehan, 2003; Kabat-Zinn, 2003) have acknowledged the paradox between seeking emotional, cognitive, or behavioral change and accepting emotions, cognitions, and behaviors as they are. In fact, Linehan's (1993a) DBT posits the relationship between acceptance and change as the central dialectic encountered by the patient (Linehan, 1994). The practice of mindfulness orients the patient toward acceptance through its exclusive focus on the present moment, not on expectations of change that focus on a future imagined self and its discrepancy with the real self in the here and now. Once these expectations of change are neutralized, the patient can focus on the mindful acceptance of all thoughts and feelings and practice the Zen concept that "'all is as it should be'" (Robins, Schmidt, and Linehan, 2004, p. 38). In structural psychoanalytic terms, the relief of superego pressure associated with relinquishing expectations of change produces a greater level of self-acceptance and, consequently, lower levels of anxiety and depression (e.g., see Feldman and Hayes, in press; Roemer and Orsillo, 2002; Segal et al., 2002; Wells, 1999, 2002).

The proliferation of mindfulness-based treatments could not have occurred if cognitive-behavioral techniques could account for the effective track record of CBT. S. C. Hayes (2004), a researcher trained in the cognitive-behavioral tradition and the founder of ACT, a mindfulness-based intervention, has concluded that the evidence against the unique effectiveness of cognitive-behavioral techniques propelled the search for other techniques that might account for outcome more consistently. Specifically, clinical improvement often occurs before cognitive-behavioral techniques have been implemented (Ilardi and Craighead, 1994, 1999; Wilson, 1999), which prompted two cognitive-behavioral experts to conclude that there is "no additive benefit to providing cognitive interventions in cognitive therapy" (Dobson and Khatri, 2000, p. 913).

According to S. C. Hayes (2004), the solution for the CBT field was to move away from direct, first-order change strategies of specific thoughts and cognitive schemas, and to embrace an indirect, "principle-focused" (p. 5) approach that would "considerably broaden the focus of change" (p. 6) to emphasize patient experience. This shift paved the way for the third wave of mindfulness-based treatments. If the reader doubts that the third wave signifies a shift toward a more psychoanalytic understanding and approach to treatment, then he or she might be convinced by what some might find an ironic quotation from Linehan and her colleagues (Robins et al., 2004): "In contrast to the experimental evidence required by psychology, Zen [mindfulness practice] emphasizes experiential evidence as a means of understanding the world" (p. 39). Of course, over the past fifty years, members of the cognitive-behavioral community have sharply criticized psychoanalysts for privileging just this kind of evidence in their clinical work (e.g., see Wolpe and Rachman, 1960).

OPERATIONAL DEFINITION OF MINDFULNESS

To their credit, the proponents of mindfulness-based treatments have attempted to operationalize their construct so that it can be standardized across treatments and empirically measured in both process and outcome studies. An early definition that appeared in the literature described mindfulness as a process of "paying attention in a particular way: on purpose, in the present moment, and nonjudgmentally" (Kabat-Zinn, 1994, p. 4). For Kabat-Zinn (2003) mindfulness is a meditation practice, which is the vehicle, or delivery system, by which mindfulness is most skillfully practiced. Meditation practice represents the heart of MBSR intervention—a radical "nonattachment to outcome" (p. 148) that fixes the patient squarely in the here and now in a state of attention to all internal and external stimuli, which facilitates "acceptance of the full gamut of emotional expression held in awareness" (p. 153). Further, Kabat-Zinn (2003) has characterized mindfulness as "an inherent human capacity" (p. 146) that varies across situations and across persons. Meditation cultivates and refines the capacity for mindfulness through the attentive observation of "the interconnectedness of apparently separate aspects of experience, many of which tend to hover beneath our ordinary level of awareness regarding both inner and outer experience" (p. 149). Another characteristic of mindfulness and the third-wave treatments, therefore, is their emphasis on unconscious phenomena and their need for integration, which clearly resembles a psychoanalytic approach to treatment (e.g., Kernberg, 1975).

In 2004, Bishop and his colleagues (Bishop et al., 2004) responded to the need to publish an operational definition that could be used to construct empirical instruments to assess mindfulness. Their model of mindfulness consisted of two components: (1) the self-regulation of attention maintained on immediate experience in the present moment and (2) an orientation to immediate experience in the present moment characterized by curiosity, openness, and acceptance. The self-regulation of attention occurs when the person observes and monitors internal and external experiences, notes them, and lets them go. In structural psychoanalytic terms the patient uses his or her self-observing ego (Freud, 1933b; Sterba, 1934) to free associate to all mental phenomena that enter into preconscious awareness (Freud, 1900).

S. C. Hayes (2004) provides a striking illustration of the patient as a dispassionate observer of mental phenomena. Called "the soldiers in the parade" mindfulness exercise, the patient is instructed to imagine that little soldiers are marching out of his or her ear and then in front of him or her as though parading in front of a reviewing stand. Each soldier is carrying a sign with a thought or feeling printed on it in the form of words or pictures. The patient must try to let the parade go by without joining the parade. When the patient inevitably joins the parade and leaves the reviewing stand, he or she must see what happened right before the observation of the parade stopped. Having been in my personal analysis for over ten years, I nevertheless found this exercise extraordinarily difficult to accomplish on my own for more than a few minutes. The exercise is designed to teach the patient "how to look at thoughts as thoughts rather than looking at the world through thoughts, and to learn how to detect the difference" (p. 20). Such an exercise can help to introduce a space between the patient's perception and response, which would permit the patient to respond to situations "more reflectively (as opposed to reflexively)" (Bishop et al., 2004, p. 232). One can imagine how mindfulness as practiced in DBT might help borderline patients diminish their impulsivity.

The practice of mindfulness differs from free association, however, because exploration of the implications and meanings of the thoughts and feelings that enter awareness would be like joining the parade: the patient is to remain anchored to the present moment and observe the parade going by, not be swept up in the parade of associations. The exclusive focus on the here and now prevents the patient from holding onto thoughts and feelings. Proponents (e.g., Ma and Teasdale, 2004) have argued that mindfulness practice is particularly effective for depressed patients plagued by ruminative thoughts because it helps them to let go of such thoughts and instead attend to the present moment. Mindfulness practice develops a flexibility of attention from one thought, feeling, or urge to the next, without privileging any particular internal or external experience. This process lessens the attachment to any one pattern or style of thinking and lends the patient "psychological freedom" (Martin, 1997, p. 291) to entertain alternate modes of experience. Mindfulness supposedly opens the patient to new modes of experience by releasing attentional resources used to increase access to information "that might otherwise remain outside awareness, resulting in a wider perspective on experience" (Bishop et al., 2004, p. 233). The parallels to free association are obvious; however, the exploration of particular strands of meaning within the flow of associations would represent the termination of the mindfulness state, not a continuation of it.

The second component of mindfulness—an orientation characterized by curiosity, openness, and acceptance—is critical to this state of consciousness because a judgmental, critical stance would inevitably suppress thoughts and produce a state of "experiential avoidance" (S. C. Hayes, 2004, p. 14) antithetical to the mindfulness process. In a state of mindfulness "all thoughts, feelings, and sensations that arise are initially seen as relevant and therefore subject to observation. . . . In this manner, a stance of acceptance is taken toward each moment of one's experience" (Bishop et al., 2004, p. 233). Let me compare this statement with Freud's (1913b) on free association: "Various thoughts will occur to you which you would like to put aside on the ground of certain criticisms and objections. You will be tempted to say to yourself that this or that is irrelevant here, or is quite unimportant, or nonsensical. . . . You must never give in to these criticisms, but must say it in spite of them"

(p. 135). Bishop et al. (2004) have added that an attitude of acceptance toward even painful or unpleasant feelings would begin to change the psychological context in which these experiences occur, which would make them tolerable.

The paradox between being open and accepting of all mental phenomena, yet returning to the central focus of attention such as one's breath, is understood within the context of experiencing the present moment. Lingering on any one thought or feeling would be like joining the parade of thoughts and feelings rather than observing them. In free association, the patient is acting as though he or she were "sitting next to the window of a railway carriage and describing to someone inside the carriage the changing views which you see outside" (Freud, 1913b, p. 135); however, in psychoanalysis the analyst inevitably interprets a theme running through the flow of associations that serves to increase self-understanding and facilitate further free association. From a mindfulness perspective, this exploration stops the train of associations and shifts the patient away from the present moment.

Although Bishop et al.'s (2004) operational definition of mindfulness seems to have encountered a mostly accepting attitude (see K. W. Brown and Ryan, 2004; A. M. Hayes and Feldman, 2004; S. C. Hayes and Shenk, 2004), some modifications have been suggested. K. W. Brown and Ryan (2004) have argued that openness to experience in the present moment and attention maintained on a particular focus represent "distinct aspects of meditative practice" (p. 243) that yield different therapeutic benefits. Concentration meditation strengthens the capacity to sustain attention, while awareness meditation brings consciousness to bear on the moment-to-moment flow of present experience. According to the authors (K. W. Brown and Ryan, 2003, 2004), both kinds of meditation comprise the state of mindfulness. Using the figure-ground analogy, awareness is that preconscious state of consciousness constantly monitoring the background of thoughts and feelings, while concentration or attention is the focusing of awareness on one figure from the background such as a breath or a word. It appears that psychoanalysis encourages only awareness meditation, while concentration meditation is alien to the psychoanalytic process. A psychoanalyst might identify concentration meditation as a fixation or an obsession.

Various mindfulness researchers have constructed self-report questionnaires to assess a person's level of mindfulness. Most of these attempts to quantify mindfulness have relied on Bishop et al.'s (2004) operational definition. Baer, Smith, and Allen (2004) developed the Kentucky Inventory of Mindfulness Skills (KIMS), a thirty-nine-item Likert-type questionnaire that measures four components of mindfulness as a disposition. The authors were aiming to capture the average level of daily mindfulness in the respondent.

The first component, observing, is the observation of all thoughts, feelings, and sensations within the spectrum of awareness. The second, describing, is the labeling of these observed mental phenomena with words. The third, acting with awareness, is the focusing of awareness without distraction. The fourth, accepting without judgment, is refraining from applying evaluative labels of good or bad on experience in the present moment and being open to all experiences, whether pleasant or unpleasant. A factor analysis of data collected using this instrument confirmed the presence of these four components of mindfulness.

The Toronto Mindfulness Scale (TMS; Lau et al., in press) is a thirteen-item Likert-type questionnaire that measures two components of mindfulness—curiosity and decentering. Curiosity is defined as an interest in all aspects of experience in the present moment, while decentering is defined as an awareness of experience "with some distance and disidentification" (p. 16)—an observer stance rather than a participant stance. Designed to measure mindfulness as a state, the instrument is completed immediately following a meditation exercise. A factor analysis of data collected using this instrument confirmed the presence of these two components of mindfulness. Interestingly, the authors' data did not support Bishop et al.'s (2004) first component of mindfulness, self-regulation of attention, presumably because this aspect of mindfulness highly correlated with their curiosity factor. In other words, curiosity toward experience presumes an attention to and awareness of experience.

K. W. Brown and Ryan (2003) introduced the Mindful Attention Awareness Scale (MAAS), a fifteen-item Likert-type questionnaire that measures mindfulness as a disposition like the KIMS. Unlike the KIMS, however, the MAAS yielded a unidimensional factor structure that accounted for 95 percent of the total variance. This one factor measures the level of "attention to and awareness of what is occurring in the present rather than on attributes such as acceptance, trust, empathy, gratitude, or the various others that have been associated with mindfulness (e.g., Shapiro and Schwartz, 1999)" (p. 824). Thus, the authors used a restricted definition of mindfulness that seems to capture Bishop et al.'s first definitional component—the self-regulation of attention—but not the second definitional component—an acceptance of and curiosity about experience.

The Freiburg Mindfulness Inventory (FMI; Walach, Buchheld, Buttenmüller, Kleinknecht, and Schmidt, 2006) is a fourteen-item Likert-type questionnaire that measures mindfulness as a state and is completed immediately following a meditation exercise. The authors have reported that the instrument yields a single dimension of mindfulness that they define as "an alert mode of perceiving all mental contents . . . [and] a warm and friendly, accepting and non-judgmental attitude towards those elements of our mind" (p. 1544). The authors cite Bishop et al.'s (2004) operational definition of mindfulness as a guiding force behind the construction of their own instrument.

A. M. Hayes and Feldman (2004) constructed the Cognitive and Affective Mindfulness Scale—Revised (CAMS-R), a twelve-item Likert-type unpublished questionnaire that measures mindfulness as a disposition like the KIMS and the MAAS (A. M. Hayes did not respond to an e-mail request for a copy of the instrument). The instrument yielded four factors—attention, awareness of internal experiences, acceptance of internal experiences, and present-focus—that predicted a second-order variable of mindfulness. Here again, we notice the two components of the Bishop et al. (2004) operational definition represented in these four factors.

Finally, the Mindfulness Questionnaire (MQ; Chadwick, Hember, Mead, Lilley, and Dagnan, 2005) is a sixteen-item Likert-type unpublished questionnaire that measures mindfulness as a disposition (Chadwick did not respond to an e-mail request for a copy of the instrument). The items measure four aspects of mindfulness—mindful observation, letting go, nonaversion, and nonjudgment—but a factor analysis yielded just one dimension of mindfulness. "Letting go" shares conceptual overlap with the MAAS's decentering factor.

In an important study to determine the various facets of mindfulness measured by the KIMS, MAAS, FMI, CAMS-R, and MQ (the TMS was not included), Baer, Smith, Hopkins, Krietemeyer, and Toney (2006) conducted both exploratory and confirmatory factor analyses on all the items of these five questionnaires using two samples of 613 and 268 undergraduate students. The results confirmed the presence of five facets of mindfulness. Four of these facets approximate the four factors of the KIMS—observing, describing, acting with awareness (concentration), and accepting without judgment. The authors identified the fifth facet as "nonreactivity to inner experience" (p. 34). In reviewing the items that load onto this factor, it appears that the MQ and FMI were the only contributors. While nonreactivity to inner experience seems to be consistent with a definition of mindfulness—for example, letting go of distressing feelings to continue observing the parade—some researchers (Bishop et al., 2004) believe that nonreactivity is actually an outcome of mindfulness, not a component of it.

In spite of all the recent work published on the definition of mindfulness, confusion lingers over distinguishing the construct from its outcomes. Qualities such as patience, trust, nonreactivity or calmness (already mentioned), wisdom (self-knowledge), and compassion (empathy for oneself) reflect the many putative benefits of an active mindfulness practice rather than mindfulness per se (Bishop et al., 2004). Other qualities associated with mindfulness include relaxation, empathy, happiness, and affect tolerance (K. W. Brown and Ryan, 2003, 2004; Davidson and Kabat-Zinn, 2004; Kabat-Zinn, 2003). Perhaps what is most important to grasp about mindfulness is that it is a mode of perception—a moment-by-moment process of observing internal and external experience—rather than a stable personality trait. A person can turn mindfulness on and off at will; it is a voluntary state of consciousness. Qualities such as patience and compassion often characterize aspects of personality that do not necessarily depend on mindful awareness. One can be calm or compassionate without attending to one's experience in the present moment.

A final task of those researchers who seek to define a construct is to distinguish it from neighboring constructs. Bishop et al. (2004) have suggested that constructs such as introspection, observing self, presence, reflective functioning or mentalization, decentering (already mentioned), psychological mindedness, insight, and self-awareness all share conceptual overlap with mindfulness. Because the authors define mindfulness as a *process* or *mode* of self-observation rather than self-knowledge per se, introspection, observing self, and mentalization seem to share greater conceptual overlap with mindfulness than psychological mindedness, insight, and self-awareness. Teasdale (1999) seems to agree when he draws a conceptual distinction between metacognitive knowledge—*knowing* that thoughts are not necessarily accurate—and metacognitive insight—*experiencing* thoughts as events in the field of awareness rather than as reflections of reality. The distinction could be summarized as the difference between a perceptual process of paying attention in the present moment and the storage of perceptual information for use in the present moment.

Two kinds of research have been conducted on mindfulness: outcome studies of the efficacy of mindfulness-based intervention programs that contain mindfulness training and studies of the correlates of mindfulness using the assessment instruments reviewed earlier. Baer (2003) conducted a review of twenty-one outcome studies of MBSR and MBCT, two treatment programs that place mindfulness at the center of their intervention. Baer (2003) excluded DBT, ACT, and RP outcome studies from her review because these treatment programs use cognitive-behavioral strategies in addition to mindfulness. Overall, these programs were able to diminish chronic pain, stress, anxiety, depressive relapse, and binge eating. In addition, MBCT prevented recurrence of depressive episodes at the one-year follow-up only in those patients who had experienced three or more lifetime depressive episodes (see Teasdale et al., 2000). MBSR was associated with quicker skin clearing among psoriasis patients who received MBSR in addition to the treatment-as-usual (TAU) light therapy sessions (see Kabat-Zinn et al., 1998) and diminished levels of mood disturbance and stress among cancer patients

(Speca, Carlson, Goodey, and Angen, 2000), which were maintained at six-month follow-up (Carlson, Ursuliak, Goodey, Angen, and Speca, 2001).

The overall mean effect size of these twenty-one outcome studies was .59, and the overall mean effect sizes of the follow-up outcome studies was also .59—both considered medium effect sizes (Baer, 2003). The methodological flaws associated with many of these outcome studies included the lack of control groups, the lack of specification of TAU conditions, small sample sizes, the lack of assessments of therapist competence or treatment adherence, the lack of assessment of clinical significance of outcomes through the measurement of diagnostic or symptomatic change into the nonclinical range of functioning, the restricted range of outcome measures that ignore constructs such as well-being, and the lack of interest in studying the processes by which mindfulness produces change (see also S. C. Hayes and Shenk, 2004). Interestingly, Kabat-Zinn and his colleagues (Davidson et al., 2003) have broadened the scope of outcome measures to include electroencephalography (EEG) assessments, which showed that meditation increased brain electrical activity in areas previously associated with positive affect. In summary, MBSR and MBCT seem to be associated with moderate improvement in some common psychiatric symptoms in some clinical and nonclinical samples. Researchers need to address the methodological flaws when designing and conducting future studies that assess the efficacy of mindfulness-based treatment programs.

The advent of the aforementioned mindfulness assessment instruments has produced initial research that documents increases in mindfulness after completion of an eight-week MBSR treatment program (K. W. Brown and Ryan, 2003; Lau et al., in press), a similar mindfulness-based meditation program (A. M. Hayes and Feldman, 2004), and an eight-hour, mindfulness-based meditation retreat (Walach et al., 2006). Notably, these studies treat mindfulness as a treatment outcome, not a process of therapeutic change. K. W. Brown and Ryan (2003) found that although changes in the levels of mindfulness of cancer patients were not significant, these changes nevertheless predicted changes in tension/anxiety, depression, fatigue, confusion, and stress. Lau et al. (in press) found that their two mindfulness factors—decentering and curiosity—significantly increased and that positive changes in decentering predicted decreases in psychological distress and stress. A. M. Hayes and Feldman (2004) used an eight-week mindfulness meditation training to increase levels of mindfulness among depressed patients. Positive changes in mindfulness were associated with decreases in experiential avoidance and rumination, two self-regulation strategies that perpetuate depression. Walach et al. (2006) reported that levels of mindfulness also positively changed after the eight-hour meditation retreat. Unfortunately, none of these four studies used control groups or attempted to study the processes by which mindfulness techniques such as meditation produce changes in the level of mindfulness. Further research is needed to isolate and test the effective ingredient in mindfulness and the processes by which this effective ingredient is activated in patients.

PROCESSES OF THERAPEUTIC CHANGE BELIEVED TO UNDERLIE MINDFULNESS

Although there is a growing body of evidence to suggest that mindfulness-based treatment programs produce therapeutic change (Baer, 2003), it is still not clear how mindfulness acts on the patient. Mindfulness researchers have proposed several hypotheses. One hypothesis is that mindfulness produces cognitive changes associated with greater well-being (Baer, 2003). These cognitive changes are believed to be associated with the decentering process described earlier—the implicit assumption that "'thoughts are not facts'" or "'I am not my thoughts'" (p. 127). For example, mindfulness therapists teach their patients to think, "'I'm having the thought that I'm a bad person,' rather than 'I'm a bad person'" (Kohlenberg, Hayes, and Tsai, 1993, p. 588). Another way of putting it is that mindfulness treatments change "one's *relationship to* one's thoughts and feelings, encouraging the viewing of thoughts as thoughts rather than as reality" (Roemer and Orsillo, 2003, p. 173). Mindfulness treatments place the focus of therapeutic change on the process of thinking rather than on the content of thought. A similar shift of emphasis is occurring within the psychoanalytic community (e.g., Bruschweiler-Stern et al., 2002; Lyons-Ruth, 1999), where the process of relating replaces the content of associations as the locus of therapeutic change.

A second hypothesis is that mindfulness improves a patient's self-management (Baer, 2003). Specifically, mindfulness promotes the use of a range of coping skills such as an increased recognition of satiety cues, binge urges, and behavioral consequences of binge eating or cues associated with the onset of a panic attack or depressive episode. Attending to experiences in the here and now affords one the opportunity to catch subtle warning signs of an event before it occurs as well as take greater advantage of environmental resources that facilitate therapeutic change (Roemer and Orsillo, 2003).

A third hypothesis is that mindfulness creates a gap or space for thinking to take place, which is associated with an attitude of nonreactivity to mental phenomena (Bishop et al., 2004; Martin, 1997). When the patient places automatic thought sequences on hold by attending only to internal and external perceptual phenomena, psychological space becomes available to make more reflective, less impulsive choices. This psychological space could also increase tolerance of distressing affect, which could in turn reduce the impulsivity typical of patients diagnosed with borderline personality disorder (Linehan et al., 1991).

A fourth hypothesis is that mindfulness produces a feeling of relaxation, which could reduce stress and the psychiatric symptoms associated with stress (Baer, 2003). Mindfulness proponents, however, have debunked this process of therapeutic change for two reasons. First, relaxation is not a goal of mindfulness practice although one could consider it a positive side effect. In fact, mindfulness practice consists of "being with and observing states of mind and body that are extremely painful or dysphoric. . . . It is hardly a trip to a luxury spa" (Davidson and Kabat-Zinn, 2004, p. 150). Letting go of expectations—even the expectation of relaxation—is the challenge posed by this practice (Kabat-Zinn, 2003, p. 148). Second, relaxation is not an outcome unique to mindfulness-based treatments. Other psychotherapy interventions also produce the effects of relaxation (Kabat-Zinn, 2003). Thus, mindfulness proponents do not consider relaxation as a bona fide process of therapeutic change in mindfulness-based treatments.

A fifth hypothesis is that mindfulness valorizes acceptance of one's current mental state, regardless of the intensity of pain associated with it (Baer, 2003). The patient can therefore stop using valuable mental resources to avoid unpleasant, even distressing, mental states in favor of directly experiencing and even embracing these states. As mentioned earlier, the central paradox of DBT and other mindfulness-based treatments is that change comes about only through acceptance of one's reality in the present moment—no matter how uncomfortable. For example, a drug addict might take drugs to avoid a distressing affect such as anxiety or guilt or grief or a combination of these. Mindfulness challenges the patient to give these feelings their due, to allow them into consciousness without judgment or disapproval. This practice supposedly neutralizes the defensive maneuvers that patients often deploy to avoid the distress often associated with these affects.

Finally, a sixth hypothesis is that mindfulness actually resembles a mild form of interoceptive exposure therapy (Baer, 2003; Barlow and Craske, 2000). In interoceptive exposure therapy, the therapist instructs the patient to recreate the symptom such as panic, then the patient practices exercises that aid the patient in tolerating the associated distress. In mindfulness practice, the patient does not distract him or herself from the panic but rather observes the feelings associated with this mental state as it occurs. Repeated exposure to all the internal and external precipitants of a panic attack, coupled with repeated exposure of the distressing affects that emerge, reduces the distress and consequently, the need for avoidance behaviors. It is possible that mindfulness is a less coercive version of interoceptive exposure therapy because the patient experiences the troubling symptoms as they arise rather than intentionally activating them. Other researchers (Baer et al., 2004; Bishop et al., 2004; A. M. Hayes and Feldman, 2004; S. C. Hayes and Shenk, 2004; S. C. Hayes et al., 1999; S. C. Hayes, Wilson, Gifford, Follette, and Strosahl, 1996; Kabat-Zinn, 1982; Linehan, 1993a, 1993b) have suggested that the exposure to distressing affects actually changes the context of these affects and thus their subjective meaning. The affect "terror"—typically associated with a panic attack—becomes something other than "terror" when the patient allows himself or herself to experience this affect repeatedly without avoidance. Thus, according to these researchers, mindfulness exposes the patient to distressing affects that become transformed into more tolerable affects through the exposure afforded by mindfulness exercises or mindfulness meditation.

COMMENTARY ON MINDFULNESS AS A PROCESS OF THERAPEUTIC CHANGE

In 1997, Martin proposed that mindfulness is a common factor "within all psychotherapy orientations" (p. 291). In this intriguing paper, he further suggested two forms of mindfulness: open-form attention and focused-form attention. His description of these two forms seems to correlate with K. W. Brown and Ryan's (2003) two components of mindfulness: awareness and attention. As already mentioned, awareness is the monitoring of all internal and external stimuli hovering in the background—what psychoanalysts would consider preconscious material. Attention is a process of focused awareness on a limited range of experience. I previously noted the paradox between these two components of mindfulness. K. W. Brown and Ryan (2004) referred to awareness and attention as "distinct aspects of meditative practice" (p. 243). Martin (1997) compared open-form attention to the psychoanalytic concepts of free association and evenly hovering attention (Freud, 1900), and focused-form attention to the cognitive-behavioral concepts of cognitive restructuring and exposure (as previously discussed).

Martin (1997) defended both forms of mindfulness as essential ingredients of therapeutic change. Psychodynamic therapy expands awareness to highlight alternative points of view and conflicts within the patient, while cognitive-behavioral therapy focuses the patient on a less dominant, previously identified schema (thought pattern) to help free the patient from the habitual schema. Further, Martin (1997) has suggested that psychodynamic interpretation of transference phenomena compares to "a decentering, a tilting off balance of [a] patient's center of awareness" (p. 304)—an open-form attention that resembles the first component of Bishop et al.'s (2004) definition of mindfulness. According to Martin (1997), transference blocks open-form attention while interpretation restores it. Once open-form attention is restored, cognitive-behavioral techniques such as repeated suggestion guide the patient out of habitual schemas—what Martin (1997) has called "*translat[ing] insight into action*" (italics in original, p. 304). Both psychodynamic and cognitive-behavioral techniques are therefore required to help the patient adopt healthier schemas.

I agree that mindfulness shares an important conceptual resemblance with the concept of free association, but it is an open question whether the second form of mindfulness identified by Martin (1997)—focused-form attention—is an essential ingredient of therapeutic change. I will argue that free association in and of itself is therapeutic because it allows unconscious, avoided thoughts, feelings, wishes, and sensations to emerge into consciousness, be metabolized by the therapist, and returned to the patient in a modulated form. This therapeutic activity requires the presence of an "Other" who processes the patient's "beta elements" into "alpha function" suitable for integration with the rest of the personality. The crucial feature of this process, of course, is the "K-link" established between patient and therapist (Bion, 1962, 1967). Mindfulness is an effective ingredient of therapeutic change because the fantasy of a K-link exists somewhere in the patient's mind, regardless of the mindfulness therapist's disavowal of such a link.

I am suggesting three problems with the construct of mindfulness as defined by its cognitive-behavioral proponents. First, in spite of all the attempts at formulating an operational definition of mindfulness, its meaning and mode of therapeutic action still seem nonspecific. I recently asked an experienced DBT therapist and trainer what mindfulness meant to her, to which she replied without hesitation, "Paying attention!" Does that mean that all a patient has to do is pay attention to get better, regardless of theoretical orientation? How common can a common factor be while retaining its meaningfulness? Second, the detachment from all internal and external experiences promoted and cultivated by mindfulness practice (Bishop et al., 2004; A. M. Hayes and Feldman, 2004) could minimize genuine conflict within the patient and discourage exploration and understanding of specific experiences. The patient accepts these experiences "without making judgments about it or elaborating on its implications, additional meanings, or need for action" (Bishop et al., 2004, p. 232). In fact, S. C. Hayes and his colleagues (S. C. Hayes, 2004; S. C. Hayes and Shenk, 2004; Masuda, Hayes, Sackett, and Twohig, 2004) use a technique called "cognitive defusion" in conjunction with mindfulness practice in which the patient rapidly repeats a single-word variant of a troublesome thought for one minute until the word loses its meaning and becomes just a sound.

Third, and most important, the construct of mindfulness omits any recognition of an interpersonal component. Even as psychoanalysis has increasingly embraced a two-person psychology in which both therapist and patient are mutually influencing each other in ways that promote therapeutic change (Aron, 1990), the third wave of behavioral therapy seems to be mired in a one-person psychology. One way of understanding what a construct represents is to study the empirical measures of that construct. I was able to obtain copies of four of the six existing measures of mindfulness (Baer et al., 2004; K. W. Brown and Ryan, 2003; Lau et al., in press; Walach, Buchheld, Buttenmüller, Kleinknecht, and Schmidt, 2006). Out of a combined total of eighty-one items that comprise these four measures, only two items allude to an interpersonal component: "I forget a person's name almost as soon as I've been told it for the first time" (Mindful Attention Awareness Scale [MAAS], item 6; K. W. Brown and Ryan, 2003, p. 826), and "I find myself listening to someone with one ear, doing something else at the same time" (MAAS, item 11; K. W. Brown and Ryan, 2003, p. 826). The content of these "interpersonal" items (p. 825) clearly reflects an interest in attentional skills, not an acknowledgment of an interpersonal component of mindfulness.

In fact, almost nothing in the mindfulness literature even suggests that the interaction between the therapist and patient influences the patient's capacity to engage in a state of mindfulness, sustain it, or practice it outside psychotherapy sessions. The emphasis is clearly on the private experience of the patient, not on a relationship: "Mindfulness can thus be further conceptualized as a process of investigative awareness that involves observing the ever-changing flow of private experience" (Bishop et al., 2004, p. 234). In mindfulness-based treatments it is the exposure to "disturbing emotions" that is the essential ingredient (A. M. Hayes and Feldman, 2004, p. 258), not an understanding of what these emotions might mean or might be communicating within the context of relationships (Malatesta-Magai, 1991). Commenting on the positive results of his outcome study of psoriasis patients randomly assigned to two conditions—with and without guided meditation instructions delivered by audiotape—Kabat-Zinn (2003) cheerfully concluded that "social support [removed by the use of audiotape] . . . cannot be a major factor in the observed outcome" (p. 152)—as if the therapist's audiotaped voice could not serve this function.

Three authors (Dimidjian and Linehan, 2003; Epstein, 1999; Kabat-Zinn, 2003) have suggested that mindfulness extends beyond a mere set of skills taught by therapists, however. For example, mindfulness includes "attitudes and behaviors that the therapist emits, as opposed to behaviors that the therapist teaches the client to do" (Dimidjian and Linehan, 2003, p. 169). Therapist modeling of mindfulness could contribute to a positive outcome in mindfulness-based treatments independent of direct skill acquisition. Kabat-Zinn (2003) advocates that mindfulness therapists engage in a "sustained personal practice over days, weeks, months, and years" (p. 149), which echoes Freud's (1912b) requirement that psychoanalysts in training must undergo their own analysis to become aware of and remove blind spots that could interfere with the analysis. Kabat-Zinn (2003), however, makes it clear that he recommends mindfulness practice for therapists for purposes of treatment adherence—to prevent mindfulness-based treatments from "becoming caricatures of mindfulness" (p. 150).

What is glaringly absent from these accounts of essential therapist characteristics is the therapist's use of mindfulness as a tool to help understand the patient in his or her totality. Freud (1912b) envisioned the therapist's unconscious as a perceptual tool used to make a connection with the unconscious of the patient—what Schore (2006) has referred to as a connection between the right hemispheres of two brains. This deep, intuitive connection facilitated by the psychoanalytic process is believed to promote a number of therapeutic changes, some of which occur outside the rational domain of the left hemisphere. In mindfulness-based treatments, the therapist's practice of mindfulness merely facilitates "therapist modeling" (Dimidjian and Linehan, 2003, p. 169) of mindful outcomes such as spontaneity, nonjudgment, moment-to-moment awareness, nonattachment to outcome, and compassion. Presumably, these authors are suggesting that the patient will observe these qualities of the therapist and want to acquire them for him or herself. The therapist's mindfulness, however, does not serve the purpose of modifying the intervention technique to facilitate mindfulness in the patient, or containing and metabolizing the patient's unbearable internal experiences, or even facilitating the patient's affect regulation. Mindfulness-based treatments focus strictly on the patient's relationship to mental phenomena—observing these phenomena and letting them go. Proponents of mindfulness would probably consider the relationship with the therapist as a distraction from the central task of observing mental phenomena without attachments or judgments.

Related to this point, mindfulness researchers underscore self-regulation rather than interactive regulation. Consider the title of a key article on mindfulness: "Intentional Systemic Mindfulness: An Integrative Model for Self-Regulation and Health" (Shapiro and Schwartz, 1999). The idea that interdependence on others can serve to regulate emotional states is alien to mindfulness, considered "a form of *mental training* to reduce cognitive vulnerability to reactive modes of mind" (italics in original; Bishop et al., 2004, p. 231). The mindfulness literature ignores a central purpose of interpersonal interaction—the benefit of humanity's psychological well-being. Persons who train their minds to become mindful develop relationships with their thoughts and feelings, not other persons. Consider the anthropomorphization of emotions in this Buddhist monk's description of a mindfulness exercise: "Look straight in the eye of the disturbing emotion and understand what it is and how it works. . . . When one genuinely looks at it, it suddenly loses its strength" (Goleman, 2003, p. 81). One might draw the conclusion that in this therapeutic model, one's relationships to one's emotions replace one's relationships to real persons.

If the construct of mindfulness indeed lacks an interpersonal component, then what makes mindfulness an effective ingredient of mindfulness-based treatment packages? One potential process of therapeutic change overlooked by mindfulness researchers is the enhanced capacity produced by mindfulness to shift flexibly between states of consciousness. Rosegrant (2005) has suggested that free association, long considered a condition of psychoanalytic psychotherapy, is actually an effective ingredient of therapeutic change independent of any therapist intervention. Free association is a state of consciousness marked by heightened awareness of internal experience—thoughts, feelings, wishes, sensations—and a complementary reduced awareness of domains of reality such as time, therapeutic goals, and therapist scrutiny.

Mindfulness researchers have described similar characteristics associated with mindfulness, including the intense focus on internal experience in the present moment, nonattachment to therapeutic goals, and a nonjudgmental attitude. Rosegrant (2005) has forcefully argued that even in a free-associative state of consciousness, the elements of reality are still powerfully present in their "absence" (p. 742). Thus, tension exists even under these highly controlled conditions between the free-associative state of consciousness and usual states of consciousness that include awareness of the demands of reality. In psychoanalytic psychotherapy the patient always experiences shifts between the free-associate state and the usual states of consciousness. Narcissistic patients have particular difficulty regulating the transition between these states (Bach, 1985, 1994).

A goal of treatment with narcissistic patients, or with any patient (Rosegrant, 2005), is to create the conditions under which the patient can continue to experience the free-associative state of consciousness as well as the flexible regulation of various self-states. Psychoanalytic interpretation, according to Rosegrant (2005), facilitates the process of free association and the flexible transition between the free-associative state of consciousness and the reality-based states of consciousness. Martin (1997) has proposed a similar function of interpretation—to promote and sustain open-form attention. Although mindfulness researchers pay no attention to the importance of less mindful states of consciousness, perhaps what is therapeutic about mindfulness is the patient's experience of shifting flexibly between a mindful state of consciousness and reality-based states of consciousness—perhaps unwittingly facilitated by the presence of the mindfulness therapist.

Another process of therapeutic change potentially activated by mindfulness is the differentiation created between the self and the mental activity of the self. Mindfulness researchers have called this process "decentering" (Lau et al., in press; Teasdale et al., 2002)—"awareness of one's experience with some distance and disidentification rather than being carried away by one's thoughts and feelings" (Lau et al., in press, p. 16). In this sense, both mindfulness and mentalization (e.g., Bateman and Fonagy, 2004b) are neighboring constructs. Mentalization consists of taking an inventory of one's thoughts, feelings, and desires, which also promotes a differentiation between the self and the mental activity of the self. Both constructs also define openness and curiosity about one's own states of mind as hallmark qualities of their respective constructs.

The constructs of mindfulness and mentalization are conceptually distinct, however, in two ways. First, mentalization also consists of formulating hypotheses of others' states of mind (two-person psychology), while mindfulness consists of paying attention only to one's own state of mind (one-person psychology). Second, the goal of mentalization is to discover the meaning of states of mind in interaction with others' states of mind, whereas mindfulness has no stated goal (Kabat-Zinn, 2003). The decentering inherent in the mindfulness process, by contrast, is to liberate the person from the domination of literal language and, consequently, the literal meanings associated with language (S. C. Hayes, 2004; S. C. Hayes and Wilson, 2003). Related to this idea is the role of causality in the two constructs. Central to mentalization is the idea that states of mind mutually influence each other, a process of causality that facilitates the formation of behavioral expectations of self in relation to others. By contrast, central to mindfulness is the suspension of belief in causality—that all internal and external experiences exist only in this moment, not in any past or future moments. Causality implies the passage of time; therefore, any process of exploring causal relationships between states of mind would be considered mindless, not mindful. Thus, mentalization and mindfulness are neighboring constructs with some conceptual overlap, yet in some ways also have incompatible therapeutic objectives.

This liberation of the self from the mental activity of the self—thoughts, feelings, wishes, and sensations—serves the purpose of psychic differentiation and separateness. One could conceptualize the holding onto versus letting go of mental phenomena within an attachment paradigm. Perhaps patients categorized as having a preoccupied/entangled attachment pattern—emotionally hyperactivated, lacking differentiation from parental relationships, and embroiled in past experiences (Goodman, 2002; Kobak, Cole, Ferenz-Gillies, Fleming, and Gamble, 1993; Main and Goldwyn, 1994; Main et al., 1985)—could benefit from a therapeutic approach designed to promote separation of self from feelings. Based on her empirical work, Dozier (2003) has suggested that intervention is most effective when the therapist provides "gentle challenge" (p. 254) to the patient. In other words, separation-promoting interventions are provided to patients with preoccupied states of mind that reflect discomfort with autonomy. Perhaps the therapeutic success of DBT in treating patients with borderline personality disorder (BPD; Linehan et al., 1991; Linehan et al., 1993; Linehan et al., 1994)—previously associated with a preoccupied attachment pattern (Agrawal, Gunderson, Holmes, and Lyons-Ruth, 2004; Bateman and Fonagy, 2004b)—is related to the gentle challenge to these patients to detach from their hyperactivated emotional states. This detachment would promote a more modulated regulation of emotional states that could reduce impulsive behaviors typically associated with BPD.

How would a mindfulness-based treatment package work for patients who feel disconnected from interpersonal relationships—those patients categorized as having a dismissing attachment pattern? Dismissing persons "limit the influence of attachment relationships and experiences in thought, in feeling, or in daily life" (Main and Goldwyn, 1994, p. 126). Mindfulness lacks an interpersonal dimension that could provide the gentle challenge that dismissing patients need to resolve their fears of closeness and dependence on others. In fact, it seems plausible to suggest that mindfulness reinforces a dismissing attachment pattern, characterized by defensive exclusion (Bowlby, 1973) of attachment needs. Consider the words of its originator, the Buddha (Siddhartha Gautama): "He who loves 50 people has 50 woes; he who loves no one has no woes. . . . Do not depend on others" ("Buddha quotes," 2006, pp. 2, 6). These words reflect the attitude of the prototypical dismissing person. Achieving distance between the self and the self's thoughts and feelings might prove beneficial for someone struggling with issues of separation and differentiation, but this approach might also strengthen the defenses of a patient walled off from needs for dependence and intimacy.

In spite of the bias toward separateness from internal and external experience espoused by mindfulness proponents, there is also an odd avoidance of separateness inherent to the construct. Because the "Other" does not exist in mindfulness, it is as if no separation from the "Other" has occurred. One might even suggest that mindfulness represents a regression to a preverbal, symbiotic state of consciousness. According to S. C. Hayes and Shenk (2004), mindfulness meditation "undermines the power of particular events to occasion verbally based streams of behavior designed to understand, predict, evaluate, avoid, soothe, control, or otherwise create a situation other than the situation that is present" (p. 253). These are precisely the verbally based streams of behavior that mentalization is designed to activate.

S. C. Hayes (2004) also discusses "experiential avoidance"—the patient's unwillingness "to remain in contact with particular private experiences" (p. 14)—as a form of psychopathology that mindfulness can ameliorate. Because it is impossible "to remove or eliminate language processes that create difficulty for human beings" (p. 15), one technique mentioned earlier is to defuse the meaning of language by rapidly repeating a single-word variant of a troublesome thought for one minute until the word loses its meaning and becomes just a sound. Interestingly, the word initially chosen for this exercise is "milk" (pp. 19, 20)—symbolically associated with mother and the early symbiotic relationship.

Interestingly, school-aged children categorized as having an anxious-avoidant attachment pattern (analogous to the adult dismissing attachment pattern) tend to undo or deny separations in their narrative responses to attachment-relevant story stems using a family of dolls (Solomon, George, and De Jong, 1995). Mindfulness seems to promote a denial of separateness and an oneness with oneself and one's surroundings that belies the reality of other persons who have separate states of mind and separate agendas. At the same time, however, mindfulness-based treatment packages do produce positive outcomes for at least some kinds of patients (e.g., BPD patients).

I mentioned earlier that free association, embodied in mindfulness practice, allows unconscious, avoided thoughts, feelings, wishes, and sensations to emerge into consciousness. Rosegrant (2005) has argued that this process in and of itself is therapeutic. I argue that in addition to its facilitation of flexible shifts between states of consciousness, free association is therapeutically effective because it activates a fantasy, held by the patient, that the therapist is containing the unbearable thoughts, feelings, wishes, and sensations now permitted into conscious experience, and is metabolizing these mental phenomena and returning them to the patient in a modulated form (Bion, 1962, 1967). As Rosegrant (2005) has noted, elements of reality, including the presence of the therapist, are powerfully present even in their "absence" during the free-associate state of consciousness (p. 742). Thus, in a mindful state of consciousness the awareness of the relationship with the therapist must nevertheless be powerfully present.

Kabat-Zinn (2003) has cheerfully denied the importance of social support in his audiotaped mindfulness instruction; however, I am arguing that the fantasy of a listening, nonjudgmental, supportive therapist ready to contain whatever unbearable material emerges is simultaneously alive in the patient's mind and empowering the patient to sustain a mindful state of consciousness.

In Bion's (1962, 1967) terms, there is an implied "Other" who processes the patient's "beta elements" into "alpha function" suitable for integration with the rest of the personality. The K-link—the missing link in the mindfulness literature—enables mindfulness to occur and endows it with its therapeutic properties. This implied relationship in the mind of the patient between the therapist and the patient, whether fantasized or real, powerfully affects both the establishment of a mindful state of consciousness as well as its practice outside therapy sessions. The gradual metabolization of beta elements through the K-link increases the patient's tolerance of future arousal states and enables the patient to depend on interpersonal relationships to enhance affect regulation without an overreliance on these relationships to compensate for dysregulated self-states. The patient's commitment to this process depends on the loyalty to the person who is conducting the intervention—the person offering to help the patient with his or her troubled mind. This is what makes mindfulness an effective ingredient of therapeutic change. Psychoanalytic psychotherapy presents a clinical advantage over mindfulness-based treatments because it explicitly identifies the therapist-patient relationship as the fulcrum of therapeutic change, applied to the products of free association as the raw material to be turned over and eventually understood.

CONCLUSIONS

Originating in Asia over 2,500 years ago, mindfulness has been co-opted by cognitive-behavioral psychologists to relieve mental suffering across a variety of patient populations. Symptoms treated by mindfulness-based treatment packages include chronic pain, stress, anxiety, depressive relapse, binge eating, substance abuse, and parasuicidal behavior in BPD. Researchers have defined mindfulness as the awareness of all internal and external stimuli experienced in the present moment. Thoughts, feelings, wishes, and sensations are observed and noted, and yield to other mental and sensory phenomena in the present moment. Openness, curiosity, acceptance, and a nonjudgmental attitude characterize the quality of this process.

Mindfulness and the psychoanalytic term "free association" are highly conceptually related constructs. Both include the idea of observing and describing all mental phenomena without criticism or concern for propriety. Mindfulness and the psychoanalytic term "mentalization" share the idea of nonjudgmental observation of all mental phenomena. Mindfulness, however, is a process of experiencing the moment with no concern for the past or the future, while mentalization is a process of not only observing but also seeking to understand mental phenomena and their causal relations in one's own mind as well as in interaction with the minds of others.

Mindfulness proponents (Baer, 2003; Bishop et al., 2004; Martin, 1997) have suggested six processes of therapeutic change believed to underlie mindfulness: cognitive change, self-management, creation of mental space, relaxation, acceptance, and exposure. From a psychoanalytic view, mindfulness might be an effective ingredient of therapeutic change because it facilitates the regulation of shifts between a mindful state of consciousness and reality-based states of consciousness, the dysregulation of which is presumed to lie at the heart of at least some forms of psychopathology. Mindfulness might also be an effective ingredient of therapeutic change because it helps some patients become detached from their preoccupation with certain states of mind (e.g., hyperactivated emotional states or painful memories of parental relationships from childhood) associated with psychopathology. I suggested, however, that the emphasis that mindfulness practice places on detachment and letting go of thoughts, feelings, wishes, and sensations could reinforce a deactivation of attachment needs in some patients who fear intimacy and dependence on others. Mindfulness, therefore, might be effective for only one category of insecurely attachment patients.

Finally, mindfulness might be an effective ingredient of therapeutic change because the process is always practiced in the presence of an implied "Other," who serves as a container for all the unbearable, dangerous, objectionable mental experiences prohibited from entering consciousness under normal circumstances. Through the K-link, this "Other" contains the toxic material, metabolizes or neutralizes it, and makes the material tolerable, which thus removes a source of psychopathology. I suggested that just as no baby can develop peace of mind in splendid isolation, so too no effective mindfulness practice could occur in the absence of another person capable of holding a troubled mind in his or her mind and making it feel safe and whole again.

Chapter Six

Mentalize This: Mentalization as an Effective Ingredient of Therapeutic Change

> The ego is in its very essence a subject; how can it be made into an object? Well, there is no doubt that it can be. The ego can take itself as an object, can treat itself like other objects, can observe itself, criticize itself, and do Heaven knows what with itself. In this, one part of the ego is setting itself over against the rest. So the ego can be split; it splits itself during a number of its functions—temporarily at least. Its parts can come together again afterwards. . . . I formed the idea that the separation of the observing agency from the rest of the ego might be a regular feature of the ego's structure.
>
> Sigmund Freud, "New Introductory Lectures on Psycho-Analysis: Lecture XXXI: The Dissection of the Psychical Personality"

> I have had good reason for asserting that everyone possesses in his own unconscious an instrument with which he can interpret the utterances of the unconscious in other people.
>
> Sigmund Freud, "The Disposition to Obsessional Neurosis, a Contribution to the Problem of the Choice of Neurosis"

Over the past fifteen years, mentalization has captured the attention of the psychoanalytic community as a potentially effective ingredient of therapeutic change. Mentalization has been specifically targeted for change in mentalization-based treatment for patients with borderline personality disorder (Bateman and Fonagy, 2004a, 2004b). Mentalization has also been operationalized in an empirically valid and reliable instrument (Fonagy, Target, Steele, and Steele, 1998) used to assess both psychotherapy process and outcome (Bateman and Fonagy, 2004a, 2004b; Josephs et al., 2004; Josephs and Fatzer, 2006; Karlsson and Kermott, 2006; Levy, Meehan, et al., 2006). Indeed, according to Bateman and Fonagy (2004a), "The potential effectiveness of all treatments depends not so much on their frame but on their ability to increase a patient's capacity to mentalize" (p. 46). It therefore seemed prudent to explore the construct of mentalization, its historical antecedents and neighboring constructs, its location in psychoanalytic developmental theory, and its empirical support. I also want to discuss several problems with the construct of mentalization and its measurement and pose a solution to some of these problems. Finally, I want to apply the construct of mentalization to Freud's (1905b) traditional stages of psychosexual development.

MENTALIZATION ACCORDING TO PETER FONAGY

Because Peter Fonagy is largely responsible for introducing the psychoanalytic community to the construct of mentalization, I will be focusing on his definition of the term and his assessment instrument, the Reflective Functioning Scale (RFS; Fonagy et al., 1998). In his first full treatment of the construct, Fonagy (1991) defined the capacity to mentalize as "the capacity to conceive of conscious and unconscious mental states in oneself and others" (p. 641). The defining feature of a mental state, according to Fonagy, is its intentionality, which includes "beliefs, thoughts, desires, expectations, etc." (p. 640). Fonagy also referred to this capacity as a theory of mind, which a person uses to understand and predict the behavior of oneself and others.

Fonagy and his colleagues (Fonagy, Gergely, et al., 2002) later used another term—reflective functioning—to describe "the operationalization of the psychological processes underlying the capacity to mentalize" (p. 24). Reflective functioning, according to these authors, is "the ability to give plausible interpretations of one's own and others' behavior in terms of underlying mental states" (p. 26). What does mentalization look like? You are walking down the street, and a runner is approaching you. About fifty yards away from you, he suddenly crosses the street. Why did he cross the street? Perhaps he lives across the street. You turn around and realize that he has crossed back over onto your side of the street to continue his run. Why did he do that? You realize that you are walking your scary-looking German shepherd and reason that the runner must have been afraid of being bitten and crossed the street to avoid a possible altercation. You attribute the man's crossing the street to the possibility that he was experiencing an underlying mental state of fear in relation to your dog's menacing appearance.

Fonagy and his colleagues (Fonagy, Gergely, et al., 2002) have argued that deficits in this mentalizing process are related to underlying psychopathology. In the previous example, you might notice the runner crossing the street and say to yourself, "That's weird," and continue walking—not realizing that your German shepherd might look scary to someone. You failed to mentalize the experience of the other person and your own influence on the other person's behavior. Alternatively, you might notice the runner crossing the street and say to yourself, "I look so out of shape that this runner doesn't even want to run by me." You mentalized the other person's mental state—disgust at your self-perceived unsightly appearance—but the attribution is implausible. Why would the runner care so much about your physical appearance that he would go out of his way to cross the street? It is a possibility (the runner's mental state is actually opaque to us), but not a reasonable possibility.

All Fonagy's writings on mentalization seem to emphasize (1) the intersubjective nature of mental states, and (2) the connection between the mental states of self and others and the behavior of self and others. Steele and Steele (in press), colleagues of Fonagy who developed the RFS with him, have suggested that the emergence of relational psychoanalysis in the 1980s (e.g., J. R. Greenberg, 1986; J. R. Greenberg and Mitchell, 1983) influenced their conceptualization of mentalization. They undertook the task of using relational theory to update familiar core constructs such as psychological mindedness (see chapter 7), the self-observational agency of the ego (Freud, 1933b), insight (Freud, 1913b), and reality testing (Freud, 1911). The intersubjective component of mentalization distinguishes it conceptually from both mindfulness and psychological mindedness (see chapter 7). The fact that the mental states of self and other persons mutually influence each other and underlie the mutual influence of the behaviors of self and other persons provides a key ingredient for the regulation of affects, the predictability of interactions, and the organization of the self (Fonagy, Gergely, et al., 2002).

Fonagy and Target (1997) defined two forms of memory—autobiographical, declarative memory and implicit, nonreflective memory. Emotional and impressionistic information dominates implicit or procedural memory and is accessible only through performance. Schematic representations of object relations are examples of procedural memories. Mentalization can rely on explicit (declarative) or implicit (procedural) memory (Allen, 2003). Mentalizing about the runner in the illustration above occurred in conscious awareness in a deliberate manner—explicit mentalization. Instinctively holding your German shepherd's leash more tightly when you first spot the runner occurs in a nonconscious, procedural, nonreflective manner. Such mentalizing illustrates intuitive empathy for what the runner might be feeling as he approaches your dog. No thoughts need appear in your conscious awareness to grasp the leash more firmly. In psychotherapy, "implicit and explicit mentalization are brought together" (Bateman and Fonagy, 2004a, p. 48). Thus, according to these authors, the therapist's capacity to mentalize the patient's mind explicitly, in collaboration with the patient, is the driving force behind effective psychotherapy.

Explicit mentalization seems to be the therapeutic process by which implicit and explicit mentalization are brought together: "The explicit content of interpreting is merely the vehicle for the implicit process that has therapeutic value" (Bateman and Fonagy, 2004a, p. 47). On the other hand, "the foundation of any therapeutic work must by definition be implicit mentalization" (p. 47). The therapist's creation of a secure base experience in the therapist-patient relationship fosters a sense of safety in the patient to explore the contents of the therapist's mind, where he or she will find a more accurate appraisal of the patient's mind. From this conceptualization, it is not clear whether the relationship constructed by the therapeutic partners enhances mentalization or whether mentalization enhances the relationship. Later in the chapter, I will return to this point.

In their later writing, Fonagy and his colleagues (Fonagy, Gergely, et al., 2002) suggested that humans' mentalizing capacity is performed by the interpersonal interpretive mechanism (IIM), which is located in the frontal region of the brain. According to the authors, the IIM functions within self-object-affect triads (Kernberg, 1983) and is divided into two substructures, the IIM-a and the IIM-c. The IIM-a is responsible for processing affect and empathic reactions and is located in the orbital frontal region (Anderson, Bechara, Damasio, Tranel, and Damasio, 1999; Blair, Morris, Frith, Perrett, and Dolan, 1999). The IIM-c is responsible for processing cognition and reasoning and is located in the medial frontal region (Baron-Cohen et al., 1994; Blair, Jones, Clark, and Smith, 1997; Gallagher et al., 2000; Goel, Grafman, Sadato, and Hallett, 1995). The functional connection between the IIM-a and IIM-c is presumed to mediate the ability to predict and experience the emotions of others. The capacity to mentalize occurs through "linking the representations of epistemic states of the mind in the medial prefrontal cortex (IIM-c) with the emotional control centers (IIM-a) in the orbital frontal cortex (OFC) and temporal lobe" (Fonagy, Gergely, et al., 2002, p. 138). Malfunctions in this connection produce impaired empathy typically found in persons with antisocial personality disorder. A focus on mentalization in psychotherapy can enhance the functioning of the IIM-a and IIM-c and their connection and even moderate the mechanisms of specific gene expression (Fonagy, Gergely, et al., 2002, pp. 139, 140).

HISTORY OF MENTALIZATION

Tracing back the historical antecedents of the construct of mentalization, we must start with Freud (1933b), who discussed the observing agency of the ego as that part of the ego that observes itself as well as others. Freud described this self-observing ego as closely aligned with the superego and its judging and punishing functions. The following year, Sterba (1934) suggested that the self-observing ego serves an essential purpose in psychoanalysis, which has nothing to do with the superego and punishment. In fact, this splitting of the ego into observing and nonobserving agencies occurs through the unobjectionable positive transference, or working alliance, that forms between the therapist and patient. Sterba (1934) described this splitting as "a demand for a balancing contemplation, kept steadily free of affect, whatever changes may take place in the contents of the instinct-cathexes and the defensive reactions" (p. 122). We notice the intimate relation between the self-observing ego and affect regulation—also a key product of mentalization (Fonagy, Gergely, et al., 2002). According to Sterba (1934), therapeutic interpretations reduce the instinctual and defensive demands placed on the ego "in favour of intellectual contemplation, reflection and correction by the standard of reality" (p. 122). The patient thus gains "a first measure of 'psychic distance' in relation to her own behavior" (p. 124). Considerable conceptual overlap exists between Sterba's self-observing ego and Hartmann's (1950) conflict-free sphere of the ego in which intellectual contemplation unfettered by drive demands can take place. Overall, the focus here seems to be on the acquisition of insight into the relations between the id and the ego, not on interpersonal and intersubjective experiences.

Psychological mindedness, thoroughly covered in chapter 7, was first defined by Wallerstein and Robbins in 1956 to operationalize the functioning of the self-observing ego. Almost thirty years later, Farber (1985) updated the definition to include an interpersonal component: "A trait which has at its core the disposition to reflect upon the meaning and motivation of behavior, thoughts, and feelings in oneself *and others*" (italics added, p. 170). The definition of mentalization encompasses psychological mindedness and includes a bidirectional, intersubjective component: understanding the mutual influence of mental states and the likely behavior following from these states (see figure 7.1). If I am the German shepherd's owner, I might be feeling sadistic and let go of the leash as the runner approaches, which might scare him enough to make him sprint away in the opposite direction. The runner's fear, which made him sprint away, might in turn fill me with pleasurable feelings of power and dominance. If I am the runner, I might feel challenged and run right up to the dog, pepper spray in hand, which might startle the dog's owner and make him call the dog back before I get there.

These two mentalizing stances include not only an understanding of the meanings and motivation of thoughts, feelings, and behavior, but also an understanding of the mutual influence of these mental states and the potential behavioral consequences of these mental states. These potential behavioral consequences in turn might influence the mental states of both parties in a bidirectional cycle. The definition of mentalization is consistent with a transactional model of psychological phenomena, first applied to mutually causal influences in caregiver-infant interactions (Sameroff, 1975; Sameroff and Chandler, 1975). This bidirectional, intersubjective component is not present in the definition of psychological mindedness, a product of a one-person psychology (see Aron, 1990). In chapter 7, I suggest that perhaps psychological mindedness as a construct has lost its utility, superseded by the construct of mentalization, a product of a two-person, transactional psychology.

Mentalization, a construct introduced by French psychoanalysts in the 1960s (Fain and David, 1963; Fain and Marty, 1964), referred to the early developmental activity of transforming somatic drive-affect excitations into symbolized mental contents. Lecours and Bouchard (1997), however, dimensionalized this definition such that a person can vary in increasing mentalizing quality from somatization—a lack of symbolization—to insight—fully symbolized mental contents. Fonagy (1991) restricted this definition to include only the symbolization of the mental states of self and others and their links to behavior. Lecours and Bouchard (1997) have suggested that Fonagy's definition of mentalization is "a result of the basic mentalisation process" (p. 858), originally defined in more global, abstract terms by Fain and his colleagues.

Neighboring constructs that might have filled some of the lexical space now occupied by the construct of mentalization need to be considered to determine whether the introduction of this term into the psychoanalytic vocabulary adds something new to our understanding of the human mind. Empathy is one such construct that shares conceptual overlap with mentalization. Carl Rogers (1959), who championed empathy as an agent of therapeutic change, initially defined empathy as "perceiv[ing] the internal frame of reference of another with accuracy and with the emotional components and meanings which pertain thereto as if one were the person, but without ever losing the 'as if' condition" (Rogers, 1959, pp. 210, 211). Twenty-one years later, Rogers (1980) dropped the "as if" condition, suggesting that therapists "secure enough in themselves . . . know they will not get lost in what may turn out to be the strange or bizarre world of the other" (Rogers, 1980, p. 143). Although I argued elsewhere (Goodman, 1991) that empathizing implicitly requires an interpretive frame of reference, Rogers's definition principally focuses on the therapist's feeling like the patient and communicating those feelings to the patient. The definition of mentalization encompasses empathy and includes a cognitive component and a dual focus on self and others and their mutual intersubjective interaction. Fonagy and his colleagues (Bleiberg, Fonagy, and

Target, 1997; Fonagy, 2003; Fonagy, Gergely, et al., 2002) have speculated that the empathic response originates specifically in the IIM-a; however, a mentalizing response includes the dual, interconnected functioning of the IIM-a and the IIM-c (Fonagy, Gergely, et al., 2002). Mentalization is therefore a broader construct.

Insight, originally defined by Wallerstein and Robbins (1956) as a patient's awareness of the connection among symptoms, behavior, and underlying conflict (see chapter 7), also shares some conceptual overlap with the construct of mentalization. Recently, Grant (2001) defined insight as a form of metacognitive knowledge produced by the process of reflective inquiry. The construct of mentalization reflects a process of interpretation of the mental states of self and others and their mutual influence on behavior, the product of which might be insight. Person X could mentalize that the runner is crossing the street because of Person X's disgusting appearance, but the product of this mentalization is certainly not insight. Person X would be demonstrating insight if he exhibited the knowledge that his feelings of low self-worth sometimes make him misinterpret whether others want to be around him because he perceives himself to have a disgusting appearance. Insight represents a form of conscious awareness, whereas mentalization represents a process that usually takes place implicitly, without any awareness, until "we hit an interactive snag" (Bateman and Fonagy, 2004a, p. 47), at which point mentalization explicitly enters our awareness. Mentalization is limited to the processing of interpersonal interactions, whereas insight also includes awareness of other mental phenomena such as one's own symptoms and underlying conflict (Wallerstein and Robbins, 1956).

Recently, infant researchers (Koren-Karie, Oppenheim, Dolev, Sher, and Etzion-Carasso, 2002; Oppenheim and Koren-Karie, 2002) have modified the definition of insight and renamed it "insightfulness": "Maternal insightfulness involves the capacity to see things from the child's point of view, and is based on insight into the child's motives, a complex view of the child, and openness to new information about the child" (Oppenheim and Koren-Karie, 2002, p. 593). This modified definition seems more aligned with definitions of psychological mindedness and mentalization than it is with traditional definitions of insight. Except for these researchers and a few psychotherapy outcome researchers (Crits-Christoph, Barber, Miller, and Beebe, 1993), no one seems to be using the assessment of insight as a measure of treatment outcome, perhaps favoring the specificity and operationalization of reflective functioning (Karlsson and Kermott, 2006).

Introspection is another construct with conceptual ties to mentalization. Although the two constructs share the idea of self-examination, mentalization concerns itself with knowledge of minds in general rather than only one's own mind (Fonagy, Gergely, et al., 2002; Fonagy and Target, 1997). Additionally, introspection refers to one's own mental states readily accessible to consciousness, while mentalization often takes place as a nonconscious automatic procedure used to interpret the interrelations between mental states and behavior. Again, we notice that introspection is not conceptually appropriate for the era of two-person psychology (Aron, 1990).

Mindfulness, thoroughly covered in chapter 5, has spawned "the third wave" of behavior therapy with a proliferation of mindfulness-based treatments (S. C. Hayes, 2002, 2004) and has prompted some therapists to promote it as a common factor of therapeutic change (e.g., Martin, 1997). Baer and her colleagues (Baer, Smith, Hopkins, Krietemeyer, and Toney, 2006) empirically identified five components of mindfulness: (1) observing all thoughts, feelings, and sensations within the spectrum of awareness; (2) labeling these observed mental phenomena with words; (3) focusing awareness without distraction; (4) refraining from applying evaluative labels of good or bad on experience in the present moment and being open to all experiences, whether pleasant or unpleasant; and (5) not reacting to inner experience. Most practitioners of mindfulness-based treatments agree that the first four components comprise a consensual operational definition of mindfulness.

In chapter 5, I argued that mindfulness shares considerable conceptual overlap with the psychoanalytic construct of free association. The concept of the other, however, is conspicuously absent from the construct of mindfulness and reflects a one-person psychology (Aron, 1990). I further argued that mindfulness-based treatments might appeal to patients who want to avoid or dismiss interpersonal interactions and their meaning and motivation. I suggested that mindfulness-based treatments might be effective because they activate a fantasy, held by the patient, that the therapist is containing the unbearable thoughts, feelings, wishes, and sensations now permitted into conscious experience, and is metabolizing these mental phenomena and returning them to the patient in a modulated form (Bion, 1962, 1967). Both mentalization and mindfulness refer to the observation and labeling of mental phenomena, yet mentalization also includes an explicit reference to interpersonal interactions and the mutual influence of mental states (see figure 7.1). This process of bidirectional causality facilitates the formation of behavioral expectations of self in relation to others. By contrast, central to the practice of mindfulness is the suspension of belief in causality—that all internal and external experiences exist only in this moment, not in any past or future moments. Thus, temporal linkages between the mental states of self and other or between mental states and behavior are not part of the practice of mindfulness. Clearly, mentalization and mindfulness share some conceptual overlap but also have incompatible therapeutic objectives.

The quality and complexity of self- and object representations as defined by object relations researchers also have features in common with mentalization. These researchers have attempted to assess various features of mental representations (for reviews, see Goodman, 2002; Stricker and Gooen-Piels, 2004). Two researchers, Sidney Blatt (Blatt, 1974; Blatt, Brenneis, Schimek, and Glick, 1976; Blatt, Chevron, Quinlan, Schaffer, and Wein, 1992; Blatt and Lerner, 1983; Blatt, Tuber, and Auerbach, 1990) and Drew Westen (Westen, 1991a, 1991b, 1993, 1995), developed coding systems that can be applied to various forms of qualitative data, including dreams, early memories, the Rorschach test, the thematic apperception test, and open-ended descriptions of emotionally significant persons (most often parents). Blatt and his colleagues (Auerbach and Blatt, 2002; Blatt et al., 1992; Diamond, Blatt, Stayner, and Kaslow, 1992) focused on three features of self- and object representations: conceptual level (overall organization of the mental representation as measured by its cohesiveness, elaboration, and integration), scorable attributes (affective and relational components of the mental representation), and differentiation-relatedness (see below). Subjects were originally instructed simply to describe their mother orally or in writing, then their father, self, and therapist (if applicable). Blatt and his colleagues then applied their coding system to these open-ended descriptions.

Interestingly, the nine-point rating scale that measures the conceptual level of self- and object representations resembles aspects of the construct of mentalization as measured by the RFS. At the lower end of this scale, the description is rated as concrete, emphasizing "what the person looks like in his/her external characteristics or physical properties" (Blatt et al., 1992, p. 14). A somewhat higher rating indicates that the description focuses on "functional activities and attributes" (p. 15) such as typical behaviors. At the highest end of this scale, the description is rated as complex and integrated, with "an appreciation of internal dimensions in their own right as well as in contrast to the external . . . [and] an appreciation of change and variation" (p. 16). Thus, the conceptual levels are hierarchically organized from a description of physical characteristics to behavioral characteristics, and finally, to internal psychological characteristics such as "feelings or values" (p. 16).

Fonagy and his colleagues (Fonagy, Gergely, et al., 2002; Fonagy et al., 1998) have discussed the reflective functioning (the operationalization of mentalization) of mental representations in similar terms:

> Certain internal working models include considerable reflective components—expectations incorporating the mental states of self and other—while other working models of relationships appear impoverished, indicating only minimal mentalizing skills. In the latter contexts the subject will offer only stereotyped,

> simple, concrete, low level descriptions. (Fonagy, Gergely, et al., 2002, p. 62; Fonagy et al., 1998, p. 7)

In other work, Fonagy and his colleagues (Fonagy, Steele, Steele, Higgitt, and Target, 1994) have hypothesized a prereflective self (established by the first six months) and a reflective self (gradually emerging by the fourth year). The mental representations contained in the prereflective self are characterized by "representations of interpersonal relations based on physical attributes, superficial categorizations of people over concrete interpretations of their actions, and other inaccuracies based on the failure to consider subjective states" (p. 247). By contrast, mental representations contained in the reflective self are characterized by "represent[ations of] interactions between self and other which contain mental experiences, feelings, perceptions, beliefs, and so on, as well as reflections upon these experiences in mental state terms" (p. 247). These conceptualizations of mental representations of the prereflective self and reflective self sound strikingly similar to Blatt's conceptual levels of self- and object representations.

In their first empirical article that reported on reflective functioning (RF), Fonagy and his colleagues (Fonagy, Steele, Steele, Moran, and Higgitt, 1991) described the research participants with high RF as perceiving their parents' mental states and their own mental states as separate and distinct, while the research participants with low RF resorted to descriptions of behavior and personality rather than feelings or internal states underlying behavior. Could the conceptual level rating scale of Blatt and his colleagues be measuring the same underlying construct as the RFS of Fonagy and his colleagues?

As Blatt and his colleagues' (Auerbach and Blatt, 2002; Diamond et al., 1992) interests shifted to a more intersubjective conceptualization of self- and object representations, they realized that their nine-point conceptual-level rating scale was "too static" (Auerbach and Blatt, 2002, p. 87). Thus, they developed the ten-point Cohesion, Differentiation, and Relatedness of Self and Other Scale, later shortened to the Differentiation-Relatedness Scale, which measures differentiation and relatedness among the subject's self- and object representations based on the subject's oral or written descriptions of mother, father, self, and therapist (if applicable).

In one of only two known studies to assess both self- and object representations and RF, Diamond and her colleagues (Diamond et al., 1999, p. 853) reported on the RF scores (Fonagy et al., 1998) and differentiation-relatedness scores (Diamond et al., 1992) of two patients diagnosed with borderline personality disorder, based on oral descriptions collected after four months and twelve months of treatment. The differentiation-relatedness scores were coded on a ten-point rating scale from open-ended descriptions of mother, father, self, and therapist. At four months, the RF score of Patient 1 was 3, while the differentiation-relatedness scores derived from the four descriptions ranged from 4 to 5 ($M = 4.6$). At twelve months, Patient 1's RF score was 5, while the differentiation-relatedness scores ranged from 5 to 7.5 ($M = 6.3$). At four months, the RF score of Patient 2 was 3, while the differentiation-relatedness scores ranged from 4 to 5 ($M = 4.6$). At twelve months, Patient 2's RF score was unchanged at 3, while the differentiation-relatedness scores ranged from 3 to 5.5 ($M = 4.6$). Admittedly, the sample size is tiny; however, visual inspection of the data points suggests that RF varies over time as the differentiation-relatedness scores vary over time. This positive correlation might reflect conceptual relatedness between the constructs of object representation and RF, as operationalized by these assessment instruments.

In the other known study, Auerbach and Blatt (2002) reported on the RF scores and differentiation-relatedness scores of a female adolescent inpatient diagnosed with conduct disorder, based on oral descriptions collected on admission (time 1), after twenty-four months of hospitalization (time 2), and at discharge after forty-three months of hospitalization (time 3). As in the previous study, the differentiation-relatedness scores were coded on a ten-point rating scale from open-ended descriptions of mother, father, self, and therapist. Interestingly, the authors applied the RFS to these same data sources—the four oral descriptions—not to independently collected Adult Attachment Interviews (AAI; George et al., 1996; Main and Goldwyn, 1994; Main et al., 1985). Thus, there were twelve sets of observations and scores: the RF scores and differentiation-relatedness scores for all four oral descriptions collected at three different points in time (Auerbach and Blatt, 2002, p. 98). I entered these twelve data points into SPSS® and performed my own calculations to complement the calculations reported in the article. The Pearson correlation between the patient's RF scores and differentiation-relatedness scores was significant, $r = .68, p < .05$. Again, this positive correlation might reflect conceptual relatedness between the constructs of object representation and RF.

Although these two studies strongly suggest conceptual relatedness between these two constructs, Blatt's definition and assessment of the quality and complexity of self- and object representations differ in nontrivial ways from Fonagy's definition and assessment of mentalization. Whereas Blatt's work focuses on the presence and cohesiveness of internal states assigned to the mental representation as evidence of representational quality and complexity, Fonagy's work focuses on the relations among mental states within and between persons and their relationship to behavior. Blatt's construct (even in its more recent intersubjective incarnation) appears static and fixed, while Fonagy's construct appears dynamic and fluid—a measure of how one thinks about minds—one's own and others' in mutual interaction—rather than a measure of one mind considered in isolation. Blatt's procedure itself betrays this bias: subjects are asked "to describe mother" (Auerbach and Blatt, 2002, p. 92)—not one's relationship to mother.

Interestingly, the data presented by Blatt, Diamond, Auerbach, and their colleagues suggest that the quality of a person's RF and the quality of his or her object representation tend to be conceptually related. Perhaps among certain clinical populations, such as those who avoid relationships, the correlation between these two constructs might be attenuated because such persons might have a high conceptual level of a mental representation but a low RF score that reflects difficulty with mentalizing the mutual influence of the mental states of multiple persons. Interestingly, the adolescent inpatient's RF scores dropped precipitously at discharge, while her differentiation-relatedness scores remained stable (Auerbach and Blatt, 2002, p. 98), which suggests that the high arousal level stimulated by discharge differentially diminished the patient's RF scores (see below; see also Allen, 2003). Only research using both instruments to assess a variety of populations under varying degrees of stress will provide definitive answers about the observed conceptual overlap between these two constructs.

Drew Westen's (1991a, 1991b, 1993, 1995) coding system purports to measure "dimensions of object relations and social cognition" (Westen, 1991b, p. 445). The five dimensions defined by Westen (1993) are: (1) complexity of representations of people (conceptually related to Blatt's instrument); (2) affect tone of relationship paradigms; (3) capacity for emotional investment in relationships; (4) capacity for emotional investment in values and moral standards; and (5) understanding of social causality. Westen (1995) later added three dimensions: (6) management of aggression; (7) self-esteem; and (8) identity and self-coherence (see also Hilsenroth et al., 2004; Peters et al., 2006). The fifth dimension, understanding of social causality, shares some conceptual overlap with mentalization because its definition resembles that of mentalization: "Tendency to attribute causes of behaviors, thoughts, and emotions in complex, logical, accurate, and psychologically minded ways" (Westen, 1991b, p. 445). Understanding of social causality focuses on "internal psychological processes rather than on surface-level, observable, behavioral causes," and includes an "understanding of unconscious processes" (p. 446). This dimension is rated on a five-point scale and ranges from level 1 ("noncausal or grossly illogical depictions of psychological and interpersonal events") to level 5 ("complex appreciation of the role of mental processes in generating thoughts, feelings, behaviors, and interpersonal interactions; understanding of unconscious motivational processes," p. 447).

Judging from these anchor points, Westen's construct of understanding of social causality appears to resemble Fonagy's construct of mentalization in the attention it pays to the causal linkages among thoughts, feelings, and behavior in interpersonal interactions. The major conceptual difference between these two constructs, in my view, consists of context-specificity. Westen's instrument purportedly measures understanding of social causality across interpersonal and situational contexts, while Fonagy's instrument (discussed in detail below) purportedly measures reflective functioning within a specific relationship and situation (Bateman and Fonagy, 2004a; Fonagy, Gergely, et al., 2002; Fonagy et al., 1998). Thus, reflective functioning can deteriorate when conflict emerges in a relationship and arousal levels become excessive (Allen, 2003; Fonagy, Gergely, et al., 2002). This dynamic, fluid feature of mentalization seems to be missing from Weston's understanding of social causality.

DEVELOPMENTAL HISTORY OF MENTALIZATION

Perhaps the most impressive aspect of Fonagy's construct of mentalization is that it is anchored in empirically based developmental theory. Fonagy and his colleagues have been conducting attachment research since the early 1990s (e.g., Fonagy et al., 1996; Fonagy, Redfern, and Charman, 1997; Fonagy, Steele, and Steele, 1991; Fonagy et al., 1994; Fonagy, Steele, Steele, Moran, and Higgitt, 1991) and have concluded that mentalization develops primarily within attachment relationships (Fonagy, Gergely, et al., 2002; Fonagy and Target, 1996a, 1997; Target and Fonagy, 1996). These authors have taken a strong environmentalist position in the debate over the acquisition of mentalization and have concluded that both the presence and quality of mentalization depend on the quality of the caregiver-infant relationship, not merely on introspection and the private observation of behavior in the context of a genetically determined unfolding of maturational processes. In fact, according to these authors, mentalization is not a prewired ability but rather "a developing or constructed capacity that evolves out of the earliest relationships" (Fonagy, Gergely, et al., 2002, p. 126).

In spite of Fonagy's (1999a, 1999b, 2001) enthusiasm for the findings of attachment research and their implications for advancing psychoanalytic developmental theory, he seems equivocal about any mediational role that attachment might play in the development of mentalization. In the view of Fonagy and his colleagues (Fonagy, Gergely, et al., 2002), although "attachment processes provide the key evolutionarily prepared paths for an interpersonal interpretive capacity to develop" (p. 131), still "the focus of study should not be attachment security, which . . . has little stability and possibly little predictive value" (p. 132). How do we understand this apparent contradiction?

Fonagy and his colleagues (Fonagy, Gergely, et al., 2002) have argued that early attachment relationships lay the groundwork for the existence of "a structure to represent object relationships, the processing skills required to deal with interpersonal interaction, the robustness of the model, the extent to which this interpretive mechanism can function under stress and process emotionally charged information, and so forth. The mechanism of predictive significance is the interpersonal interpretive mechanism" (p. 132). In other words, specific caregiver-infant interactions are responsible for the development of both the IIM-a and IIM-c and self- and object representations and, ultimately, the quality of the attachment relationship. In this passage, the authors seem to have suggested a model in which early caregiver-infant interactions independently influence both attachment security and mentalization (see part a of figure 6.1).

Elsewhere, however, attachment security seems to mediate the relation between caregiver-infant interactions and mentalization. A secure attachment relationship "provides the psychosocial basis for acquiring an understanding of mind" because "the secure infant feels safe in making attributions of mental states to account for the behavior of the caregiver" (Fonagy, Gergely, et al., 2002, p. 55). The process by which the securely attached infant comes to understand how minds work is the infant's "exploration of the mental state of the sensitive caregiver, which enables the child to find in the caregiver's mind (that is, in the hypothetical representation of her mind that he constructs to explain her behavior toward him) an image of himself as motivated by beliefs, feelings, and intentions" (p. 55). In this second model, caregiver-infant interactions determine the quality of the attachment relationship, which in turn facilitates the development of mentalization (see part b of figure 6.1). In a variation of this second model (see part c of figure 6.1), the attachment relationship, in turn, indirectly influences the development of mentalization through other mediating variables such as pretend play, conversations about feelings and motivations of behavior, and peer group and sibling interactions (Fonagy, Gergely, et al., 2002; Fonagy and Target, 1997).

Perhaps caregiver-infant interactions both directly and indirectly influence the development of mentalization (part d of figure 6.1). Indeed, a path analysis indicated that mothers' willingness to treat their three-year-old children as mental agents both directly and indirectly predicted the later development of the children's mentalizing abilities at age five (Meins, Fernyhough, Russell, and Clark-Carter, 1998). Thus, we can tentatively conclude that both the caregiver's mentalizing communication to the child and the child's attachment security directly facilitate the exploration of others' minds, most notably the primary caregiver's, and thus enable the child ultimately to make

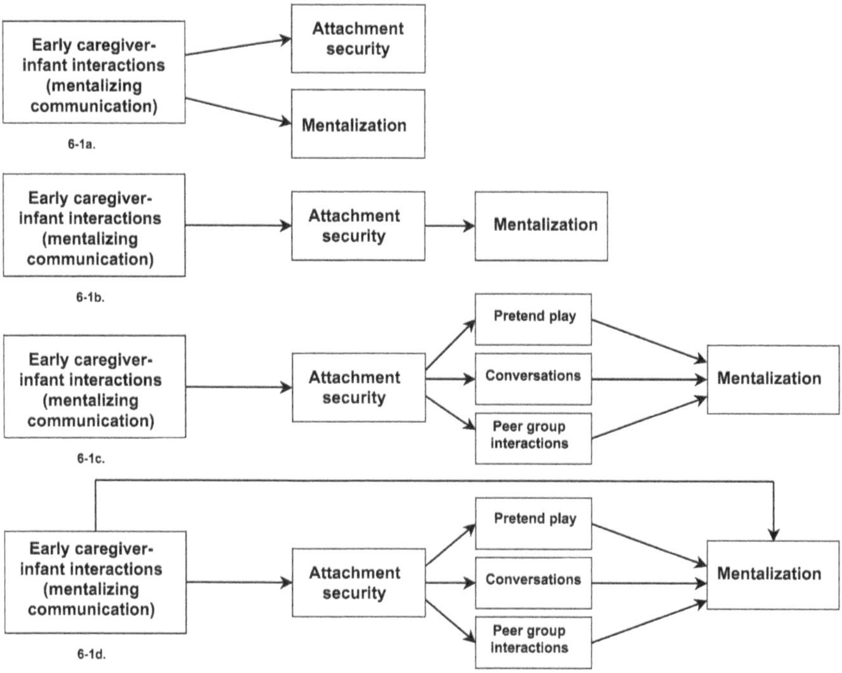

Figure 6.1. Developmental Pathways Model of Mentalization

plausible interpretations of the mental states underlying his or her own and others' behavior.

What is the nature of these caregiver-infant interactions that facilitate the development of mentalization? Fonagy and his colleagues (Fonagy, Gergely, et al., 2002; Gergely, 2000; Gergely and Watson, 1996) have articulated the "social biofeedback model" to account for the early symbolization of mental phenomena such as thoughts and feelings. Based on the empirical study of caregiver-infant interactions, these authors have suggested that the caregiver who is empathically attuned to his or her infant mentalizes the infant's needs and affect states and reflects them back to the infant to communicate to him or her that the caregiver understands these needs and affect states. The mentalizing caregiver communicates this understanding through the process of "marking"—using exaggerated facial and vocal expressions to indicate that (1) the caregiver is aware of the infant's mental state, and (2) the caregiver is not experiencing what the infant is experiencing (see Goodman, in press, chapter 4). Marking can take a variety of forms. The most common form—"motherese"—directs the infant's attention to the caregiver and communicates to the infant that the caregiver is holding the infant in mind. I recently learned that even female rhesus monkeys use motherese with their infants (Whitham, Gerald, and Maestripieri, 2007), which suggests that marking is not unique to humans and has a genetic basis.

The function of marking is to provide the infant with the experience of feeling understood in a variety of contexts. Fonagy and his colleagues (Fonagy, Gergely, et al., 2002; Fonagy and Target, 1997) have emphasized distress situations and play situations as two key contexts in which marking takes place. By introducing an exaggerated variation into the representation of the infant's mental state, the caregiver reflects back the infant's mental state in a similar but not identical form. This variation is critical to the development of symbolization and, ultimately, mentalization, because it enables the infant to recognize that the caregiver's response is only a facsimile of the infant's experienced mental state. That the caregiver both understands this mental state and is not personally experiencing it communicates to the infant that he or she "is not dying and will get over it" (Aron, 2006, p. 358). Thus, through this process of early symbol formation (see also Segal, 1957), the caregiver assists the infant in regulating affects that could be considered the essence of affective containment (see also Bion, 1962, 1967). In fact, Fonagy and his colleagues (Fonagy, Gergely, et al., 2002; Fonagy et al., 1998) have drawn a parallel between the caregiver's mentalization and Bion's (1962, 1967) alpha function. The emotionally responsive, mentalizing caregiver uses the alpha function to interpret the infant's message of distress (e.g., need for protection, hunger, discomfort); acts as a container for these primitive, dysregulated affects ("beta elements") through the process of marking; and transforms them into modulated, coherent affects. The infant then introjects these metabolized affects, thus accumulating experiences that can ultimately be symbolized to form self- and object representations "capable of self-knowledge and communication between different aspects of themselves" (Britton, 1998, p. 23).

Of course, not all caregivers mentalize their infants' dysregulated affects and thus assist them in symbol formation and affect regulation. The caregiver's reaction instead might suggest that the infant's mental states are intolerable or even nonexistent (Fonagy and Target, 1998). If the caregiver does not introduce any variation into the representation of the infant's mental state and instead reflects back the infant's mental state in its original, unmodulated form, the infant will introject an image of his or her mental state as intolerable. For example, an anxious, inept caregiver who panics when the infant spits up food communicates through facial and vocal expressions the same level of distress that the infant is feeling. This reaction does not assist the infant with regulating the distress but rather conveys to the infant that the external world is as frightening as the internal world. Relief from distress cannot be found in either world.

Fonagy and his colleagues (Bateman and Fonagy, 2004a, 2004b; Fonagy, Gergely, et al., 2002; Fonagy and Target, 1997, 1998) have referred to this infant's experience as "psychic equivalence mode." The caregiver reflects back to the infant a frighteningly accurate representation of the infant's dysregulated affects and thus fails to contain them. The caregiver's panic robs the resultant visual and auditory communication of its symbolic potential so that internal reality and external reality are identical. Although the authors have not made an explicit connection between the psychic equivalence mode and Klein's (1946, 1952) paranoid-schizoid position, the two constructs are conceptually similar. The infant in the paranoid-schizoid position is projecting and introjecting primitive, affectively charged, unmodulated part-objects that turn external reality into a funhouse full of distorted mirrors. Grotstein (1998) has referred to these projected and introjected maternal part-objects as comprising "the infant in drag," which vividly captures the idea that these introjected part-objects are composed of the infant's projections of his or her own mental states. The psychic equivalence of internal reality and external reality seems to be the essence of the paranoid-schizoid position in British object relations theory.

By contrast, the caregiver's nonreaction to the infant's dysregulated affects might suggest that the infant's mental states are nonexistent or at least not related to the external world (Fonagy and Target, 1998). The infant is abandoned to find his or her own strategies for regulating affects. Alternatively, the caregiver has a reaction that nevertheless bears no resemblance to the infant's mental state. In other words, the variation introduced by the caregiver has little or nothing to do with the infant's mental state. For example, a caregiver uncomfortable with distress might attempt to stop the infant from crying by making funny faces or showing the infant a toy rather than acknowledging and marking the distress. This reaction does not assist the infant with regulating the distress but rather conveys to the infant that the external world does not recognize or symbolically represent distress. Relief from distress can be found only in the internal world.

Fonagy and his colleagues (Bateman and Fonagy, 2004a, 2004b; Fonagy, Gergely, et al., 2002; Fonagy and Target, 1998) have referred to this infant's experience as "pretend mode." The caregiver reflects back to the infant an inaccurate, unfaithful representation of the infant's dysregulated affects and thus fails to contain them. The caregiver's denial of distress, represented in a reaction having little or no correspondence to the infant's distress, serves to replace the infant's constitutionally experienced mental state with a mental state alien to this internal experience. The pretend mode is strikingly conceptually similar to Winnicott's (1965) false self. The false self develops when the infant introjects the caregiver's invalidating reactions to the infant's cues. These reactions come from the caregiver's own mental state (or defensive reaction to his or her own mental state) rather than the infant's own internal experience reflected back from the caregiver. The infant's resultant dependence on him or herself for affect-regulating strategies is reminiscent of the development of Kernberg's (1970, 1975, 1984, 1986a, 1986b) pathological grandiose self characterized by an inability to depend on others. According to Fonagy and his colleagues (Bateman and Fonagy, 2004a, 2004b; Fonagy, Gergely, et al., 2002; Fonagy and Target, 1998), the unfortunate outcome of the pretend mode is the development of an alien self that provides "illusory stability" but is "dissociated" from internal reality (Bateman and Fonagy, 2004a, p. 38), or Winnicott's (1965) true self. In fact, we can surmise that the pretend mode serves to protect the infant from the annihilation anxiety associated with the psychic equivalence mode, just as the false self "hides and protects" the true self (Winnicott, 1956, p. 387).

The good-enough mother (Winnicott, 1965)—through mentalizing and containing the infant's affects (especially intense negative affects)—provides the necessary conditions for the integration of these two modes of experience by the age of four. The reflective mode (Fonagy, Gergely, et al., 2002; Fonagy and Target, 1997, 1998) permits the child to begin the process of rudimentary mentalization in which he or she begins to symbolize his or her intense affective experiences rather than become overwhelmed by them (psychic equivalence mode) or become withdrawn from them (pretend mode). In my view, this mode of functioning resembles that of Klein's (1933, 1937, 1952) depressive position in which the infant has begun the process of integrating split-off objects and mentally representing whole persons rather than parts of persons dominated by unmodulated affects loosely structured as fantasies. The infant's awareness that his or her aggressive impulses have been trained against the loved object—now perceived as a whole person—as well as the infant's anxiety associated with the potential damage to and loss of the loved object both signify the symbolization of this loved object. The reason is that the infant cannot feel the absence of the external object if an internal representation of this object were not still present to serve as a painful reminder to the infant of this external loss (and the infant's fantasized role in it).

In the reflective mode, however, what the child integrates are not objects but rather two distinct modes of processing affective experience. The child begins to understand that the caregiver's responses are neither identical to nor dissociated from his or her internal experiences; rather, these responses are marked as reasonable facsimiles of the child's experience that confirm an emotional understanding of this experience as well as a separateness from it that encompass both the psychic equivalence and pretend modes. This mentalizing process begins in interaction with the caregiver during infancy. Grienenberger and his colleagues (Grienenberger, Kelly, and Slade, 2005) have referred to the caregiver's response as simultaneously mirroring the infant's experience and mastering it on behalf of the infant. This combination of mirroring and mastery represents a marked response that allows the infant to develop over time a reflective mode of experience, first observed in four-year-olds in which the internal world and external reality are meaningfully interconnected (Fonagy and Target, 1998). Affective experience has a beginning, middle, and end, and can be shared by others or experienced alone. It can be hidden from others' awareness or symbolized in play or words. Alexythymia, defined as the difficulty identifying and verbally describing feelings (Conte and Ratto, 1997; Sifneos, 1973), signifies a deficit in the ability to symbolize affective experience. Future research could examine whether persons suffering from this condition tend to demonstrate low RF and function primarily within the psychic equivalence or pretend mode.

These three modes of early childhood experience have not been operationalized and are thus not currently subject to empirical investigation. I would hypothesize, however, that the reflective mode would be most closely associated with a secure infant attachment, while the psychic equivalence mode would be most closely associated with an anxious-resistant infant attachment and the pretend mode most closely associated with an anxious-avoidant infant attachment (see below). I have argued earlier (Goodman, 2002) that an anxious-resistant attachment is a behavioral manifestation of Klein's (1946, 1952) paranoid-schizoid position dominated by splitting and other primitive defensive processes. One sees the oscillation between good and bad objects unfold within the infant's mind in a reunion episode of the Strange Situation (Ainsworth, 1979; Ainsworth et al., 1978), where the child demands to be picked up by the caregiver, only to demand to be put down again in an anxiety-driven cycle of ambivalence.

On the other hand, an anxious-avoidant attachment is a behavioral manifestation of Kernberg's (1986a, 1986b) pathological grandiose self dominated by a condensation of pathologically idealized object representations imbedded within a nexus of real and pathologically idealized self-representations (Rosenfeld [1964] developed a similar construct he called the "omnipotent narcissistic self" [p. 337]). One sees the rigid self-sufficiency played out by the infant in snubbing the caregiver in the reunion episode, where the child hides his or her separation anxiety by pretending to ignore the caregiver's return. By contrast, a secure attachment is a behavioral manifestation of Klein's (1933, 1937, 1952) depressive position dominated by a recognition of the caregiver's temporary loss and sustaining presence of a symbolic representation of this caregiver as a whole person that effectively contains the separation anxiety and renders the reunion episode only briefly upsetting.

Fonagy (1999b) has suggested conceptual associations between the paranoid-schizoid position of Kleinian theory and insecure attachment and between the depressive position and secure attachment. Like the paranoid-schizoid position, "[Attachment] insecurity (rather than security) is the 'basic position,' and that the persistence of splitting is a consequence" (p. 617). Each mode of mental functioning—psychic equivalence or pretend—represents one form of distorted, split-off thinking that requires integration with the other form to understand accurately and comprehensively the relations between one's internal world and external reality. According to Fonagy and his colleagues (Fonagy, Gergely, et al., 2002), "The child integrates these two modes to arrive at the stage of *mentalization*—or reflective mode—in which mental states can be experienced as representations" (p. 57, italics in original). I am suggesting that a secure attachment in infancy is a necessary condition for the integration of these two primitive modes of mental functioning and the onset of the reflective mode—perhaps the conceptual counterpart of Klein's depressive position. Aside from the differences in developmental timing, Klein's and Fonagy's theories of the development of the mind converge with each other. I will further discuss the connections among mentalization-based developmental theory, attachment theory, and personality organization later in this chapter.

OPERATIONALIZATION OF MENTALIZATION

As I discussed earlier, Fonagy and his colleagues (Fonagy, Gergely, et al., 2002) operationalized the mentalization construct and used the term, reflective functioning, to describe "the operationalization of the psychological processes underlying the capacity to mentalize" (p. 24). Reflective functioning, according to these authors, is "the ability to give plausible interpretations of one's own and others' behavior in terms of underlying mental states" (Fonagy, Gergely, et al., 2002, p. 26; Fonagy et al., 1998, p. 4). These researchers developed the Reflective Functioning Scale (RFS) to capture individual differences in this capacity and to relate these differences to the quality of attachment assessed using the Adult Attachment Interview (AAI; George et al., 1996; Main and Goldwyn, 1994; Main et al., 1985). If attachment quality indeed mediates the development of children's mentalization (Fonagy, Gergely, et al., 2002; Fonagy and Target, 1997; Meins et al., 1998), then one would expect attachment quality to be associated with level of RF. Thus, Fonagy and his colleagues used AAI transcriptions to assess RF, reasoning that an accurate measure of RF can be made only when the attachment system is activated—that is to say, when sufficient anxiety is aroused and mentalization is most needed to cope with this interview-induced stress associated with the recall of the vicissitudes of the childhood relationships to the primary caregivers.

Main and Goldwyn's (1994) AAI attachment classification coding system features a series of seventeen nine-point rating scales divided into three groups: inferred parental behavior during childhood, patterned or organized states of mind, and unresolved states of mind (for a more thorough discussion of this coding system, see Goodman, 2002). One of these rating scales, listed under patterned or organized states of mind, is called "metacognitive monitoring" (see Main, 1991). This rating scale measures the extent to which the interviewee is monitoring his or her own discourse for slips of the tongue and other illogical utterances. Main and Goldwyn (1994) found that interviewees who experienced lapses or temporary deficits in the metacognitive monitoring of reasoning during a discussion of loss, abuse, or other traumatic events were experiencing an unresolved state of mind with respect to attachment. An unresolved (U) attachment pattern has been associated with disorganized attachment in infancy (Lyons-Ruth and Jacobvitz, 1999; van IJzendoorn, 1995).

Fonagy and his colleagues (Fonagy, Gergely, et al., 2002; Fonagy et al., 1998) wanted to design an instrument that assessed not just the interviewee's awareness of their own discourse reasoning but also their awareness of their own and others' (principally, the primary caregivers') mental states and the interrelations between them. For example, how does the interviewee explain why their parents behaved as they did during childhood? The authors divided the AAI's twenty questions into two groups: demand and permit questions. Demand questions demand interviewees to demonstrate RF—as is the case with the previous question. Permit questions instead permit interviewees to demonstrate RF but do not demand them to. For example, the question that asks interviewees to recall a childhood separation from the parents allows for interviewees to elaborate on their own and their parents' mental states and the interrelations between them but does not require it.

RF is measured using an eleven-point scale ranging from -1 (negative or limited RF) to 9 (exceptional RF; Fonagy et al., 1998). A rating of -1 would reflect the level of RF of someone diagnosed with antisocial personality disorder, while a rating of 9 would be reserved, perhaps, for Fonagy himself. The RF assessed from my own AAI transcription was rated as a 6—somewhere between "definite or ordinary" (5) and "marked" (7)—not what I was hoping for as a psychoanalytic candidate with over twelve years of personal analysis. In the only published study of RF in seven experienced therapists who were interviewed about their relationships with their ten BPD patients, the RF scores ranged from 3 to 8, with a mean of 5.75 (Diamond, Stovall-McClough, Clarkin, and Levy, 2003, p. 242; see also Goodman, in press, chapter 5).

As demonstrated by this study of therapist RF (Diamond, Stovall-McClough, et al., 2003), RF scores are context-dependent—both to persons and to situations. One of these seven therapists, who was treating three BPD patients, obtained scores of 3, 6, and 7 in three separate interviews about his or her relationships with these three BPD patients. The nature of the therapeutic relationships that developed between this therapist and these three BPD patients varied to the extent that they differentially affected the therapist's RF capacity. Similarly, discussion of specific situations also affects a person's RF. Fonagy and his colleagues (Fonagy et al., 1998) suggested that a psychoanalyst with high RF in a clinical context might experience a loss of RF in discussing a situation involving his or her own family relationships. Because of this context-dependency, Fonagy and his colleagues also suggested that RF develops through multiple pathways of experience. As I suggested earlier, these pathways include play situations, conversational experiences, peer group and sibling interactions, the quality of the attachment pattern (and thus the perceived level of freedom to explore one's own and others' minds), and the quality of the caregiver-child relationship. These different pathways could yield different RF capacities, reflected in varying RF assessed in different situations. Just as an AAI interviewee might shift between attachment patterns (e.g., dismissing to preoccupied) when discussing one or the other parent or one episodic memory or another (Goodman, 2002), so too can RF shift between high and low levels depending on the conversational context.

It is also important to mention that RF is not subject to fixation or regression like the libidinal drive, but rather develops in complexity over time, even at low levels (Fonagy et al., 1998). In this sense, RF is considered a task-based skill, whose level varies according to the task and whose coordination across persons and situations is a continuous process. One can observe an unevenness of RF skill level, also known as décalage, across contexts. RF also tends to diminish as affective experience tends to increase. This idea has spread to the popular literature, which tells us that emotional IQ (a neighboring construct of RF) drops when we are feeling angry or depressed (Goleman, 1995).

If RF is indeed context-dependent, then does it have to be measured in the context of an interview about childhood caregiver relationships? In other words, does RF have to be measured using the AAI? Furthermore, is RF considered a unidimensional or multidimensional construct? Although the RFS yields only one score, one could argue that RF can be assessed across multiple dimensions. Slade and her colleagues (Slade, Grienenberger, Bernbach, Levy, and Locker, 2005) have suggested that "subtypes on the RFS can be used to capture differences in narrative or reflective style, as there are ways of being reflective that are more avoidant and dismissing, and others that are more preoccupied and undifferentiated" (p. 295). Fonagy and his colleagues (Fonagy et al., 1998) have suggested several categories of absent, low, or questionable RF for scores of 3 or lower (e.g., "self-serving" and "hyperactive"). Subtypes of RF, however, have not yet been empirically validated. I will return to these issues later in this chapter.

Fonagy and his colleagues (Fonagy et al., 1998) examined hundreds of AAIs and collected thousands of examples of RF for scores higher than 3. They then classified these examples into four general categories: (1) awareness of the nature of mental states; (2) explicit effort to tease out mental states underlying behavior; (3) recognizing developmental aspects of mental states; and (4) mental states in relation to the AAI interviewer. Unfortunately, these four categories have never been used to predict anything such as infant attachment classifications or psychotherapy outcomes. Yet one would imagine that an empirically derived, multidimensional conceptualization of RF would yield dimensions resembling these four categories.

In rating RF, the coder uses these four categories to determine whether the AAI interviewee demonstrates RF. In the first category, the interviewee demonstrates an awareness of the nature of mental states. In other words, the interviewee must demonstrate an understanding of how mental states work in either him-/herself or others. The *RF Manual* (Fonagy et al., 1998) lists five general characteristics of mental states. First, mental states can be opaque, which means that a person cannot be confident of his or her understanding of another person's intentions or wishes. Returning to the illustration at the beginning of this chapter, if I am the German shepherd's owner, I might have thought that the runner crossed to the other side of the street because he was scared of my dog, but I am not certain of his motive. I could not read his mind. Second, mental states are susceptible to disguise. In other words, what a person is thinking and feeling might differ from the thoughts and feelings that he or she is displaying. Using my illustration, the runner appears calm and relaxed as he is crossing to the other side of the street, but perhaps he is feeling scared inside and does not want to show it. Third, mental states are sometimes limited in their ability to provide insight. This characteristic resembles that of the opaqueness of mental states. Fourth, mental states can be normative or deviant, which means that a person has a sense of how another person would generally think or feel in a particular situation. The possibility of being bitten by a scary-looking German shepherd would make any runner want to cross to the other side of the street. Fifth, mental states can serve defensive functions. In other words, a person can use a mental state to reduce unpleasant affects. I tell myself that my German shepherd is not that scary-looking to avoid feeling guilty for having made the runner cross to the other side of the street.

In the second category, the interviewee demonstrates an explicit effort to tease out mental states underlying behavior. In other words, the interviewee must demonstrate an understanding of which mental states could plausibly influence behavior and how these mental states could plausibly influence behavior. The *RF Manual* (Fonagy et al., 1998) lists seven general aspects of identification and causal influence. First, a person makes accurate attributions of mental states to others, which means that a mental state plausibly accounts for a behavior. The runner crossed to the other side of the street because he felt scared of my dog. Second, a person's feelings concerning a situation could be unrelated to observable aspects of it. In other words, a person might be feeling a certain way about a situation because he or she is preoccupied with feelings over a different situation altogether. The runner might have crossed to the other side of the street because another dog might have recently bitten him while running. Third, a person recognizes the presence of diverse perspectives, which means that different persons might perceive a given behavior or situation differently. The runner probably has no idea how friendly, sweet, and loving my German shepherd is toward people—especially runners.

Fourth, a person takes into account one's own mental state in interpreting another person's behavior. In other words, a person's interpretation of another person's behavior critically depends on one's own mental state. I think that the runner crossed to the other side of the street to avoid having to look at me, but perhaps I think that because I look disgusting to myself. Fifth, a person's mental states can potentially influence one's own or another person's behavior. In other words, a person's mental state might have behavioral manifestations in oneself or another person. I think that because I was feeling nervous for the runner, I held my dog's leash more tightly. Sixth, a person understands that other persons perceive them and in what ways these other persons might perceive them. In other words, other persons' perceptions can influence one's own or others' behaviors or reactions. When I saw the runner flinch as he approached my dog and me, I thought he might be scared of my dog, so I held the leash more tightly. Seventh, a person's recall of and thinking about mental states are unrehearsed and spontaneous, which means that the person can be flexible in their perspective on a situation. At the time, I thought the runner was afraid of my German shepherd, but come to think of it, I was wearing my cat burglar Halloween costume, so maybe that is what scared him.

In the third category, the interviewee demonstrates an awareness of the developmental aspects of mental states. In other words, the interviewee must demonstrate the idea that mental states can change over time and depend on one's age and level of maturity. The *RF Manual* (Fonagy et al., 1998) lists seven general developmental aspects of mental states. First, a person understands that generations mutually influence each other. In other words, a person's childhood experiences with parents influence his or her child's own experiences with this person. The runner, who is much younger than I am, crossed to the other side of the street, perhaps because he felt uncomfortable asking an older adult to muzzle his dog. Second, a person takes a developmental perspective with regard to his or her own or others' mental states, which means that the person understands that the mental states of oneself or others can change with age. At the time, I felt powerful making runners cross to the other side of the street with my scary-looking German shepherd, but now I realize that I was feeling insecure about my ability to have an impact on others. Third, a person revises mental states from childhood in the context of understanding gained since childhood. In other words, childhood perceptions change as a person's understanding of him or herself and others expands in adulthood. As a child, I always let go of my dog's leash whenever I saw a runner coming because I thought the runner would like to meet my dog. Now I realize that my dog's mad rush to greet them probably scared them to death.

Fourth, a person anticipates future changes in mental states of him or herself or others, which means that a person understands that mental states will change over time as circumstances change. My German shepherd will be less threatening to runners when I buy a muzzle for him to wear. Fifth, a person understands that parent and child mental states are mutually influential, which means that a person understands that his or her mental states affected his or her parents as his or her parents' mental states affected him. My father gave me a German shepherd because he knew that I worried about my safety but refused to carry a cell phone during my nightly walks, which also worried him. Sixth, a person understands a child's need for affect regulation and the behaviors that could regulate his or her affects. In other words, a person realizes how a child's relative helplessness in changing his or her mental states requires developmentally appropriate intervention. My infant son became so manically excited whenever my dog licked his face that I had to limit the amount of time my dog spent with him so that he would not become so overstimulated. Seventh, a person demonstrates an awareness of the interdependent nature of mental states within the family system, which means that a person understands how the dynamics of the entire family system affect each individual family member's mental state, which in turn affects the entire family system. The dog's presence in my family gives us all something to talk about and play with, but, oddly enough, it seems to make us all feel more distant toward each other—perhaps because the dog gives us all an excuse to avoid each other.

In the fourth category, the interviewee demonstrates an awareness of mental states in relation to the AAI interviewer. In other words, the interviewee must demonstrate the idea that he or she is willing to entertain mental states in the context of other relationships. The *RF Manual* (Fonagy et al., 1998) lists three general aspects of an awareness of mental states in relation to the AAI interviewer. First, a person acknowledges the separateness of his or her mind from the interviewer's mind. In other words, a person demonstrates an appreciation that the interviewer might not share his or her mental state. I know that the interviewer might think I am weird, but I actually enjoyed watching the runner flinch and run away in fear when he saw my scary-looking German shepherd. Second, a person does not assume shared knowledge between him or her and the interviewer. In other words, a person appreciates that the interviewer needs additional information or clarification to make sense of the conversation. You might not know this if you are not a runner, but many runners—like me—have a secret fear of dogs because we have all been chased or bitten by one at one time or another. Third, a person is emotionally attuned to the probable impact his or her conversation will have on the interviewer's mental state. In other words, the person both acknowledges that the conversation might affect the interviewer's mental state and understands the reason behind this impact. I suspect my telling you that I actually enjoy making runners fearful of me might make you uncomfortable because you might be wondering whether I could scare you the same way.

I hope that I have done justice to explaining the comprehensive RFS criteria. By the way, I am not and have never been a dog owner, but have been trying to mentalize some of the mental states that certain dog owners might experience in relation to themselves and to runners (which I am). I purposely chose a nonfamilial illustration to underscore the point that we mentalize all the time, in innumerable situations. Our capacity to mentalize might increase or decrease depending on the context, and our mentalizing might be implicit or explicit, but mentalization is always happening, like thinking, feeling, or breathing. It also happens to be an effective ingredient of therapeutic change (see below).

Researchers have attempted to operationalize mentalization beyond the context of the AAI—an interview designed to evaluate the quality of a person's childhood relationships with primary caregivers. While some researchers have defined RF as "mentalization measured in the context of attachment" (Fonagy and Target, 2005a, p. 334), others have decided to develop instruments that assess RF in contexts other than the AAI. These attempts at operationalization can be divided into two groups: (1) instruments designed to measure caregiver RF in relation to their children, and (2) instruments designed to measure patient or therapist RF in psychotherapy sessions. I will briefly review these instruments now.

In the first group, Meins and her colleagues (Meins, Fernyhough, Fradley, and Tuckey, 2001; Meins et al., 1998; Meins et al., 2003; Meins et al., 2002) have operationalized mentalization in the context of the caregiver's interactions with the infant and child and have labeled it "mind-mindedness." In their early work (Meins et al., 1998), mentalization was operationalized as a mother's "inclination to use mental characteristics in describing their children" (p. 9). The mother's use of "mentalistic attributes" (p. 11) was measured while the mother was interviewed about her three-year-old child. The interview procedure is strikingly reminiscent of Blatt et al.'s (1992) procedure for assessing the quality and complexity of object representations. The mother is asked, "Can you describe [child] for me?" (Meins et al., 1998, p. 9). No other instructions are provided. Interviews are recorded and transcribed verbatim and later coded for maternal attributes, which are classified into four categories: mental (references to the child's mental life), behavioral (references to the child's behavior), physical (references to the child's physical attributes), and general (references not fitting into the other three categories). The coding system also resembles Blatt and his colleagues' (Blatt et al., 1992) nine-point rating scale of the conceptual level of object representation except that it yields categories rather than scores. The authors, however, constructed scores by dividing the sum of the mother's mental attributes by the sum of the mother's attributes from all four categories. Thus, higher scores signify greater mentalizing capacity with respect to the child's mind.

In contrast to the RFS, this procedure has the advantage of assessing RF within a context different from childhood relationships with primary caregivers (i.e., the AAI). This measure affords the opportunity of assessing the primary caregiver's mentalization of the child. This measure does not, however, assess the mother's own mental states in relation to her child.

In their later work, Meins and her colleagues (Meins et al., 2001; Meins et al., 2003; Meins et al., 2002) developed an *in vivo* measure of mind-mindedness—now defined as the ability to "'read' the mental states underlying a child's behaviour [which] is most likely to be apparent in situations where the child's physical and emotional needs are satisfied" (Meins et al., 2001, p. 639). This instrument is designed to measure a mother's mind-mindedness with her six-month-old infant in a twenty-minute free-play situation in which the mother and infant play as they would do if they had a few spare minutes together at home. The mother's behaviors toward the infant are coded along five dimensions: (1) maternal responsiveness to change in infant's direction of gaze (calculated as a proportion of the total number of changes in direction of gaze); (2) maternal responsiveness to infant's object-directed action (calculated as a proportion of the total number of object-directed actions); (3) imitation (calculated as a proportion of the total number of infant vocalizations); (4) encouragement of autonomy (calculated as a proportion of the total number of maternal behaviors); and (5) appropriateness of maternal mind-related comments (calculated as a proportion of the total number of the mother's verbal comments) (Meins et al., 2001). All five scores are used to define mind-mindedness, although only appropriateness of maternal mind-related comments significantly predicted infant attachment security.

Like Meins and her colleagues' (Meins et al., 1998) earlier procedure, this procedure has the advantage of assessing RF within a context different from childhood relationships with primary caregivers. In addition, mind-mindedness is measured *in vivo*, while the mother is actively engaged with her infant. One would expect that such a procedure would more likely access relational procedural knowledge (e.g., Lyons-Ruth, 1999; Stern et al., 1998; Tronick et al., 1998)—which would presumably be less susceptible to secondary elaboration (Freud, 1940)—than declarative symbolic knowledge. In other words, because this instrument assesses mentalization while the mother is actually engaged in interaction with her child rather than in an interview removed from the child where, under less demanding conditions, she can calmly provide more socially desirable mental-state discourse, one would expect this instrument's external validity to be superior to the RFS. Fonagy and Target (2005a), however, disagree with this point of view and have instead claimed that maternal RF measured in an interview by Slade and her colleagues (Aber, Slade, Berger, Bresgi, and Kaplan, 1985; Slade, 2005) actually provides "greater accuracy of prediction" (p. 336) than the *in vivo* procedure developed by Meins and her colleagues (Meins et al., 2001). I will return to this controversy later in this chapter.

Another instrument designed to measure parent RF in relation to their children is the insightfulness assessment (IA; Oppenheim and Koren-Karie, 2002). These authors have defined insightfulness as "the parent's capacity to invoke motives that underlie the child's behavior" (p. 596)—a definition that clearly resembles mind-mindedness. Insightfulness is assessed in the context of the parent's viewing and commenting on their previously videotaped interactions with their infant (free-play episode) or young child (building a house together). Specifically, the parent is interviewed afterward regarding their perceptions of the child's thoughts and feelings during the videotaped interactions as well as their own thoughts and feelings. The verbatim transcripts of these interviews are then rated on ten seven-point scales: (1) insight into child's motives; (2) openness; (3) complexity in description of child;

(4) maintenance of focus on child; (5) richness of description of child; (6) coherence of thought; (7) acceptance; (8) anger; (9) worry; and (10) separateness from child. The anchor points of each scale range from 1 (an absence of the insightfulness characteristic being measured) to 7 (exemplary examples of the insightfulness characteristic being measured). The resulting ten scores are then used to classify the parent into one of four categories: (1) positively insightful (PI; seeing through the child's eyes and understanding the motives underlying his or her behavior); (2) one-sided (Os; imposing a conception onto the child that does not appear open to change); (3) disengaged (De; lack of emotional involvement throughout the interview); and (4) mixed (Mx; a mixture of categories). Among these four categories of parents, PI parents are considered to have the highest degree of insightfulness.

Again in contrast to the RFS, this procedure, like the mind-mindfulness procedure, has the advantage of assessing RF within a context different from childhood relationships with primary caregivers (i.e., the AAI). This measure affords the opportunity of assessing the primary caregiver's mentalization of the child. Because IA is not assessed "in the heat of battle," so to speak, but rather during a calmer moment while watching the interactions on videotape, the IA appears to resemble the RFS more than the mind-mindfulness measure. The parent, however, engages in mental-state discourse regarding actual footage of his or her interactions with the child, which I believe still offers fewer opportunities for secondary elaboration than the RFS. Fonagy and Target (2005a), however, have criticized the IA as well as the mind-mindfulness measure for measuring only "a particular moment of interaction" rather than "an aggregate across many episodes of interaction" (p. 335) as is the case with maternal RF measured in an interview without videotaped interactions by Slade and her colleagues (Aber et al., 1985; Slade, 2005). I will discuss this controversy further below.

The final instrument designed to measure caregiver RF in relation to their children is the Parent Development Interview (PDI; Aber et al., 1985; Slade, 2005). Designed to resemble the AAI as closely as possible, the PDI consists of forty-five questions designed to assess the parent's attachment representation of the relationship with the child. Slade and her colleagues (Slade, Bernbach, Grienenberger, Levy, and Locker, 2004) later adapted the RFS (Fonagy et al., 1998) for use with the PDI. According to Slade (2005), this adaptation of the RFS "offers what can be presumed to be an inherently complementary assessment of reflective functioning in a different relational context" (p. 280). Like the RFS, it is scored on an eleven-point rating scale with anchor points identical to the RFS (Slade, Grienenberger, Bernbach, Levy, and Locker, 2005).

Slade (2005) has compared Meins and her colleagues' (Meins et al., 2001) mind-mindfulness measure unfavorably with her own adaptation of the RFS because mind-mindfulness fails to capture the parent's "capacity to link [an] awareness of her child's or her own internal state to behavior or to other internal states that is the hallmark of true reflective functioning" (p. 278). While it is true that RF seems to have a broader definition than mind-mindedness, it is not clear which instrument is more closely associated with successful socioemotional child outcomes. The two constructs could be so highly correlated with each other that they are statistically redundant and thus predict these outcomes equally well. Slade (2005) neglects to address the fact that her adaptation, like the RFS itself, measures RF in the relatively calm setting of an interview rather than the demanding conditions of actual interaction with the child. This difference in setting could differentially affect the prediction of socioemotional child outcomes (see below).

In the second group of instruments designed to operationalize mentalization, researchers are interested in moving beyond the caregiver-child setting altogether, instead capturing patient or therapist RF in psychotherapy sessions. The Reflective Function Multidimensional Rating Scale (Levy, Meehan, and Hill, 2005) is a fifty-three-item questionnaire constructed directly from the *RF Manual* (Fonagy et al., 1998). The items are rated on a Likert-type scale from 1 ("not true at all") to 5 ("very true") (Hill, Levy, Meehan, and Reynoso, 2007). The goal of this instrument is twofold: (1) to provide a measure of the patient's RF in psychotherapy sessions, and (2) to examine a possible multidimensional structure of RF via factor analysis. The authors have applied these items to AAI transcripts to establish convergent validity with the RFS; however, it is clear from the wording of the items that the authors' ultimate goal is to apply their questionnaire to psychotherapy transcripts. Sample items include the following: "The patient makes spontaneous efforts to clarify confusing aspects of his/her narrative in session"; "The patient often acknowledges how his/her perception of an event might have been distorted by what he/she was feeling or thinking at the time"; and "The patient acknowledges that one can be internally experiencing emotions different from what is being overtly displayed (i.e., I felt sad but didn't want to show that to her)" (p. 312). This measure is currently under construction; the authors are working on establishing its validity and reliability. It is not clear whether the measure is designed for use with an entire psychotherapy session or only a portion of it.

Another instrument designed to measure patient RF in psychotherapy sessions is a computerized text analysis measure of RF (CRF; Fertuck, Mergenthaler, Target, and Clarkin, 2004). Still in its infancy, the CRF is derived from earlier work (Mergenthaler and Bucci, 1999) that uses a computer software program to identify fifty-four word markers indicative of RF used by forty-nine interviewees on the AAI. These word markers were then used to identify RF in a second batch of forty-nine AAIs. The authors demonstrated a Spearman-Brown correlation of $r = .63$, $p < .01$, between the CRF and the RFS applied to these same AAIs. The goal is to apply this methodology to psychotherapy transcripts to obtain patient RF. Changes in RF over time can then be documented and used to predict psychotherapy outcomes in other domains or as an outcome itself.

The RFS has been directly applied to psychotherapy transcripts in two process and outcome studies (Karlsson and Kermott, 2006). The *RF Manual* (Fonagy et al., 1998) was modified for use with psychotherapy transcript data: attachment figures mentioned in sessions include not only parents but also other significant persons in patients' current lives such as partners, children, colleagues, and the therapist. The patient also demonstrates an awareness of mental states in relation to the therapist rather than the AAI interviewer. The patient's RF is based on the highest RF score from each session rather than an aggregated RF score, which is the procedure used to code the AAI. The authors reported an interrater reliability of .83 for this procedure. This instrument has the advantage of assessing RF over an entire psychotherapy session; however, RF is known to fluctuate, sometimes dramatically, during a session. Recording the highest RF score over an entire session fails to take into account this natural variation, which might be more pronounced among certain patient populations (e.g., borderline personality disorder).

To correct this potential problem, Josephs and his colleagues (Josephs et al., 2004; Josephs and Fatzer, 2006) applied the RFS to blocks of 150 words in thirty-six psychotherapy transcripts from one patient with interrater reliability of .75. Each block of words receives a score that reflects the highest RF only within that block. As the authors suggested, this methodology also permits researchers to determine the immediate effect of a therapist intervention on the level of RF. These RF scores are then used to reflect changes in the patient's RF over time. In their later work (Josephs and Fatzer, 2006), RF scores were averaged within each session to permit RF to be correlated with other measures that use the entire session as the unit of analysis. Josephs and his colleagues did not report whether these blocks of words were coded in random order to prevent rater bias (i.e., raters' educated guessing that RF would increase over the course of this one treatment). This method of calculating RF might seem more labor-intensive than Karlsson and Kermott's (2006) method, but this more fine-grained analysis increases the amount of information available for assessing RF change, both within and between sessions, and could also increase accuracy and thus interrater reliability. Josephs (personal communication, February 27, 2006) suggested, however, that his method of calculating patient RF could provide "an artificially low estimate of the patients' capacity for mentalization" because most blocks of words typically have low RF or none at all; thus, high RF moments have a relatively small impact on the RF session average.

Still another instrument used to assess mentalization within psychotherapy sessions is the Mentalization and Mindfulness Q-Set (M & M Q-Set; Goodman and Schneider, 2006). The M & M Q-Set consists of fifty items constructed to assess mentalization and fifty items constructed to assess mindfulness within an entire audiotaped or videotaped forty-five-minute psychotherapy session. The fifty Q-sort items designed to assess mentalization were largely inspired by the criteria contained within the *RF Manual* (Fonagy et al., 1998). The Q-sort methodology was used to develop this instrument because of its ease of use and its forced-choice procedure, which forces raters to place items in a normal distribution that uniquely characterizes both the high and low ends of the two constructs under study—two specific processes of therapeutic change often associated with psychoanalytic and cognitive-behavioral treatments. All items are therefore ranked in comparison with each other rather than rated independently of each other, as is the case with Likert-type scaling (see Block, 1978, for additional information regarding Q-sort methodology and procedures). In this forty-five-minute procedure, two raters independently assign scores of 1–9 to all one hundred items. A score of 1 indicates that the item is most uncharacteristic of the session being rated, while a score of 9 indicates that the item is most characteristic of the session being rated. A score of 5 indicates that the item is neither characteristic nor uncharacteristic of the session. A specified number of items is assigned to each score. All one hundred Q-sort items are sorted into nine piles ranging from most uncharacteristic to most characteristic of the psychotherapy session being rated.

With a sufficient number of psychotherapy sessions, this instrument is ideally suited to examining a possible multidimensional structure of RF via factor analysis. Such a factor structure might vary across sessions of one patient or across patients. These factors might also be related to patients' attachment organization. For example, I would hypothesize that dismissing patients might manifest "self-serving" or cognitively based (IIM-c–based) RF, while preoccupied patients might manifest "hyperactive" or affectively based (IIM-a–based) RF (for RF descriptions, see Fonagy et al., 1998, p. 45; see also earlier discussion). These RF factors can also be used to predict differentially both symptom outcome measures such as the Symptom Checklist-90-Revised (SCL-90-R; Derogatis, 1983) and structural outcome measures such as the Social Cognition and Object Relations Scale—Global (SCORS-G; Westen, 1995). This method thus poses an advantage over the one-session, one-score method favored by the other instruments.

The M & M Q-Set can also be used to construct an ideal prototype of RF identified in psychotherapy sessions. Experts widely recognized for their expertise in RF will be asked to sort the M & M Q-Set items according to the RF that occurs within a prototypical psychotherapy session. The resulting RF Q-sort distributions will then be composited to form an RF-expert-driven prototypical Q-sort distribution that reflects the ideal RF manifested by a patient in a psychotherapy session. Correlations between the M & M Q-sort of each psychotherapy session and the prototypical RF Q-sort distribution comprised of the RF experts reflect the extent to which the RF manifested by a patient measures up to the ideal RF in a psychotherapy session. These adherence correlations can then be treated as scores used to predict outcome measures or track changes in the quality of RF over time. The M & M Q-Set is currently under construction; its authors are working on establishing its validity and reliability.

The final instrument designed to assess patient RF in psychotherapy sessions is the patient-therapist Adult Attachment Interview (PT-AAI; Diamond, Clarkin, et al., 2003; Diamond, Stovall-McClough, et al., 2003), formerly known as the patient-therapist relationship interview (Diamond et al., 1999). Reviewed in chapter 5 of Goodman (in press), the PT-AAI assesses not only the patient's state of mind but also the therapist's state of mind with respect to attachment to the other member of the therapeutic dyad (Diamond, Stovall-McClough, et al., 2003). The *RF Manual* (Fonagy et al., 1998) is directly applied to the PT-AAI transcript. Each PT-AAI transcript receives one RF score from the eleven-point RFS used to code the AAI. interrater and test-retest reliabilities of RF scores were not reported.

This instrument has the advantage of assessing not only the patient's RF but also the therapist's RF in a psychotherapy session. The putative mutual influence of the therapist's and patient's mentalization in the session could be tested with this instrument. Although the instrument seems conceptually flawed in its assessment of the therapist's attachment to the patient (see Goodman, in press, chapter 5), therapist RF could nevertheless be assessed in this situation and be shown to vary across sessions and across patients (Diamond, Stovall-McClough, et al., 2003). That mentalization is assessed "offline"—that is, when the patient and therapist are not actively involved with each other—could represent a disadvantage similar to that discussed in relation to the PDI because the PT-AAI also seems to be accessing declarative symbolic knowledge susceptible to secondary elaboration rather than relational procedural knowledge expressed "in the heat of battle."

Only research studies that use both methods of assessing RF—both in interaction with and not in interaction with the emotionally significant other (e.g., parent, child, therapist, patient) will determine which method is more accurate in predicting outcomes of interest. Perhaps these two methods measure qualitatively different characteristics of RF that relate to qualitatively different outcome domains. Following Fonagy and his colleagues' (Fonagy, Gergely, et al., 2002) hypothesis of the IIM-a and IIM-c—the brain structures responsible for mentalization—perhaps online measures of RF tend to access IIM-a functioning, while offline measures of RF tend to access IIM-c functioning. A comprehensive assessment of RF might need to include both online and offline measures so that deficits in one or the other domains of IIM can be identified and ameliorated through specifically tailored psychotherapy treatment programs.

Perhaps cognitive-behavioral treatments work better for some patients than psychodynamic treatments because these patients have deficits in IIM-c functioning, while psychodynamic treatments work better for other patients than cognitive-behavioral treatments because these patients have deficits in IIM-a functioning. We already know that the findings of at least one study (Ablon and Jones, 1998) suggest that the effectiveness of cognitive-behavioral treatment depends on the "unlicensed" psychodynamic interventions made by the cognitive-behavioral therapists. Perhaps these unlicensed interventions assist patients in mentalizing the relational procedural (i.e., IIM-a) aspects of their mentalization of relationships. Until studies that test these hypotheses are conducted, however, the operationalization of mentalization remains incomplete.

EMPIRICAL DATA RELATED TO MENTALIZATION

I want to provide the reader with a brief overview of the major research studies published on the correlates of mentalization. I will pay particular attention to research findings related to the RFS constructed by Fonagy and his colleagues (Fonagy et al., 1998) as well as the research findings related to the two groups of instruments I reviewed earlier that assess mentalization in contexts other than the AAI. I want to demonstrate how these assessment instruments are being used to address developmental and clinical questions of relevance to transforming the internal world and attachment.

Fonagy and his colleagues (Fonagy, Steele, and Steele, 1991) published their first research findings on RF in a sample of one hundred mothers and one hundred fathers as part of the London Parent-Child Project, whose primary objective was to establish the predictive validity of parental attachment (assessed by the AAI) on infant attachment (assessed by the Strange Situation) by assessing parental attachment prior to the infant's birth. In the process of achieving this objective, these researchers coded the parents' AAIs for RF (then known as reflective-self function) and found that RF was significantly higher among mothers and fathers independently rated secure on the AAI than dismissing and preoccupied mothers and fathers—independent of socioeconomic status, ethnicity, educational level, and verbal intelligence. Among the seventeen nine-point rating scales that comprise the AAI coding system (Main and Goldwyn, 1994), coherence of transcript was most highly correlated with RF (mothers: $r = .73$; fathers: $r = .64$). In other words, those parents who were able to reflect on their own experiences with their parents and demonstrate an understanding of their own mental states, their parents' mental states, and the relations between them tended to provide the most coherent interviews. In addition, mothers' RF and fathers' RF were significantly associated with infant attachment security assessed at twelve months ($r = .51$ with mother) and eighteen months ($r = .36$ with father). Maternal RF was also significantly correlated with two rating scales used in infant attachment classification—proximity-seeking ($r = .26$) and contact-maintenance ($r = .30$). Thus, the construct of mentalization was shown to have predictive validity.

A factor analysis of these two hundred AAIs yielded six factors. On the coherence factor, RF loaded higher than on any other AAI rating scale, including coherence of mind (.91 vs. .77) and coherence of transcript (.91 vs. .67). In addition, a stepwise multiple regression equation revealed that RF accounted for 86 percent of the variance in the coherence factor, while coherence of transcript accounted for only 6 percent, and insistence upon lack of recall only 5 percent (Fonagy et al., 1998). The authors concluded: "Ratings on RF were consistently the strongest contributors to judges' assessment of [adult] attachment security, and accounted for more than half of the variance in the secure/insecure distinction" (p. 11). Further analysis revealed that all the mothers who had experienced deprivation in their childhood histories had securely attached infants when they were rated as having high RF (greater than 6), whereas only 6 percent of deprived mothers had securely attached infants when they were rated as having low RF (less than 4). The capacity for mentalization, as operationalized by the RFS, appears to have protected these high-risk mothers from allowing their childhood histories to influence their infant caregiving in an adverse manner (Fonagy et al., 1994).

In a later study of eighty-five psychiatric inpatients at Cassel Hospital in London (Fonagy et al., 1996; Fonagy et al., 1995), the authors reported that physical or sexual abuse was associated with a diagnosis of borderline personality disorder (BPD)—but only among those BPD inpatients who were categorized as having low RF (less than or equal to 3). In fact, 97 percent of inpatients who had reported abuse in the low RF group were diagnosed with BPD, while only 17 percent who had reported abuse in the high RF group (greater than 3) were so diagnosed. These findings suggest that RF protected the abused persons from manifesting borderline symptoms. In other words, these inpatients were able to mentalize their abusive experiences and thus avoid becoming symptomatic. Finally, 64 percent of adult male prison inmates were rated as having low RF (less than 4), while only 23 percent of adult male psychiatric inpatients were so rated (Fonagy, Gergely, et al., 2002; Fonagy et al., 1998). These findings demonstrate that high mentalization protects persons from developing severe criminality, while low mentalization facilitates it.

Previously, I also reviewed instruments that operationalize caregivers' mentalization in relation to their children: maternal mentalistic attributes, measured in a description of a three-year-old child (Meins et al., 1998); maternal mind-mindedness, measured in a free-play situation with a six-month-old infant (Meins et al., 2001); the insightfulness assessment (IA), measured in an interview while the caregiver watches a videotape of him or herself interacting in either a free-play episode with an infant or building a house together with a young child (Oppenheim and Koren-Karie, 2002); and the parent development interview (PDI), measured in an interview about a child of unspecified age (Aber et al., 1985; Slade, 2005). What were the authors' major findings using these instruments?

Regarding maternal mentalistic attributes, mothers of securely attached infants were more likely to use mentalistic attributes to describe their three-year-old children than mothers of insecurely attached infants. Mentalistic attributes also influenced their five-year-old children's developing mentalizing abilities (Meins et al., 1998). In their later work (Meins et al., 2001; Meins et al., 2003; Meins et al., 2002), appropriate mind-related comments was the only one of five indices of mind-mindedness that significantly predicted infant attachment security, even after controlling for maternal sensitivity. Further, maternal sensitivity and mind-mindedness were found to characterize related but distinct aspects of infant-mother interaction. Construct stability was confirmed by correlating mothers' scores at six months with their scores at forty-eight months in an interview in which they used mentalistic attributes. In spite of the conceptual criticisms leveled against this construct and the procedure for measuring it (Fonagy and Target, 2005a; Slade, 2005), mind-mindedness was shown to have predictive validity and stability over three and a half years.

Regarding maternal insightfulness, positively insightful (PI) mothers tended to have securely attached infants, while one-sided (Os) mothers tended to have anxious-resistant infants, and mixed (Mx) mothers disorganized infants (Koren-Karie, Oppenheim, Dolev, Sher, and Etzion-Carasso, 2002; Oppenheim and Koren-Karie, 2002). These classifications were also unrelated to maternal vocabulary and educational level. PI mothers were also found to be more sensitive in their interactions with their infants than mothers from the other categories were. Finally, mothers of clinically referred preschoolers who received intervention to increase their levels of insightfulness showed improvements over six months, which coincided with improvements in their children's internalizing and externalizing behaviors—but only for children of PI mothers (Oppenheim, Koren-Karie, and Sagi, 2001). Like mind-mindedness, insightfulness is linked with infant attachment security. Interestingly, this research group also examined the relations between their construct and all four patterns of infant attachment rather than dichotomizing the data into secure and insecure categories as the previous research group had done. This research therefore suggests different subtypes of mentalization associated with different attachment patterns, first proposed by Slade and her colleagues (Slade, Grienenberger, et al., 2005).

Turning now to maternal RF measured by the PDI, prenatally assessed maternal attachment was associated with maternal RF, assessed when the infant was ten months old (Slade, Grienenberger, et al., 2005), thus establishing the PDI's postdictive validity. Securely attached mothers tended to have higher levels of maternal RF than mothers classified in the other three attachment categories. Maternal RF was also associated with infant attachment quality assessed at fourteen months, with securely attached infants tending to have mothers with higher levels of maternal RF than anxious-resistant and disorganized infants (but not anxious-avoidant infants). This research group also presented preliminary evidence for maternal RF as mediating the relation between maternal attachment and infant attachment. The authors noted that the correlation between maternal RF and infant attachment ($r = .41$) exceeds that between maternal sensitivity and infant attachment ($r = .32$) reported in van IJzendoorn's (1995) often-cited meta-analysis of the relation between maternal sensitivity and infant attachment. In addition, the correlation between maternal RF and maternal attachment ($r = .51$) also exceeds that between maternal sensitivity and maternal attachment ($r = .34$) also reported in van IJzendoorn's (1995) meta-analysis. Based on this weakness of caregiver sensitivity in serving as a mediator, van IJzendoorn (1995) identified an intergenerational transmission gap in which "[caregiver] sensitivity has lost its privileged position as the only important causal factor" (De Wolff and van IJzendoorn, 1997, p. 583) in determining infant attachment security. Slade and her colleagues (Slade, Grienenberger, et al., 2005) have claimed that maternal RF rather than maternal sensitivity might account for the transmission gap that had baffled attachment researchers for ten years.

Slade and her colleagues (Grienenberger et al., 2005) also examined the relations between maternal RF and maternal behavior characterized by frightened or frightening behavior expressed by mothers toward their infants in the "strange situation." Main and Hesse (1990) had originally hypothesized that these maternal behaviors were responsible for infant attachment disorganization, which was later supported empirically (Hesse and Main, 1999; Lyons-Ruth, Bronfman, and Parsons, 1999; Schuengel et al., 1999). Using the atypical maternal behavior instrument for assessment and classification (AMBIANCE; Bronfman, Parsons, and Lyons-Ruth, 1999), Slade and her colleagues (Grienenberger et al., 2005) found that maternal RF was negatively correlated with the overall level of disrupted maternal communication as measured by the AMBIANCE ($r = -.48$). This finding demonstrates that maternal mentalization strongly influences caregiving behaviors in separation-reunion situations—the crucible where internal working models are formed (Bowlby, 1973). In addition, the overall level of disrupted maternal communication was found to mediate the relation between maternal RF and infant attachment security. Thus, this research group seems to be proposing a pathways model of development in which the maternal internal working model influences maternal mentalization, which in turn influences maternal behaviors directed toward the infant, which in turn influences infant attachment security (for an attachment-based model of intervention loosely based on this model of intergenerational transmission, see volume II, chapter 7).

In a high-risk sample, cocaine-abusing pregnant women had lower PDI-derived RF scores than their nonabusing counterparts matched on other key dimensions of risk (Truman, Levy, and Mayes, in press). At time 2, maternal RF was also negatively correlated with parent distress, parent-child dysfunction, and child withdrawal and positively correlated with child attention, social skills, and adaptability. Maternal RF also mediated the effects of maternal cocaine abuse on child social skills, parent distress, and parent-child dysfunction. Thus, evidence of maternal RF's contribution to key domains of children's socioemotional development goes beyond low-risk populations.

Taken as a whole, these four research groups (Fonagy, Meins, Oppenheim, and Slade) have established mentalization as a critical aspect of mental functioning whose relative presence or absence can profoundly influence a person's severity of psychopathology. Furthermore, mentalization also profoundly affects caregiving responses during critical moments of infant and child development (e.g., separation-reunion situations) and both indirectly and directly influences infant attachment security and later mentalizing abilities in children up to age five. These early findings not only underscore the presence of mentalization as a buffer against psychopathology and its absence as a risk factor for psychopathology, but also suggest points of intervention in psychotherapy that might produce therapeutic change.

The second group of instruments designed to operationalize mentalization captures patient or therapist RF in psychotherapy sessions. Fonagy, whose RFS (Fonagy et al., 1998) is now widely used to assess mentalization, has developed mentalization-based treatment (MBT), a manualized psychotherapy approach to treating borderline personality disorder that enhances mentalization (Bateman and Fonagy, 2004a, 2004b). These authors nevertheless acknowledged that "we were unable to show that the target of our interventions, mentalization, had been enhanced in patients treated within the PH [partial hospital] program, compared with control patients" (Bateman and Fonagy, 2004a, p. 38). The authors suggested that they would assess mentalization in future treatment outcome studies. It is likely that they would use pre- and post-AAI administrations to measure RF change over the course of treatment rather than use an *in vivo* RF measure that would assess psychotherapy transcript data.

The reflective function multidimensional rating scale (Levy, Wasserman, et al., 2006) has never been empirically validated; however, Levy and his colleagues (Levy, Meehan, et al., 2006) did use the RFS to assess the outcome of patients treated with one year of transference focused psychotherapy (TFP; Clarkin et al., 1999). The RF of patients treated in twice-weekly TFP significantly improved over the course of one year from a mean of 2.86 to a mean of 4.11, while the RF of patients treated in two other manualized treatments (dialectical behavior therapy and supportive-psychodynamic therapy) did not improve over one year of treatment. In spite of the fact that TFP, unlike MBT, was not designed to enhance mentalization but rather to integrate split-off self- and object representations (Clarkin et al., 1999), it is puzzling that the authors would assess therapeutic change using the RFS rather than an instrument better suited to assessing the quality of self- and object representations (e.g., Blatt et al., 1992; Westen, 1995). In their discussion of the observed RF change, Levy and his colleagues (Levy, Meehan, et al., 2006) concluded, "We conceptualized [RF and attachment organization] as putative mechanisms of change," which they had done "on the basis of prior theorizing" (p. 1035). That TFP produced RF change, when it was never conceptualized to accomplish such change (Clarkin et al., 1999), suggests that perhaps most psychodynamic therapies share RF-changing properties as an effective therapeutic ingredient—a potential common factor recently suggested by Bateman and Fonagy (2004a): "The potential effectiveness of all treatments depends . . . on their ability to increase a patient's capacity to mentalize" (p. 46). Thus, the TFP study provides initial evidence that one's mentalization ability can actually change in psychotherapy (regardless of what that therapy purports to change).

The second instrument designed to measure patient RF in psychotherapy sessions, the CRF, has not been empirically validated yet; however, as I already reported, Fertuck and his colleagues (Fertuck et al., 2004) have taken the initial step by correlating their word-marker-derived RF with the RFS applied to forty-nine transcribed AAIs. The authors intend to assess RF in psychotherapy sessions using the CRF in the future.

The RFS has been directly applied to psychotherapy transcripts in two process and outcome studies (Karlsson and Kermott, 2006). In the first study, cognitive-behavioral therapy (CBT) was compared with interpersonal therapy (IPT) near the beginning of treatment (session 4) and near the end (session 12). At session 4, IPT patients had higher RF than CBT patients, but this significant difference vanished by session 12. Patients in both treatment groups unexpectedly experienced a decrease in RF from session 4 to session 12. RF was also correlated with aspects of psychotherapy process identified by the Psychotherapy Process Q-Set (PQS; Jones, 2000). The process most positively correlated with RF and successful outcome (as measured by symptom improvement) included high patient commitment, the acquisition of insight into his or her problems, the therapist's empathy with and containment of unacceptable feelings, and the therapist's awareness of the patient's experience. On the other hand, the process most negatively correlated with RF and successful outcome included high patient passivity and suspiciousness of the therapist, therapist overcontrol, characteristic rejection of the therapist's comments, and the patient's lack of feeling understood.

In the second study, thirty patients receiving brief psychodynamic psychotherapy (BPDT) were assessed for RF near the beginning of treatment (session 1), middle of treatment (session 5), and near the end (session 14). Unexpectedly, RF did not change for these patients over the fourteen sessions examined. As in the first study, RF was also correlated with aspects of psychotherapy process identified by the PQS. The process most positively correlated with RF and successful outcome (as measured by symptom improvement) included discussion of interpersonal relationships and the patient's active exploration and expression of angry feelings. The process most negatively correlated with RF and successful outcome included high patient passivity and resistance to exploration of mental states related to problems. The authors explained the lack of RF change by pointing to the supportive, structured nature of all three treatments (Karlsson and Kermott, 2006, pp. 78, 79).

I would add that it takes an enormous level of trust to engage in the mentalizing process of exploring the mental states in one's own mind as well as the mind of the other person. Bateman and Fonagy (2004a) have similarly underscored the importance of feeling understood in MBT: "The experience of being understood generates an experience of security, which facilitates 'mental exploration,' the exploration of the mind of the other to find oneself therein" (p. 47). In any fifteen- to twenty-session course of treatment, regardless of whether the therapist uses supportive techniques, the patient is not going to have spent enough time with the therapist to have developed an attachment to him or her to permit unfettered mental exploration (see Goodman, in press, chapter 3). Just as the exploratory system is deactivated when a stranger is present in the Strange Situation (Ainsworth et al., 1978), so too is the exploration of one's mental apparatus deactivated in the presence of a stranger—in this case, the therapist.

In chapter 3 of Goodman (in press), I argue that attachment to the therapist is formed after many experiences in which the therapist has seen the patient through periods of distress when the attachment system has been activated. Only after a secure attachment has formed can a patient meaningfully explore the mental contents of his or her mind. As Karlsson and Kermott (2006) suggested, supportive techniques might partially account for the lack of RF improvement manifested in these treatments; however, the patient's knowledge of these treatments' time-limited nature probably also constrained RF development. The awareness of an impending early termination prevented a secure attachment to the therapist from forming, thus also limiting the patient's sense of freedom to explore the mental states in his or her own mind and the mind of the therapist. This restriction in mental exploration would necessarily limit RF development.

As I have already mentioned, Levy and his colleagues (Levy, Meehan, et al., 2006) have already demonstrated RF improvement using the RFS over the course of one year of TFP. In this study, the other two treatment approaches—DBT and SPT—did not produce RF change in spite of the fact that these treatments also lasted one year. Perhaps an interpretive, nonsupportive approach and treatment duration lasting a year or longer are necessary but not sufficient conditions for RF change to occur. Furthermore, perhaps treatment duration moderates the relation between theoretical approach and RF change. In other words, RF change occurs only in psychodynamically oriented treatments (e.g., MBT, TFP), but only of considerable duration (e.g., one year). This hypothesis, of course, awaits empirical testing. I am currently coding RF in TFP sessions with BPD patients over a shorter course of treatment (i.e., six months) to determine whether TFP can enhance RF in less time. If mentalization is indeed the secret sauce of all effective treatments, then we must determine how much secret sauce is needed and for how long to produce the desired effect—RF change.

The RFS has also been directly applied to thirty-six psychotherapy transcripts of a single case (Josephs et al., 2004; Josephs and Fatzer, 2006). As described earlier, each transcript was divided into blocks of 150 words, which were then coded for RF. The highest RF score within each block of words was averaged together with all the other highest RF scores to yield an average RF score for each session. In their first study (Josephs et al., 2004), mentalization, as measured by the RF score of each block of words, was positively correlated with time (as measured by the chronological order of blocks from session 1 to session 36; $r = .52$). This patient's RF improved significantly over the course of treatment. In this same study, RF scores were averaged over each week of three sessions, which yielded twelve RF scores (one score for each week of treatment). These RF scores were then correlated with scores on the Shedler-Westen Assessment Procedure–200 (SWAP-200; Shedler, 2002; Shedler and Westen, 1998; Westen and Shedler, 1999a, 1999b, 2000)—an instrument that quantitatively describes a person's diagnostic profile. SWAP-200 profiles were compiled for each of the twelve weeks; thus, each profile was based on three sessions. RF was positively correlated with high-functioning depressive ($r = .74$) and obsessional ($r = .55$) and negatively correlated with emotionally dysregulated dysphoric ($r = -.64$) and hostile externalizing dysphoric ($r = -.68$). The authors explained that high-functioning depressives and obsessionals score high on SWAP-200 items that one would expect to be conceptually related to mentalization such as humor, empathy, ability to perceive alternative perspectives, psychological insightfulness, and articulateness. Of course, emotional dysregulation and hostile externalization would represent an anti-mentalizing position.

In their second study (Josephs and Fatzer, 2006), RF was associated with the PQS (Jones, 2000), applied to all thirty-six psychotherapy transcripts. Rather than correlating all one hundred PQS items with the RFS as Karlsson and Kermott (2006) had done, Josephs and Fatzer (2006) instead conducted a factor analysis on the thirty-six PQS Q-sorts, which yielded five factors: (1) supportive defense analysis of an insightful but passive patient; (2) the supportive environment; (3) exploring feelings; (4) supporting while presenting a different perspective to a committed but provocative, angry, self-accusatory, and sad patient; and (5) angry patient, rejecting analyst. Of these five factors, only factor 4 was positively correlated with time ($r = .57$). RF scores for each session were then correlated with the five factor scores for each session to determine whether changes in interaction structures varied with RF. RF was positively correlated with both factor 1 ($r = .29$) and factor 4 ($r = .44$), suggesting that these two interaction structures supported the development of RF. Finally, a time-series analysis (Gottman, 1981) was conducted to determine whether changes in RF were predicting changes in interaction structures two sessions later or whether changes in interaction structures were predicting changes in RF two sessions later. Factor 4 predicted very significant changes in RF two sessions later ($r = .47$), but RF predicted only significant changes in factor 4 two sessions later ($r = .35$). Thus, the therapist's supporting while presenting a different perspective was identified as the primary causal agent in determining the most significant increases in mentalization. These results provide some tantalizing preliminary clues regarding the kinds of therapist interventions necessary to enhance a patient's mentalization over the course of treatment.

The RFS-inspired M & M Q-Set (Goodman and Schneider, 2006) will be used to assess the levels of mentalization and mindfulness observed in each session in a sample of five psychiatric inpatients diagnosed with BPD over the first six months of TFP. First, two groups of four experts who have helped to define the mentalization and mindfulness constructs in the literature will be selected to sort the M & M Q-Set to capture the prototypically mentalizing or mindful patient in a typical psychotherapy session from their theoretical perspective (see earlier discussion). Second, each of the session M & M Q-sorts will be correlated with each of the two resulting prototypical (criterion) Q-sorts, which will yield two adherence correlations associated with each session—a mentalization adherence correlation and a mindfulness adherence correlation. Third, the resulting adherence correlation scores of each session will be correlated with the weekly SCL-90-R (Derogatis, 1983) global symptom index (GSI) scores to determine which of the two sets of scores produced the most global symptomatic change over the course of treatment among each of the five patients.

Fourth, a P-technique (Luborsky, 1953, 1995) factor analysis will be conducted on the M & M Q-sorts that will yield factors of mentalization and mindfulness associated with these five treatments. Fifth, the resulting mentalization and mindfulness factor scores associated with each session will be correlated with the weekly GSI scores to determine which factors produced the most global symptomatic change over the course of treatment among each of the five patients. Sixth, a time-series analysis (Gottman, 1981) of the treatment course of each of these five patients will be conducted to determine (1) whether the adherence correlation scores and weekly GSI scores are predictive of each other and (2) whether the mentalization and mindfulness factors and weekly GSI scores are also predictive of each other. Finally, we also want to examine the correlations between these factors and the PQS Q-sort items across all sessions (see Josephs et al., 2004; Josephs and Fatzer, 2006; Karlsson and Kermott, 2006).

Taken together, these findings would help us to make conceptual comparisons between mentalization and mindfulness, identify factors of these two constructs, determine the relations between these two constructs and symptom change, establish the causal direction of these relations, and explore the relations between these two constructs and the psychotherapy process. We expect this effort to take us further toward understanding the therapeutic ingredients that enhance specific mentalization factors that ultimately produce symptom change in a sample of BPD inpatients.

The AAI and PT-AAI (Diamond et al., 1999; Diamond, Clarkin, et al., 2003; Diamond, Stovall-McClough, et al., 2003; see Goodman, in press, chapter 5) were used to assess patient RF in these two different interview contexts. The AAI was administered to ten patients at four and twelve months, while the PT-AAI was administered to ten patients and seven therapists of these patients only at twelve months (Diamond, Stovall-McClough, et al., 2003). On the AAI, the ten patients who participated in the twelve-month TFP demonstrated a mean RF change of 1.05 (M = 4.3 at twelve months), while the thirty-one patients in the twelve-month TFP condition reported on by Levy and his colleagues (Levy, Meehan, et al., 2006) demonstrated a mean RF change of 1.25 (M = 4.11 at time 2; oddly, time 1 and time 2 were not defined in this study). On the PT-AAI at twelve months, the ten patients in twelve-month TFP demonstrated a mean RF of 3.9, while the seven therapists demonstrated a mean RF of 5.8 (Diamond, Stovall-McClough, et al., 2003). The patients' AAI RF scores at four months were significantly positively correlated with their scores at twelve months (r = .93) and significantly different from each other (paired-samples $t(9)$ = -4.85, p = .001). In addition, the patients' AAI RF scores at twelve months were marginally significantly positively correlated with their PT-AAI RF scores at twelve months (r = .63) and not significantly different from each other (paired-samples $t(9)$ = .98, p = .35). These data suggest (1) that TFP can significantly increase a BPD patient's mentalizing ability over time with respect to parents and (2) that patient RF tends to remain stable across concurrently conducted interviews with respect to different attachment figures (i.e., parents and therapist).

The patients' and therapists' RF scores on the PT-AAI at twelve months were not significantly positively correlated (r = .11) and were significantly different from each other (paired-samples $t(9)$ = −3.35, p = .009). These findings indicate that the RF used by patients to describe the relationship with the therapist does not vary with and is significantly lower than the RF used by therapists to describe their relationship with the patient. Finally, this study also illustrates that one therapist can demonstrate a wide range of RF (range = four points) across concurrently conducted PT-AAIs with respect to three different patients. Therapists' interactions with their patients can enhance or inhibit their mentalizing abilities, depending on the patient relationship under discussion, yet the mentalizing abilities of both members of the therapeutic dyad are not lawfully in synchrony with each other. In chapter 5 of Goodman (in press), I suggest that therapists summon a highly sophisticated and complex RF to protect themselves from feeling overwhelmed by the mental contents of their patients' traumatic experiences reported in therapy. This phenomenon boosts therapists' RF used to describe their relationships with these patients to protect themselves from feeling so overwhelmed (see my discussion of these data in Goodman, in press, chapter 5).

Finally, Slade and her colleagues (Slade, Sadler, and Mayes, 2005) used the PDI to assess RF improvement in a weekly home-based intervention program for mothers of high-risk infants. The PDI was administered during the fifth month of pregnancy and when the infant was fourteen months old. The Strange Situation was also administered at fourteen months. Preliminary findings after eighteen months of intervention on six mother-infant dyads suggest that this intervention boosts maternal RF and protects infants from attachment disorganization. Mothers also reported lower levels of depressive symptoms and posttraumatic stress symptoms and higher levels of self-efficacy.

PROBLEMS WITH THE CONSTRUCT OF MENTALIZATION

In spite of the sound theoretical basis of mentalization, its creative operationalization, and the impressive empirical data marshaled to demonstrate its association with attachment quality, its intergenerational transmission, and its improvement in psychotherapy, problems with the construct nevertheless exist. I want to highlight several of them here. In spite of these problems, I nevertheless believe that mentalization has the potential of assuming the lofty position of the primary catalyst of therapeutic change across "all treatments" (Bateman and Fonagy, 2004a, p. 46). Many empirical studies across a variety of treatment approaches need to be conducted before the coronation ceremony is scheduled, however.

The first problem is that the developmental pathway of mentalization is unsettled. Earlier, I proposed four different developmental pathways of mentalization (see figure 6.1). If mentalization develops directly through pretend play, conversations, and peer group interactions and only indirectly through early caregiver-infant interactions (Fonagy, Gergely, et al., 2002; Fonagy and Target, 1997), then mentalization as a construct becomes more generalized to a wide variety of contexts and interpersonal situations. In this view, mentalization develops during moments when the attachment system is essentially deactivated. Mentalization, however, is also used to regulate unpleasant affects and thus develops specifically in the context of distress when the attachment system is essentially activated. Perhaps mentalization develops in both contexts (see part d of figure 6.1), with early caregiver-infant interactions making both indirect and direct contributions. The symbolization of affects, thoughts, wishes, and behaviors is obviously crucial to the development of mentalization. Symbolization of these mental phenomena can take place in a variety of contexts, both in distress (such as a caregiver telling the child she is leaving him briefly and returning) and in low-key conversations with peers (such as one peer telling another to share a toy or he will not play with him). Do different categories of mentalization develop out of these different contexts? Do these different contexts differentially contribute to an IIM-a–based mentalization and an IIM-c–based mentalization? Which one of these categories of mentalization is most important for overall psychological functioning?

Related to this problem, mentalization is defined by Fonagy and his colleagues (Fonagy, Gergely, et al., 2002; Fonagy et al, 1998) as "an automatic procedure, unconsciously invoked in interpreting human action" (Fonagy, Gergely, et al., 2002, p. 27). Procedural knowledge of minds rather than declarative self knowledge is "the defining feature" (Fonagy et al., 1998, p. 8). Yet Allen (2003) has suggested that people engage in both explicit (declarative) and implicit (procedural) mentalization. Bateman and Fonagy (2004a) have defined psychotherapy as "an integrative process where implicit and explicit mentalization are brought together" (p. 48). How this integration takes place in psychotherapy, however, has not been clearly articulated. Having read Bateman and Fonagy's (2004b) manual on how to conduct mentalization-based treatment (MBT) and having attended their MBT workshop (Bateman and Fonagy, 2006), I formed an overall impression that this treatment helps patients build explicit, cognitively based mentalization skills. Bateman and Fonagy (2004b) even underscored MBT's "emphasis on cognitive processes in the here-and-now . . . that bridges traditional cognitive and psychoanalytic techniques" (p. vii). Obviously, skill-building does not require highly trained psychoanalysts who have been through their own personal analysis. Indeed, MBT can be "implemented by mental health professionals without full psychotherapy training" (Bateman and Fonagy, 2004a, p. 37). I understand how skill-building might develop one's ability to engage in explicit mentalization, but it is not clear how implicit mentalization is attended to and enhanced using this treatment approach.

Enhancing explicit mentalization at the expense of implicit mentalization could produce a décalage, or unevenness, in overall mentalization ability that could allow some persons to engage in antisocial behavior toward others: they now have a cognitive awareness of the minds of others without the emotional awareness, or empathy, that should accompany it. This distinction between the ability to interpret the cognitions and affect states of self and others "might help to explain why narcissistic PDs and psychopaths may have a high level of RF as measured on the AAI, while not being in touch with their own or others' emotions" (Bateman and Fonagy, 2004b, p. 75). Thus, psychotherapy must address both levels of mentalization to be truly effective.

Perhaps treatment approaches that emphasize only one kind of mentalization could nevertheless help patients with mentalization deficits in that area.

For example, the mentalization skill-building of MBT could help patients with focal deficits in explicit, cognitively based mentalization skills. It is not surprising that MBT has been shown to help patients with borderline personality disorder—persons whose weak psychic structures easily permit affect dysregulation. Building explicit, cognitively based mentalization skills could serve to modulate dysregulated affects through cognitive understanding of the mental states of self and others. In addition, perhaps Rosenzweig's (1936) common factor referred to as the interdependence of aspects of the patient's personality (see chapter 3)—that a therapeutic intervention targeting one personality domain reverberates in other domains—applies here: targeting explicit mentalization also enhances the development of implicit mentalization. Research is needed to establish evidence of therapeutic change across mentalization domains when only one domain is targeted.

In contrast to MBT, the intersubjective and relational schools of psychoanalysis seem to focus on the patient's implicit, affectively based mentalization skills. For example, the Boston Process of Change Study Group (Stern et al., 1998) has defined "moment of meeting" (p. 906) as the point in a therapy session where the patient and therapist subjectively experience "a sudden shift in *implicit relational knowing*" (italics in original, p. 906). This group emphasizes the mutual regulation of state between the two members of the dyad over the conscious, verbally symbolized thinking about mental states characteristic of explicit mentalization. Fonagy (1998) commented that a therapeutic emphasis on implicit mentalization over explicit mentalization (the domain of more traditional psychotherapies) should inspire "technical innovation" rather than "the exact same technical priorities that were drawn up on the basis of traditional object relations theory" (p. 351) used to enhance explicit mentalization. Donnel Stern (D. Stern, 2006) has suggested that there is no intersubjective-free sphere of the mind, just as there is no conflict-free sphere of Hartmann's (1950) ego. New perceptions emerge spontaneously in both participants of the therapy relationship without "expert" knowledge coming from the therapist. These new perceptions, in turn, produce enhanced mentalization capacities, not the other way around, as Fonagy and Target have suggested (D. Stern, 2006). I would like to suggest that, for some patients, a focus on implicit mentalization is necessary to move the therapy process along, while for other patients, a focus on explicit mentalization is necessary. The days of one-size-fits-all treatments are over.

Another problem with the construct of mentalization, as I understand it, is the ecological validity of its operationalization. In other words, in which interpersonal contexts is mentalization validly assessed? Earlier, I reviewed all the current measures of mentalization and found that mentalization is typically measured in one of two contexts: (1) in an interview where the interviewee can reflect on the nature of the relationship (e.g., AAI, PDI), and (2) in an interactional setting where the subject is interacting with another person (e.g., mind-mindedness measure, M & M Q-Set). Fonagy and Target (2005a) have argued that mentalization assessed in an interview would provide "greater accuracy of prediction" (p. 336) than mentalization assessed *in vivo* because an interview would aggregate the subject's "many hundreds of interactions" (p. 336) with the mentalized object—ostensibly a more stable measure of mentalization than an *in vivo* measure that relies on just one interaction.

This reasoning is flawed, however, because comparing these two contexts is like comparing apples and zucchinis. If I told you how I think I would respond to the runner approaching my dog and me, do you as the listener have any confidence that I would actually respond to a real runner as I say I would respond? I would rather trust a measure of mentalization that assesses the construct under battlefield conditions than in an interview. Interviewing a police cadet about when to fire his or her firearm in the line of duty might yield different results than putting him or her out on a desolate, dangerous street late at night. Even Bateman and Fonagy (2004b) have admitted that "narcissistic PDs and psychopaths" (p. 75) can fake a high RF score on the AAI. According to Allen (2003), "Mentalizing is quick to collapse in the face of excessive arousal" (p. 101). It follows, then, that the assessment of mentalization under conditions of relatively low arousal such as those experienced in an interview might overestimate the mentalization ability of those persons prone to affect dysregulation in actual, stressful interactions. In the 1987 film *House of Games* directed by David Mamet, the cool, poised sociopath Mike is unexpectedly shot by his conned victim, Margaret. As he is bleeding to death, Mike's cool, calculating façade quickly turns to rage. I wonder whether the high-mentalizing psychopaths referred to by Bateman and Fonagy (2004b) would be as adept at mentalizing under conditions of high arousal.

Perhaps a solution to this measurement problem is to consider the possibility that the two contexts—interview and *in vivo*—assess two different facets of mentalization—explicit, cognitively based mentalization, and implicit, affectively based mentalization. Of course, one might expect some measurement overlap, but each context is ideally suited to measuring only one of them. An interview requires the interviewee to rely on declarative knowledge to symbolize in words the mental states of self and others, while an *in vivo* interaction relies on procedural knowledge that cannot be rehearsed or verbalized. In spite of his support of the interview context for assessing mentalization, Fonagy and his colleagues (Fonagy et al., 1998) have privileged procedural knowledge of minds rather than declarative self knowledge as "the defining feature" (p. 8) of mentalization. Yet a more moderate view—that people engage in both explicit (declarative) and implicit (procedural) mentalization in different contexts that elicit two different facets of mentalization—can account for the predictive accuracy of both groups of measures. Perhaps each measure is differentially accurate in assessing particular mentalization deficits found in particular populations and predicting particular outcomes. Conducting research studies that use both groups of assessments in different contexts and with different populations could provide us with the necessary data with which to test this proposition.

Perhaps it is not surprising that caregiver sensitivity (measured behaviorally) and caregiver mentalization, though significantly correlated with each other ($r = .40$), independently predicted attachment security at twelve months, accounting for 6.5 percent and 12.7 percent of the variance, respectively (Meins et al., 2001). Similarly, caregiver-disrupted affective communication (also measured behaviorally) and caregiver mentalization were significantly correlated with each other ($r = -.48$), accounting for unique amounts of the variance in predicting attachment security at fourteen months (9.2 percent and 4.7 percent, respectively) (Grienenberger et al., 2005). Perhaps these two techniques for measuring the caregiver's ways of understanding and responding to the infant's mental states actually measure these two facets of mentalization—the explicit (symbolically/verbally mediated knowledge) and the implicit (procedurally/behaviorally mediated knowledge). We might expect these two measures to be conceptually overlapping but uniquely predictive of infant outcomes—precisely what these studies found.

Related to the problem of the ecological validity of the operationalization of mentalization, it is not clear whether mentalization is a unidimensional or multidimensional construct. I have suggested that two facets of mentalization exist: (1) an explicit, cognitively based mentalization, associated with declarative symbolic knowledge and localized in the IIM-c (medial prefrontal cortex), and (2) an implicit, affectively based mentalization, associated with relational procedural knowledge and localized in the IIM-a (orbital frontal cortex). Bateman and Fonagy (2004a, p. 48) have suggested that the goal of psychotherapy for BPD patients (and one might consider extending this goal to all patients) is to bring together implicit and explicit mentalization so that implicit mentalization becomes explicit. Their therapeutic goal is reminiscent of Freud's (1917) famous dictum: "To make conscious everything that is pathogenically unconscious" (p. 282). In their therapeutic model, the nonconscious procedural memory becomes explicit and conscious.

On the other hand, Lyons-Ruth (1999) has argued that "retranscription of implicit relational knowing into symbolic knowing is . . . not how developmental change in implicit relational knowing is generally accomplished. . . . Making the unconscious conscious does not adequately describe developmental or psychoanalytic change" (pp. 579, 590). In chapter 3 of Goodman (in press), I argue in favor of the importance of the therapist's nonsymbolic interventions that target the internal working model for therapeutic change. Thus, working to enhance implicit mentalization would involve nonexplicit as well as explicit therapeutic pathways. The assessment of therapeutic change, therefore, might require two different measurement techniques for these two different facets of mentalization (see above).

Another aspect of mentalization one could consider multidimensional is the variety of patterns of verbal or behavioral responses to an assessment of one's understanding of the mental states of self and others and their mutual interaction. Slade (2005, p. 295) already suggested that mentalization might manifest itself in stylistic patterns that correspond to the insecure attachment patterns—dismissing and preoccupied. In the *RF Manual* (Fonagy et al., 1998), illustrations of mentalization can be labeled as disavowed or self-serving (i.e., dismissing), or unintegrated or hyperactive (i.e., preoccupied). Slade (2005) has placed these patterns of poor mentalization on a dimension orthogonal to a high-low RF dimension. This two-dimensional conceptualization of mentalization seems to enhance the richness of data captured by its operationalization. Just as the various insecure attachment patterns have distinct correlates (M. T. Greenberg, 1999; Weinfield et al., 1999), so too might the various patterns of poor mentalization have distinct correlates. Only future research that assesses subjects' mentalization patterns as well as their mentalization scores will be able to test this hypothesis.

CONTEXTUALIZATION OF MENTALIZATION WITHIN A THEORY OF PERSONALITY ORGANIZATION

In this section, I want to integrate the ideas of mentalization developed by Fonagy and his colleagues (Fonagy, Gergely, et al., 2002; Fonagy and Target, 1997) with my own ideas regarding attachment quality and personality organization developed in my first book (Goodman, 2002). In that book, I proposed that Kernberg's (1966, 1967, 1975, 1984, 1986a) theory of borderline personality organization could be used to place Bowlby's (1980) theory of internal working models and their various manifestations of secure and insecure attachment patterns (Ainsworth et al., 1978) within a broadly conceptualized object relations framework. Briefly, dismissing attachment, preoccupied attachment, and unresolved attachment—which comprise the three categories of insecure attachment—belong to the borderline level of personality organization, which exists on a continuum of psychopathology midway between the neurotic and psychotic levels. I am not conflating these three attachment categories with the presence of borderline personality disorder as defined by the *DSM-IV* (APA, 2000) but rather identifying them as risk factors (Rutter, 1985, 1987) of psychopathology that includes both cluster A (paranoid, schizoid, schizotypal) and cluster B (antisocial, borderline, histrionic, narcissistic) personality disorders.

Following Kernberg (1986a, 1986b), I suggested that borderline personality organization is characterized by two modes of functioning. The first mode manifests itself through interpersonal instability related to identity diffusion, split-off self- and object representations, nonspecific ego weaknesses, and defensive processes characterized by splitting, projection, projective identification, and introjection. The second mode manifests itself through superficial interpersonal stability supported by a pathological grandiose self, the condensation of split-off self- and object representations that permits a surface adaptation, and defensive processes characterized by splitting, denial, primitive idealization, derogation, omnipotent control, and narcissistic withdrawal. Though differing in levels of adaptation, both modes of functioning share "the predominance of mechanisms of splitting . . . or split-off ego states" (Kernberg, 1986b, p. 246).

I proposed that (1) the dismissing attachment pattern, characterized by a deactivating secondary attachment strategy of affect overregulation (Kobak et al., 1993), is conceptually related to the second mode of borderline personality functioning, and (2) the preoccupied and unresolved attachment patterns, characterized by a hyperactivating secondary attachment strategy of affect underregulation (Kobak et al., 1993), is conceptually related to the first mode of borderline personality functioning (Goodman, 2002, p. 66). I also proposed that the secure attachment pattern, characterized by a primary attachment strategy of optimal affect regulation, is conceptually related to a neurotic level of personality organization.

Persons classified as having a dismissing state of mind with respect to attachment (Main et al., 1985) tend to deny or minimize the importance of attachment relationships in their lives and often derogate the very meaning of being attached to someone. Similarly, persons characterized by a pathological grandiose self (the second mode of borderline personality functioning) demonstrate an inability "to depend on anybody because of their deep distrust and depreciation of others" (Kernberg, 1986a, p. 292) and, consequently, "a persistent absence of separation anxiety or mourning reactions at weekends, vacation, or illness of the analyst" (Kernberg, 1986b, p. 255). Diagnostically, Kernberg (1986a) associated the pathological grandiose self—the first mode of borderline personality functioning—with the narcissistic and antisocial personality disorders ("a subgroup of the narcissistic personality" [p. 292]), and the first mode of borderline personality functioning with the borderline, paranoid, and histrionic personality disorders. Kernberg (1986b) explained this diagnostic distinction:

> The absence of the capacity to depend upon others on the part of narcissistic personalities, in contrast to the clinging dependency and persistent capacity for a broad spectrum of object relations in borderline patients, contributes fundamentally to the differential diagnosis of narcissistic personalities functioning on an overt borderline level [of personality organization] from usual borderline patients. (pp. 255, 256)

The obvious attachment metaphor for these two modes of borderline personality functioning is the Strange Situation (Ainsworth et al., 1978). The anxious-avoidant infant (the analogue of the dismissing adult) snubs the caregiver on reunion and behaves as if he or she did not exist, while the anxious-resistant infant (the analogue of the preoccupied adult) clings to the caregiver even before separation and ambivalently oscillates between clinging to the caregiver and resisting contact with him or her on reunion.

Kernberg and his colleagues (Kernberg et al., 1989) and Mahler and her colleagues (Mahler, 1972; Mahler et al., 1975) both viewed borderline personality organization as originating within the first two years of life, when dyadic relations are prominent—prior to the Oedipus complex and triadic relations. By contrast, a neurotic personality organization, which represents a developmental advance, originates in the preschool years and reflects a lack of resolution of the Oedipus complex. I proposed that persons classified as having a secure state of mind with respect to attachment were able to resolve their preoedipal conflicts and function minimally at an oedipal level of psychosexual development (Goodman, 2002). These persons experience whole object relations and defend against forbidden wishes with a more sophisticated arsenal of defensive processes (A. Freud, 1936).

To integrate the ideas of mentalization developed by Fonagy and his colleagues (Bateman and Fonagy, 2004a, 2004b; Fonagy, Gergely, et al., 2002; Fonagy and Target, 1997, 1998) into my attachment-based model of personality organization, we must first consider the three modes of mental functioning introduced by these authors: the psychic equivalence mode, the pretend mode, and the reflective mode (see above). In the psychic equivalence mode, the infant's early awareness of mental states begins with confusion between the internal world and external reality. The series of projections and introjections vividly described in Melanie Klein's (1946, 1952) work can create a frightening experience because the boundaries between self and other and between fantasy and reality have not been clearly demarcated in the infant's mind. The caregiver can facilitate this mode by reflecting back the infant's internal experience without marking that permits its symbolization, containment, and differentiation between internal and external experience.

In the pretend mode, the infant's early awareness of mental states excludes an awareness of the connection between the internal world and external reality. In Kernberg's (1986a, 1986b) language, the infant forms a pathological grandiose self that provides an illusion of protection against the noncontingencies or impingements of the external world. The caregiver can facilitate this mode by reflecting back an experience subjectively different from the internal experience the infant is actually having. This discrepancy between what the caregiver is communicating externally and what the infant is experiencing internally does not permit the symbolization and containment of the infant's internal experience and promotes an overdifferentiation between internal and external experience—Winnicott's (1965) false self. The false self develops when the infant introjects the caregiver's invalidating reactions to the infant's cues. These reactions come from the caregiver's own mental state (or defensive reaction to his or her own mental state) rather than the infant's own internal experience reflected back from the caregiver. The infant then depends on him or herself for affect-regulating strategies.

In the reflective mode, an integration of the psychic equivalence and pretend modes occurs in which the infant's experiences in external reality are neither identical to nor dissociated from his or her internal experiences. The caregiver's responses are marked as reasonable facsimiles of the infant's experience that confirm an emotional understanding of the infant's internal experience as well as a separateness from it that encompass both the psychic equivalence and pretend modes. Mental states can be experienced as representations that have a connection to external reality.

In my model of attachment and personality organization (see figure 6.2), the pretend mode of mental functioning as outlined by Fonagy and his colleagues (Bateman and Fonagy, 2004a, 2004b; Fonagy, Gergely, et al., 2002; Fonagy and Target, 1997, 1998) can be observed on the left side of the diagram, where the various trajectories of dismissing attachment subclassifications (Ds1–Ds4) are curving to the left, away from the pathway of secure attachment and toward deactivation of the attachment system. I am proposing that the pretend mode characterizes the unintegrated mentalization processes of persons classified as having a dismissing state of mind with respect to attachment. Bateman and Fonagy (2004a) have suggested that the pretend mode facilitates the development of an alien self, which provides "illusory stability" but is "dissociated" from internal reality (Bateman and Fonagy, 2004a, p. 38).

Similarly, dismissing persons tend to deny or minimize the emotional impact of the interpersonal (external) world on their mental states, which

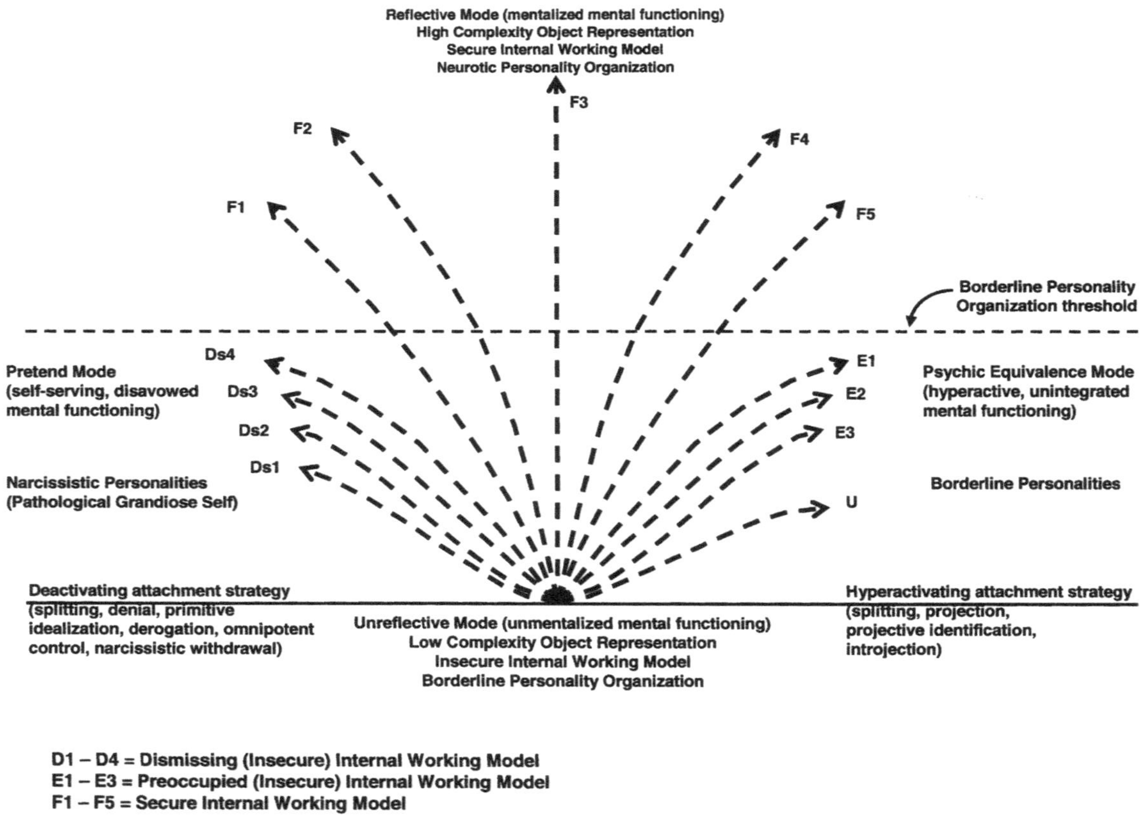

Figure 6.2. A Model of Personality and Attachment Organization and Mental Functioning

reflect a deactivated attachment system. They have difficulty understanding the mutual influence of the mental states of themselves and others because they often exist in a pathological grandiose bubble in which the reality of the interpersonal world cannot touch them (for a clinical example, see volume II, chapter 2). As I mentioned earlier, Kernberg (1986b) has described persons functioning at a borderline level of personality organization with a pathological grandiose self as having a "surface adaptation" (p. 247) at the expense of "widespread, devastating devaluation of external objects and their representations" (Kernberg, 1986b, p. 262). Winnicott (1960) would have characterized these persons as having built their personalities on turning away from the external world of impingement against the true self. Self-sufficiency—the dependence on oneself for affect-regulating strategies—becomes interwoven with a global depreciation of one's interpersonal needs and the persons who have the capacity to satisfy them. Given this underlying personality organization, narcissistic and antisocial personality disorders represent two extreme diagnostic manifestations of the pretend mode of mental functioning.

We can also include in this discussion the multidimensional nature of mentalization (see above). Bateman and Fonagy (2004b) have noted that persons diagnosed with narcissistic and antisocial personality disorders can fake a high RF score on the AAI, which I suggested measures primarily explicit, cognitively based mentalization skills originating in the domain of the IIM-c (interpreting cognitions but not affect states of self and others). Words—the symbols assigned to represent internal experience—are not connected to genuine emotional experience for these persons. Their stylistic pattern of mentalization on the AAI could often be characterized as self-serving or disavowed. As a favorite relative of mine is fond of saying whenever I ask him how his childhood experiences have influenced his personality, "Well, we were poor—we grew up in the Depression. We didn't have all these luxuries you kids have today." This person provided a concrete, sociological explanation to an abstract, psychological question that disavows the existence of his own or others' mental states.

My patient who is extricating herself from the bubble she has lived in her entire life (see volume II, chapter 2) has developed a crush on a coworker who is romantically involved with someone else. She tells me in sessions that she contorts her face, constricts her dress and gait, and even alters her voice to prevent the coworker from looking at her sexually. The fact that this coworker has never exhibited any signs of sexual interest in her does not stop my patient from engaging in these strange behaviors and mentalizing his internal experience in self-serving ways because it allows her to preserve the fantasy that this coworker would be drooling all over her if only she behaved and dressed in a sexier manner. For this patient, the pretend mode is a way of life, and to hell with external reality.

By contrast, the psychic equivalence mode of mental functioning as outlined by Fonagy and his colleagues (Bateman and Fonagy, 2004a, 2004b; Fonagy, Gergely, et al., 2002; Fonagy and Target, 1997, 1998) can be observed on the right side of the diagram (see figure 6.2), where the various trajectories of unresolved (U) and preoccupied attachment subclassifications (E1–E3) are curving to the right, away from the pathway of secure attachment and toward hyperactivation of the attachment system. I am proposing that the psychic equivalence mode characterizes the unintegrated mentalization processes of persons classified as having preoccupied or unresolved states of mind with respect to attachment. According to Bateman and Fonagy (2004a), the psychic equivalence mode facilitates the development of a fragmented self, which is "engulfed by affect, experiencing too much" (p. 38).

Similarly, preoccupied and unresolved persons tend to feel confused, frightened, and overwhelmed by the emotional impact of the interpersonal (external) world on their mental states, which reflect a hyperactivated attachment system. Unlike the persons who have developed the protective structure of the pathological grandiose self, these persons feel exquisitely vulnerable to their own and others' mental states. Their internal worlds often mirror external reality in an unmediated form because their internal experience has been inadequately symbolized, preventing them from attaining psychological distance and experiencing more modulated affect states. Kernberg (1986b) has described persons functioning at a borderline level of personality organization without a pathological grandiose self as demonstrating a "clinging dependency" (p. 255) with poor anxiety tolerance and lack of impulse control (Kernberg, 1986a). An overdependence on others for affect-regulating strategies contributes to a hostile, desperate attitude toward the persons who have the capacity to satisfy their interpersonal needs yet fail them, or even worse, leave them. Given this underlying personality organization, borderline personality disorder represents the extreme diagnostic manifestation of the psychic equivalence mode of mental functioning.

Regarding the multidimensional nature of mentalization (see above), Fonagy and his colleagues (Fonagy et al., 1996; Fonagy et al., 1995) found that low RF moderated the relation between a history of abuse and borderline personality disorder. Persons functioning at a borderline level of personality organization without the pathological grandiose self are particularly vulnerable to dysregulated affect states and typically score in the lower range of the RFS measured with the AAI (Diamond, Stovall-McClough, et al., 2003; Levy, Meehan, et al., 2006). It appears that high-risk persons (e.g., persons with a history of abuse) who have an impairment in mentalizing their own and others' affect states tend to be at their mercy and eventually become symptomatic. These persons often have difficulty finding words to represent their affect states. In a nonclinical sample, alexythymia has been positively associated with borderline psychopathology (Modestin, Furrer, and Malti, 2004). The stylistic pattern of mentalization on the AAI of persons diagnosed with borderline personality disorder could often be characterized as hyperactive or unintegrated. Persons who exhibit hyperactive mentalization compulsively search in vain for the words to represent their thoughts and feelings, but the links among words, thoughts, and feelings are incomplete or no longer exist (see Bion, 1959). Explicit, cognitively based mentalization skills originating in the domain of the IIM-c (interpreting cognitions but not affect states of self and others) seem to be lacking or misfiring.

My financially successful analytic patient diagnosed with borderline personality disorder (see volume II, chapter 3) tells me that she thinks she was sexually abused because she is a lesbian woman with a drug and alcohol problem. When asked about it, she tells me that she has problems with alcohol, drugs, and her sexuality; there must be a reason behind it, and the reason must be that she was sexually abused even though she has no memories to support her claim. I should mention here that I am lending a considerable amount of coherence to her hyperactive mentalization. When I point out that many women without sexual abuse histories share her sexual orientation and struggles with addiction, my patient labors to find the links that will magically explain the origin of her problems. The search is ultimately unproductive, however. Although Fonagy and his colleagues (Fonagy, Gergely, et al., 2002, p. 383) have suggested that hyperactive mentalization occurs in the pretend mode, I am suggesting instead that the futile search for thoughts, feelings, and the verbal links between them occurs when the internal world becomes frightening and threatens to contaminate the safe haven of my office. This patient, who as a child was physically abused, has severed these links to avoid a collapse of the tenuous boundary between the frightening internal world and external reality. She has unconsciously displaced the emotional impact of the experience of her frightening physical abuse onto a fictitious belief in the experience of sexual abuse to protect her abusive mother—and me as a maternal transference object—from her rage and to protect herself from potential retaliation. The thoughts and feelings associated with the physical abuse remain disconnected and unarticulated (see volume II, chapter 3).

Unintegrated mentalization seems to reflect the activation of different states of mind during the mentalization process. This same analytic patient tells me that (1) her peace of mind is worth more to her than anything else, (2) I am worth every penny I charge, and (3) she would never pay much more than the $15 per session she is currently paying—all in the same session.

When I point out that one of these statements does not belong with the others, she casually replies, "What don't you understand?" At other times, this patient has said that therapists should not charge any money for their services because they have taken an oath of poverty like Mother Theresa. The psychic equivalence mode requires that external reality—that therapists charge a fee for their emotional care—conform to her internal world—that her childhood neglect entitles her to free services. She exhibits no awareness that her internal mental state—a feeling of resentment over having been neglected—is not linked to therapists' economic reality.

The reflective mode of mental functioning as outlined by Fonagy and his colleagues (Fonagy, Gergely, et al., 2002; Fonagy and Target, 1997, 1998) can be observed in the upper part of the diagram (see figure 6.2), where the various trajectories of secure attachment subclassifications (F1–F5) are curving upward. F1 and F2 are curving slightly to the left, toward deactivation, while F4 and F5 are curving slightly to the right, toward hyperactivation. I am proposing that the reflective mode characterizes the integrated mentalization processes of persons classified as having a secure state of mind with respect to attachment. According to Fonagy and Target (1997), the reflective mode develops as the product of the integration of the psychic equivalence mode and the pretend mode. In the reflective mode, mental states are experienced as mental representations, in which the internal world and external reality are related to each other but neither identical to nor dissociated from each other.

Similarly, secure persons tend to be more reflective of their childhood relationship experiences with their caregivers than insecure persons. Fonagy and his colleagues revealed that RF scores were the strongest predictors of adult attachment security (Fonagy et al., 1998) and their infants' attachment security (Fonagy, Steele, and Steele, 1991), which suggests a strong association between the reflective mode and secure attachment. Even during infancy, securely attached infants achieve person permanence before object permanence, while insecurely attached infants achieve object permanence before person permanence (Bell, 1968, 1970). Securely attached infants, however, achieve object permanence earlier than insecurely attached infants do. According to Bell (1968), "Babies who consistently have significantly higher scores on person-permanence are, because of their experience with persons at the higher levels, facilitated in the development of the permanence of inanimate objects" (p. 48). Thus, securely attached infants internalize mental representations (both animate and inanimate) earlier than their insecurely attached counterparts do. This earlier representational capacity suggests earlier and more advanced metarepresentational skills, such as the capacity to reflect on the mental states of oneself and others—aspects of complex, differentiated, and integrated mental representations (Auerbach and Blatt, 2002; Blatt, 1995).

A person functioning in the reflective mode would be expected to have developed whole, integrated mental representations and triadic relations. His or her personality would also be organized at a neurotic level rather than a borderline level (Kernberg, 1986a, 1996). This person can depend not only on others to regulate affect states but also on his or her own meta-representational structures (both IIM-a and IIM-c substructures) that function to link representations of the mental states of self and others.

Regarding the multidimensional nature of mentalization (see above), a person functioning in the reflective mode would exhibit an awareness that one's behaviors are connected to one's mental states rather than impersonal personality traits and that these mental states can affect the mental states and behaviors of others and *vice versa*. This person's mentalization skills might exhibit a self-serving flavor (i.e., F1, F2) or a hyperactive flavor (i.e., F4, F5), depending on the attachment subclassification and resultant trajectory toward the pretend mode (curving left) or psychic equivalence mode (curving right). Overall, however, the hallmarks of mentalization in the reflective mode would be evident: (1) awareness of the nature of mental states; (2) explicit effort to tease out mental states underlying behavior; (3) recognizing developmental aspects of mental states; and (4) mental states in relation to the AAI interviewer (Fonagy et al., 1998). Words—the symbols assigned to represent internal experience—are connected to genuine emotional experience and are used to link thoughts and feelings. Explicit, cognitively based mentalization skills originating in the domain of the IIM-c seem to be functioning in synchrony with implicit, affectively based mentalization skills originating in the domain of the IIM-a.

In rare moments of clarity, my analytic patient who is extricating herself from the bubble she has lived in her entire life (see volume II, chapter 2) realizes that her coworker does not love her or hold her in his mind. With my help, she understands that she uses the fantasy of being in a relationship with him to protect herself from the terrifying reality that, at age thirty-eight, she is completely alone with no prospects for a committed relationship or a family of her own. My patient is becoming aware of how she uses self-deception to disguise her coworker's internal states for her own self-aggrandizement and ultimate protection from the barrenness of external reality. Interestingly, she has also used her knowledge of the opaqueness of mental states—another illustration of mentalization—in the service of denial: she sometimes questions the realization that her coworker does not hold her in his mind, claiming that he might after all because, of course, she cannot know what is in his mind.

I also want to suggest that the two modes of borderline personality functioning—pretend and psychic equivalence—do not necessarily function as stable processes over time but rather exhibit more fluid properties like

Klein's (1933, 1937, 1946, 1952) paranoid-schizoid and depressive positions. On the contrary, each mode of mental functioning might occur in the same person in different contexts or at different developmental periods. Under the influence of the pathological grandiose self, the pretend mode protects the person from the awareness of the links between his or her internal world and external reality. The person can then live out life as a daydream, as is the case with my analytic patient. Under high levels of stress, however, a person with a weakened pathological grandiose self could exhibit a loosening of the omnipotent defensive structure (Goodman, 2002) that could result in a collapse of the superficial dissociation between the internal world and external reality and a shift to the psychic equivalence mode—the default position. In this default position, without the protective bubble of the pathological grandiose self, the person exhibits unintegrated mentalization while desperately attempting to reduce the anxiety produced by this collapse. The person must therefore mentalize external reality, and the persons who inhabit it, to conform to his or her internal world to avoid the possibility that external reality is utterly barren of emotional supplies. Developmentalists and therapists alike are increasingly considering the question of multiple states of mind and their meanings for socioemotional development, psychopathology, and intervention. I have therefore proposed a potential theoretical framework with which to consider this question.

MENTALIZATION IN THE TRADITIONAL STAGES OF PSYCHOSEXUAL DEVELOPMENT

In my previous book (Goodman, 2002), I proposed a model for understanding the relation between libido and attachment. Briefly, I want to apply this model to the functioning of mentalization in the traditional stages of psychosexual development. I explained my rationale for devoting space to what many theoreticians and therapists believe to be an arcane developmental model—the traditional stages of psychosexual development:

> The current trend of treating oral, anal, and phallic clinical material as only a series of metaphors for relational concerns minimizes the subjective reality of pleasurable infantile bodily sensations—a trend that I believe reflects the imagined dangers associated with such pleasurable bodily sensations long ago repressed in the deepest layers of the unconscious. (p. 253)

I also cited both Klein (1957) and Freud (1940) in support of the hypothesis that the erotogenic zones can be simultaneously activated and appear in no particular order. Following Anna Freud's (1963) concept of developmental lines, I also suggested that the traditional stages of psychosexual development do not belong to one invariant, universal developmental line. Instead, each erotogenic zone occupies its own distinct developmental line from birth, "with its own distinct developmental trajectory and peak level of intensity, and . . . its own distinct impact on mental representation and later psychopathology" (Goodman, 2002, p. 253). I then redefined a psychosexual stage as "that period of development when an erotogenic zone has gained ascendancy and achieved its peak level of intensity of stimulation. Genetic potentialities as well as caregiving experiences influence the shape and amplitude of each developmental trajectory, which, in turn, influences and is influenced by other domains of development" (pp. 253, 254). I then explained how attachment both influences and is influenced by these psychosexual stages.

As I have already shown, mentalization is both person-specific and situation-specific; in other words, a person's mentalization skills vary according to the relationship and situation the person is mentalizing. A therapist might mentalize his or her relationships with two different patients at two very different levels (Diamond, Stovall-McClough, et al., 2003) or mentalize his or her relationship with the same person in two different situations at two very different levels (e.g., going to dinner with a spouse vs. watching the spouse have a heart attack). I am suggesting that a child's capacity for mentalization similarly influences and is influenced by the quality of the attachment relationship to the caregiver and the psychosexual phase most prominent at that point in development.

My argument centers on two assumptions: (1) a child can form two different attachment patterns based on independent interactions with each caregiver (Main and Weston, 1981), and (2) "mentalizing is quick to collapse in the face of excessive arousal" (Allen, 2003, p. 101). We know that a person's mentalization skills vary with that person's quality of attachment (Fonagy, Steele, Steele, Moran, and Higgitt, 1991) and that high levels of arousal accompany the ascendancy of each psychosexual phase (Lustman, 1956). Thus, it is plausible that a child's mentalization skills depend on (1) the quality of attachment relationship he or she has formed with the particular caregiver being mentalized, and (2) the level of psychosexual arousal the child is experiencing in this relationship. Conversely, a child's attachment quality and level of psychosexual arousal depend on his or her mentalization skills.

Let us assume that a preschool-aged girl, who by twelve months has formed secure attachments with both parents and by age five has already developed rudimentary mentalization skills, enters the oedipal period by turning her attention away from her mother and toward her father. She therefore announces to her parents that she will marry her father when she grows up. The heightened arousal level directed toward her father arouses sexual feelings in him, which he feels guilty about. He unconsciously turns away from his daughter, who feels rejected by him and associates her father's recent coldness with her own increasing libidinal interest in her father. This series of events could adversely affect the girl's attachment relationship to her father, whom she might no longer rely on as a secure base. She might also associate rejection and emotional abandonment with her libidinal needs and thus repress them or turn to her mother instead. This scenario of burgeoning oedipal desire, parental rejection, and child withdrawal, defiance, or compulsive submission to parental rejection depends on the quality of the child's mentalizing skills. A child who has developed a rudimentary understanding of her own mental states and those of her parents might realize that her father feels uncomfortable with her burgeoning sexual interest and begin to turn her attention to someone like her father. A father with moderately high mentalization skills might also help his daughter understand her feelings and his reactions by having a talk with her about the interrelationships among mother, father, daughter, and anyone else in the family.

The mentalization skills of both father and daughter could buffer the daughter's attachment relationship from becoming insecure. She might feel disappointed that her father cannot gratify her libidinal needs, but her understanding of her own and her father's mental states—facilitated by her father's scaffolding (Vygotsky, 1978) of these mentalization processes—might help the girl to process the narcissistic trauma and avert relationship difficulties and later psychopathology. If the mentalization skills of both father and daughter are lacking, however, then the attachment relationship could become insecure, and the narcissistic trauma of the father's rejection of the girl's sexual desire could contribute to pathological sexual attitudes and behaviors.

The parent's scaffolding of these mentalization processes for the child is critical to resolving the conflict because the child's arousal level, heightened by the psychosexual phase, interferes with the child's rudimentary mentalization skills and thus hinders the child from arriving at a benign interpretation of the father's rejection and regulating the associated unpleasant affect states. Can certain familial contexts erode mentalization skills and render them ineffective as a buffer against subsequent psychopathology? Mentalization skills can protect abused persons from manifesting borderline symptoms (Fonagy et al., 1996), but how can mentalization skills develop or be preserved in a context of abuse, especially caregiver abuse? It is possible that parental scaffolding occurs in the context of nonabusive caregiving relationships, such as a relationship with the other parent or a close relative like a grandparent. Pretend play and peer group interactions, including sibling interactions, might also contribute to the development or preservation of mentalization skills (Fonagy, Gergely, et al., 2002).

The timing of the onset of the adverse familial context (e.g., abuse) might also influence the acquisition or erosion of previously acquired mentalization skills. If the child is abused prior to the establishment of a reflective mode of mental functioning at age four, then the acquisition of mentalization skills might be disrupted, leaving the child vulnerable to the affective experiences associated with any resultant trauma. The onset of an adverse familial context after age four, however, might spare the child from any erosion in his or her mentalization skills, particularly if other caregivers can facilitate the scaffolding of the mentalization processes required to regulate the unpleasant affects associated with any resultant trauma.

Applying these ideas to the traditional psychosexual stages of development, a child who has not received scaffolding of his or her mentalization skills will be unable to rely on these skills when he or she becomes overwhelmed with peak levels of sexual arousal. This scaffolding process can occur, however, in the context of another caregiving relationship. If the girl's libidinal wishes toward her father and aggressive wishes toward her mother (or *vice versa*) render these two figures unavailable for processing the oedipal dynamics, then perhaps a trusted aunt, grandfather, or therapist can scaffold the girl's mentalizion processes, which could ameliorate the potential susceptibility to affect dysregulation caused by preexisting mentalization deficits.

In addition, considering the fact that two of the three traditional stages of psychosexual development—oral and anal—typically occur prior to age four, any conflicts that arise during these periods of development will be subject to the psychic equivalence or pretend mode of mental functioning. Caregiver scaffolding of mentalization processes would be critical to the resolution of these conflicts. Of course, conflicts that occur prelinguistically would require the caregiver to mirror the unsymbolized affects by marking them as both similar and different from the infant's actual affective experience (see above). Alternative caregivers could facilitate these proto-mentalization processes as well. A three-year-old boy with only rudimentary language skills was having difficulty with toilet training until he stayed with his aunt for a few days. By the end of his stay, he was completely toilet-trained. Through a combination of (1) talking with the boy about his parents' expectations and his feelings about the process, and (2) engaging him in an affirming affective communication through vocal tone and facial expression (and other factors), the aunt was able to contain his anxiety and frustration and allow him to represent these affects in his mind. This boy could begin to feel that the contents of his mind were being held and contained in the mind of his aunt, which re-regulated his affect states and thus removed the symptom.

IMPLICATIONS OF MENTALIZATION SCAFFOLDING FOR CLINICAL INTERVENTION

I have tried to demonstrate that the influences between mentalization and the psychosexual stages are bidirectional in nature, such that caregiver scaffolding of mentalization processes can help to resolve psychosexual conflicts, while psychosexual conflicts at peak arousal levels can interfere with mentalization processes—of both child and caregiver. Mentalization-based developmental theory has implications for clinical intervention with both children (see volume II, chapter 7) and adults (see volume II, chapters 2 and 3). I want to share some additional clinical implications below.

In his superbly written book integrating developmental theory and clinical process, Pine (1985) has suggested that the therapist "*strike while the iron is cold*" (p. 153, italics in original). From a mentalization-promoting point of view, the therapist needs to scaffold the patient's mentalization processes either before or after an affective storm. During my postdoctoral fellowship, one of my BPD inpatients used to attack me verbally throughout the duration of an entire session, for days at a time. My clinical supervisor provided me with sage advice: "Dig a trench and hunker down until the enemy fire begins to subside. The goal is survival." And survive I did. To my surprise (and relief), I found that the patient gradually became more available for processing these experiences after the affect storms than at earlier points in the treatment. The peak arousal levels experienced by the patient during these sessions seemed to neutralize any rudimentary mentalization skills possessed by this patient, which consequently spoiled the impact of all interventions made by me. The goal of my interventions after the affect storms would be to facilitate the development of her mentalization skills so that they could remain functional *during* an affect storm. Later in treatment, the goal of my interventions was to cultivate her mentalization skills to a level that could assist her with modulating her affects at critical moments in our interactions and thus averting these affect storms altogether.

It is also important to consider whether the patient treats external reality as directly mirroring his or her internal world (psychic equivalence mode), or whether the patient is turning away from external reality to live in the internal world (pretend mode). My BPD patient (see volume II, chapter 3) thought that her mother was going to die if she spoke badly about her mother in session. She had to say the words, "God forbid," to undo the fantasized impact of her unconscious wishes. She truly believed that her unacceptable thoughts—what amounted to unconscious wishes to murder her mother—would result in the actual death of her mother in external reality unless she took some preventative measure such as an incantation. In the psychic equivalence mode, the therapist needs to mark the patient's unsymbolized mental state—murderous wishes against the mother—in a nonalarmist manner that suggests that wishes do not cause events in external reality. The mother is not in imminent danger.

Although Fonagy and his colleagues (Bateman and Fonagy, 2004a, 2004b; Fonagy, Gergely, et al., 2002) might disagree with me, facilitating mentalization skills in the transference could present an ideal opportunity to shift the patient from the psychic equivalence mode to a reflective mode of mental functioning. Interpreting a patient's wishes in the transference would (1) mark the patient's mental state in relation to the therapist; (2) establish the acceptability of this mental state as a representation in the patient's mind and therapist's mind; and (3) demonstrate to the patient *in vivo* that the therapist has survived these unconscious wishes—both physically and emotionally—because they are not causally connected to external reality. This transference focused intervention would enhance the patient's mentalization skills by demarcating a boundary between the patient's mental states and external reality (which includes the therapist's mental states), not lead to "a dissociative experience" in which the patient is "thrown into a pretend mode" (Bateman and Fonagy, 2004a, p. 44). As I illustrate in chapter 3 of volume II, the therapist needs to accentuate firm boundaries and differentiation for patients with a hyperactivating/preoccupied attachment strategy, functioning in the psychic equivalence mode.

I am also treating a man struggling with emotional intimacy as he nears his wedding date. As this date approaches, he has noticed an increase in his use of pornographic websites and binge eating. The man describes these moments of online masturbation and binge eating as if he lived in a fantasy world far removed from the reality of his life—where he is becoming emotionally intimate with his future wife. He has reserved a hidden, private mental space dissociated from external reality where he can still depend on objects rather than her for the gratification of his emotional needs. In confronting the pretend mode, the therapist needs to establish the connection between his growing emotional intimacy with his future wife and his avoidance of the associated mental states by setting up an alternate universe without attachments in external reality.

As in the first example, facilitating mentalization skills in the transference presents an ideal opportunity to shift the patient from the pretend mode to a reflective mode of mental functioning. Interpreting this patient's unconscious separation anxiety associated with increased emotional intimacy in the transference and his defensive processes mobilized against awareness of these mental states would (1) identify the existence of his counterdependent mental state (i.e., part of the pathological grandiose self or alien self); (2) establish a causal connection between the patient's denied mental states (closeness, dependence, anxiety) and his defensive behavior in external reality (e.g., coming to sessions late, not noticing the therapist); and (3) demonstrate to the patient *in vivo* that the therapist accepts all his mental states, including his dependent mental state, without rejecting or abandoning him in external reality. This transference-focused intervention would enhance the patient's mentalization skills by loosening the boundary that helps the patient dissociate his mental states from external reality. As I illustrate in chapter 2 of volume II, the therapist needs to accentuate flexible boundaries and moderate differentiation for patients with a deactivating/dismissing attachment strategy, functioning in the pretend mode.

I am using the language of mentalization-based developmental theory to restate my thesis in chapter 6 of Goodman (in press)—namely, that noncomplementary interaction structures in the therapeutic relationship offer the most effective means of creating enduring changes in the patient's intrapsychic and interpersonal life. If mentalization is a common factor of all effective treatments (Bateman and Fonagy, 2004a, p. 46), then the therapist must decide how to promote mentalization skills in every patient. I have suggested that dismissing and preoccupied patients manifest mentalization deficits in two different modes—the pretend mode and the psychic equivalence mode. In the pretend mode, the therapist must find ways of getting close to the patient's emotional experience and helping him or her to make connections with external reality—the therapist being one such representative. In the psychic equivalence mode, the therapist must find ways of marking the patient's emotional experience and helping him or her represent it to facilitate the establishment of a boundary between his or her mental states and external reality. In both cases, both explicit mentalization (i.e., verbalizing mental states and their interrelations with each other and with behaviors of self and others) and implicit mentalization (i.e., nonverbal, intuitive understanding of mental states through nonconscious communication channels such as vocal tone and facial expression) contribute to the ultimate therapeutic outcome: a secure attachment to the therapist "conducive to exploring [the patient's] mind in the mind of the [therapist] who has [the patient's] mind in mind" (Allen, 2003, p. 100). And thus secure attachment and mentalization mutually influence and modify each other in an infinite regress of cause and effect that produce an enduring transformation of both the internal world and attachment.

Chapter Seven

The Evolution of the Construct of Psychological Mindedness: A Victim of Natural Selection?

> The somewhat outdated notion of psychological-mindedness . . . has always been a rather vague construct which was poorly operationalized, and our work may be viewed as an attempt to fill this gap.
>
> P. Fonagy, M. Steele, H. Steele, G. S. Moran, and A. C. Higgitt, "The Capacity for Understanding Mental States: The Reflective Self in Parent and Child and Its Significance for Security of Attachment"

In 1991, Fonagy and his colleagues introduced a new term to the psychoanalytic literature—"reflective-self function," which was later (Fonagy, Target, Steele, and Steele, 1998) changed to "reflective functioning." The quotation cited above suggests that the authors considered their new construct of reflective functioning (RF) as an extension, perhaps even a replacement, of the older psychoanalytic term "psychological mindedness." Before we relegate the construct of psychological mindedness (PM) to the dustbin of psychoanalytic history along with terms such as "cathexis," "libidinization," and "actual neurosis," perhaps we should pause to reflect on the history of a construct that focused our attention on a process of self-reflection believed to be a primary criterion of suitability for psychoanalysis and psychoanalytic psychotherapy (Wallerstein and Robbins, 1956). Through such reflection, we can therefore decide whether to resuscitate PM or memorialize it.

Perhaps the central problem with the construct of PM has been its evolving definition. I will argue that the definition of PM has changed since its inception in 1956 (Wallerstein and Robbins, 1956) to accommodate major changes accompanying the evolution of psychoanalytic theory over the past fifty years. During this time, psychoanalytic theory has moved from a one-person to a two-person psychology (Aron, 1990). The writings of Sandor Ferenczi (1932/1988), Melanie Klein (1946), Theodor Reik (1948), and others heralded this paradigm shift from the analyst as a blank screen for the patient's fantasies and projections to the patient's transference and analyst's countertransference mutually influencing each other to create a co-constructed, dyadic experience. Keeping in step with the times, PM evolved from a construct the purview of which was exclusively the self (Wallerstein and Robbins, 1956) to a construct the purview of which includes others as well as the self (Farber, 1985).

I will also argue that the perspective on the etiology of PM has also changed over the past fifty years. Initially, theoreticians defined PM as consisting of primarily a genetic component that manifested itself irrespective of diagnostic characteristics (Wallerstein and Robbins, 1956). Recently, however, PM has been conceptualized as an awareness that develops within the context of the caregiver-child relationship (Alvarez, Farber, and Schonbar, 1998; Beitel and Cecero, 2003) and becomes increasingly complex during the course of development (Hatcher and Hatcher, 1997; Hatcher, Hatcher, Berlin, Okla, and Richards, 1990).

Similarly, PM was considered a primary criterion for analyzability or suitability for treatment in addition to diagnostic and structural considerations, assessed during a diagnostic interview (Coltart, 1988; Wallerstein and Robbins, 1956). PM was believed to provide a fertile ground for the analyst's interpretive work. Thus, a psychologically minded person would be able to apply the understanding provided by an interpretation of his or her resistances, which would make drive derivatives more conscious and available to the ongoing work of analysis. Recently, researchers (e.g., Beutler and Clarkin, 1990; Beutler, Clarkin, and Bongar, 2000; Beutler and Harwood, 2000; Beutler and Hodgson, 1993) have begun to target specific interventions to patients with specific psychological characteristics such as level of distress and functional impairment as well as quality of defensive processes. This research program of patient-treatment matching has been extended to PM in which more psychologically minded patients are hypothesized to have better treatment outcomes in interpretive psychotherapies than in supportive psychotherapies, while less psychologically minded patients are hypothesized to have better treatment outcomes in supportive psychotherapies than in interpretive psychotherapies (Piper et al., 2002). Thus, PM is now perceived not only as a predictor but also as a moderator of treatment outcome.

Finally, I will argue that PM seems to be evolving in the direction of Fonagy et al.'s (1991) RF. But is this evolution too late to salvage the construct? Curiously, I found no reference to RF in the PM literature, and no reference to PM in the RF literature except for the quotation cited. It is plausible to speculate that no one wants to acknowledge that the construct of PM has already been eclipsed by a newer and more contemporary construct. Alternatively, perhaps RF has co-opted the essential elements of PM for its own purposes. As I will demonstrate, RF, from its inception, incorporated not only a two-person psychology into its definition but also an understanding of the intersubjective nature of mental states (Fonagy, Steele, Steele, Moran, and Higgitt, 1991; Fonagy et al., 1998; Fonagy, Gergely, et al., 2002). If the reader holds this theoretical perspective, then RF will represent a theoretical advance over its conceptual rival.

In addition, RF was built upon a solid foundation of empirically based developmental theory out of the caregiver-infant matrix and child research on theory of mind (Fonagy, Gergely, et al., 2002). It is clear that these authors consider a person's level of RF to depend on the quality of this caregiver-infant relationship, not on a particular genetic loading (Fonagy, Gergely, et al., 2002, p. 99). Further, deficits in RF are not considered regressions or fixations to an earlier level of development or genetically determined but rather manifestations of highly complex and well-developed defensive processes that interfere with this genetically inherited capacity (Fonagy, Gergely, et al., 2002, p. 61). The developmental perspective that these authors lend to the construct of RF provides it with a richness and complexity that the construct of PM lacks.

RF has also been conceptualized as a state construct rather than a trait construct. In other words, RF is a context-dependent construct that varies with specific situations and specific persons. By contrast, PM is considered a trait whose level remains constant across situations and persons (e.g., Conte et al., 1990; Farber, 1985). Even when theoreticians (Farber and Golden, 1997; Fogel, 1995) discuss the defensive properties of PM, their descriptions tend to reflect a global personality style rather than a context-dependent process.

In their mentalization-based treatment (MBT), designed for patients with borderline personality disorder, Bateman and Fonagy (2004b) placed RF at the center of the process of therapeutic change. Therapists work with patients to increase their level of RF, believed to mediate structural and symptomatic outcomes. Thus, RF is considered a mediator of successful treatment outcome as well as an outcome in and of itself. As mentioned before, PM has been considered only as a predictor or moderator of successful treatment, not as a patient characteristic that itself could be targeted for change. I will conclude that RF co-opted certain facets of the PM construct, but RF also represents a significant theoretical and clinical extension of PM that reflects a contemporary understanding of psychoanalytic theory. I will suggest ways in which the PM construct might be resuscitated if it is to survive the process of natural selection of theoretical constructs in psychoanalytic theory.

HISTORICAL REFLECTIONS ON THE THEORETICAL DEFINITIONS OF PM

The first known reference of PM in the literature was located in a paper by Wallerstein and Robbins (1956) that described concepts used in their group's Psychotherapy Research Project of the Menninger Foundation: "The patient's capacity—and readiness—to see some relationship between his symptoms or behavior and his emotional state. To what extent is he able to see significant relationships between his thought, feeling, and action? To what extent does his ego have the capacity to split into an observing (introspecting) and experiencing part?" (p. 246). PM is defined here as both a capacity or an ability, demonstrated by the patient during an evaluation, as well as an interest or preference to use PM, reflected in the patient's readiness to see relationships between symptoms and emotional states. PM is also defined as a strictly intrapsychic process, whose purview is exclusively the self—which reflects the one-person psychology of that era. The observing ego (Sterba, 1934) takes only the experiencing ego as its object of observation, not other persons. The definition is also restricted to the suitability of the person for treatment, reflected in the reference to symptoms. If the patient understands that his or her symptoms are derived from emotional states, then an insight-oriented therapy would have a chance of broadening and deepening these connections.

Interestingly, Wallerstein and Robbins (1956) considered PM as a patient variable, listed along with "intelligence," "constitutionally endowed aspects of ego strength," and "capacity for sublimations" under the heading "Capacities Factors," which they defined as "probably largely constitutionally based and only in part experientially determined or modified" (p. 246). Although not explicit to their pioneering definition, the authors nevertheless considered PM to be largely genetically based and immutable. Given these assumptions, it is not surprising that the psychoanalysts of that era treated PM as a predictor of treatment rather than a mediator or an outcome of treatment. What is not addressed is the curious person who comes in for treatment with a high capacity for PM but low interest. According to the definition, this person would be considered unsuitable for treatment in spite of the high capacity for PM. The authors do not consider the possibility that uncovering the resistances that hinder his or her interest could restore this function and make the person suitable for an insight-oriented treatment. The counterargument would be that the person would first have to be interested in psychological understanding for the uncovering of these resistances to succeed. Implicit to the definition is the belief that both an innate capacity for and interest in PM are necessary but not sufficient conditions for interpretive work to effect change.

An earlier definition provided by Edwards (1953), which he termed "intraception," consisted of the analysis of "one's motives and feelings, to observe others, to understand how others feel about problems, to put one's self in another's place, to judge people by why they do things rather than by what they do, to analyze the behavior of others, to analyze the motives of others, to predict how others will act" (p. 11). In contrast to the 1956 definition of PM, this definition focuses exclusively on the understanding of the other, which resembles a common definition of empathy. Again, the definition reflects a one-person psychology—in this case, an understanding of the self is absent. This conflict between PM related to the self versus PM related to others recurs throughout the literature and reached its zenith in the empirical work of Hatcher and his colleagues (Hatcher and Hatcher, 1997; Hatcher, Hatcher, Berlin, Okla, and Richards, 1990). They conceptualized PM toward the self and PM toward others as separate constructs and provided data collected on adolescents to support their hypothesis that in most groups classified by age and gender, these two constructs are uncorrelated.

Another definition of PM provided by Holt and Luborsky (1958) during this classical era of psychoanalysis contains the same themes as Wallerstein and Robbins's (1956) definition: "An interest in, orientation toward, and/or ability to grasp the psychological dimension of experience; particularly, an understanding of behavior in terms of its motivation" (p. 143). In this definition, the target of explanation is not clear. Understanding the relationship between behavior and its motivation is the definition's central element, although the terms "psychological dimension" and "motivation" obscure its meaning. This definition also indicates that one must have both ability and an interest in PM to be considered psychologically minded.

These definitions seemed to suffice for a number of years until Appelbaum's classic paper on PM published in 1973. His definition of PM is still widely cited in the psychoanalytic literature: "A person's ability to see relationships among thoughts, feelings, and actions, with the goal of learning the meanings and causes of his experiences and behaviors" (p. 36). Again, we see the influence of a one-person psychology typical of that era: the object of observation is one's own experiences and behaviors. Appelbaum (1973) later underscored this aspect of the definition: "The direction of a person's psychological thinking for purposes of treatment must be toward himself" (p. 37). The implication is that any thinking directed toward others is not psychologically minded. In addition, the connection between PM and a clinical context is clear.

Both ability and interest are woven into the definition; in other words, the person must be able to see connections as well as want to learn about the explanations behind these connections. This definition seems to be directed to therapists evaluating a patient to determine whether "the goal of learning" is present. Others (e.g., Shill and Lumley, 2002; Valbak, 2004; Wallerstein and Robbins, 1956) have separated motivation for change from PM because more psychologically minded persons might have both ability and interest, yet not feel compelled to change—especially if they feel emotionally secure. The absence of the word "symptoms," however, suggests that PM could be conceived of outside a clinical context. In fact, Appelbaum (1973) later mentioned that "a kind of low-key, implicit psychological-mindedness [is] at work even during such apparently non-psychological problem-solving moments" (p. 44)—which opens the door to considering PM as a constant mental activity that everyone engages in at all times.

Appelbaum (1973) was also the first author to recognize the paradox between requiring PM for treatment and freeing up PM from "dynamic conflicts" for further work: "The process of modulating and resolving conflicts should release the patient's potential capacity for psychological thinking. Something of a conundrum is implied here since the process that is to release psychological thinking is in itself dependent upon it" (p. 44). Appelbaum (1973) resolved the paradox by reasoning that "the process of analysis exploits and builds upon the capacities for psychological thinking that are available at any given moment" (p. 44). If this reasoning about PM is correct, then why has PM been considered only as a predictor of treatment in the psychotherapy research literature? Why could PM not also be considered a mediator or an outcome of a successful treatment? One would expect that a successful treatment would have sufficiently worked through resistances to liberate increasing quantities of PM, which might be expected not only to produce symptomatic change but also to facilitate continued clinical work.

Other theoretical definitions were also offered in the 1970s and early 1980s that similarly confined the construct of PM to a clinical context that required both ability and interest. Some of these definitions (e.g., Baekeland and Lundwall, 1975) contain tautological aspects such as "the patient's ability to . . . see himself in psychological terms" (p. 756). This definition uses a word ("psychological") to define the same word used in the construct "psychological mindedness." Others (e.g., Dollinger, Reader, Marnett, and Tylenda, 1983) use vague language to fix the direction of causality from thoughts and feelings to verbalization and behavior: "The ability to read between the lines of what a person does or says" (p. 183). The reciprocal influence of behaviors on thoughts and feelings is not considered. It should also be noted that PM is defined here as an understanding of others' behaviors rather than of one's own. Again, a one-person psychology prevails because the self is not also taken as an object of observation. The centrality of the verbalization of internal experience, and the self as the focus of inquiry, are taken to extremes in a definition offered by Rogawski (1982): "The ability to verbalize one's internal experience as a product of one's mind . . . and not as caused by . . . another" (pp. 109, 110). As Hall (1992) pointed out, some definitions of PM resemble the construct of internal locus of control (Rotter, 1966), which unfortunately diminishes PM's unique stature in the literature. Ironically, Werman (1979) defined one manifestation of PM as the belief that not all experiences are under one's internal control.

The dawn of a two-person psychology (Aron, 1990) brought about a new era in the definition of the construct of PM. Among theoreticians, Farber (1985) was the first to acknowledge that the target of explanation in PM could be both the self and others: "A trait which has at its core the disposition to reflect upon the meaning and motivation of behavior, thoughts, and feelings in oneself and others" (p. 170). This flexible and elegant definition assumes that not only behavior but also thoughts and feelings are motivated phenomena that merit reflection. The depiction of PM as a trait rather than a context-dependent state also suggests that PM has a genetic component. The use of the word "disposition" implies a habitual inclination or a tendency to be psychologically minded, which implies both an ability and an interest in such reflection.

In spite of this breakthrough, some authors continued to define PM exclusively toward the self (e.g., Coltart, 1988) or others (e.g., McCallum and Piper, 1990). At the same time, however, the definition began to broaden. For example, Coltart (1988) suggested that PM includes characteristics as wide-ranging as "imagination" and "realistic self-esteem" (p. 820), while Conte, Ratto, and Karasu (1996) included "access to one's feelings, a willingness to try to understand oneself and others, a belief in the benefit of discussing one's problems, an interest in the meaning and motivation of one's own and others' thoughts, feelings, and behavior, and a capacity for change" (p. 254). This latter definition was derived from five factors that had emerged from an empirical study of PM in 256 psychiatric outpatients. This research, based on a flawed assessment instrument (Shill and Lumley, 2002), produced what could be considered a prime example of construct bloating that ultimately renders a construct meaningless.

Recognizing that the definition of PM consists of components with unspecified relations among them, Hall (1992) attempted to construct a complex yet precise definition. The components of PM included "interest, ability, affect, and intellect" (p. 139). Hall (1992) also concerned herself with the accuracy of PM. She reasoned that both a person's interest and ability in both the affective and cognitive domains of PM determine the accuracy of PM: "Accurate psychological mindedness is defined as reflectivity about psychological processes, relationships, and meanings . . . displayed by an individual to the extent that he or she displays both interest in and ability for such reflectivity, and across both affective and intellectual dimensions" (pp. 139, 140). In other words, accuracy depends on both interest and ability. She further clarified that ability depends on the level of interest so that a person with a high ability in PM might nevertheless be inaccurate when called on to engage in psychologically minded activity because he or she lacks interest in such activity or the results of such activity.

The cognitive-behaviorist Grant (2001) took the final step in the evolution of the PM construct by reconceptualizing it as a form of metacognition. He criticized previous definitions of PM for their circularity (including Hall's [1992] definition of PM as reflectivity about "psychological" processes), their exclusive focus on the self or others, their exclusive emphasis on explanations of behavior rather than thoughts or feelings, and their psychoanalytic, clinical bias that could alienate those from other theoretical backgrounds. Grant (2001) defined PM as "a predisposition to engage in acts of affective and intellectual inquiry into how and why oneself and/or others behave, think, and feel in the way that they do" (p. 12). He explicitly defined "predisposition" as incorporating "both abilities and motivations" (p. 11). In contrast to Hall (1992), the level of interest in PM depends on ability just as ability in PM depends on the level of interest. Both ability and interest mutually reinforce each other and are necessary conditions for PM to occur.

Grant (2001) also specified the cognitive and motivational characteristics required to engage in PM. Among these cognitive characteristics are the ability to recognize causal relationships, the ability to categorize events according to theory, and metacognitive abilities—thinking about thinking. Motivational characteristics include anxiety reduction, self-actualization, need for cognition, and desire for social acceptability. Although not mentioned in his article, one might also wonder whether PM represents a survival strategy for making predictions about not only the emotional availability of protectors but also the threatening behaviors of rivals and enemies. These predictions could modify one's own behavior to increase the probability of emotional availability and decrease the probability of threat.

According to Grant (2001), PM is a predisposition or potential that can be activated by an "initiating event" that produces "the act of reflective inquiry" (p. 14). Thus, he made a distinction between the person's interest and ability and the actual reflective process of affective and intellectual inquiry into meaning and motivation. The product of this process is insight, a form of metacognitive knowledge that can in turn modify the level of PM. Because PM represents the potential to engage in reflectivity, Grant (2001) suggested that researchers interested in assessing PM should more productively direct their efforts at assessing the actual process of reflective inquiry or insight. He pointed out that a person might have the interest and the ability to reflect on meaning and motivation, "yet engage in little reflectivity and exhibit minimal insight" (p. 15). It is not clear from Grant's (2001) conceptualization why a person high in interest and ability would not use it at the time of an "initiating event." Appelbaum (1973) was the first to suggest that PM can acquire symbolic meanings that could hinder its functioning; however, this inhibition would reduce the person's ability to reflect on meaning and motivation. In other words PM would decrease, which would account for its lack of use.

Although I disagree with Grant's (2001) argument that favors the conceptual independence of PM and the act of reflective inquiry, the distinction that he has made between PM as a predisposition and PM as an active process represents a significant conceptual advance. One of the difficulties encountered in assessing PM (see below) has been a lack of attention paid during the assessment to activating the process of reflective inquiry. Because PM has been defined as a trait or predisposition, some analysts and therapists of other theoretical backgrounds have treated PM as a criterion of suitability for treatment rather than as an active process that can itself be modified through uncovering resistances to PM and acquiring insight. Another significant conceptual advance that Grant (2001) introduced is the identification of an "initiating event" that activates PM and thus causes the person to engage in the process of reflective inquiry. Although he does not discuss its significance, the initiating event could be interpreted as a conceptual shift toward a context-dependent understanding of PM. The initiating event could thus be a specific person or situation more likely to elicit this process than other persons or situations. Grant's (2001) twin emphases on "the act of reflective inquiry" (a process) and the "initiating event" (a context) move the definition of PM away from a trait-based construct in the direction of Fonagy et al.'s (1998) RF, a context-dependent construct.

OPERATIONAL DEFINITIONS OF PM

Clinical researchers have attempted to operationalize the PM construct so that its assessment can be standardized across treatments and empirically measured as a predictor of treatment outcome. These attempts vary widely both in content and scope. Gough (1957) developed the California Psychological Inventory (CPI), designed to assess a combination of personality, intellectual, and interpersonal dimensions. The Psychological Mindedness Scale (Py), one of eighteen CPI subscales, consists of twenty-two true-false items that collectively measure PM in a person who "is interested in, and responsive to, the inner needs, motives, and experiences of others" (p. 11). The problem with this definition, as discussed earlier, is that it emphasizes others as the target of observation rather than the self. The instrument also has poor face validity. Puzzling items include "I would like to hear a great singer in an opera," "I do not have a great fear of snakes," "I would like to write a technical book," and "We ought to pay our elected officials better than we do." Test-retest reliability and internal consistency of items has been found to be poor (Conte and Ratto, 1997; Grant, 2001), and pretreatment scores on Py were uncorrelated with interviewer ratings of improvement in psychosocial adjustment following dynamic group therapy (Yalom, Houts, Zimerberg, and Rand, 1967).

Considering PM as a "relevant prognostic indicator" (p. 26), Wolitzky and Reuben (1974) used a projective technique—the thematic apperception test (TAT)—to assess PM in a sample of fourteen male undergraduates. Each subject told nine TAT stories, and then read two TAT stories told by Person A and two by Person B, both of whom were the subjects of a prior intensive investigation of personality assessment. The examiner then instructed each subject to give his separate impressions of the personality of Person A and of Person B. Each set of impressions was coded for the presence or absence of ten PM characteristics: (1) projection; (2) motives, needs, or wishes; (3) conflict; (4) affect; (5) defense; (6) personality traits; (7) attitudes and values; (8) relates the two stories; (9) self-awareness; and (10) reasoning that underlies the inferences drawn. The categories used are summed to arrive at the total PM score. Notably, the quality of reasoning used by the subject is not coded in this system.

In addition the authors coded the TAT stories told by each subject on a six-point scale (not published) that indicated "the degree to which the subjects, in their own TAT stories, attributed motives, conflicts, feelings, interpersonal strategies, etc., to the story characters" (p. 28). Wolitzky and Reuben (1974) reported a modest interrater reliability, $r = .66$, for this six-point scale, and only a marginally significant correlation, $r = .40$, $p < .10$, between these ratings of the subjects' own TAT stories and the PM ratings of the subjects' impressions of Person A's and Person B's TAT stories. Finally, the authors compared the subjects' impressions of Person A's and Person B's TAT stories with impressions of these stories provided by an expert in personality assessment. The degree of similarity between each set of impressions, rated on a six-point scale by two independent raters, became a measure of accuracy of the subject's PM. The large significant correlations between the accuracy ratings and the PM ratings, $r = .70$, $p < .01$, and $r = .56$, $p < .05$, for personality descriptions A and B, respectively, suggested that level of PM is associated with its accuracy.

In interpreting their findings, Wolitzky and Reuben (1974) concluded, "A subject cannot score high in accuracy and low in PM, although he could score high in PM and low in accuracy" (p. 29). In other words, the authors defined level of PM as a necessary but not sufficient condition of accuracy of PM—similar to Hall's (1992) later definition of interest in PM as a necessary but not sufficient condition of ability in PM. As Grant (2001) pointed out, however, a person's ability in PM can also influence his or her interest in PM. This instrument also defines PM as exclusively focused on reflection on the understanding of others, not on the understanding of the self. The subjects were asked to reflect on the meaning and motivation of their own story characters but not themselves. At best, this instrument might be considered an incomplete assessment of PM.

This trend to operationalize PM as exclusively focused on the meaning and motivation of others reached its zenith with McCallum and Piper's (1990) psychological mindedness assessment procedure (PMAP). Working from a definition of PM as "the ability to identify dynamic (intrapsychic) components and to relate them to a person's difficulties" (p. 412), these researchers show subjects a fifteen-minute videotape of a simulated patient-therapist interaction in which the patient verbalizes conflictual wishes and fears, defense mechanisms, and connections among thoughts, feelings, and behavior. Afterward, the administrator asks the subject, "What seems to be troubling this woman?" The subject's response is rated on a nine-point scale in which higher levels require more sophisticated and complex explanations than those for the lower levels. A high PM score on this scale "reflect[s] several of the basic assumptions held by psychodynamic therapists concerning human pathology" (p. 413). Thus, the PMAP explicitly defines PM using psychodynamic concepts in the context of the patient-therapist interaction.

In a sample of thirty adults, the PMAP was positively correlated with the Py subscale of the CPI, $r = .42, p < .05$, and uncorrelated with social desirability, intelligence, anxiety, or depression (McCallum and Piper, 1990). Test-retest reliability after one month was $r = .76, p < .001$. In a second sample of seventy-nine adult outpatients participating in twelve-week, analytically oriented, group psychotherapy, test-retest reliability after three months was $r = .59, p < .001$. PM scores obtained at admission were positively correlated with therapists' seven-point ratings of their patients' PM exhibited in group therapy, $r = .30, p < .05$. Finally, PM scores were not significantly associated with any of the thirteen outcome variables assessed, which included interpersonal functioning, psychiatric symptomatology, self-esteem, and personalized target objectives; however, PM scores were negatively associated with dropping out of treatment, X^2 $(1, N = 54) = 17.46, p < .001$, and positively associated with engaging in psychodynamic work in group, $r = .42, p < .01$.

Perhaps PM scores on the PMAP were not associated with treatment outcomes because the PMAP assesses a person's psychodynamic understanding of others, not the self. A more complex understanding of others might not help a person to become more understanding of the meaning and motivation of his or her own behavior, thoughts, and feelings, and thus reduce symptoms or increase self-esteem. The PMAP, therefore, seems ill-suited to predict treatment outcomes—a conclusion supported by the fact that this research group has come up empty-handed in other attempts to demonstrate the PMAP's value in predicting or moderating outcomes in both interpretive and supportive treatments (e.g., Ogrodniczuk, Piper, Joyce, and McCallum, 2001; Piper et al., 2002). I would suggest that the *discrepancy* between a person's psychological understanding of him or herself and his or her psychological understanding of others predicts treatment outcome. Defensive processes might interfere with one's own self-observational functioning to protect the self from awareness of painful intrapsychic conflicts, whereas making sense out of others' thoughts, feelings, and behavior does not carry the same psychological costs. The size of the discrepancy between PM toward others and PM toward the self could reflect the extent to which defensive processes are interfering with the person's ability to engage in PM toward the self, which could in turn impede the person's receptivity to interpretive work, whose target is the self. Thus, the PMAP could also be considered an incomplete instrument for assessing PM.

In an attempt to improve on Gough's (1957) Py subscale of the CPI, Conte et al. (1990) developed the Psychological Mindedness Scale (PM Scale), a forty-five-item Likert-type self-report questionnaire that assesses PM as a disposition—the average level of daily PM in the respondent. According to the authors, the PM Scale was specifically designed "to measure suitability for dynamically oriented psychotherapy" (p. 427). Relying on the earlier definitions of PM by Appelbaum (1973) and Farber (1985), Conte and Ratto (1997) defined PM as "an ability to be introspective about one's own feelings, thoughts, and behavior as well as an interest in understanding why others feel, think, and behave as they do" (p. 13). It is unclear why this definition matches one's ability with PM toward the self and one's interest with PM toward others. According to Hall (1992) and Grant (2001), a person must also have an interest in PM toward the self and ability in PM toward others.

In Conte et al.'s (1990) initial study (which did not seek to validate the instrument), forty-four adult outpatients were administered the PM Scale at admission. Like McCallum and Piper (1990), these authors found that PM scores were negatively associated without dropping out of treatment. PM scores were positively correlated with number of sessions attended, $r = .37$, $p < .01$. PM scores were also positively correlated with the Global Assessment Scale (GAS), $r = .33$, $p < .05$, and negatively correlated with the Psychiatric Outpatient Rating Scale (PORS; a symptom checklist), $r = -.37$, $p < .05$—both instruments administered at discharge. In a larger study of 256 adult outpatients (Conte et al., 1996), a principal components analysis of the PM Scale yielded five factors: (1) willingness to try to understand oneself and others; (2) openness to new ideas and capacity for change; (3) access to one's feelings; (4) belief in benefits of discussing one's problems; and (5) interest in meaning and motivation of own and others' behavior. This finding produced the unwieldy and impractical definition of PM as "an attribute of an individual that presupposes a degree of access to one's feelings, a willingness to try to understand oneself and others, a belief in the benefit of discussing one's problems, an interest in the meaning and motivation of one's own and others' thoughts, feelings, and behavior, and a capacity for change" (p. 254). The definition encompasses constructs unrelated to traditional definitions of PM such as belief in the benefits of psychotherapy and a capacity for change—two components that nevertheless reflect the historical association between PM and suitability for treatment. In this second study, the significant correlations between PM scores and the GAS and PORS outcome measures were not replicated; however, the significant correlation between PM scores and number of sessions attended was replicated, $r = .25$, $p < .01$.

Significant problems with the construction of the PM Scale might explain its lack of association with treatment outcomes. Shill and Lumley (2002) conducted their own factor analysis of the PM Scale on a nonclinical sample of 397 undergraduates, which yielded two factors that reflect the valence of the items. The first factor consisted of positively worded items, while the second factor consisted of negatively worded items. This finding suggests that method variance influenced the factor structure, which naturally throws the instrument's construct validity into question. Content analysis of the PM Scale also revealed that the items loading onto each factor lacked a unifying theme. In fact, Shill and Lumley (2002) identified four clusters of items loading onto the first factor. Following a different statistical procedure, Shill and Lumley (2002) then conducted a second factor analysis, which yielded five factors: (1) belief in the benefits of discussing one's problems; (2) access to one's feelings; (3) willingness to discuss problems with others; (4) interest in the meaning and motivation of own and others' behavior; and (5) openness to change. A comparison of this factor structure with the original factor structure of Conte et al. (1996) revealed that only Shill and Lumley's (2002) first and second factors conceptually replicated Conte et al.'s (1996) fourth and third factors, respectively—belief in the benefits of discussing one's problems and access to one's feelings. Unfortunately, "openness to change" bears little resemblance to the most frequently cited theoretical definitions of PM, and factors 1, 3, and 4 are exclusively related to interest rather than ability.

In a literature that has inexplicably marginalized the existence and development of PM in children, Hatcher and his colleagues (Hatcher and Hatcher,

1997; Hatcher et al., 1990) attempted to measure PM toward others using one-page oral presentations of two fairytale stories—"Cinderella" and "The Emperor's New Clothes." After the presentation of each story, the researcher asks the child to write down his or her responses to three questions related to each story. The written responses to these six total questions constitute the basis for the assessment of PM toward others. Questions include "Why were the stepsisters so mean to Cinderella?" and "Why did the emperor believe that he was wearing a beautiful new outfit?" Responses are coded on a four-point scale that assesses "Psychological Mindedness Toward Others." In a separate assessment procedure designed to measure PM toward the self, the child is shown two photographs and asked to write a story about each one that includes a beginning, a middle, and an end, and to tell what the people in each story are thinking and feeling. After writing both stories, the child is asked to reflect on each story separately, write what each story might tell about himself or herself, and explain the connections between the story and the child's ideas about what the story reveals about himself or herself. The responses to both written stories are coded on a six-point scale that assesses "Psychological Mindedness Toward the Self."

A validation study was conducted using a sample of sixty fifth-, sixty eighth-, and fifty-nine twelfth-grade students. Hatcher and his colleagues (Hatcher and Hatcher, 1997; Hatcher et al., 1990) correlated the PM-toward-others (PO) scores with the PM-toward-the-self (PS) scores for each grade level and found that the two sets of scores were significantly positively correlated only for twelfth-grade girls, $r = .47$, $p < .01$. All scores increased with grade level. Girls also obtained higher PO and PS scores than boys did at all grade levels. Believing that PO and PS would be associated with abstract reasoning skills, the authors assessed the children on a task of verbal abstract reasoning and a task of spatial/mathematical reasoning and combined the scores on each task to form a total abstract reasoning score. The authors found that PO was positively correlated with the total abstract reasoning score only for fifth-grade boys, $r = .49$, $p < .01$, and eighth-grade girls, $r = .46$, $p < .01$. On the other hand, PS was positively correlated with the total abstract reasoning score only for eighth-grade boys, $r = .57$, $p < .01$, and uncorrelated for girls at any grade level. The lack of a clear pattern of findings suggests that abstract reasoning skills are only indirectly related to PM toward others or the self. PM toward others and PM toward the self appear to develop separately, and only by twelfth grade become connected to each other—but only for girls.

The assessment procedures outlined by Hatcher and his colleagues (Hatcher and Hatcher, 1997; Hatcher et al., 1990) identified the quantitative differences between PM toward others and PM toward the self. This finding suggests that other assessment instruments that measure only one form of PM (e.g., PMAP; McCallum and Piper, 1990) or yield a total score for items that cover both forms of PM (e.g., PM Scale; Conte et al., 1990) are not valid measures of PM. As already discussed, the degree of PM toward self depends on the severity of defensive processes interfering with its function. These defensive processes would be less likely to interfere with PM toward others because the psychological cost of understanding others is less.

NEIGHBORING CONSTRUCTS OF PM

To develop a better understanding of the nature of PM, research has identified many variables associated with PM. Using the admittedly flawed PM Scale (Conte et al., 1990), these studies associated PM with a series of personality traits, ego functions, and attachment variables (Alvarez et al., 1998; Beitel and Cecero, 2003; Beitel, Ferrer, and Cecero, 2004, 2005; Conte, Buckley, Picard, and Karasu, 1995; Taylor, 1995; Trudeau and Reich, 1995). With respect to personality traits, PM was positively correlated with assertiveness, sociability, and activity (Conte et al., 1995), and openness and extroversion (Beitel and Cecero, 2003), and negatively correlated with neuroticism (Beitel and Cecero, 2003). I would interpret these results to mean that psychologically minded persons are presumably highly equipped to understand the meaning and motivation of others' thoughts, feelings, and behaviors; thus, they are sufficiently trusting of others to be assertive, sociable, open, extroverted, and actively engaged with others. PM also seems to protect against neuroticism, perhaps also because psychologically minded persons have a coherent set of expectations of themselves and others, which permits them to experience low levels of anxiety and stress. When these conditions do occur, psychologically minded persons are able to reflect on their emotional reactions and understand how their circumstances contribute to these reactions, which would be expected to lower their levels of anxiety and stress.

PM has also been related to cognitive styles of thinking. Specifically, PM was positively correlated with ambiguity tolerance and negatively correlated with external locus of control and magical thinking (Beitel et al., 2004). Psychological processes are inherently ambiguous because they cannot be directly observed; thus, psychologically minded persons must be able to tolerate ambiguity to make meaning out of their interior lives and those of others. Psychologically minded persons must also be able to observe their internal selves and their emotional landscape rather than dwell on external events. Perhaps this experience fosters a sense of self-directedness that epitomizes an internal locus of control. Because psychologically minded persons seek plausible explanations for their thoughts, feelings, and behaviors, magical thinking is not part of their cognitive repertoire. Psychologically minded persons can tolerate the ambiguity of their emotional experience without resorting to externalizing or even magical explanations for their thoughts, feelings, and behavior.

Beitel et al. (2005) also found positive correlations between PM and perspective taking and empathic concern, and negative correlations between PM and personal distress and social anxiety. To understand the emotional life of another person, the psychologically minded person must take the other person's perspective; thus, PM would be expected to be associated with perspective taking. Consequently, this perspective taking would naturally establish an emotional connection between psychologically minded persons and other persons. Psychologically minded persons do not experience high levels of social anxiety because they are able to reflect on the meaning and motivation of this anxiety and make sense out of their experiences with others. Psychologically minded persons are also able to appreciate their emotional responses associated with an emergency and respond calmly rather than react with high levels of personal distress. Making connections among thoughts, feelings, and behavior enables comparisons with previous emergencies and helps these persons to predict a variety of outcomes, which can reduce the experience of personal distress.

Trudeau and Reich (1995) found that PM was also positively correlated with mental well-being as measured by the Happy Scale (Ryff, 1989), which suggests that psychologically minded persons are also well adjusted. In contrast, Farber (1989) reported that private self-consciousness (as measured by the Self-Consciousness Scale) was negatively correlated with self-esteem. Farber (1989) concluded that PM "may leave one feeling more emotionally attuned but also more aware of disturbing aspects of oneself that cannot be overcome and of possibilities in oneself that cannot be realized" (p. 216). The discrepancy between the two findings might be related to the differences in assessment instruments used. The Self-Consciousness Scale (Fenigstein, Scheier, and Buss, 1975) identifies highly self-conscious persons who "constantly think about themselves, scrutinize their behavior (or appearance), and mull over their thoughts—to the point of obsessiveness" (p. 522). Items such as "I'm constantly examining my motives" and "I never scrutinize myself" (reverse scored) reflect a preoccupation with internal processes that suggests a lack of psychological adjustment. In addition, the focus of the instrument is exclusively on the self rather than the self and others. Given the differences between the PM Scale, used by Trudeau and Reich (1995), and the Self-Consciousness Scale, used by Farber (1989), we might expect differences in how these two instruments relate to measures of mental well-being and self-esteem. Interestingly, Beitel et al. (2005) recently reported a positive correlation between private self-consciousness, as measured by the Self-Consciousness Scale, and PM, as measured by the PM Scale, $r = .27$, $p < .05$. Clearly, further research is needed to determine the relations between PM and mental well-being and self-esteem.

Regarding ego functions measured by the Self-Evaluation Questionnaire (Conte et al., 1995), PM was positively correlated with mastery-competence, synthetic-integrative functioning, and autonomous functioning (Conte et al., 1995). Because of their deep understanding of the meaning and motivation of their own and others' thoughts, feelings, and behaviors, psychologically minded persons experience mastery over their environments, synthesize a wide range of internal and external information, and consequently experience a full sense of self-directedness. A limitation of this research, however, is that the same research group (Conte et al., 1995) designed both instruments, which could spuriously inflate the correlations.

Attachment variables have also been associated with the PM Scale. Contrary to their hypothesis, Alvarez et al. (1998) found that PM was negatively correlated with the extent to which the adult subjects experienced their mothers as having been rejecting during childhood, defined as having been too busy for the child, having spent a minimal amount of time with the child, and having complained about the child. PM, however, was uncorrelated with adult subjects' current attachment to mother or father and positively correlated with current attachment to peers (Beitel and Cecero, 2003). Perhaps adults have closer relationships to peers than to parents because they are able to understand their peers' internal worlds and thus feel comfortable getting close to and depending on them. Notably, attachment as defined by these studies bears little resemblance to attachment as defined by attachment researchers in the tradition of Bowlby (see Bowlby, 1982; Main et al., 1985).

Other constructs have also been at least theoretically associated with PM. These constructs include self-consciousness, self-awareness, introspection, insight, alexithymia, mindfulness, and, of course, reflective functioning. Self-consciousness and self-awareness are twin concepts with slightly different definitions. Self-consciousness has been defined as a "relatively permanent tendency of individuals to direct more or less attention to the self" (Fenigstein, 1997, p. 106), while self-awareness has been defined as a "psychological *state* of being attentive to the self, whether as a result of transient situational variables, chronic dispositions, or both" (p. 106). Self-consciousness and PM therefore have both been categorized as a trait or a permanent tendency rather than a current process that someone is actively engaging in such as self-awareness. The focus of observation—exclusively on the self rather than on the self and others—conceptually distinguishes PM from both self-consciousness and self-awareness. In addition, self-consciousness and self-awareness could reflect either a preoccupation with one's internal processes or an open receptivity to them (K. W. Brown and Ryan, 2003), whereas PM has always been associated with an open receptivity to internal experience. As mentioned earlier, PM was positively correlated with private self-consciousness, $r = .27$, $p < .05$ (Beitel et al., 2005), which accounts for only 7.3 percent of the variance between the two constructs. I would consider PM to be a broader construct because of its dual focus on both the self and others.

Introspection is another term often associated with PM. Introspection is considered a process of "microscopic examination of experience as well as openness to affects" (Appelbaum, 1973, p.43). PM, however, has traditionally been defined as a trait rather than a process. PM is also focused on both the self and others rather than exclusively on the self. PM is also more broadly conceptualized than simply the examination of experience. PM also refers to the "manipulation of ideas and the creation of abstractions" (p. 43). The construct of introspection has not been operationalized in an assessment instrument; therefore, no research has been conducted on the relation between PM and introspection.

Insight is another neighboring construct of PM. As part of the Psychotherapy Research Project of the Menninger Foundation, Wallerstein and Robbins (1956) offered this definition of insight under the heading "Ego Factors (and Defenses)" (p. 244): "How much of the total disturbed functioning (both symptomatic and characterologic) the patient sees as maladaptive and as the proper object of therapy. . . . Is it at some level of *awareness of connections* between symptoms, behavior, and underlying conflict?" (italics in original, p. 245). This definition of insight refers to knowledge about whether a person has a problem. Appelbaum (1973) made the conceptual distinction between PM as a process of discovery and insight as "*a result* of the process of discovery" (italics in original, p. 37). Similarly, Bishop et al. (2004) categorized insight as self-knowledge rather than a process of self-observation. Grant (2001, p. 14) also considered insight as the ultimate product of PM, but added that insight then modifies PM in a feedback loop in line with the insight gained through the inquiry phase of PM.

The only known instrument constructed to measure insight is the insight test (Tolor and Reznikoff, 1960). The authors operationally defined insight as the accurate ability to comprehend the causative influences on the attitudes and behaviors of others. This instrument's reliability and internal consistency have been questioned (Conte and Ratto, 1997); moreover, the target of observation is focused on others rather than the self. Hatcher and his colleagues have already pointed out that PM toward others is not synonymous with PM toward the self (Hatcher and Hatcher, 1997; Hatcher et al., 1990). The construct of insight as measured by this instrument is not in line with the emphasis on self-knowledge made by other authors. No research has been conducted on the relation between PM and insight.

Alexithymia has received considerable attention as the conceptual converse of PM (Conte and Ratto, 1997). Defined originally by Sifneos (1973) as difficulty identifying and verbally describing feelings, Taylor (1995) operationalized alexithymia in the Toronto Alexithymia Scale–20 (TAS-20), a twenty-item Likert-type questionnaire, which yielded three factors: (1) difficulty identifying feelings; (2) difficulty describing feelings to others; and (3) externally oriented thinking. This factor structure was replicated in both clinical and nonclinical samples and in other cultural settings. The Py subscale of the CPI was negatively correlated with an earlier version of the TAS-20, $r = -.33$, $p < .01$ (Bagby, Taylor, and Parker, 1986). The PM Scale was also negatively correlated with the TAS-20, $r = -.68$, $p < .01$, with factor 1, $r = -.44$, $p < .01$, with factor 2, $r = -.51$, $p < .01$, and with factor 3, $r = -.54$, $p < .01$ (Taylor, 1995). In another study the PM Scale was also negatively correlated with the TAS-20, $r = -.31$, $p = .01$. Two factors of the PM Scale—(4) interest in the meaning and motivation of own and others' behavior and (5) openness to change—were uncorrelated with the TAS-20 total score (Shill and Lumley, 2002). The authors suggested that factor 4 of the PM Scale measures an interest in meaning and motivation, while the factors of the TAS-20 measure the lack of ability. One can have an interest without ability and vice versa; therefore, no strong negative correlation was found. Regarding factor 5—openness to change—the authors disputed its inclusion in the PM construct because it seems to be more closely associated with motivation for psychotherapy than PM. If PM is the converse of alexithymia, and if openness to change is conceptually unrelated to PM, then openness to change would also be expected to be uncorrelated with alexithymia.

Alexithymia is conceptually related to PM because both constructs underscore the importance of identifying and describing feelings and focusing on one's internal world—with alexithymia defined as the converse of PM. PM, however, could be considered a broader construct that includes not only the converse of alexithymia but also reflection on the meaning and motivation of feelings, as well as of thoughts and behavior, and an external focus toward others as well as an internal focus toward the self. Perhaps this conceptual difference accounts for the moderate magnitude of the correlation between the two constructs.

Mindfulness has also been characterized as a neighboring construct of PM. Originating in Buddhism and co-opted by the cognitive-behavioral literature, mindfulness has been associated with the so-called third wave of behaviorism (S. C. Hayes, 2002, 2004). According to Bishop et al. (2004), mindfulness "involves the self-regulation of attention so that it is maintained on immediate experience, thereby allowing for increased recognition of mental events in the present moment [and] adopting a particular orientation toward one's experiences in the present moment, an orientation that is characterized by curiosity, openness, and acceptance" (p. 232). Among some cognitive-behaviorists, mindfulness is considered an essential ingredient of therapeutic change. Several treatment packages have been designed with mindfulness training as the centerpiece (Baer, 2003). It has even been suggested as a common factor shared across effective treatments (Martin, 1997). Unlike PM and other related constructs with psychoanalytic origins, mindfulness has spawned a cadre of self-report instruments used by researchers to assess therapeutic change (for reviews, see Baer, Smith, Hopkins, Krietemeyer, and Toney, 2006; Lau et al., in press).

Three attempts have been made to correlate mindfulness with PM or constructs conceptually related to PM. K. W. Brown and Ryan (2003) developed the Mindful Attention Awareness Scale (MAAS), a fifteen-item Likert-type questionnaire, which yielded a unidimensional factor structure that accounted for 95 percent of the total variance. In four independent samples, the internal state awareness subscale of the Self-Consciousness Scale (Fenigstein, Scheier, and Buss, 1975), previously used to measure PM (Farber, 1989), was modestly and positively correlated with the MAAS, $r = .17–.23$, which modestly supported the discriminant validity of the MAAS in relation to a construct conceptually related to PM. In a different study (Beitel, Ferrar, and Cecero, 2005), the MAAS was positively correlated with the PM Scale, (Conte et al., 1990), $r = .41$, $p < .01$. In a third study, Lau et al. (in press) introduced the Toronto Mindfulness Scale (TMS), a thirteen-item Likert-type questionnaire, which yielded two factors—curiosity and decentering. Curiosity was defined as an interest in all aspects of experience in the present moment, while decentering was defined as an awareness of experience "with some distance and disidentification" (p. 16)—an observer stance rather than a participant stance. The TMS curiosity and decentering factors were positively correlated with the PM Scale, $r = .22$, $p < .01$, and $r = .19$, $p < .05$, respectively. The modest magnitude of these correlations again supported the discriminant validity of the TMS in relation to PM.

These positive correlations, however, reflect some conceptual overlap between mindfulness and PM. Both constructs consist of "an enhanced attention to and awareness of current experience or present reality" (K. W. Brown and Ryan, 2003, p. 822). The construct of PM, however, has a broader conceptual scope that includes additional components such as the connections among thoughts, feelings, and behavior to form patterns of meaning and motivation, not only in oneself but also in others. These components, of course, require an enhanced attention to and awareness of current experience. PM also transcends the present to include the past and future. A psychologically minded person might reevaluate his or her current behavior in the context of feelings experienced the previous day, or predict the emotional reaction of a colleague at work if he or she were to share an observation with the colleague. These are aspects of PM excluded by the definition of mindfulness. Bishop and his colleagues (Bishop et al., 2004) also pointed out that mindfulness is "a *process* of self-observation" (italics in original, p. 235), while PM has been defined as "a trait" (Farber, 1985, p. 170) or "a person's ability" (Appelbaum, 1973, p. 36).

The other neighboring construct of PM to be reviewed is reflective functioning (RF), originally called "reflective-self functioning" and defined by Fonagy and his colleagues (Fonagy, Steele, Steele, Moran, and Higgitt, 1991) as "the internal observation of mental activities. . . . The evolution and awareness of mental processes in the self and other are intrinsically linked" (p. 203). Later, the authors added this definition: "The ability to take account of one's own and others' mental states and, thus, to understand why people behave in specific ways" (p. 203). Astonishingly, no researcher has sought to assess the correlation between the constructs of RF and PM. Only Fonagy and his colleagues (Fonagy, Steele, Steele, Moran, and Higgitt, 1991) have even mentioned PM in connection with RF, as cited at the beginning of this chapter. Perhaps one reason behind the paucity of empirical inquiry has to do with the method of measurement of RF. The only official method available is through administering the Adult Attachment Interview (AAI; George et al., 1996), an hour-long, semi-structured interview that elicits information about a person's childhood relationships with his or her parents or primary caregivers. The forty-seven-page, single-spaced coding system developed for assessing RF (Fonagy et al., 1998) is time-consuming to learn (requiring attendance at a three-day RF training workshop and subsequent coding of fifteen practice AAIs to calculate interrater reliability with the authors) and labor-intensive to apply (one to two hours per AAI). This grueling process makes RF research prohibitive for many. Fonagy and Target (2005b) have mentioned, however, that an RF questionnaire is under construction.

One might also account for this lack of acknowledgment of the existence of each other's construct as evidence of a quiet turf war between two twin siblings who do not know whether they are fraternal or identical. One might also suggest that RF has eclipsed PM as a newer and more contemporary construct. Perhaps RF has co-opted the essential elements of PM and placed them in a contemporary developmental and psychoanalytic context, which would render PM "outdated" (Fonagy, Steele, Steele, Moran, and Higgitt, 1991, p. 215).

Fonagy and his colleagues (Fonagy, Gergely, et al., 2002) have defined RF as the operationalization of mentalization, a construct introduced by French psychoanalysts in the 1960s (Fain and David, 1963; Fain and Marty, 1964) that referred to the early developmental activity of transforming somatic drive-affect excitations into symbolized mental contents. Lecours and Bouchard (1997), however, dimensionalized this definition such that a person can vary in increasing mentalizing quality from somatization—a lack of symbolization—to insight—fully symbolized mental contents. One can easily make an analogy to alexithymia as representing the low end of mentalization. Does PM, considered by some to be the conceptual converse of alexithymia (Conte and Ratto, 1997), represent the high end of mentalization?

PM as well as RF can be conceptually distinguished from mentalization because both constructs represent broader concerns than the mere symbolization of mental contents. In addition, both PM and RF refer to reflection on the causal connections among mental contents (e.g., feelings, thoughts, wishes, fears, intentions) as well as behavior in both the self as well as others. One might think of mentalization as having only to do with identifying and describing feelings and wishes rather than deriving meaning from the organization of all forms of mental phenomena and their products in both the self and others. Notably, Fonagy and his colleagues (Fonagy et al., 1998) used the terms "RF" and "mentalization" interchangeably (p. 4).

The primary conceptual distinction between PM and RF appears to be an additional component of RF—the intersubjective nature of mental states. Farber's (1985) definition of PM indicates that a person can reflect on the meaning and motivation of mental and behavioral phenomena in himself or herself and others, but the mutual influence of each other's mental states is not explicitly specified. Here is an illustration of the intersubjective nature of RF:

> My boss seems angry with me because I have been arriving late for work. I have been late because I have been feeling angry that I was passed over for a promotion. I did not get the promotion because I have been working under duress. I have become distracted at work because my mother feels worried that she will not recover from her stroke, and her worry worries me. I think my boss sees me as distracted, however, because she thinks I don't know what I'm doing.

The focus in this illustration is on the intersubjective influence of mental states rather than on the mental states of the self or of others exclusively.

An illustration of PM toward the self might sound something like this: "I have been feeling angry at work because I was passed over for that promotion. I have been distracted at work lately, which might account for my diminished work performance. My worry about my mother is making me distracted." An illustration of PM toward others might sound something like this: "My boss seems angry lately. She is under a lot of pressure from her boss to meet fourth-quarter expectations and needs everyone to work at their optimal capacity. She gets angry when her boss yells at her because she feels she is doing everything in her power to meet his demands." The interconnectivity of meaning and motivation between the self and others is missing in these last two illustrations.

According to Fonagy and his colleagues (Fonagy, Gergely, et al., 2002, p. 60), the quality of one's RF can be uneven, depending on the context in which RF is invoked to make sense out of one's experience. A psychoanalyst who demonstrates high RF when discussing his clinical work "may be far less so in the context of discussing his own family relationships" (Fonagy et al., 1998, p. 6). These authors privilege RF in contexts in which the person is relating to others in whom he or she has a significant emotional investment. RF demonstrated under these conditions reveals something about the quality of the person's reasoning ability when his or her defensive processes are most likely to be activated. RF is therefore assessed using the AAI (George et al., 1996), in which the person is asked to engage in RF regarding childhood relationships with primary caregivers. The response to the following AAI question, "Why do you think your parents behaved as they did during your childhood?" (p. 53), illustrates high RF in the context of high emotional arousal:

> I think my dad behaved the way he did to me because after his mother died, my mother was seven years older than him. I think he saw my mom as a replacement, so she in turn would mother him, and as soon as he realized that she wanted him to be a husband and she already had one child, he beat that child, my half brother, so much that it had to be taken away. My brother was born, but he didn't seem to have much contact with him, and when I was born, a girl, mothers are supposed to be closer to their daughters, and I think he saw me as a potential threat to their relationship. So he beat me, and he saw me sexually, and it's a shame how he felt towards his own daughter [that] led him to beat me, and he also beat my mom, and I think he beat my mom because she wouldn't be a mother to him.

The respondent presents a coherent explanation for her father's behavior toward her mother and her—specifically, how certain circumstances (father's loss of mother) and family characteristics (respondent's gender, mother's age) converged to influence the father's attitude and behavior, which in turn influenced the respondent.

The theoreticians who have defined PM through the years might respond that this illustration from the AAI indeed reflects PM. Yet Fonagy and his colleagues would argue that RF—with its focus on the intersubjective connections between mental states—is like new wine that must be poured into new wineskins because the old wineskins cannot contain it. PM was initially defined in the heyday of ego psychology as an ego function (Appelbaum, 1973) with a large genetic component (Wallerstein and Robbins, 1956) that applies only to the mental phenomena of the ego. It was later considered a trait that could be applied to understand the self as well as others (Farber, 1985). Recent authors (Hatcher and Hatcher, 1997) suggested considering PM toward the self and PM toward others as conceptually independent constructs with separate developmental lines. The advent of a two-person psychology (Aron, 1990) and attachment theory (Bowlby, 1982) necessitates that PM undergo a facelift to keep pace with the paradigm shifts underway in psychoanalytic theory.

PM AS A COMMON FACTOR OF THERAPEUTIC CHANGE

Consistent with the view of PM as a genetically based ego function (Appelbaum, 1973; Wallerstein and Robbins, 1956), PM has traditionally been considered a primary criterion of suitability for treatment. Influenced by recent attempts at patient-treatment matching (e.g., Beutler and Clarkin, 1990; Beutler, Clarkin, and Bongar, 2000; Beutler and Harwood, 2000; Beutler and Hodgson, 1993), PM has been empirically tested not only as a predictor but also as a moderator of treatment outcome (Piper et al., 2002). Quality of object relations was shown to be predictive of the rate of change in treatment outcomes for patients in supportive therapy but not interpretive therapy, while PM was not associated with treatment outcomes (Conte et al., 1996; Ogrodniczuk, Piper, Joyce, and McCallum, 2001; Piper et al., 2002). PM was instead negatively associated with dropping out of treatment and positively associated with engaging in psychodynamic work in group therapy.

One could conclude that PM is not a criterion of suitability for treatment. Alternatively, flaws in the assessment of PM could account for the absence of findings. Another possibility, however, is that the construct itself is also flawed. PM directed toward only the self or toward only others—without considering the mutual influence of mental states and behaviors—eliminates a critical aspect of human experience that one would imagine to be closely associated with treatment outcome. The interaction structures that form between patient and therapist can change over time through the mutative effects of both interpretation and interpersonal interaction, which in turn affect symptomatic and structural change (Jones, 2000). Preliminary research that treats RF as a psychotherapy-process variable (Josephs et al., 2004; Josephs and Fatzer, 2006; Karlsson and Kermott, 2006) suggests that RF fluctuates as a function of changes in these interaction structures over time. For the construct of PM to demonstrate similar changes during the process of therapy, perhaps the field needs to consider making changes both to the construct and to the methods of its assessment.

Another possible reason for the absence of findings of a positive association between PM and treatment outcome is the treatment itself. Psychoanalytically oriented psychotherapies have traditionally focused on the acquisition of insight as the goal of therapeutic work (H. P. Blum, 1979), yet the report of the Psychotherapy Research Project of the Menninger Foundation concluded, "The most common change in conflicts was increased awareness of them but without resolution of them [which] occurred infrequently" (Wallerstein, 1989, p. 204). Perhaps PM is not associated with treatment outcome because we fail to target PM explicitly in our treatments. Insight can easily become intellectualized and used defensively, which could diminish the likelihood of a satisfactory treatment outcome. Working toward developing the patient's own nascent capacity for PM, however, either through the interpretation of defensive processes formed against PM or through clarifying work in the transference, could help the patient to acquire insight on his or her own. Give a man a fish, and he will eat for a day; teach him how to fish, and he will eat for a lifetime. Perhaps our treatments feed our patients insight but fail to teach them how to acquire insight on their own through engaging in psychologically minded functioning both in and out of sessions.

Bateman and Fonagy (2004b) have developed MBT, a treatment package that purports to help patients with borderline personality disorder develop a reflective function, which provides the patient with "a capacity to distinguish inner from outer reality, intrapersonal mental and emotional processes from interpersonal communications, and what is self from what is not" (p. 123). The development of RF in patients engaged in MBT "critically depends upon interaction with more mature minds, which are both benign and reflective in their turn" (p. 123). Undoubtedly, most psychoanalytically oriented psychotherapies do provide experiences in which patients develop this reflective function as they acquire insight; however, MBT places the development of RF at the heart of the therapeutic process. Perhaps if our treatments made the acquisition of PM a priority rather than the acquisition of insight, empirical studies of treatment outcome might reveal PM as a mediator of outcome rather than as a predictor or moderator.

If the construct of PM can be reconceptualized as a therapeutic process rather than as a primary criterion of suitability for therapy, then one can speculate whether PM could be considered a common factor of therapeutic change. In other words, does treatment effectiveness depend on the acquisition of PM, regardless of theoretical orientation? One can also speculate whether PM and two of its neighboring constructs—mindfulness and RF—share certain features of therapeutic change. Both mindfulness (Martin, 1997) and RF (Bateman and Fonagy, 2004b) have been given consideration as common factors of therapeutic change. I have already outlined the commonalities among the constructs of PM, mindfulness, and RF. What specific features are common to these putative common factors?

Figure 7.1 contains a Venn diagram of the common and distinctive features among these three constructs. According to exploratory and confirmatory factor analyses conducted by Baer et al. (2006), mindfulness consists of five factors—(1) observing mental phenomena, (2) describing/labeling mental phenomena, (3) acting with awareness/concentration, (4) nonjudging of mental phenomena, and (5) nonreactivity to mental phenomena. According to an exploratory factor analysis conducted by Shill and Lumley (2002), PM also consists of five factors: (1) belief in the benefits of discussing one's problems; (2) access to one's feelings; (3) willingness to discuss problems with others; (4) interest in the meaning and motivation of own and others' behavior; and (5) openness to change. Although the RF coding system created by

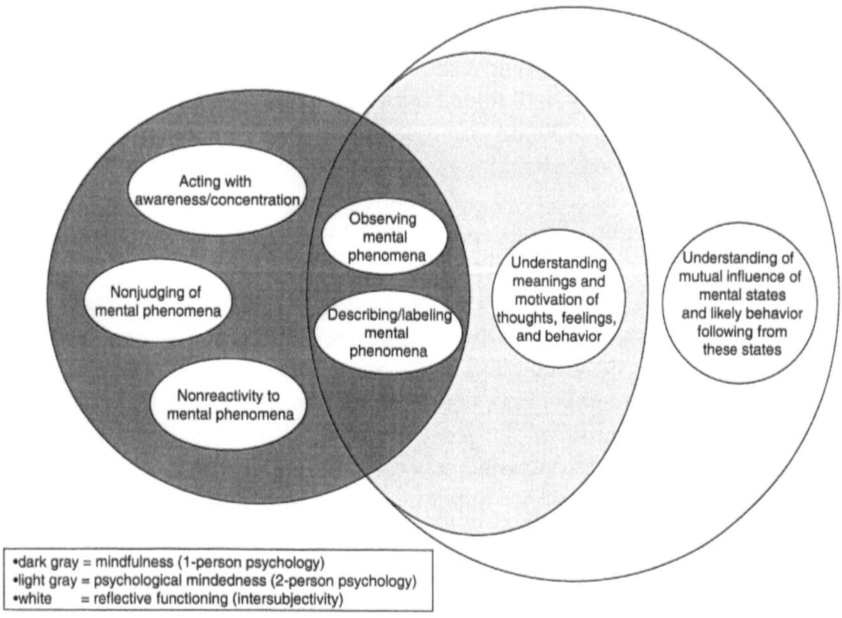

Figure 7.1. Common and Distinctive Features among Mindfulness, Psychological Mindedness, and Reflective Functioning

Fonagy and his colleagues (Fonagy et al., 1998) cannot be factor-analyzed, we can extrapolate from their operational definition of RF four components: (1) observing mental phenomena; (2) describing/labeling mental phenomena; (3) interest in the meaning and motivation of own and others' behavior; and (4) understanding the intrinsic linkage and mutual influence of mental processes in self and other. Figure 7.1 demonstrates that all three constructs conceptually overlap on two features: (1) observing mental phenomena, and (2) describing/labeling mental phenomena. Perhaps these two common features of the three putative common factors of therapeutic change are the true common factors of therapeutic change.

An alternative explanation for these findings is that the other features that did not conceptually overlap, such as interest in the meaning and motivation of one's own and others' behavior, and understanding the intrinsic linkage and mutual influence of mental processes in self and other, might wield an unacknowledged influence over the therapeutic process of all effective treatments. Citing Strupp (1988) as a source, Grant (2001), a cognitive behaviorist, concluded, "All attempts at directed purposeful change, regardless of theoretical orientation, are directed at fostering reflectivity" (p. 8), which he defined as "*inquiry into how and why oneself and/or others behave, think, and feel in the way that they do*" (italics in original, p. 12). Thus, Grant (2001) suggested that interest in meaning and motivation implicitly operates in every successful treatment. Similarly, Appelbaum (1973) suggested that PM, which he defined as seeing "relationships among thoughts, feelings, and actions" (p. 36), operates at an implicit level "even during such apparently non-psychological problem-solving moments. It is only 'as if' the requirements for psychological thinking had been put aside" (p. 44). Again, the feature of interest in meaning and motivation is implicated as a common factor even in problem-solving treatments.

Recent research supports the idea that this interest in meaning and motivation wields an unacknowledged influence over the therapeutic process of all effective treatments. Treatments that adhere to a cognitive-behavioral orientation nevertheless contain psychodynamic interventions, which prove to be most predictive of positive outcome (Ablon and Jones, 1998; Ablon et al., 2006). In one study (Ablon and Jones, 1998), typical psychodynamic interventions included "Therapist interprets warded-off or unconscious wishes, feelings, or ideas," "Patient's feelings or perceptions are linked to situations or behavior of the past," and "Therapist comments on changes in patient's mood or affect" (p. 75). Of course, these interventions are designed to foster the patient's interest in meaning and motivation. Thus, perhaps the interest in meaning and motivation, while not identified in figure 7.1 as a feature common to all three putative common factors, might be implicitly fostered even in treatments that do not officially support such interventions. Farber and Golden (1997) observed, "There are a great many clinicians who treat problems using a cognitive-behavioral perspective but who continue to think of their own issues and those of their patients in more or less dynamic terms" (p. 216).

Although not explicitly included as a psychodynamic intervention in Ablon and Jones's (1998) study, the unique feature of RF, understanding the intrinsic linkage and mutual influence of mental processes in self and other (the only feature unique to the construct of RF; see figure 7.1), might also be operating implicitly in treatments of varying theoretical orientations. Preliminary evidence suggests that RF is associated with treatment outcome in treatments of varying theoretical orientations (Karlsson and Kermott, 2006). Thus, this unique feature of RF might also be implicitly fostered in treatments of diverse theoretical orientations. Additional research is needed to determine (1) whether observing mental phenomena and describing/labeling mental phenomena are the two specific features shared by all three putative common factors responsible for producing therapeutic change across theoretical orientations, or (2) whether other specific features implicitly operate as effective ingredients of therapeutic change, even among treatments that do not officially sanction such features.

Farber and Golden (1997), however, have suggested that fostering PM is not appropriate for some patients. Interest in meaning and motivation might occur across treatments of varying theoretical orientations, but some patients do not benefit from any kind of treatment. For such patients, increasing PM might do more harm than good: "There are those patients who are facing life situations so realistically bleak that a psychological understanding of the condition is beside the point and may only serve to exacerbate the despair" (p. 226). Elsewhere, Farber (1989) concluded that PM increases awareness "of disturbing aspects of oneself that cannot be overcome and of possibilities in oneself that cannot be realized . . . [which makes one] wiser but also sadder" (p. 216). Therapists must be careful not to overestimate the effectiveness of common factors for all patients.

THE FUTURE OF PM

If PM is to survive in the jungle of constructs and not fall victim to natural selection, theoreticians need to redesign it in accordance with contemporary advances in psychoanalytic theory such as attachment theory. One of the many advances made by attachment theory on behalf of psychoanalytic theory in the past fifteen years is the adoption of a two-dimensional model of psychopathology (Goodman, 2002, 2005). Object relations researchers such as Blatt and his colleagues (Blatt, Chevron, Quinlan, Schaffer, and Wein, 1992) articulated a structural model of object representations that operationalized the views of American object relations theoreticians such as Mahler and her colleagues (Mahler, 1968; Mahler, Pine, and Bergman, 1975) and Jacobson (1964) into a one-dimensional model of psychopathology. Object representations varied in their overall quality from complex, differentiated, and integrated to simple, undifferentiated, and unintegrated. Psychopathology was conceptually positioned at various levels of this one-dimensional model, depending on the hypothesized developmental stage at which the fixation or regression occurred. For example, depression is a form of psychopathology whose position on this spectrum depends on the overall quality of the object representation, which in turn depends on developmental antecedents. Thus, the etiology of the primitive anaclitic depression developmentally precedes that of the more mature introjective depression, empirically differentiated by the overall quality of the patient's object representation (Blatt, 1974; Blatt and Maroudas, 1992).

Attachment theory reconceptualized psychopathology as a two-dimensional model with a security-anxiety dimension and an orthogonally positioned deactivating-hyperactivating dimension (Kobak, Cole, Ferenz-Gillies, Fleming, and Gamble, 1993). Bowlby's (1973) construct of the internal working model, conceptually related to the construct of object representation (Goodman, 2005), was classified into three categories: secure (B), anxious-avoidant (A), and anxious-resistant (C) (Ainsworth, Behar, Waters, and Wall, 1978). The A and C categories were conceptualized as two forms of insecure attachment. If these three categories were dimensionalized, the B category would represent one dimension and range from security to insecurity, while the A and C categories would represent opposite ends of an orthogonally positioned second dimension and range from extreme anxious-avoidance to extreme anxious-resistance. Kobak and his colleagues (Kobak et al., 1993) relabeled this second dimension "deactivating-hyperactivating" to capture the state of the attachment system when it is activated in a stressful or dangerous situation that requires protection. Humans who have no confidence in a caregiving response that confers protection would deactivate this system, while humans who feel uncertain about a caregiving response that confers protection would hyperactivate this system in a desperate attempt to insure a response.

Because these categories form by twelve months of age (Ainsworth et al., 1978) and remain relatively stable throughout the lifespan (Hamilton, 2000; van IJzendoorn, 1995; Waters, Merrick, Treboux, Crowell, and Albersheim, 2000), psychopathology in this model is assigned a position along the

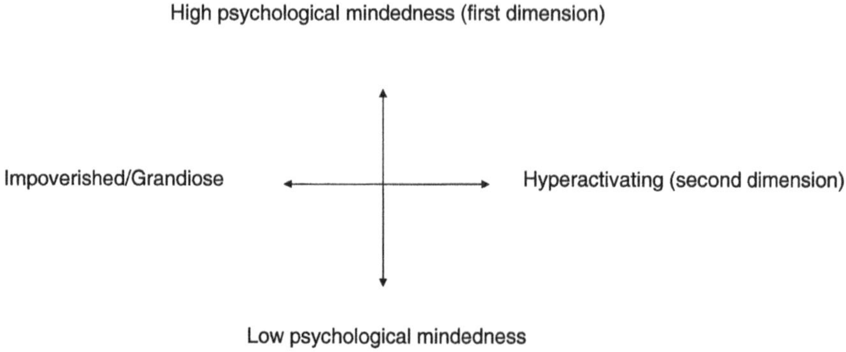

Figure 7.2. Proposed Two-Dimensional Construct of Psychological Mindedness

deactivating-hyperactivating dimension (Goodman, 2002), not to a particular developmental stage to account for its etiology, as in the object relations model. Considering this two-dimensional model of psychopathology, one can speculate whether PM could also be reconceptualized as a two-dimensional construct with a high-low dimension and an orthogonally positioned impoverished/grandiose-hyperactivated dimension (see figure 7.2). In other words, low levels of PM might take two different forms, depending on the nature of the defensive processes interfering with this capacity. It has often been noted in the literature that PM can be used for defensive purposes (Appelbaum, 1973; Fogel, 1995; McCallum and Piper, 1997).

An impoverished/grandiose PM would resemble brief, barren responses that show little reflection on the meaning and motivation of oneself or others or responses intended to inflate themselves and devalue others. This form of PM would be associated with the dismissing internal working model (adult version of the anxious-avoidant category), which has been associated with defensive processes such as denial, devaluation, omnipotent control, and narcissistic withdrawal (Goodman, 2002). The PM of a dismissing person would both maintain and reflect a defensive structure that protects against feelings of loss or rejection by accentuating the person's supreme autonomy and independence of others. One would expect that the dismissing internal working model of relationships between the self and others would carry over into his or her reasoning about the meaning and motivation of oneself and others. Patients who use PM as a defensive process have been labeled "narcissistic" and typically rely on primitive defenses to protect themselves from "fragmentations" (Fogel, 1995, p. 804). For these persons, PM has been recruited in the service of increasing "security and self-esteem or gain[ing] the admiration and protection of others," not to "spontaneously express and live out personal experience" (p. 795). A self-aggrandizing PM would characterize dismissing persons who resolve underlying feelings of vulnerability by holding onto a fantasy of invincibility in the face of others who could hurt them. Alternatively, an impoverished PM would characterize dismissing persons who resolve these underlying vulnerable feelings by denying the importance of understanding the meaning and motivation of themselves and others altogether.

On the other hand, a hyperactivated PM would resemble loquacious, meandering, affectively dysregulated responses that fail to provide useful information about the meaning and motivation of oneself or others. This form of PM would be associated with the preoccupied internal working model (adult version of the anxious-resistant category), which has been associated with defensive processes such as splitting, projection, projective identification, and introjection (Goodman, 2002). The PM of a preoccupied person would both maintain and reflect a defensive structure that protects against feelings of loss or rejection by remaining emotionally entangled with significant others such as parents with no understanding of the nature of this entanglement. One would expect that the preoccupied internal working model of relationships between the self and others would carry over into his or her reasoning about the meaning and motivation of oneself and others. Unlike persons who use impoverished/grandiose PM, persons who use hyperactivated PM are attempting to maintain an emotional connection with an ambivalently experienced object, split into all good and all bad features. Although these persons might be interested in understanding the meaning and motivation of themselves and others, the fear of what they might find out—for example, that the other person is planning to abandon them—hinders their efforts at PM from succeeding. A hyperactivated PM would characterize preoccupied persons who spin their wheels to gain understanding but whose faulty reasoning never really takes them anywhere because their ambivalence toward significant others spoils the attempt and renders their reasoning implausible. These persons can provide highly complex, sophisticated explanations for their own and others' thoughts, feelings, and behavior that nevertheless lack coherence and plausibility.

I will illustrate these two forms of PM with two examples from the Adult Attachment Interview. In the first example, the person (MF)—categorized as dismissing—mentions that her mother had refused to take her to the hospital as a child when she had had a serious head injury, and later, that her mother had warned her as an adolescent that if she came home pregnant, the mother would break both her legs. In response to the question "How do you think your overall experiences have affected your adult personality?" MF replies: "I think, if anything, it gave me a great deal of confidence in myself. I could certainly appreciate what they've done for me at this point and even certainly earlier. And I guess that they just gave me a great example for how I can raise my own children." MF dismisses the neglectful and threatening experiences with her mother while convincing herself and the interviewer that her childhood experiences gave her confidence. MF does not explain the meaning of her childhood experiences for her adult personality or for her own parenting. She seems to be manifesting a false confidence about the positive influence of her childhood experiences on her adult personality, but the explanation seems impoverished. She offers few connections among thoughts, feelings, and behavior, then and now.

In response to the question "Are there any aspects to your early experiences that you feel were a setback in your development?" MF replies: "No, not really, because, I mean, the things I really wanted to do, I kind of did. . . . If I wanted to take ballet lessons, I'd take ballet lessons. . . . If I wanted to pursue something, I guess they thought it was okay." MF denies any setbacks in her development and instead focuses on her pursuit of hobbies as evidence. In spite of her supreme confidence in the positive nature of her childhood experiences, she expresses mild uncertainty about whether her parents approved of her hobbies. Again, her PM is impoverished and reflective of an attitude about her adult personality characterized by flawlessness and invulnerability to disappointment.

In the second example, the person (MR)—categorized as preoccupied—mentions that her mother forced her to go shopping, while her father never changed her diapers. Her mother was "always there" for her, yet later she states without explanation, "There were times I knew that [my mother] didn't want to be there, not for me, but she just didn't want to be there." In response to the question "How do you think your overall experiences have affected your adult personality?" MR replies:

> See, I'm the kind of person that likes to see a lot of positive in things. So I don't want to remember the bad and the ugliness or the crying or the feelings that I thought hurt or whatever, because that doesn't help. . . . But if I had to take, I could take a positive, the fact that they made a family an issue, the fact that we had family outings, the fact that my parents or my father found a way to take care of us having no medical insurance. Who would figure? The fact that he lived on a fixed income even though he was self-employed. . . . We were Roman Catholic, so we celebrated, well, obviously, Thanksgiving, and then sure enough Christmas, and New Year's, and Three Kings Day, and then Easter, and the whole bit, and every time, we had new clothing. . . . Fight with my father for it, but we had always new clothing. It was like, I don't know, I can't even explain what it was; it was, it just that just the way it was. That family unit and that family setting, I brought into my family.

MR struggles to answer the question with an abundance of words that signify her feelings of ambivalence but little else. She suggests that she experienced a childhood filled with anguish, but then presents a picture of a family that valued family ties, presumably because they celebrated holidays together. MR always had new clothing on these holidays, but fighting with her father to obtain it was a prerequisite. By the end of the passage, MR tries to relate her childhood experiences to her adult personality, but ultimately she gives up: "I don't know, I can't even explain what it was; it was, it just that just the way it was." MR expends a lot of mental energy attempting to make sense out of her thoughts and feelings and assign some overall meaning to her childhood experiences, but the attempt ultimately fails. MR's hyperactivated search for meaning, like a hyperactivated baby's search for her mother, ends without the psychological answers she is seeking. Perhaps she does not "want to remember the bad and the ugliness."

In response to the question "Are there any aspects to your early experiences that you feel were a setback in your development?" MR replies: "If I could have been taught to express a little bit more, I might have been more aggressive, I think. 'Cause I, I'm more passive, I think. I, it's funny because with my kids I'm aggressive. . . . I fight for them tooth and nail. But when it comes to myself, I'm very laid back." MR acknowledges implicitly that her parents could have done more to nurture her self-expression, yet she seems puzzled that self-expression for the sake of her children comes easily for her. Again, unlike MF, MR is struggling to make sense out of her childhood experiences and their influence on her adult personality. In the end, however, her efforts are in vain. Her PM fails her when she tries to understand how she could be so verbally expressive on behalf of her children but not verbally expressive on her own behalf.

These two illustrations suggest that low levels of PM can be expressed in different forms, depending on the quality of the person's internal working model (see figure 7.2). It is important to keep in mind that these illustrations occurred under conditions in which the respondent was talking about primary caregivers. In a different context, the PM of these two persons might function differently. For example, talking about the meaning and motivation of Barry Bonds's alleged steroid use might produce a significantly higher level of PM than talking about one's parents or about oneself because talking about a stranger does not have the same potential to dysregulate affect and activate defensive processes to protect against this dysregulation that talking about significant others or the self does. PM can no longer be conceptualized as a trait that manifests stable functioning across contexts but rather as a state or process that depends on a particular context for its functioning, whether that context is a person or a situation.

Theoreticians of PM have not adequately accounted for the uneven functioning of PM across contexts. Only Hatcher and Hatcher (1997) have suggested that PM toward others and PM toward the self are qualitatively different constructs, at least in adolescence. According to these authors, "it is a different and less difficult task to see others' motives and affects than it is to see our own . . . [because of our] efforts to get free of painful affects" (pp. 66, 67). Later in their chapter, however, they also suggest, "The activation of conflict [between oneself and others] may make the task of recognizing others' motives more difficult [than recognizing one's own motives]" (p. 73). These quotations suggest that perhaps the quality of PM depends not on whether the target of observation is the self or others but on whether the target of observation is more likely to dysregulate affective homeostasis and activate defensive processes that deteriorate the quality of PM.

On the other hand, Grant (2001) has argued that PM toward others and PM toward the self must be conceptually overlapping phenomena because "the psychological mechanisms mediating behavior, thought, and feelings in *oneself* [would not differ] significantly from those mechanisms in *others*. . . . Thus . . . PM must be conceptualised in terms of both *self and other*" (italics in original, p. 10). While it is indisputable that the psychological mechanisms that mediate PM toward others and PM toward the self are shared, Grant's position nevertheless ignores the potential for defensive processes to incapacitate, or at least deteriorate, the functioning of PM in one of these areas. In fact, according to Grant (2001), defining PM by reference to defensive processes "clearly limits the usefulness of the PM construct to those from different [nonpsychoanalytic] theoretical backgrounds" (p. 10). For those of us who do believe in the power of defensive processes to affect PM, the unevenness in PM described by Hatcher and Hatcher (1997) makes perfect sense. I would add, however, that it is not the target of observation (i.e., PM toward others vs. PM toward the self) but rather the potential of the context in which PM is occurring to dysregulate affect and activate defensive processes that determines the quality of PM.

I would suggest that, paradoxically, a high level of PM is not only the product of affect regulation but also its origin. Effective PM (i.e., not impoverished/grandiose or hyperactivated) can protect against any organizational vulnerabilities to affect dysregulation by integrating fragments of meaning into a coherent whole, which in turn further supports PM. On the other hand, ineffective PM offers porous protection against these organizational vulnerabilities, which results in a proneness to affect dysregulation, which in turn further disrupts PM. Bion (1959) described how in the paranoid-schizoid position, destructive forces attack any attempts at linking thoughts and feelings together, thus producing a state of psychic fragmentation. Using contemporary language, affect dysregulation disrupts attempts at understanding the meaning and motivation of behavior, thoughts, and feelings, which, if these attempts were successful, could serve to re-regulate affect and restore psychic homeostasis. In those persons whose affect seldom becomes too dysregulated but whose internal working models have nevertheless become vulnerable (e.g., inexplicable loss of contact with a loved one), PM can serve to maintain affect regulation in the context of such psychic stressors. Paradoxically, then, affect dysregulation hinders PM, while PM has the potential to restore it.

We can therefore view the two forms of low-level PM as specific forms of disrupted thinking produced by affect dysregulation. Impoverished/grandiose PM manifests itself as a dismissal or derogation of thinking or self-serving thinking that diminishes its interpersonal significance. On the other hand, hyperactivated PM manifests itself as possibly obsessive or ruminative thinking that lacks the necessary attachment to meaning. In either case, PM becomes degraded to the point of being ineffective in facilitating affect re-regulation and restoring psychic homeostasis. Primitive defensive processes must therefore be summoned at the cost of psychic differentiation, integration, and reality testing. This state of affairs carries implications for therapeutic intervention.

Therapists routinely observe fluctuations in the PM of patients depending on the state of the transference. During negative transferential moments, patients with more primitive personality organizations tend to stop thinking in the midst of their affective storms. Their capacity to symbolize thoughts diminishes, and the equation "therapist = bad parent" becomes concretized and dangerously real to the patient. These situations often result from subtle empathic misattunements perpetrated by the therapist that can nevertheless significantly dysregulate affect and cause transient psychic fragmentation.

During this rupture in the treatment alliance (Zetzel, 1956), the therapist can assist the patient to restore the functioning of PM by (1) containing the dysregulated, unprocessed affects associated with the negative transference, and (2) lending the patient his or her own PM to permit the patient to begin to process the unbearable, dysregulated affects contained by the therapist (Bion, 1962, 1967). In a sense the therapist serves as an auxiliary ego for the patient by helping him or her to restore thinking or reattach meaning to thinking—a process that during an affective storm the patient is unable to accomplish on his or her own. Once thinking is restored, the patient can resume exploring collaboratively with the therapist the meaning and motivation of the therapist's thoughts, feelings, and behavior as well as his or her own. This process reestablishes links among thoughts and feelings (Bion, 1959) and serves to restore the symbolic quality of the transference.

This process of reparation serves to increase the patient's confidence that he or she can tolerate future states of arousal using PM, gradually appropriated from the therapist's use of PM during such states. This confidence facilitates the patient's self-regulation of affective states. Reparation also serves to increase the patient's confidence that he or she can tolerate conflicts that arise in interpersonal relationships and can work toward reconciliation with others. This confidence facilitates the patient's interactive regulation of affective states. Developmentally, attachment researchers (Lyons-Ruth, Bronfman, and Atwood, 1999; Solomon and George, 1999) have highlighted the importance of the reparative process initiated by the caregiver after a rupture caused by the caregiver's frightening or frightened behavior. These authors have suggested that this reparative process buffers children from frightening caregiver behaviors that typically contribute to the formation of a disorganized attachment (Hesse and Main, 1999; Lyons-Ruth, Bronfman, and Parsons, 1999; Main and Hesse, 1990; Schuengel, Bakermans-Kranenburg, and van IJzendoorn, 1999). A future line of research could examine the buffering qualities of these processes of caregiver reparation. Perhaps these early reparative experiences represent the precursors of PM that the caregiver lends to the frightened child after a rupture.

The therapist can facilitate the success of this reparative process by paying attention to the defensive processes used against PM and adjusting the delivery of the "auxiliary PM" accordingly. If the therapist notices that the PM is impoverished/grandiose, the auxiliary PM lent to the patient needs to preserve the patient's self-esteem while helping the patient to understand the shameful vulnerability that the patient is desperately trying to protect himself or herself from. If the therapist notices that the PM is hyperactivated, the auxiliary PM needs to help the patient gain traction to use PM more effectively by reattaching the meaning to thinking.

CONCLUSIONS

During its fifty-year history, PM has evolved to accommodate major changes in the evolution of psychoanalytic theory. Following the paradigm shift from a one-person to a two-person psychology (Aron, 1990), PM evolved from a construct focused on the connections between one's own symptoms, behaviors, and emotional states to a construct focused on these connections in the self as well as others (Farber, 1985). PM also evolved from a construct presumed to have a large genetic component to a construct that develops over time (Hatcher and Hatcher, 1997) and possibly originates in the caregiver-infant relationship (Alvarez, Farber, and Schonbar, 1998; Beitel and Cecero, 2003). Finally, PM evolved from a construct considered a primary criterion of suitability for treatment to a construct considered a potential moderator of treatment (Ogrodniczuk et al., 2001; Piper et al., 2002). But do these conceptual advances go far enough to save PM from extinction?

I have made four suggestions to update the construct of PM. First, I suggested a reconceptualization of PM as a two-dimensional construct, with the first dimension that characterizes a range from high to low levels of complexity and plausibility and an orthogonally positioned dimension that characterizes a range from impoverished/grandiose PM to hyperactivated PM. Second, I suggested that PM is not a trait the level of which remains constant across situations and persons (e.g., Conte et al., 1990; Farber, 1985) but rather a context-dependent, porous state of awareness. The quality of a person's PM can vary with the level of emotional investment in the target of observation and the situation under consideration. Under conditions of high affective arousal, the quality of PM can deteriorate and become ineffective, particularly in persons with organizational vulnerabilities. Third, I suggested that effective PM facilitates affect regulation, while affect regulation facilitates effective PM. Conversely, ineffective PM facilitates affect dysregulation, while affect dysregulation facilitates ineffective PM. These interrelated processes frequently appear in the therapeutic context. Fourth, I suggested that PM could be considered a process of therapeutic change, facilitated by the therapist's lending the patient an auxiliary PM during transference-induced affective storms, which could restore affect regulation. Ultimately, the patient will use this newly acquired PM during moments of affect dysregulation outside therapy sessions. In this sense, PM could also be thought of as an outcome of an effective treatment.

In spite of these suggestions, PM still faces notable challenges from its competitor, RF. Depending on one's theoretical perspective, one could view RF as PM Turbo—PM plus a powerful intersubjective component that transforms the entire meaning of PM. While PM might produce the question "What is she thinking about that made her cry?" RF might produce the question "What view of me does she hold in her mind that made her interpret what I said in a way that made her cry?" An even more complex variant of this question might be "What view of her does she think I hold in my mind that made her interpret what I said in a way that made her cry?" The construct of RF adds an important layer of complexity to an interpersonal situation that the construct of PM fails to capture.

Fonagy and his colleagues (Fonagy, Gergely, et al., 2002; Fonagy, Steele, Steele, Moran, and Higgitt, 1991; Fonagy et al., 1998) have suggested that this complex awareness actually begins to emerge in the context of the caregiver-infant relationship, when the infant sees himself or herself in the eyes of the caregiver. Over time, this awareness emerges as an image of the infant that the caregiver holds in mind. The infant gradually internalizes this image of himself or herself, held in the caregiver's mind, which forms the core of the self-representation. The caregiver representation, which the infant also internalizes, also contains this core self-image held in the caregiver's mind. Difficulties in the development of the self occur when the caregiver does not hold an image of the infant in mind or when the caregiver holds an image of the infant in mind incongruent with the infant's actual mental states (e.g., irritable because of hunger, not because of a rejection by the caregiver). Based on this developmental framework, Fonagy and his colleagues have concluded that the human mind is essentially intersubjective—that we form representations of others' representations of us and that we think, feel, and behave in accordance with (or in reaction to) these representations-within-representations. RF is an awareness of these mental processes and their mutual influence on persons in interpersonal relationships. PM lacks both this intersubjective component and a comprehensive developmental framework to explain its origins.

Except for the suggestion that PM be reconceptualized as a two-dimensional construct, my suggestions for updating the construct of PM have more or less already been incorporated into the literature on RF (Fonagy, Gergely, et al., 2002; Fonagy, Steele, Steele, Moran, and Higgitt, 1991; Fonagy et al., 1998). RF is a context-dependent construct, assessed using an interview (i.e., the AAI) designed to increase affective arousal (George et al., 1996). As a facilitator of affect regulation, the therapist can use RF as a mediating process of therapeutic change (Bateman and Fonagy, 2004b). The measurement of RF has already begun to be applied to psychotherapy transcripts (Josephs et al., 2004; Josephs and Fatzer, 2006; Karlsson and Kermott, 2006) to assess the mediating influence of RF on treatment outcome. A Q-sort instrument that assesses RF in psychotherapy sessions is also under construction (Goodman and Schneider, 2006). A coding system has also been developed for assessing maternal RF during an interview about her infant (Slade, 2005). Fonagy and Target (2005b) have also begun to construct an RF questionnaire. Given the importance of assessing RF when the mental apparatus is under stress, however, it is unknown whether a self-report questionnaire could demonstrate convergent validity with the stress-inducing AAI.

Based on the analysis of both constructs, PM and RF, I have concluded that PM in its current form is indeed an "outdated" (Fonagy, Steele, Steele, Moran, and Higgitt, 1991, p. 215) construct—a victim of natural selection in the context of the ascendancy of attachment theory as the principal framework for understanding the development of affect regulation and psychopathology in psychoanalytic theory. RF has taken full advantage of this new psychoanalytic environment and has eclipsed its predecessor in conceptual significance for the understanding of intrapsychic development and functioning, psychopathology, and therapeutic change. RF might have co-opted the skeletal remains of PM—reflection on the meaning and motivation of behavior, thoughts, and feelings in oneself and others (Farber, 1985)—however, the introduction of a context-dependent intersubjective component, with its own etiological narrative and applications to the therapeutic process, forms the basis of a complete transformation of PM into something original and inherently therapeutic. For those psychoanalytically oriented theoreticians and therapists who have difficulty holding intersubjective theory in mind, I have made four suggestions how to resuscitate the construct of PM independent of this theory. Some might argue that the interplay of mental states is already implicitly embodied in the spirit, if not the formal definition, of PM. If this is the case, then the constructs could be considered synonyms for each other.

References

Aber, J. L., Slade, A., Berger, B., Bresgi, I., & Kaplan, M. (1985). *The Parent Development Interview*. Unpublished manuscript, Columbia University, New York.

Ablon, J. S., & Jones, E. E. (1998). How expert clinicians' prototypes of an ideal treatment correlate with outcome in psychodynamic and cognitive-behavioral therapy. *Psychotherapy Research, 8*, 71–83.

——. (1999). Psychotherapy process in the National Institute of Mental Health Treatment of Depression Collaborative Research Program. *Journal of Consulting and Clinical Psychology, 67*, 64–75.

——. (2002). Validity of controlled clinical trials of psychotherapy: Findings from the NIMH Treatment of Depression Collaborative Research Program. *American Journal of Psychiatry, 159*, 775–83.

——. (2005). On analytic process. *Journal of the American Psychoanalytic Association, 53*, 541–68.

Ablon, J. S., Levy, R. A., & Katzenstein, T. (2006). Beyond brand names of psychotherapy: Identifying empirically supported change processes. *Psychotherapy: Theory, Research, Practice, Training, 43*, 216–31.

Ablon, J. S., & Marci, C. (2004). Psychotherapy process: The missing link: Comment on Westen, Novotny, & Thompson-Brenner (2004). *Psychological Bulletin, 130*, 664–68.

Achenbach, T. M. (1991). *Manual for the Child Behavior Checklist/4-18 and 1991 Profile*. Burlington: University of Vermont, Department of Psychiatry.

Achenbach, T. M., & Edelbrock, C. S. (1981). Behavioral problems and competencies reported by parents of normal and disturbed children aged four through sixteen. *Monographs of the Society for Research in Child Development, 46*, 1–82.

Agras, W. S., Crow, S. J., Halmi, K. A., Mitchell, J. E., Wilson, G. T., & Kraemer, H. C. (2000). Outcome predictors for the cognitive behavior treatment of bulimia nervosa: Data from a multisite study. *American Journal of Psychiatry, 157*, 1302–8.

Agrawal, H. R., Gunderson, J., Holmes, B. M., & Lyons-Ruth, K. (2004). Attachment studies with borderline patients: A review. *Harvard Review of Psychiatry, 12*, 94–104.

Ahn, H., & Wampold, B. E. (2001). Where oh where are the specific ingredients? A meta-analysis of component studies in counseling and psychotherapy. *Journal of Counseling Psychology, 48*, 251–57.

Ainsworth, M. D. S. (1979). Infant-mother attachment. *American Psychologist, 34*, 932–37.

Ainsworth, M. D. S., Blehar, M. C., Waters, E., & Wall, S. (1978). *Patterns of attachment: A psychological study of the strange situation*. Hillsdale, NJ: Erlbaum.

Alexander, F., & French, T. M. (1946). *Psychoanalytic therapy: Principles and application*. Oxford: Ronald.

Allen, J. G. (2003). Mentalizing. *Bulletin of the Menninger Clinic, 67*, 91–112.

Alvarez, J. R., Farber, B. A., & Schonbar, R. A. (1998). The relationship of psychological-mindedness to adult perceptions of early parental rejection. *Journal of Clinical Psychology, 54*, 1079–84.

American Psychiatric Association. (2000). *Diagnostic and statistical manual of mental disorders* (Fourth ed., text revision). Washington, DC: Author.

Anderson, S., Bechara, A., Damasio, H., Tranel, D., & Damasio, A. (1999). Impairment of social and moral behavior related to early damage in human prefrontal cortex. *Natural Neuroscience, 2*, 1032–37.

Appelbaum, A. H. (2005). Supportive psychotherapy. In J. Oldham, A. Skodol, and D. Bender (Eds.), *The American Psychiatric Publishing textbook of personality disorders* (pp. 311–26). Washington, DC: American Psychiatric Publishing.

Appelbaum, S. A. (1973). Psychological-mindedness: Word, concept and essence. *International Journal of Psycho-Analysis, 54*, 35–46.

Aron, L. (1990). One person and two person psychologies and the method of psychoanalysis. *Psychoanalytic Psychology, 7*, 475–85.

———. (2006). Analytic impasse and the third: Clinical implications of intersubjectivity theory. *International Journal of Psycho-Analysis, 87*, 349–68.

Assay, T. P., & Lambert, M. J. (1999). The empirical case for the common factors in therapy: Quantitative findings. In M. A. Hubble, B. L. Duncan, and S. D. Miller (Eds.), *The heart and soul of change: What works in therapy* (pp. 33–56). Washington, DC: American Psychological Association.

Auerbach, J. S., & Blatt, S. J. (2002). The concept of mind: A developmental analysis. In R. Lasky (Ed.), *Symbolization and desymbolization: Essays in honor of Norbert Freedman* (pp. 75–117). New York: Other Press.

Auerbach, C. F., & Silverstein, L. B. (2003). *Qualitative data: An introduction to coding and analysis*. New York: New York University Press.

Bach, S. (1985). *Narcissistic states and the therapeutic process*. New York: Jason Aronson.

———. (1994). *The language of perversion and the language of love*. Northvale, NJ: Jason Aronson.

Baekeland, F., & Lundwall, L. (1975). Dropping out of treatment: A critical review. *Psychological Bulletin, 82*, 738–83.

Baer, R. A. (2003). Mindfulness training as a clinical intervention: A conceptual and empirical review. *Clinical Psychology: Science and Practice, 10*, 125–43.

Baer, R. A., Smith, G. T., & Allen, K. B. (2004). Assessment of mindfulness by self-report: The Kentucky Inventory of Mindfulness Skills. *Assessment, 11*, 191–206.

Baer, R. A., Smith, G. T., Hopkins, J., Krietemeyer, J., & Toney, L. (2006). Using self-report assessment methods to explore facets of mindfulness. *Assessment, 13*, 27–45.

Bagby, R. M., Taylor, G. J., & Parker, J. D. A. (1986). Construct validity of the Toronto Alexithymia Scale. *Psychotherapy and Psychosomatics, 50*, 29–34.

Bakeman, R., & Gottman, J. M. (1986). *Observing interaction: An introduction to sequential analysis*. New York: Cambridge University Press.

Barlow, D. H., & Craske, M. G. (2000). *Mastery of your anxiety and panic* (Third ed.). New York: Psychological Corporation.

Baron-Cohen, S., Ring, H., Moriarty, J., Schmitz, B., Costa, D., & Ell, P. (1994). Recognition of mental state terms: Clinical findings in children with autism and a functional neuroimaging study of normal adults. *British Journal of Psychiatry, 165*, 640–49.

Baskin, T. W., Tierney, S. C., Minami, T., & Wampold, B. E. (2003). Establishing specificity in psychotherapy: A meta-analysis of structural equivalence of placebo controls. *Journal of Consulting and Clinical Psychology, 71*, 973–79.

Bateman, A. W., & Fonagy, P. (2004a). Mentalization-based treatment of BPD. *Journal of Personality Disorders, 18*, 36–51.

———. (2004b). *Psychotherapy for borderline personality disorder: Mentalization-based treatment*. Oxford: Oxford University Press.

———. (2006, May). *Mentalisation based therapy workshop*. Workshop presented at the City College of New York, New York.

Beitel, M., & Cecero, J. J. (2003). Predicting psychological mindedness from personality style and attachment security. *Journal of Clinical Psychology, 59*, 163–72.

Beitel, M., Ferrer, E., & Cecero, J. J. (2004). Psychological mindedness and cognitive style. *Journal of Clinical Psychology, 60*, 567–82.

———. (2005). Psychological mindedness and awareness of self and others. *Journal of Clinical Psychology, 61*, 739–50.

Beitman, B. D. (2005). To the editor: Defining the core processes of psychotherapy. *American Journal of Psychiatry, 162*, 1549, 1550.

Bell, S. M. (1968). *The relationship of infant-mother attachment to the development of the concept of object permanence*. Unpublished doctoral dissertation, Johns Hopkins University, Baltimore, Maryland.

———. (1970). The development of the concept of object as related to infant-mother attachment. *Child Development, 41*, 292–311.

Benjamin, L. S. (1993). *Interpersonal diagnosis and treatment of personality disorders*. New York: Guilford Press.

Bergin, A. E. (1971). The evaluation of therapeutic outcomes. In A. E. Bergin and S. L. Garfield (Eds.), *Handbook of psychotherapy and behavior change* (pp. 217–70). New York: Wiley.

Bergin, A. E., & Lambert, M. (1978). The evaluation of therapeutic outcomes. In S. L. Garfield and A. E. Bergin (Eds.), *Handbook of psychotherapy and behavior change* (Second ed., pp. 139–89). New York: Wiley.

Bernier, A., & Dozier, M. (2002). The client-counselor match and the corrective emotional experience: Evidence from interpersonal and attachment research. *Psychotherapy: Theory/Research/Practice/Training, 39*, 32–43.

Bernier, A., Larose, S., & Soucy, N. (2005). Academic mentoring in college: The interactive role of student's and mentor's interpersonal dispositions. *Research in Higher Education, 46*, 29–51.

Bernstein, S. B. (1992). Guidelines: Comments on treatment report writing and the written description of analytic process (from the Committee on Certification, American Psychoanalytic Association). *Journal of Clinical Psychoanalysis, 1*, 469–78.

Beutler, L. E. (1979). Toward specific psychological therapies for specific conditions. *Journal of Consulting and Clinical Psychology, 47*, 882–97.

Beutler, L. E., & Clarkin, J. (1990). *Differential treatment selection: Toward targeted therapeutic interventions*. New York: Brunner/Mazel.

Beutler, L. E., Clarkin, J. F., & Bongar, B. (2000). *Guidelines for the systematic treatment of the depressed patient*. New York: Oxford University Press.

Beutler, L. E., & Harwood, T. M. (2000). *Prescriptive psychotherapy: A practical guide to systematic treatment selection*. New York: Oxford University Press.

Beutler, L. E., & Hodgson, A. B. (1993). Prescriptive psychotherapy. In G. Stricker and J. R. Gold (Eds.), *Comprehensive handbook of psychotherapy integration* (pp. 151–63). New York: Plenum Press.

Binder, J. L., & Strupp, H. H. (1997). "Negative process": A recurrently discovered and underestimated facet of therapeutic process and outcome in the individual psychotherapy of adults. *Clinical Psychology: Science and Practice, 4*, 121–39.

Bion, W. R. (1959). Attacks on linking. *International Journal of Psycho-Analysis, 40*, 308–15.

——. (1962). *Learning from experience*. London: Heinemann.

——. (1967). *Second thoughts*. London: Heinemann.

Bishop, S. R., Lau, M., Shapiro, S., Carlson, L., Anderson, N. D., Carmody, J., Segal, Z. V., Abbey, S., Speca, M., Velting, D., & Devins, G. (2004). Mindfulness: A proposed operational definition. *Clinical Psychology: Science and Practice, 11*, 230–41.

Blagys, M. D., & Hilsenroth, M. J. (2000). Distinctive features of short-term psychodynamic-interpersonal psychotherapy: A review of the comparative psychotherapy process literature. *Clinical Psychology: Science and Practice, 7*, 167–88.

——. (2002). Distinctive activities of cognitive-behavioral therapy: A review of the comparative psychotherapy process literature. *Clinical Psychology Review, 22*, 671–706.

Blair, R., Jones, L., Clark, F., & Smith, M. (1997). The psychopathic individual: A lack of responsiveness to distress cues? *Psychophysiology, 34*, 192–98.

Blair, R., Morris, J., Frith, C., Perrett, D., & Dolan, R. (1999). Dissociable neural responses to facial expressions of sadness and anger. *Brain, 122*, 883–93.

Blatt, S. J. (1974). Levels of objective representation in anaclitic and introjective depression. *Psychoanalytic Study of the Child, 29*, 107–57.

——. (1995). Representational structures in psychopathology. In D. Cicchetti and S. L. Toth (Eds.), *Rochester Symposium on Developmental Psychopathology: Vol. 6. Emotion, cognition, and representation* (pp. 1–33). Rochester, NY: University of Rochester Press.

Blatt, S. J., Brenneis, C. B., Schimek, J. G., & Glick, M. (1976). Normal development and psychopathological impairment of the concept of the object on the Rorschach. *Journal of Abnormal Psychology, 85*, 364–73.

Blatt, S. J., Chevron, E. S., Quinlan, D. M., Schaffer, C. E., & Wein, S. (1992). *The assessment of qualitative and structural dimensions of object representations* (Rev. ed.). Unpublished manuscript, Yale University, New Haven, Connecticut.

Blatt, S. J., & Felsen, I. (1993). Different kinds of folks may need different kinds of strokes: The effect of patients' characteristics on therapeutic process and outcome. *Psychotherapy Research, 3*, 245–59.

Blatt, S. J., & Ford, R. (1994). *Therapeutic change: An object relations perspective.* New York: Plenum.

Blatt, S. J., & Lerner, H. (1983). Investigations in the psychoanalytic theory of object relations and object representations. In J. Masling (Ed.), *Empirical studies of psychoanalytic theories* (pp. 189–249). Hillsdale, NJ: Analytic.

Blatt, S. J., & Maroudas, C. (1992). Convergences among psychoanalytic and cognitive-behavioral theories of depression. *Psychoanalytic Psychology, 9*, 157–90.

Blatt, S. J., Quinlan, D. M., Pilkonis, P. A., & Shea, T. M. (1995). Impact of perfectionism and need for approval on the brief treatment of depression: The National Institute of Mental Health Treatment of Depression Collaborative Research Program revisited. *Journal of Consulting and Clinical Psychology, 63*, 125–32.

Blatt, S. J., & Shahar, G. (2004). Das dialogische selbst: Adaptive und maladaptive dimesionen [The dialogic self: Adaptive and maladaptive dimensions]. In P. Giampieri-Deutsch (Ed.), *Psychoanalyse im dialog der wissenschaften. Band 2. Anglo-Amerikanische perspektiven [Psychoanalysis as an empirical, interdisciplinary science: An Anglo-American perspective]* (Vol. 2, pp. 285–309). Stuttgart: Kohlhammer.

——. (2005). Psychoanalysis—with whom, for what, and how? Comparisons with psychotherapy. *Journal of the American Psychoanalytic Association, 52*, 393–447.

Blatt, S. J., Shahar, G., & Zuroff, D. C. (2002). Anaclitic (sociotropic) and introjective (autonomous) dimensions. In J. C. Norcross (Ed.), *Psychotherapy relationships that work: Therapist contributions and responsiveness to patients* (pp. 306–24). New York: Oxford University Press.

Blatt, S. J., Tuber, S. B, & Auerbach, J. S. (1990). Representation of interpersonal interactions on the Rorschach and level of psychopathology. *Journal of Personality Assessment, 54*, 711–28.

Blatt, S. J., & Zuroff, D. C. (2005). Empirical evaluation of the assumptions in identifying evidence based treatments in mental health. *Clinical Psychology Review, 25*, 459–86.

Bleiberg, E., Fonagy, P., & Target, M. (1997). Child psychoanalysis: Critical overview and a proposed reconsideration. *Psychiatric Clinics of North America, 6*, 1–38.

Block, J. (1978). *The Q-sort method in personality assessment and psychiatric research.* Palo Alto, CA: Consulting Psychologists. (Original work published 1961)

Blum, H. P. (1979). The curative and creative aspects of insight. *Journal of the American Psychoanalytic Association, 27*(Suppl.), 41–70.

Blum, J. M. (1978). *Pseudoscience and mental ability: The origins and fallacies of the IQ controversy.* New York: Monthly Review Press.

Bohart, A. (2000). The client is the most important common factor. *Journal of Psychotherapy Integration, 10*, 127–49.

Borckardt, J. J., Nash, M. R., Murphy, M. D., Moore, M., Shaw, D., & O'Neill, P. (2008). Clinical practice as natural laboratory for psychotherapy research: A guide to case-based time-series analysis. *American Psychologist, 63*, 77–95.

Borus, J. F. (1981). Deinstitutionalization of the chronically mentally ill. *New England Journal of Medicine, 305*, 339–42.

Bowlby, J. (1973). *Attachment and loss: Vol. 2. Separation: Anxiety and anger.* New York: Basic Books.

———. (1980). *Attachment and loss: Vol. 3. Loss, sadness and depression.* New York: Basic Books.

———. (1982). *Attachment and loss: Vol. 1. Attachment* (Second ed.). New York: Basic Books.

———. (1988). *A secure base: Parent-child attachment and healthy human development.* New York: Basic Books.

Britton, R. (1998). *Belief and imagination: Exploration in psychoanalysis.* London: Tavistock/Routledge.

Bronfman, E., Parsons, E., & Lyons-Ruth, K. (1999). *Atypical Maternal Behavior Instrument for Assessment and Classification (AMBIANCE): Manual for coding disrupted affective communication, Version 2.* Unpublished manuscript, Harvard Medical School, Cambridge, Massachusetts.

Brown, T. A., & Barlow, D. H. (1995). Long-term outcome in cognitive-behavioral treatment of panic disorder: Clinical predictors and alternative strategies for assessment. *Journal of Consulting and Clinical Psychology, 63*, 754–65.

Brown, K. W., & Ryan, R. M. (2003). The benefits of being present: Mindfulness and its role in psychological well-being. *Journal of Personality and Social Psychology, 84*, 822–48.

———. (2004). Perils and promise in defining and measuring mindfulness: Observations from experience. *Clinical Psychology: Science and Practice, 11*, 242–48.

Bruschweiler-Stern, N., Harrison, A. M., Lyons-Ruth, K., Morgan, A. C., Nahum, J. P., Sander, L. W., Stern, D. N., & Tronick, E. Z. (2002). Explicating the implicit: The local level and the microprocesses of change in the analytic situation. *International Journal of Psychoanalysis, 83*, 1051–62.

Butler, S. F., & Strupp, H. H. (1986). Specific and nonspecific factors in psychotherapy: A problematic paradigm for psychotherapy research. *Psychotherapy, 23*, 30–39.

Calhoun, K. S., Moras, K., Pilkonis, P. A., & Rehm, L. (1998). Empirically supported treatments: Implications for training. *Journal of Consulting and Clinical Psychology, 66*, 151–62.

Campbell, D. T., & Stanley, J. C. (1963). *Experimental and quasi-experimental designs for research.* Boston: Houghton Mifflin.

Carlson, L. E., Ursuliak, Z., Goodey, E., Angen, M., & Speca, M. (2001). The effects of a mindfulness meditation-based stress reduction program on mood and symptoms of stress in cancer outpatients: 6-month follow-up. *Supportive Care in Cancer, 9*, 112–23.

Carroll, L. (1865). *Alice's Adventures in Wonderland.* New York: Penguin.

Castonguay, L. G. (1993). "Common factors" and "nonspecific variables": Clarification of the two concepts and recommendations for research. *Journal of Psychotherapy Integration, 3*, 267–86.

Castonguay, L. G., Goldfried, M. R., Wiser, S., Raue, P. J., & Hayes, A. M. (1996). Predicting the effect of cognitive therapy for depression: A study of unique and common factors. *Journal of Consulting and Clinical Psychology, 64*, 497–504.

Castonguay, L. G., & Holtforth, M. G. (2005). Change in psychotherapy: A plea for no more "nonspecific" and false dichotomies. *Clinical Psychology: Science and Practice, 12*, 198–201.

Chadwick, P., Hember, M., Mead, S., Lilley, B., & Dagnan, D. (2005). *Responding mindfully to unpleasant thoughts and images: Reliability and validity of the Mindfulness Questionnaire.* Unpublished manuscript.

Chambless, D., & Ollendick, T. (2000). Empirically supported psychological interventions: Controversies and evidence. *Annual Review of Psychology, 52*, 685–716.

Chi, T. C., & Hinshaw, S. P. (2002). Mother-child relationships of children with ADHD: The role of maternal depressive symptoms and depression-related distortions. *Journal of Abnormal Child Psychology, 30*, 387–400.

Christensen, A., & Jacobson, N. (1994). Who (or what) can do psychotherapy: The status and challenge of nonprofessional therapies. *Psychological Science, 5*, 8–14.

Clarkin, J. F. (2008). Clinical approaches to Axis II comorbidity: Commentary. *Journal of Clinical Psychology, 64*, 222–30.

Clarkin, J. F., Foelsch, P. A., Levy, K. N., Hull, J. W., Delaney, J. C., & Kernberg, O. F. (2001). The development of a psychodynamic treatment for patients with borderline personality disorder: A preliminary study of behavioral change. *Journal of Personality Disorders, 15*, 487–95.

Clarkin, J. F., Hull, J. W., & Hurt, S. W. (1993). Factor structure of borderline personality disorder criteria. *Journal of Personality Disorders, 7*, 137–43.

Clarkin, J. F., Levy, K. N., Lenzenweger, M. F., & Kernberg, O. F. (2007). Evaluating three treatments for borderline personality disorder: A multiwave study. *American Journal of Psychiatry, 164*, 922–28.

Clarkin, J. F., Yeomans, F. E., & Kernberg, O. F. (1999). *Psychotherapy for borderline personality.* New York: Wiley.

———. (2006). *Psychotherapy for borderline personality: Focusing on object relations.* Washington, DC: American Psychiatric Publishing.

Cohen, J. (1992). A power primer. *Psychological Bulletin, 112*, 155–59.

Coltart, N. E. C. (1988). The assessment of psychological-mindedness in the diagnostic interview. *British Journal of Psychiatry, 153*, 819, 820.

Conte, H. R., Buckley, P., Picard, S., & Karasu, T. B. (1995). Relations between psychological mindedness and personality traits and ego functioning: Validity studies. *Comprehensive Psychiatry, 36*, 11–17.

Conte, H. R., Plutchik, R., Jung, B. B., Picard, S., Karasu, T. B., & Lotterman, A. (1990). Psychological mindedness as a predictor of psychotherapy outcome: A preliminary report. *Comprehensive Psychiatry, 31*, 426–31.

Conte, H. R., & Ratto, R. (1997). Self-report measures of psychological mindedness. In M. McCallum and W. E. Piper (Eds.), *Psychological mindedness: A contemporary understanding* (pp. 1–26). Mahwah, NJ: Lawrence Erlbaum.

Conte, H. R., Ratto, R., & Karasu, T. B. (1996). The Psychological Mindedness Scale: Factor structure and relationship to outcome of psychotherapy. *Journal of Psychotherapy Practice and Research, 5*, 250–59.

Craighead, W. E., Sheets, E. S., Bjornsson, A. S., & Arnarson, E. O. (2005). Specificity and nonspecificity in psychotherapy. *Clinical Psychology: Science and Practice, 12*, 189–93.

Crits-Christoph, P., Baranackie, K., Kurcias, J., Beck, A., Carroll, K., Perry, K., Luborsky, L., McLellan, A., Woody, G., Thompson, L., Gallagher, D., & Zitrin, C. (1991). Meta-analysis of therapist effects in psychotherapy outcome studies. *Psychotherapy Research, 1*, 81–91.

Crits-Christoph, P., Barber, J., Miller, N., & Beebe, K. (1993). Evaluating insight. In N. Miller, L. Luborsky, J. Barber, and J. Docherty (Eds.), *Psychodynamic psychotherapy research: A handbook for clinicians* (pp. 407–22). New York: Basic Books.

Crits-Christoph, P., & Mintz, J. (1991). Implications of therapist effects for the design and analysis of comparative studies of psychotherapies. *Journal of Consulting and Clinical Psychology, 59*, 20–26.

Cummings, N. A. (2008, July/August). Are graduate students being deceived? *The National Psychologist, 17*, 14.

Cutler, J. L., Goldyne, A., Markowitz, J. C., Devlin, M. J., & Glick, R. A. (2004). Comparing cognitive behavior therapy, interpersonal psychotherapy, and psychodynamic psychotherapy. *American Journal of Psychiatry, 161*, 1567–73.

——. (2005). Dr. Cutler and colleagues reply. *American Journal of Psychiatry, 162*, 1550.

Davidson, R. J., & Kabat-Zinn, J. (2004). Response. *Psychosomatic Medicine, 66*, 149–52.

Davidson, R. J., Kabat-Zinn, J., Schumacher, J., Rosenkranz, M., Muller, D., Santorelli, S. F., Urbanowski, F., Harrington, A., Bonus, K., & Sheridan, J. F. (2003). Alterations in brain and immune function produced by mindfulness meditation. *Psychosomatic Medicine, 65*, 564–70.

Depue, R. A., & Lenzenweger, M. F. (2005). A neurobehavioral dimensional model of personality disturbance. In M. F. Lenzenweger and J. F. Clarkin (Eds.), *Major theories of personality disorder* (Second ed., pp. 391–453). New York: Guilford Press.

De Wolff, M., & van IJzendoorn, M. H. (1997). Sensitivity and attachment: A meta-analysis on parental antecedents of infant attachment. *Child Development, 68*, 571–91.

Derogatis, L. (1983). *SCL-90-R: Administration, scoring, and procedures manual II.* Towson, MD: Clinical Psychometric Research.

———. (1993). BSI: *Administration, scoring, and procedures manual.* Minneapolis: National Computer Systems.

Derogatis, L. R., & Melisaratos, N. (1983). The Brief Symptom Inventory: An introductory report. *Psychological Medicine, 13*, 595–605.

DeRubeis, R. J., Brotman, M. A., & Gibbons, C. J. (2005). A conceptual and methodological analysis of the nonspecifics argument. *Clinical Psychology: Science and Practice, 12*, 174–83.

Diamond, D., Blatt, S. J., Stayner, D., & Kaslow, N. (1992). *Differentiation, cohesion and relatedness of self and other representations: A developmental scale.* Unpublished manuscript, Yale University, New Haven, Connecticut.

Diamond, D., Clarkin, J., Levine, H., Levy, K., Foelsch, P., & Yeomans, F. (1999). Borderline conditions and attachment: A preliminary report. *Psychoanalytic Inquiry, 19*, 831–84.

Diamond, D., Clarkin, J. F., Stovall-McClough, K. C., Levy, K. N., Foelsch, P. A., Levine, H., & Yeomans, F. E. (2003). Patient-therapist attachment: Impact on the therapeutic process and outcome. In M. Cortina and M. Marrone (Eds.), *Attachment theory and the psychoanalytic process.* London: Whurr.

Diamond, D., Stovall-McClough, C., Clarkin, J. F., & Levy, K. N. (2003). Patient-therapist attachment in the treatment of borderline personality disorder. *Bulletin of the Menninger Clinic, 67*, 227–59.

Diener, M. J., Hilsenroth, M. J., & Weinberger, J. (2007). Therapist affect focus and patient outcomes in psychodynamic psychotherapy: A meta-analysis. *American Journal of Psychiatry, 164*, 936–41.

Dimidjian, S., & Linehan, M. M. (2003). Defining an agenda for future research on the clinical application of mindfulness practice. *Clinical Psychology: Science and Practice, 10*, 166–71.

Dobson, K. S., & Khatri, N. (2000). Cognitive therapy: Looking backward, looking forward. *Journal of Clinical Psychology, 56*, 907–23.

Dollinger, S. J., Reader, M. J., Marnett, J. P., & Tylenda, B. (1983). Psychological-mindedness, psychological-construing, and the judgment of deception. *Journal of General Psychology, 108*, 183–91.

Dozier, M. (2003). Attachment-based treatment for vulnerable children. *Attachment and Human Development, 5*, 253–57.

Dozier, M., & Bates, B. C. (2004). Attachment state of mind and the treatment relationship. In L. Atkinson and S. Goldberg (Eds.), *Attachment issues in psychopathology and intervention* (pp. 167–80). Mahwah, NJ: Erlbaum.

Dozier, M., Cue, K. L., & Barnett, L. (1994). Clinicians as caregivers: Role of attachment organization in treatment. *Journal of Consulting and Clinical Psychology, 62*, 793–800.

Dozier, M., & Tyrrell, C. (1998). The role of attachment in therapeutic relationships. In J. A. Simpson and W. S. Rholes (Eds.), *Attachment theory and close relationships* (pp. 221–48). New York: Guilford Press.

Duncan, B. L. (2002). The legacy of Saul Rosenzweig: The profundity of the Dodo bird. *Journal of Psychotherapy Integration, 12*, 32–57.

Eagle, M. (1995). The developmental perspectives of attachment and psychoanalytic theory. In S. Goldberg, R. Muir, and J. Kerr (Eds.), *Attachment theory: Social, developmental, and clinical perspectives* (pp. 123–50). Hillsdale, NJ: Analytic.

——. (1996). Attachment theory and psychoanalytic theory. In J. M. Masling and R. F. Bornstein (Eds.), *Psychoanalytic perspectives on developmental psychology* (pp. 105–49). Washington, DC: American Psychological Association.

——. (1997). Attachment and psychoanalysis. *British Journal of Medical Psychology, 70*, 217–29.

——. (2003). Clinical implications of attachment theory. *Psychoanalytic Inquiry, 23*, 27-53.

——. (2006). Attachment, psychotherapy, and assessment: A commentary. *Journal of Consulting and Clinical Psychology, 74*, 1086–97.

Edwards, A. L. (1953). *Manual for the Edwards Personal Preference Schedule*. New York: Psychological Corporation.

Ehrenreich, B., & English, D. (1978). *For her own good: 150 years of expert advice to women*. New York: Anchor Books.

Epstein, M. (1996). *Thoughts without a thinker*. New York: Basic Books.

Epstein, R. M. (1999). Mindful practice. *Journal of the American Medical Association, 282*, 833–39.

Fain, M., & David, C. (1963). Aspects fonctionnels de la view onirique. *Revue Francaise de Psychosomatique, 27*, 241–343.

Fain, M., & Marty, P. (1964). Perspective psychosomatique sur la fonction des fantasmes. *Revue Francaise de Psychosomatique, 28*, 609–22.

Fairburn, C. G. (1997). Interpersonal psychotherapy for bulimia nervosa. In D. M. Garner and P. E. Garfinkel (Eds.), *Handbook of treatment for eating disorders* (Second ed., pp. 278–94). New York: Guilford Press.

Fairburn, C. G., Jones, R., Peveler, R. C., Carr, S. J., Solomon, R. A., O'Connor, M. E., Burton, J., & Hope, R. A. (1991). Three psychological treatments for bulimia nervosa: A comparative trial. *Archives of General Psychiatry, 48*, 463–69.

Fairburn, C. G., Marcus, M. D., & Wilson, G. T. (1993). Cognitive behaviour therapy for binge eating and bulimia nervosa: A comprehensive treatment manual. In C. G. Fairburn and G. T. Wilson (Eds.), *Binge eating: Nature, assessment, and treatment* (pp. 361–404). New York: Guilford Press.

Farber, B. A. (1985). The genesis, development, and implications of psychological-mindedness in psychotherapists. *Psychotherapy: Theory, Research, Practice, Training, 22*, 170–77.

——. (1989). Psychological-mindedness: Can there be too much of a good thing? *Psychotherapy: Theory, Research, Practice, Training, 26*, 210–17.

Farber, B. A., & Golden, V. (1997). Psychological mindedness in psychotherapists. In M. McCallum and W. E. Piper (Eds.), *Psychological mindedness: A contemporary understanding* (pp. 211–35). Mahwah, NJ: Lawrence Erlbaum.

Fassinger, R. E. (2005). Paradigms, praxis, problems, and promise: Grounded theory in counseling psychology research. *Journal of Counseling Psychology, 52*, 156–66.

Feldman, G. C., & Hayes, A. M. (in press). Preparing for problems: A measure of anticipatory coping processes. *Journal of Research in Personality*.

Fenigstein, A. (1997). Self-consciousness and its relation to psychological mindedness. In M. McCallum and W. E. Piper (Eds.), *Psychological mindedness: A contemporary understanding* (pp. 105–31). Mahwah, NJ: Lawrence Erlbaum.

Fenigstein, A., Scheier, M. F., & Buss, A. H. (1975). Public and private self-consciousness: Assessment and theory. *Journal of Consulting and Clinical Psychology, 43*, 522–27.

Ferenczi, S. (1932). The clinical diary of Sandor Ferenczi (M. Balint and N. Z. Jackson, Trans.). In J. Dupont (Ed.), *The clinical diary of Sandor Ferenczi*. Cambridge, MA: Harvard University Press, 1988.

Ferenczi, S., & Rank, O. (1924). *The development of psychoanalysis*. Madison, CT: International Universities Press.

Fertuck, E. A., Mergenthaler, E., Target, M., & Clarkin, J. F. (2004). Initial validity of a computerized text analysis measure of reflective function. *Journal of the American Psychoanalytic Association, 52*, 1215–17.

Fogel, G. I. (1995). Psychological-mindedness as a defense. *Journal of the American Psychoanalytic Association, 43*, 793–822.

Fonagy, P. (1991). Thinking about thinking: Some clinical and theoretical considerations in the treatment of a borderline patient. *International Journal of Psycho-Analysis, 72*, 639–56.

——. (1998). Moments of change in psychoanalytic theory: Discussion of a new theory of psychic change. *Infant Mental Health Journal, 19*, 346–53.

——. (1999a). Points of contact and divergence between psychoanalytic and attachment theories: Is psychoanalytic theory truly different? *Psychoanalytic Inquiry, 19*, 448–80.

——. (1999b). Psychoanalytic theory from the viewpoint of attachment theory and research. In J. Cassidy and P. R. Shaver (Eds.), *Handbook of attachment: Theory, research, and clinical applications* (pp. 595–624). New York: Guilford Press.

——. (2001). *Attachment theory and psychoanalysis*. New York: Other Press.

——. (2003). The development of psychopathology from infancy to adulthood: The mysterious unfolding of disturbance in time. *Infant Mental Health Journal, 24*, 212–39.

Fonagy, P., & Bateman, A. W. (2006). Mechanisms of change in mentalization-based treatment of BPD. *Journal of Clinical Psychology, 62*, 411–30.

Fonagy, P., Gergely, G., Jurist, E. L., & Target, M. (2002). *Affect regulation, mentalization, and the development of the self*. New York: Other Press.

Fonagy, P., Leigh, T., Steele, M., Steele, H., Kennedy, R., Mattoon, G., Target, M., & Gerber, A. (1996). The relation of attachment status, psychiatric classification, and response to psychotherapy. *Journal of Consulting and Clinical Psychology, 64*, 22–31.

Fonagy, P., Redfern, S., & Charman, T. (1997). The relationship between belief-desire reasoning and a projective measure of attachment security (SAT). *British Journal of Developmental Psychology, 15*, 51–61.

Fonagy, P., Steele, H., & Steele, M. (1991). Maternal representations of attachment during pregnancy predict organization of infant-mother attachment at one year of age. *Child Development, 62*, 891–905.

Fonagy, P., Steele, M., Steele, H., Higgitt, A., & Target, M. (1994). The theory and practice of resilience. *Journal of Child Psychology and Psychiatry, 35*, 231–57.

Fonagy, P., Steele, M., Steele, H., Leigh, T., Kennedy, R., Mattoon, G., & Target, M. (1995). Attachment, the reflective self, and borderline states: The predictive specificity of the Adult Attachment Interview and pathological emotional development. In S. Goldberg, R. Muir, and J. Kerr (Eds.), *Attachment theory: Social, developmental, and clinical perspectives* (pp. 233–78). Hillsdale, NJ: Analytic Press.

Fonagy, P., Steele, M., Steele, H., Moran, G. S., & Higgitt, A. C. (1991). The capacity for understanding mental states: The reflective self in parent and child and its significance for security of attachment. *Infant Mental Health Journal, 12*, 201–18.

Fonagy, P., & Target, M. (1996a). Playing with reality: I. Theory of mind and the normal development of psychic reality. *International Journal of Psycho-Analysis, 77*, 217–33.

——. (1996b). Predictors of outcome in child psychoanalysis: A retrospective study of 763 cases at the Anna Freud Centre. *Journal of the American Psychoanalytic Association, 44*, 27–77.

——. (1997). Attachment and reflective function: Their role in self-organization. *Development and Psychopathology, 9*, 679–700.

——. (1998). Mentalization and the changing aims of child psychoanalysis. *Psychoanalytic Dialogues, 8*, 87–114.

——. (2005a). Bridging the transmission gap: An end to an important mystery of attachment research? *Attachment and Human Development, 7*, 333–43.

——. (2005b, September). *Mentalization and split psychic reality: An attachment theory approach to PTSD*. Paper presented at the conference, "Reflecting on the future of psychoanalysis: Mentalization, internalization and representation," City College of New York.

Fonagy, P., Target, M., Cottrell, D., Phillips, J., & Kurtz, Z. (2002). *What works for whom? A critical review of treatments for children and adolescents*. New York: Guilford Press.

Fonagy, P., Target, M., Steele, H., & Steele, M. (1998). *Reflective-functioning manual, version 5: For application to Adult Attachment Interviews*, University College, London.

Frank, E., & Spanier, C. (1995). Interpersonal psychotherapy for depression: Overview, clinical efficacy, and future directions. *Clinical Psychology: Science and Practice, 2*, 349–69.

Frank, J. D. (1973). *Persuasion and healing*. Baltimore: Johns Hopkins University Press. (Original work published 1961).

Freud, A. (1936). *The ego and the mechanisms of defense*. New York: International Universities Press.

——. (1963). The concept of developmental lines. *Psychoanalytic Study of the Child, 18*, 245–65.

——. (1971). Foreword. In *The Wolf-Man, with the case of the Wolf-Man by Sigmund Freud* (pp. ix-xii). New York: Basic Books.

Freud, S. (1893). Katharina, case histories from studies on hysteria. In J. Strachey (Ed. and Trans.), *The standard edition of the complete psychological works of Sigmund Freud* (Vol. 2, pp. 125–34). London: Hogarth Press, 1955.

——. (1896). Further remarks on the neuro-psychoses of defence. In J. Strachey (Ed. and Trans.), *The standard edition of the complete psychological works of Sigmund Freud* (Vol. 3, pp. 157–85). London: Hogarth Press, 1961.

——. (1900). The interpretation of dreams. In J. Strachey (Ed. and Trans.), *The standard edition of the complete psychological works of Sigmund Freud* (Vols. 4 and 5, pp. 1–625). London: Hogarth Press, 1961.

——. (1905a). Fragment of an analysis of a case of hysteria. In J. Strachey (Ed. and Trans.), *The standard edition of the complete psychological works of Sigmund Freud* (Vol. 7, pp. 7–122). London: Hogarth Press, 1961.

——. (1905b). Three essays on the theory of sexuality. In J. Strachey (Ed. and Trans.), *The standard edition of the complete psychological works of Sigmund Freud* (Vol. 7, pp. 135–243). London: Hogarth Press, 1961.

——. (1909a). Analysis of a phobia in a five-year-old boy. In J. Strachey (Ed. and Trans.), *The standard edition of the complete psychological works of Sigmund Freud* (Vol. 10, pp. 1–150). London: Hogarth Press, 1961.

——. (1909b). Notes upon a case of obsessional neurosis. In J. Strachey (Ed. and Trans.), *The standard edition of the complete psychological works of Sigmund Freud* (Vol. 10, pp. 151–318). London: Hogarth Press, 1961.

——. (1910). The future prospects of psycho-analytic therapy. In J. Strachey (Ed. and Trans.), *The standard edition of the complete psychological works of Sigmund Freud* (Vol. 11, pp. 139–52). London: Hogarth Press, 1961.

——. (1911). Formulations on the two principles of mental functioning. In J. Strachey (Ed. and Trans.), *The standard edition of the complete psychological works of Sigmund Freud* (Vol. 12, pp. 215–26). London: Hogarth Press, 1961.

——. (1912a). The dynamics of transference. In J. Strachey (Ed. and Trans.), *The standard edition of the complete psychological works of Sigmund Freud* (Vol. 12, pp. 97–108). London: Hogarth Press, 1961.

——. (1912b). Recommendations to physicians practising psycho-analysis. In J. Strachey (Ed. and Trans.), *The standard edition of the complete psychological works of Sigmund Freud* (Vol. 12, pp. 109–20). London: Hogarth Press, 1961.

——. (1913a). The disposition to obsessional neurosis, a contribution to the problem of the choice of neurosis. In J. Strachey (Ed. and Trans.), *The standard edition of the complete psychological works of Sigmund Freud* (Vol. 12, pp. 311–26). London: Hogarth Press, 1958.

——. (1913b). On beginning the treatment (Further recommendations on the technique of psycho-analysis I). In J. Strachey (Ed. and Trans.), *The standard edition of the complete psychological works of Sigmund Freud* (Vol. 12, pp. 123–44). London: Hogarth Press, 1958.

——. (1915). Observations on transference-love (Further recommendations on the technique of psycho-analysis III). In J. Strachey (Ed. and Trans.), *The standard edition of the complete psychological works of Sigmund Freud* (Vol. 12, pp. 157–71). London: Hogarth Press, 1961.

——. (1917). Introductory lectures on psycho-analysis. In J. Strachey (Ed. and Trans.), *The standard edition of the complete works of Sigmund Freud* (Vol. 16, pp. 241–463). London: Hogarth Press, 1955.

——. (1918). From the history of an infantile neurosis. In J. Strachey (Ed. and Trans.), *The standard edition of the complete psychological works of Sigmund Freud* (Vol. 17, pp. 1–124). London: Hogarth Press, 1961.

——. (1919a). Lines of advance in psycho-analytic therapy. In J. Strachey (Ed. and Trans.), *The standard edition of the complete psychological works of Sigmund Freud* (Vol. 17, pp. 157–68). London: Hogarth Press, 1955.

——. (1919b). On the teaching of psycho-analysis in universities. In J. Strachey (Ed. and Trans.), *The standard edition of the complete psychological works of Sigmund Freud* (Vol. 17, pp. 169–74). London: Hogarth Press, 1955.

——. (1925). An autobiographical study. In J. Strachey (Ed. and Trans.), *The standard edition of the complete psychological works of Sigmund Freud* (Vol. 20, pp. 1–74). London: Hogarth Press, 1961.

——. (1933a). New introductory lectures on psycho-analysis. In J. Strachey (Ed. and Trans.), *The standard edition of the complete psychological works of Sigmund Freud* (Vol. 22, pp. 1–182). London: Hogarth Press, 1964.

——. (1933b). New introductory lectures on psycho-analysis: Lecture XXXI: The dissection of the psychical personality. In J. Strachey (Ed. and Trans.), *The standard edition of the complete psychological works of Sigmund Freud* (Vol. 22, pp. 57–80). London: Hogarth Press, 1964.

——. (1940). An outline of psycho-analysis. In J. Strachey (Ed. and Trans.), *The standard edition of the complete psychological works of Sigmund Freud* (Vol. 23, pp. 144–207). London: Hogarth Press, 1961.

Gabbard, G. O., & Westen, D. (2003). Rethinking therapeutic action. *International Journal of Psychoanalysis, 84*, 823–41.

Gallagher, H. L., Happe, F., Brunswick, N., Fletcher, P. C., Frith, U., & Frith, C. D. (2000). Reading the mind in cartoons and stories: An fMRI study of "theory of mind" in verbal and nonverbal tasks. *Neuropsychologia, 38*, 11–21.

Garfield, S. L. (1978). *Research on client variables in psychotherapy* (Second ed.). New York: Wiley.

Gautama Buddha. (2006). Wikipedia. Retrieved June 30, 2006, from en.wikipedia .org/wiki/Gautama_Buddha.

Gelso, C. J. (1973). Effect of audiorecording and videorecording on client satisfaction and self-expression. *Journal of Consulting and Clinical Psychology, 40*, 455–61.

George, C., Kaplan, N., & Main, M. (1996). *Adult Attachment Interview* (Third ed.). Unpublished manuscript, University of California, Berkeley.

Gergely, G. (2000). Reapproaching Mahler: New perspectives on normal autism, symbiosis, splitting and libidinal object constancy from cognitive developmental theory. *Journal of the American Psychoanalytic Association, 48*, 1197–1228.

Gergely, G., & Watson, J. (1996). The social biofeedback model of parental affect-mirroring. *International Journal of Psycho-Analysis, 77*, 1181–1212.

Giesen-Bloo, J., & Arntz, A. (2007, May). In reply [Letter to the editor]. *Archives of General Psychiatry, 64*, 610, 611.

Giesen-Bloo, J., van Dyck, R., Spinhoven, P., van Tilburg, W., Dirksen, C., van Asselt, T., Kremers, I., Nadort, M., & Arntz, A. (2006). Outpatient psychotherapy for borderline personality disorder. *Archives of General Psychiatry, 63*, 649–58.

Glaser, B. G., & Strauss, A. L. (1967). *The discovery of grounded theory: Strategies for qualitative research*. Chicago: Aldine.

Goel, V., Grafman, N., Sadato, M., & Hallett, M. (1995). Modeling other minds. *Neuroreport, 6*, 1741–46.

Goldfried, M. R., & Wolfe, B. E. (1996). Psychotherapy practice and research: Repairing a strained alliance. *American Psychologist, 51*, 1007–16.

———. (1998). Toward a more clinically valid approach to therapy research. *Journal of Consulting and Clinical Psychology, 66*, 143–50.

Goleman, D. (1995). *Emotional intelligence*. New York: Bantam Books.

———. (2003). *Destructive emotions: A scientific dialogue with the Dalai Lama*. New York: Bantam.

Goodman, G. (1991). Feeling our way into empathy: Carl Rogers, Heinz Kohut, and Jesus. *Journal of Religion and Health, 30*, 191–205.

———. (2002). *The internal world and attachment*. Hillsdale, NJ: The Analytic Press.

———. (2005). Empirical evidence supporting the conceptual relatedness of object representations and internal working models. *Journal of the American Psychoanalytic Association, 53*, 597–617.

———. (in press). *Therapeutic attachment relationships: Interaction structures and the processes of therapeutic change*. Lanham, MD: Jason Aronson.

Goodman, G., Bass, J. N., Geenens, D. L., & Popper, C. W. (2006). The MAVRIC-C and MAVRIC-P: A preliminary reliability and validity study. *Journal of Personality Assessment, 86*, 273–90.

Goodman, G., Hans, S. L., & Bernstein, V. J. (2005). Mother expectation of bother and infant attachment behaviors as predictors of mother and child communication at 24 months in children of methadone-maintained women. *Infant Mental Health Journal, 26*, 549–69.

Goodman, G., Hull, J. W., Clarkin, J. F., & Yeomans, F. E. (1998). Comorbid mood disorders as modifiers of treatment response among inpatients with borderline personality disorder. *Journal of Nervous and Mental Disease, 186*, 616–22.

Goodman, G., Sapp, M. S., Stroh, M., & Valdez, A. (2007). Maternal depression, prepubertal children's representations of attachment disorganization, and the development of aggression and depression: A mediational model. In C. Yoon (Ed.), *Focus on family relations in the 21st century* (pp. 43–68). New York: Nova Science.

Goodman, G., & Schneider, C. (2006). *Mentalization and Mindfulness Q-Set*. Unpublished manuscript, Long Island University, Brookville, New York.

Gorman, B. S., & Allison, D. B. (1996). Statistical alternatives for single-case designs. In R. D. Franklin, D. B. Allison, and B. S. Gorman (Eds.), *Design and analysis of single-case research*. Mahwah, NJ: Erlbaum.

Gottman, J. M. (1981). *Time series analysis*. New York: Cambridge University Press.

Gottman, J. M., & Ringland, J. (1981). The analysis of dominance and bidirectionality in social development. *Child Development, 52*, 393–412.

Gottman, J. M., & Roy, J. M. (1990). *Sequential analysis: A guide for behavioral researchers*. New York: Cambridge University Press.

Gough, H. G. (1957). *Manual of the California Psychological Inventory*. Palo Alto, CA: Consulting Psychologists Press.

Grant, A. M. (2001). Rethinking psychological mindedness: Metacognition, self-reflection, and insight. *Behaviour Change, 18*, 8–17.

Green, A. (1996). What kind of research for psychoanalysis? *International Psychoanalysis: The Newsletter of the IPA, 5*, 10–14.

Greenberg, J. R. (1986). Theoretical models and the analyst's neutrality. *Contemporary Psychoanalysis, 22*, 89–106.

Greenberg, J. R., & Mitchell, S. A. (1983). *Object relations in psychoanalytic theory*. Cambridge, MA: Harvard University Press.

Greenberg, M. T. (1999). Attachment and psychopathology in childhood. In J. Cassidy and P. R. Shaver (Eds.), *Handbook of attachment: Theory, research, and clinical applications* (pp. 469–96). New York: Guilford Press.

Grencavage, L. M., & Norcross, J. C. (1990). Where are the commonalities among the therapeutic common factors? *Professional Psychology: Research and Practice, 21*, 372–78.

Grienenberger, J., Kelly, K., & Slade, A. (2005). Maternal reflective functioning, mother-infant affective communication, and infant attachment: Exploring the link between mental states and observed caregiving behavior in the intergenerational transmission of attachment. *Attachment and Human Development, 7*, 299–311.

Grotstein, J. S. (1998, November 7). Workshop on Kleinian therapeutic technique presented to the New York Freudian Society, New York.

Hall, J. A. (1992). Psychological-mindedness: A conceptual model. *American Journal of Psychotherapy, 46*, 131–40.

Hamilton, C. E. (2000). Continuity and discontinuity of attachment from infancy through adolescence. *Child Development, 71*, 690–94.

Harris, M. J., & Rosenthal, R. (1985). Mediation of interpersonal expectancy effects: 31 meta-analyses. *Psychological Bulletin, 97*, 363–86.

Hart, E. L., Lahey, B. B., Loeber, R., & Hanson, K. S. (1994). Criterion validity of informants in the diagnosis of disruptive behavior disorders in children: A preliminary study. *Journal of Consulting and Clinical Psychology, 62*, 410–14.

Hartmann, H. (1950). Psychoanalysis and developmental psychology. *Psychoanalytic Study of the Child, 5*, 7–17.

Hatcher, R. L., Hatcher, S., Berlin, M., Okla, K., & Richards, J. (1990). Psychological mindedness and abstract reasoning in late childhood and adolescence: An exploration using new instruments. *Journal of Youth and Adolescence, 19*, 307–26.

Hatcher, R. L., & Hatcher, S. L. (1997). Assessing the psychological mindedness of children and adolescents. In M. McCallum and W. E. Piper (Eds.), *Psychological mindedness: A contemporary understanding* (pp. 59–75). Mahwah, NJ: Lawrence Erlbaum.

Hayes, A. M., & Feldman, G. (2004). Clarifying the construct of mindfulness in the context of emotion regulation and the process of change in therapy. *Clinical Psychology: Science and Practice, 11*, 255–62.

Hayes, S. C. (2002). Acceptance, mindfulness, and science. *Clinical Psychology: Science and Practice, 9*, 101–6.

———. (2004). Acceptance and commitment therapy and the new behavior therapies: Mindfulness, acceptance, and relationship. In S. C. Hayes, V. M. Follette, and M. M. Linehan (Eds.), *Mindfulness and acceptance: Expanding the cognitive-behavioral tradition* (pp. 1–29). New York: Guilford Press.

Hayes, S. C., & Shenk, C. (2004). Operationalizing mindfulness without unnecessary attachments. *Clinical Psychology: Science and Practice, 11*, 249–54.

Hayes, S. C., Strosahl, K. D., & Wilson, K. G. (1999). *Acceptance and commitment therapy: An experiential approach to behavior change*. New York: Guilford Press.

Hayes, S. C., & Wilson, K. G. (2003). Mindfulness: Method and process. *Clinical Psychology: Science and Practice, 10*, 161–65.

Hayes, S. C., Wilson, K. G., Gifford, E. V., Follette, V. M., & Strosahl, K. (1996). Experiential avoidance and behavioral disorders: A functional dimensional approach to diagnosis and treatment. *Journal of Consulting and Clinical Psychology, 64*, 1152–68.

Henry, W. P., & Strupp, H. H. (1994). The therapeutic alliance as interpersonal process. In A. O. Horvath and L. S. Greenberg (Eds.), *The working alliance: Theory, research, and practice* (pp. 51–84). Oxford: Wiley.

Hesse, E., & Main, M. (1999). Second-generation effects of unresolved trauma in non maltreating parents: Dissociated, frightened, and threatening parental behavior. *Psychoanalytic Inquiry, 19*, 481–540.

Hill, C. E., O'Grady, K. E., & Elkin, I. (1992). Applying the Collaborative Study Psychotherapy Rating Scale to rate adherence in cognitive-behavioral therapy, interpersonal therapy, and clinical management. *Journal of Consulting and Clinical Psychology, 60*, 73–79.

Hill, L. L., Levy, K. N., Meehan, K. B., & Reynoso, J. S. (2007). Reliability of a multidimensional measure for scoring reflective function. *Journal of the American Psychoanalytic Association, 55*, 309–13.

Hilliard, R. B. (1993). Single-case methodology in psychotherapy process and outcome research. *Journal of Consulting and Clinical Psychology, 61*, 373–80.

Hilsenroth, M. J., Blagys, M. D., Ackerman, S. J., Bonge, D. R., & Blais, M. A. (2005). Measuring psychodynamic-interpersonal and cognitive-behavioral techniques: Development of the Comparative Psychotherapy Process Scale. *Psychotherapy: Theory, Research, Practice, Training, 42*, 340–56.

Hilsenroth, M. J., Stein, M., & Pinsker, J. (2004). *Social Cognition and Object Relations Scale: Global rating method (SCORS-G).* Unpublished manuscript, Adelphi University, Garden City, New York.

Hoffman, I. Z. (1994). Dialectical thinking and therapeutic action in the psychoanalytic process. *Psychoanalytic Quarterly, 63*, 187–218.

Høglend, P., Bøgwald, K.-P., Amlo, S., Marble, A., Ulberg, R., Sjaastad, M. C., Sørbye, Ø., Heyerdahl, O., & Johansson, P. (2008). Transference interpretations in dynamic psychotherapy: Do they really yield sustained effects? *American Journal of Psychiatry, 165*, 763–71.

Holt, R. R., & Luborsky, L. (1958). *Personality patterns of psychiatrists* (Vols. 1 and 2). New York: Basic Books.

Horvath, A., & Symonds, B. (1991). Relation between working alliance and outcome in psychotherapy: A meta-analysis. *Journal of Counseling Psychology, 38*, 139–49.

Horvath, A. O., & Bedi, R. P. (2002). The alliance. In J. C. Norcross (Ed.), *Psychotherapy relationships that work: Therapist contributions and responsiveness to patients* (pp. 37–69). New York: Oxford University Press.

Howard, K. I., Cornille, T. A., Lyons, J. S., Vessey, J. T., Lueger, R. J., & Saunders, S. M. (1996). Patterns of mental health service utilization. *Archives of General Psychiatry, 53*, 696–703.

Howard, K. I., Kopta, S. M., Krause, M. S., & Orlinsky, D. E. (1986). The dose-effect relationship in psychotherapy. *American Psychologist, 41*, 159–64.

Howard, K. I., Lueger, R., Maling, M., & Martinovich, Z. (1993). A phase model of psychotherapy: Causal mediation of outcome. *Journal of Consulting and Clinical Psychology, 54*, 106–10.

Hubble, M. A., Duncan, B. L., & Miller, S. D. (1999). Directing attention to what works. In M. A. Hubble, B. L. Duncan, and S. D. Miller (Eds.), *The heart and soul of change: What works in therapy* (pp. 407–48). Washington, DC: American Psychological Association.

Hull, J. W., Yeomans, F., Clarkin, J., Li, C., & Goodman, G. (1996). Factors associated with multiple hospitalizations of patients with borderline personality disorder. *Psychiatric Services, 47*, 638–41.

Huppert, J. D., Bufka, L. F., Barlow, D. H., Gorman, J. M., Shear, M. K., & Woods, S. W. (2001). Therapists, therapist variables, and cognitive-behavioral therapy outcome in a multicenter trial for panic disorder. *Journal of Consulting and Clinical Psychology, 69*, 747–55.

Ilardi, S. S., & Craighead, W. E. (1994). The role of nonspecific factors in cognitive-behavior therapy for depression. *Clinical Psychology: Science and Practice, 1*, 138–56.

———. (1999). Rapid early response, cognitive modification, and nonspecific factors in cognitive behavior therapy for depression: A reply to Tang and DeRubeis. *Clinical Psychology: Science and Practice, 6*, 295–99.

Jacobson, E. (1964). *The self and the object world.* New York: International Universities Press.

Jacobson, N. S., & Truax, P. (1991). Clinical significance: A statistical approach to defining meaningful change in psychotherapy research. *Journal of Consulting and Clinical Psychology, 41*, 51–65.

Jones, E. E. (1993). Introduction to special section: Single-case research in psychotherapy. *Journal of Consulting and Clinical Psychology, 61*, 371, 372.

———. (2000). *Therapeutic action: A guide to psychoanalytic therapy.* Northvale, NJ: Jason Aronson.

Jones, E. E., Cumming, J. D., & Horowitz, M. J. (1988). Another look at the nonspecific hypothesis of therapeutic effectiveness. *Journal of Consulting and Clinical Psychology, 56*, 48–55.

Jones, E. E., Ghannam, J., Nigg, J. T., & Dyer, J. F. P. (1993). A paradigm for single-case research: The time-series study of a long-term psychotherapy for depression. *Journal of Consulting and Clinical Psychology, 61*, 381–94.

Jones, E. E., Hall, S. A., & Parke, L. A. (1991). The process of change: The Berkeley Psychotherapy Research Group. In L. E. Beutler and M. Crago (Eds.), *Psychotherapy research: An international review of programmatic studies* (pp. 98–106). Washington, DC: American Psychological Association.

Jones, E. E., Krupnick, J. L., & Kerig, P. K. (1987). Some gender effects in a brief psychotherapy. *Psychotherapy: Theory, Research, Practice, Training, 24*, 336–52.

Jones, E. E., & Price, P. B. (1998). Interaction structure and change in psychoanalytic therapy. In R. F. Bornstein and J. M. Masling (Eds.), *Empirical studies of the therapeutic hour* (pp. 27–62). Washington, DC: American Psychological Association.

Jones, E. E., & Pulos, S. M. (1993). Comparing the process in psychodynamic and cognitive-behavioral therapies. *Journal of Consulting and Clinical Psychology, 61*, 306–16.

Jones, E. E., & Windholz, M. (1990). The psychoanalytic case study: Toward a method for systematic inquiry. *Journal of the American Psychoanalytic Association, 38*, 985–1015.

Josephs, L., Anderson, E., Bernard, A., Fatzer, K., & Streich, J. (2004). Assessing progress in analysis interminable. *Journal of the American Psychoanalytic Association, 52*, 1185–1214.

Josephs, L., & Fatzer, K. (2006). *Therapeutic interaction with a schizoid patient.* Manuscript submitted for publication, Adelphi University, Garden City, New York.

Kabat-Zinn, J. (1982). An out-patient program in Behavioral Medicine for chronic pain patients based on the practice of mindfulness meditation: Theoretical considerations and preliminary results. *General Hospital Psychiatry, 4*, 33–47.

———. (1990). *Full catastrophe living: Using the wisdom of your body and mind to face stress, pain and illness.* New York: Delacorte Press.

———. (1994). *Wherever you go, there you are: Mindfulness meditation in everyday life.* New York: Hyperion.

——. (2003). Mindfulness-based interventions in context: Past, present, and future. *Clinical Psychology: Science and Practice, 10*, 144–56.

Kabat-Zinn, J., Massion, A. O., Kristeller, J., Peterson, L. G., Fletcher, K., Pbert, L., Lenderking, W. R., & Santorelli, S. F. (1992). Effectiveness of a meditation-based stress reduction program in the treatment of anxiety disorders. *American Journal of Psychiatry, 149*, 936–43.

Kabat-Zinn, J., Wheeler, E., Light, T., Skillings, Z., Scharf, M. J., Cropley, T. G., Hosmer, D., & Bernhard, J. D. (1998). Influence of a mindfulness meditation-based stress reduction intervention on rates of skin clearing in patients with moderate to severe psoriasis undergoing phototherapy (UVB) and photochemotherapy (PUVA). *Psychosomatic Medicine, 50*, 625–32.

Kantrowitz, J. L. (2001). The analyst's participation: A new look [Commentary]. *Journal of the American Psychoanalytic Association, 49*, 398–406.

Karlsson, R., & Kermott, A. (2006). Reflective-functioning during the process in brief psychotherapies. *Psychotherapy: Theory, Research, Practice, Training, 43*, 65–84.

Katzenstein, T. (2005, June). *Validating change: Empirical methods and clinical work*. Paper presented at the annual meeting of the American Psychoanalytic Association, Seattle, Washington.

Kazdin, A. E. (2005). Treatment outcomes, common factors, and continued neglect of mechanisms of change. *Clinical Psychology: Science and Practice, 12*, 184–88.

——. (2006). Arbitrary metrics: Implications for identifying evidence-based treatments. *American Psychologist, 61*, 42–49.

Kazdin, A. E., & Bass, D. (1989). Power to detect differences between alternative treatments in comparative psychotherapy outcome research. *Journal of Consulting and Clinical Psychology, 57*, 138–47.

Keller, M. B., McCullough, J. P., Klein, D. N., Arnow, B., Dunner, D. L., Gelenberg, A. J., Markowitz, J. C., Nemeroff, C. B., Russell, J. M., Thase, M. E., Trivedi, M. H., Zajecka, J. (2000). A comparison of nefazodone, the cognitive behavioral-analysis system of psychotherapy, and their combination for the treatment of chronic depression. *New England Journal of Medicine, 342*, 1462–70.

Kendall, P. C., Marrs-Garcia, A., Nath, S. R., & Sheldrick, R. C. (1999). Normative comparisons for the evaluation of clinical significance. *Journal of Consulting and Clinical Psychology, 67*, 285–99.

Kernberg, O. (1966). Structural derivatives of object relationships. *International Journal of Psycho-Analysis, 47*, 236–53.

——. (1967). Borderline personality organization. *Journal of the American Psychoanalytic Association, 15*, 641–85.

——. (1970). Factors in the psychoanalytic treatment of narcissistic personalities. *Journal of the American Psychoanalytic Association, 18*, 51–85.

——. (1975). *Borderline conditions and pathological narcissism*. New York: Jason Aronson.

——. (1976). *Object relations theory and clinical psychoanalysis*. New York: Jason Aronson.

——. (1983). Object relations theory and character analysis. *Journal of the American Psychoanalytic Association, 31*, 247–71.

——. (1984). *Severe personality disorders: Psychotherapeutic strategies.* New Haven, CT: Yale University Press.

——. (1986a). Borderline personality organization. In M. Stone (Ed.), *Essential papers on borderline disorders: One hundred years at the border* (pp. 279–319). New York: New York University Press.

——. (1986b). Further contributions to the treatment of narcissistic personalities. In A. Morrison (Ed.), *Essential papers on narcissism* (pp. 245–92). New York: New York University Press.

——. (1995). *Love relations: Normality and pathology.* New Haven, CT: Yale University Press.

——. (1996). A psychoanalytic theory of personality disorders. In J. F. Clarkin and M. F. Lenzenweger (Eds.), *Major theories of personality disorder* (pp. 106–40). New York: Guilford Press.

Kernberg, O. F., Burstein, E. D., Coyne, L., Appelbaum, A., Horwitz, L., & Voth, H. (1972). Psychotherapy and psychoanalysis: Final report of the Menninger Foundation's Psychotherapy Research Project. *Bulletin of the Menninger Clinic, 36*, 1–275.

Kernberg, O. F., Selzer, M. A., Koenigsberg, H. W., Carr, A. C., & Appelbaum, A. H. (1989). *Psychodynamic psychotherapy of borderline patients.* New York: Basic Books.

Kessler, R. C., Nelson, C. B., McGonagle, K. A., Liu, J., Swartz, M., & Blazer, D. G. (1996). Comorbidity of DSM-III-R major depressive disorder in the general population: Results from the US National Comorbidity Survey. *British Journal of Psychiatry, 168* (Suppl. 30), 17–30.

Kessler, R. C., Stang, P., Wittchen, H. U., Stein, M., & Walters, E. E. (1999). Lifetime comorbidities between social phobia and mood disorders in the US National Comorbidity Survey. *Psychological Medicine, 29*, 555–67.

Kiesler, D. J. (1971). Experimental designs in psychotherapy research. In A. E. Bergin and S. L. Garfield (Eds.), *Handbook of psychotherapy and behavior change* (pp. 36–74). New York: Wiley.

Kim, D.-M., Wampold, B. E., & Bolt, D. M. (2006). Therapist effects in psychotherapy: A random-effects modeling of the National Institute of Mental Health Treatment of Depression Collaborative Research Program data. *Psychotherapy Research, 16*, 161–72.

Klein, D. N., Schwartz, J. E., Santiago, N. J., Vivian, D., Vocisano, C., Castonguay, L. G., Arnow, B., Blalock, J. A., Manber, R., Markowitz, J. C., Riso, L. P., Rothbaum, B., McCullough, J. P., Thase, M. E., Borian, F. E., Miller, I. W., & Keller, M. B. (2003). Therapeutic alliance in depression treatment: Controlling for prior change and patient characteristics. *Journal of Consulting and Clinical Psychology, 71*, 997–1006.

Klein, M. (1933). The early development of conscience in the child. In R. E. Money-Kyrle (Ed.), *Love, guilt and reparation and other works 1921–1945* (pp. 248–57). New York: Delacorte Press, 1975.

——. (1937). Love, guilt and reparation. In R. E. Money-Kyrle (Ed.), *Love, guilt and reparation and other works 1921–1945* (pp. 306–43). New York: Delacorte Press, 1975.

——. (1946). Notes on some schizoid mechanisms. In R. E. Money-Kyrle (Ed.), *Envy and gratitude and other works 1946–1963* (pp. 1–24). New York: Delacorte Press, 1975.

——. (1952). The origins of transference. In R. E. Money-Kyrle (Ed.), *Envy and gratitude and other works 1946–1963* (pp. 48–56). New York: Delacorte Press, 1975.

——. (1957). Envy and gratitude: A study of unconscious sources. In R. E. Money-Kyrle (Ed.), *Envy and gratitude and other works 1946–1963* (pp. 176–235). New York: Delacorte Press, 1975.

Klerman, G. L., & Weissman, M. M. (1993). *New applications of interpersonal psychotherapy*. Washington, DC: American Psychological Association.

Klumpner, G., & Frank, A. (1991). On methods of reporting clinical material. *Journal of the American Psychoanalytic Association, 39*, 537–51.

Kobak, R. R., Cole, H. E., Ferenz-Gillies, R., Fleming, W. S., & Gamble, W. (1993). Attachment and emotion regulation during mother-teen problem solving: A control theory analysis. *Child Development, 64*, 231–45.

Kobak, R. R., & Sceery, A. (1988). Attachment in late adolescence: Working models, affect regulation, and representations of self and others. *Child Development, 59*, 135–46.

Koenigsberg, H. W., Kernberg, O. F., Stone, M. H., Appelbaum, A. H., Yeomans, F. E., & Diamond, D. (2000). *Borderline patients: Extending the limits of treatability*. New York: Basic Books.

Kohlenberg, R. J., Hayes, S. C., & Tsai, M. (1993). Radical behavioral psychotherapy: Two contemporary examples. *Clinical Psychology Review, 13*, 579–92.

Koren-Karie, N., Oppenheim, D., Dolev, S., Sher, E., & Etzion-Carasso, A. (2002). Mothers' empathic understanding of their infants' internal experience: Relations with maternal sensitivity and infant attachment. *Development Psychology, 38*, 534–42.

Kovacs, M. (1992). *Children's Depression Inventory manual*. North Tonawanda, NY: Multi-Health Systems.

Lambert, M. J. (1992). Implications of outcome research for psychotherapy integration. In J. C. Norcross and M. R. Goldfried (Eds.), *Handbook of psychotherapy integration* (pp. 94–129). New York: Basic Books.

——. (2004). Overview, trends, and future issues. In M. J. Lambert (Ed.), *Bergin and Garfield's handbook of psychotherapy and behavior change* (Fifth ed., pp. 805–22). New York: Wiley.

Lambert, M. J., & Barley, D. E. (2001). Research summary on the therapeutic relationship and psychotherapy outcome. *Psychotherapy: Theory, Research, Practice, Training, 38*, 357–61.

Lambert, M. J., & Bergin, A. E. (1994). The effectiveness of psychotherapy. In A. E. Bergin and S. L. Garfied (Eds.), *Handbook of psychotherapy and behavior change* (Fourth ed., pp. 143–89). New York: Wiley.

Lambert, M. J., & Ogles, B. M. (2004). The efficacy and effectiveness of psychotherapy. In M. J. Lambert (Ed.), *Bergin and Garfield's handbook of psychotherapy and behavior change* (Fifth ed., pp. 139–93). New York: Wiley.

Lau, M. A., Bishop, S. R., Segal, Z. V., Buis, T., Anderson, N. D., Carlson, L., Shapiro, S., Carmody, J., Abbey, S., & Devins, G. (in press). The Toronto Mindfulness Scale: Development and validation. *Journal of Clinical Psychology.*

Lecours, S., & Bouchard, M.-A. (1997). Dimensions of mentalisation: Outlining levels of psychic transformation. *International Journal of Psycho-Analysis, 78*, 855–75.

Levy, K. N. (2008). Psychotherapies and lasting change. *American Journal of Psychiatry, 165*, 556–59.

Levy, K. N., Clarkin, J. F., Yeomans, F. E., Scott, L. N., Wasserman, R. H., & Kernberg, O. F. (2006). The mechanisms of change in the treatment of borderline personality disorder with transference focused psychotherapy. *Journal of Clinical Psychology, 62*, 481–501.

Levy, K. N., Meehan, K. B., & Hill, L. L. (2005). *Reflective Function Multidimensional Rating Scale.* Unpublished rating scale, Pennsylvania State University at State College.

Levy, K. N., Meehan, K. B., Kelly, K. M., Reynoso, J. S., Weber, M., Clarkin, J. F., & Kernberg, O. F. (2006). Change in attachment patterns and reflective function in a randomized control trial of transference-focused psychotherapy for borderline personality disorder. *Journal of Consulting and Clinical Psychology, 74*, 1027–40.

Levy, K. N., Wasserman, R. H., Scott, L. N., Zach, S. E., White, C. N., Cain, N. M., Fischer, C., Eubanks Carter, C., Clarkin, J. F., & Kernberg, O. F. (2006). The development of a measure to assess putative mechanisms of change in the treatment of borderline personality disorder. *Journal of the American Psychoanalytic Association, 54*, 1325–31.

Linehan, M. M. (1993a). *Cognitive-behavioral treatment of borderline personality disorder.* New York: Guilford Press.

———. (1993b). *Skills training manual for treating borderline personality disorder.* New York: Guilford Press.

———. (1994). Acceptance and change: The central dialectic in psychotherapy. In S. C. Hayes, N. S. Jacobson, V. M. Follette, and M. J. Dougher (Eds.), *Acceptance and change: Content and context in psychotherapy* (pp. 73–86). Reno, NV: Context Press.

Linehan, M. M., Armstrong, H. E., Suarez, A., Allmon, D., & Heard, H. L. (1991). Cognitive-behavioral treatment of chronically parasuicidal borderline patients. *Archives of General Psychiatry, 48*, 1060–64.

Linehan, M. M., Comtois, K. A., Murray, A. M., Brown, M. Z., Gallop, R. J., Heard, H. L., Korslund, K. E., Tutek, D. A., Reynolds, S. K., & Lindenboim, N. (2006). Two-year randomized controlled trial and follow-up of dialectical behavior therapy vs therapy by experts for suicidal behaviors and borderline personality disorder. *Archives of General Psychiatry, 63*, 757–66.

Linehan, M. M., Heard, H. L., & Armstrong, H. E. (1993). Naturalistic follow-up of a behavioral treatment for chronically parasuicidal borderline patients. *Archives of General Psychiatry, 50*, 971–74.

Linehan, M. M., Turek, D., Heard, H. L., & Armstrong, H. E. (1994). Interpersonal outcome of cognitive-behavioral treatment for chronically suicidal borderline patients. *American Journal of Psychiatry, 51*, 1771–76.

Lipsey, M. W., & Wilson, D. B. (1993). The efficacy of psychological, educational, and behavioral treatment: Confirmation from meta-analysis. *American Psychologist, 48*, 1181–1209.

Loeber, R., Green, S. M., Lahey, B. B., & Stouthamer-Loeber, M. (1989). Optimal informants on childhood disruptive behaviors. *Development and Psychopathology, 1*, 317–37.

———. (1991). Differences and similarities between children, mothers, and teachers as informants on disruptive child behavior. *Journal of Abnormal Child Psychology, 19*, 75–95.

Luborsky, L. (1953). Intra-individual repetitive measurements (P-technique) on understanding symptom structure and psychotherapeutic change. In O. H. Mowrer (Ed.), *Psychotherapy: Theory and research* (pp. 389–413). New York: Ronald Press.

———. (1995). The first trial of the P technique in psychotherapy research—A still lively legacy. *Journal of Consulting and Clinical Psychology, 63*, 6–14.

Luborsky, L., Diguer, L., Seligman, D. A., Rosenthal, R., Krause, E. D., Johnson, S., Halperin, G., Bishop, M., Berman, J. S., & Schweizer, E. (1999). *Clinical Psychology: Science and Practice, 6*, 95–106.

Luborsky, L., McLellan, A. T., Diguer, L., Woody, G., & Seligman, D. A. (1997). The psychotherapist matters: Comparison of outcomes across twenty-two therapists and seven patient samples. *Clinical Psychology: Science and Practice, 4*, 53–65.

Luborsky, L., Singer, B., & Luborsky, L. (1975). Comparative studies of psychotherapies: Is it true that "everyone has won and all must have prizes"? *Archives of General Psychiatry, 32*, 995–1008.

Lustman, S. L. (1956). Rudiments of the ego. *Psychoanalytic Study of the Child, 11*, 89–98.

Lyons-Ruth, K. (1991). Rapprochement or approchement: Mahler's theory reconsidered from the vantage point of recent research on early attachment relationships. *Psychoanalytic Psychology, 8*, 1–23.

———. (1999). The two-person unconscious: Intersubjective dialogue, enactive relational representation, and the emergence of new forms of relational organization. *Psychoanalytic Inquiry, 19*, 576–617.

Lyons-Ruth, K., Bronfman, E., & Atwood, G. (1999). A relational diathesis model of hostile-helpless states of mind: Expressions in mother-infant interaction. In J. Solomon and C. George (Eds.), *Attachment disorganization* (pp. 33–70). New York: Guilford Press.

Lyons-Ruth, K., Bronfman, E., & Parsons, E. (1999). Maternal frightened, frightening, or atypical behavior and disorganized infant attachment patterns. In J. Vondra and D. Barnett (Eds.), *Atypical patterns of infant attachment: Theory, research and current directions. Monographs of the Society for Research in Child Development, 64* (pp. 67–96). Malden, MA: Blackwell.

Lyons-Ruth, K., & Jacobvitz, D. (1999). Attachment disorganization: Unresolved loss, relational violence, and lapses in behavioral and attentional strategies. In J. Cassidy and P. R. Shaver (Eds.), *Handbook of attachment: Theory, research, and clinical applications* (pp. 520–54). New York: Guilford Press.

Ma, S. H., & Teasdale, J. D. (2004). Mindfulness-based cognitive therapy for depression: Replication and exploration of differential relapse prevention effects. *Journal of Consulting and Clinical Psychology, 72*, 31–40.

Mahler, M. S. (1968). *On human symbiosis and the vicissitudes of individuation*. New York: International Universities Press.

———. (1972). Rapprochement subphase of the separation-individuation process. *Psychoanalytic Quarterly, 41*, 487–506.

Mahler, M. S., Pine, F., & Bergman, A. (1975). *The psychological birth of the human infant: Symbiosis and individuation*. New York: Basic Books.

Main, M. (1991). Metacognitive knowledge, metacognitive monitoring, and singular (coherent) vs. multiple (incoherent) models of attachment: Findings and directions for future research. In C. M. Parkes, J. Stevenson-Hinde, and P. Marris (Eds.), *Attachment across the life cycle* (pp. 127–59). London: Routledge.

Main, M., & Goldwyn, R. (1994). *Adult attachment scoring and classification systems* (Sixth ed.). Unpublished manuscript, University College, London.

Main, M., & Hesse, E. (1990). Parents' unresolved traumatic experiences are related to infant disorganized attachment status: Is frightened and/or frightening parental behavior the linking mechanism? In M. T. Greenberg, D. Cicchetti, and E. M. Cummings (Eds.), *Attachment in the preschool years: Theory, research, and intervention* (pp. 161–82). Chicago: University of Chicago Press.

Main, M., Kaplan, N., & Cassidy, J. (1985). Security in infancy, childhood, and adulthood: A move to the level of representation. In I. Bretherton and E. Waters (Eds.), *Growing points in attachment theory and research. Monographs of the Society for Research in Child Development, 50*(1-2, Serial No. 209), 66–104.

Main, M., & Weston, D. R. (1981). The quality of the toddler's relationship to mother and to father: Related to conflict behavior and the readiness to establish new relationships. *Child Development, 52*, 932–40.

Malatesta-Magai, C. (1991). Development of emotion expression during infancy: General course and pattern of individual difference. In J. Garber and K. A. Dodge (Eds.), *The development of emotion regulation and dysregulation* (pp. 49-69). New York: Cambridge University Press.

Mallinckrodt, B., Gantt, D. L., & Coble, H. M. (1995). Attachment patterns in the psychotherapy relationship: Development of the Client Attachment to Therapist Scale. *Journal of Counseling Psychology, 42*, 307–17.

Mallinckrodt, B., King, J. L., & Coble, H. M. (1998). Family dysfunction, alexithymia, and client attachment to therapist. *Journal of Counseling Psychology, 45*, 497–504.

Mallinckrodt, B., Porter, M. J., & Kivlighan, D. M., Jr. (2005). Client attachment to therapist, depth of in-session exploration, and object relations in brief psychotherapy. *Psychotherapy: Theory, Research, Practice, Training, 42*, 85–100.

Marlatt, G. A. (1994). Addiction, mindfulness, and acceptance. In S. C. Hayes, N. S. Jacobson, V. M. Follette, and M. J. Dougher (Eds.), *Acceptance and change: Content and context in psychotherapy* (pp. 175–97). Reno, NV: Context Press.

Marlatt, G. A., & Gordon, J. R. (1985). *Relapse prevention: Maintenance strategies in the treatment of addictive behaviors*. New York: Guilford Press.

Martin, D. J., Garske, J. P., & Davis, M. K. (2000). Relation of the therapeutic alliance with outcome and other variables: A meta-analytic review. *Journal of Consulting and Clinical Psychology, 68*, 438–50.

Martin, J. R. (1997). Mindfulness: A proposed common factor. *Journal of Psychotherapy Integration, 7*, 291–312.

Marx, K., & Engels, F. (1848). *Communist manifesto.* New York: Penguin.

Masson, J. M. (Ed. and Trans.). (1985). *The complete letters of Sigmund Freud to Wilhelm Fliess, 1877–1904.* Cambridge, MA: Belknap Press of Harvard University Press.

Masuda, A., Hayes, S. C., Sackett, C. F., & Twohig, M. P. (2004). Cognitive defusion and self-relevant negative thoughts: Examining the impact of a ninety year old technique. *Behaviour Research and Therapy, 42*, 477–85.

McCallum, M., & Piper, W. E. (1990). The Psychological Mindedness Assessment Procedure. *Psychological Assessment: A Journal of Consulting and Clinical Psychology, 2*, 412–18.

—— (Eds.). (1997). *Psychological mindedness: A contemporary understanding.* Mahwah, NJ: Erlbaum.

Meins, E., Fernyhough, C., Fradley, E., & Tuckey, M. (2001). Rethinking maternal sensitivity: Mothers' comments on infants' mental processes predict security of attachment at 12 months. *Journal of Child Psychology and Psychiatry, 42*, 637–48.

Meins, E., Fernyhough, C., Russell, J., & Clark-Carter, D. (1998). Security of attachment as a predictor of symbolic and mentalising abilities: A longitudinal study. *Social Development, 7*, 1–24.

Meins, E., Fernyhough, C., Wainwright, R., Clark-Carter, D., Gupta, M. D., Fradley, E., & Tuckey, M. (2003). Pathways to understanding mind: Construct validity and predictive validity of maternal mind-mindedness. *Child Development, 74*, 1194–1211.

Meins, E., Fernyhough, C., Wainwright, R., Gupta, M. D., Fradley, E., & Tuckey, M. (2002). Maternal mind-mindedness and attachment security as predictors of theory of mind understanding. *Child Development, 73*, 1715–26.

Meltzoff, J., & Kornreich, M. (1970). *Research in psychotherapy.* New York: Atherton.

Mergenthaler, E., & Bucci, W. (1999). Linking verbal and nonverbal representations: Computer analysis of referential activity. *British Journal of Medical Psychology, 72*, 339–54.

Michels, R. (2000). The case history. *Journal of the American Psychoanalytic Association, 48*, 355–75.

Miller, A. L., Rathus, J. H., & Linehan, M. M. (2007). *Dialectical behavior therapy with suicidal adolescents.* New York: Guilford Press.

Modestin, J., Furrer, R., & Malti, T. (2004). Study on alexithymia in adult nonpatients. *Journal of Psychosomatic Research, 56*, 707–9.

Nathan, P. E., Stuart, S. P., & Dolan, S. L. (2000). Research on psychotherapy efficacy and effectiveness: Between Scylla and Charybdis? *Psychological Bulletin, 126*, 964–81.

Newman, D. L., Moffitt, T., Caspi, A., & Silva, P. A. (1998). Comorbid mental disorders: Implications for treatment and sample selection. *Journal of Abnormal Psychology, 107*, 305–11.

Nilsson, T., Svensson, M., Sandell, R., & Clinton, D. (2007). *Psychotherapy Research, 17*, 553–66.

Ogrodniczuk, J. S., Piper, W. E., Joyce, A. S., & McCallum, M. (2001). Investigating follow-up outcome change using hierarchical linear modeling. *Psychotherapy Research, 11*, 13–28.

Oldham, J. M., Skodol, A. E., Kellman, H. D., Hyler, S. E., Doidge, N., Rosnick, L., & Gallaher, P. E. (1995). Comorbidity of Axis I and Axis II disorders. *American Journal of Psychiatry, 152*, 571–78.

Oppenheim, D., & Koren-Karie, N. (2002). Mothers' insightfulness regarding their children's internal worlds: The capacity underlying secure child-mother relationships. *Infant Mental Health Journal, 23*, 593–605.

Oppenheim, D., Koren-Karie, N., & Sagi, A. (2001). Mothers' empathic understanding of their preschoolers' internal experience: Relations with early attachment. *International Journal of Behavioral Development, 25*, 16–26.

Orlinsky, D. E., & Howard, K. I. (1986). Process and outcome in psychotherapy. In S. L. Garfield and A. E. Bergin (Eds.), *Handbook of psychotherapy and behavior change* (Third ed., pp. 311–84). New York: Wiley.

Overall, J. E., & Gorham, D. R. (1962). The Brief Psychiatric Rating Scale. *Psychological Reports, 10*, 799–812.

Parish, M., & Eagle, M. N. (2003). Attachment to the therapist. *Psychoanalytic Psychology, 20*, 271–86.

Perls, F. S. (1969). *Gestalt therapy verbatim*. Moab, UT: Real People Press.

Peters, E. J., Hilsenroth, M. J., Eudell, E. M., Blagys, M. D., & Handler, L. (2006). Reliability and validity of the Social Cognition and Object Relations Scale in clinical use. *Psychotherapy Research, 16*, 606–14.

Pine, F. (1985). *Developmental theory and clinical process*. New Haven, CT: Yale University Press.

Piper, W. E., Joyce, A. S., McCallum, M., Azim, H. F., & Ogrodniczuk, J. S. (2002). Interaction of interpretive and supportive forms of psychotherapy and patient personality variables. In W. E. Piper, A. S. Joyce, M. McCallum, H. F. Azim, and J. S. Ogrodniczuk, *Interpretive and supportive psychotherapies: Matching therapy and patient personality* (pp. 91–120). Washington, DC: American Psychological Association.

Pole, N., & Jones, E. E. (1998). The talking cure revisited: Content analyses of a two-year psychodynamic psychotherapy. *Psychotherapy Research, 8*, 171–89.

Racker, H. (1968). *Transference and countertransference*. New York: International Universities Press.

Reik, T. (1948). *Listening with the third ear: The inner experience of a psychoanalyst*. Oxford: Farrar, Straus & Co.

Robins, C. J., Schmidt, H., III, & Linehan, M. M. (2004). Dialectical behavior therapy: Synthesizing radical acceptance with skillful means. In S. C. Hayes, V. M.

Follette, and M. M. Linehan (Eds.), *Mindfulness and acceptance: Expanding the cognitive-behavioral tradition* (pp. 30–44). New York: Guilford Press.

Rockland, L. H. (1992). *Supportive therapy for borderline patients: A psychodynamic approach*. New York: Guilford Press.

Roemer, L., & Orsillo, S. M. (2002). Expanding our conceptualization of and treatment for generalized anxiety disorder: Integrating mindfulness/acceptance-based approaches with existing cognitive-behavioral models. *Clinical Psychology: Science and Practice, 9*, 54–68.

——. (2003). Mindfulness: A promising intervention strategy in need of further study. *Clinical Psychology: Science and Practice, 10*, 172–78.

Rogawski, A. S. (1982). Current status of brief psychotherapy. *Bulletin of the Menninger Clinic, 46*, 331–51.

Rogers, C. R. (1957). The necessary and sufficient conditions of therapeutic personality change. *Journal of Consulting Psychology, 21*, 95–103.

——. (1959). A theory of therapy, personality, and interpersonal relationships, as developed in the client-centered framework. In S. Koch (Ed.), *Psychology: A study of a science* (Vol. 3, pp. 184–256). New York: McGraw-Hill.

——. (1980). *A way of being*. Boston: Houghton-Mifflin.

Rosegrant, J. (2005). The therapeutic effects of the free-associative state of consciousness. *Psychoanalytic Quarterly, 74*, 737–66.

Rosenfeld, H. (1964). On the psychopathology of narcissism: A clinical approach. *International Journal of Psycho-Analysis, 45*, 332–37.

Rosenthal, R., & Rubin, R. L. (1978). Interpersonal expectancy effects: The first 345 studies. *Behavioral and Brain Sciences, 3*, 377–86.

Rosenzweig, S. (1936). Some implicit common factors in diverse methods of psychotherapy. *American Journal of Orthopsychiatry, 6*, 412–15.

——. (1997). Letters by Freud on experimental psychodynamics. *American Psychologist, 52*, 571.

Roth, A., & Fonagy, P. (2005). *What works for whom? A critical review of psychotherapy research* (Second ed.). New York: Guilford Press.

Rotter, J. B. (1966). Generalized expectancies for internal versus external control of reinforcement. *Psychological Monographs: General and Applied, 80*, 1–28.

Rutter, M. (1985). Resilience in the face of adversity: Protective factors and resistance to psychiatric disorders. *British Journal of Psychiatry, 147*, 598–611.

——. (1987). Psychosocial resilience and protective mechanisms. *American Journal of Orthopsychiatry, 57*, 316–31.

Ryff, C. D. (1989). Happiness is everything, or is it? Explorations on the meaning of psychological well-being. *Journal of Personality and Social Psychology, 57*, 1069–81.

Safran, J. D., & Muran, J. C. (1996). The resolution of ruptures in the therapeutic alliance. *Journal of Consulting and Clinical Psychology, 64*, 447–58.

——. (2000). Resolving therapeutic alliance ruptures: Diversity and integration. *Journal of Clinical Psychology, 56*, 233–43.

Salmon, P. G., Santorelli, S. F., & Kabat-Zinn, J. (1998). Intervention elements in promoting adherence to mindfulness-based stress reduction programs in the clinical behavioral medicine setting. In S. A. Shumaker, E. B. Schron, J. K. Ockene, and W. L. Bee (Eds.), *Handbook of health behavior change* (Second ed., pp. 239–68). New York: Springer.

Sameroff, A. J. (1975). Transactional models in early social relations. *Human Development, 18*, 65–79.

Sameroff, A. J., & Chandler, M. J. (1975). Reproductive risk and the continuum of caretaking casualty. In F. D. Horowitz, E. M. Hetherington, S. Scarr-Salapatek, and G. M. Sigel (Eds.), *Review of child development research* (Vol. 4, pp. 187–244). Chicago: University of Chicago Press.

Santayana, G. (1905). *Reason in common sense: Volume one of The life of reason.* New York: Dover Publications, 1980.

Schafer, R. (1996). Authority, evidence, and knowledge in the psychoanalytic relationship. *Psychoanalytic Quarterly, 65*, 236–53.

Scheel, K. R. (2000). The empirical basis of dialectical behavior therapy: Summary, critique, and implications. *Clinical Psychology: Science and Practice, 7*, 68–86.

Schneider, C. (2004). *The development of the child psychotherapy Q-set.* Doctoral dissertation, University of California, Berkeley, 2004. *Dissertation Abstracts International, 65*(2-B), 1039.

Schneider, C., & Jones, E. E. (2004). *Child Psychotherapy Q-Set coding manual.* Unpublished manuscript, University of California, Berkeley.

Schneider, C., Pruetzel-Thomas, A., & Midgley, N. (in press). Discovering new ways of seeing and speaking about psychotherapy process: The Child Psychotherapy Q-Set. In N. Midgley, J. Anderson, E. Grainger, T. Nesic-Vuckovic, and C. Urwin (Eds.), *Child psychotherapy and research: New approaches, emerging findings.* New York: Routledge.

Schore, A. N. (2006, June). *Neurobiology and attachment theory in psychotherapy: Psychotherapy for the 21st century.* Workshop presented by PsyBC, Mount Sinai Medical Center, New York.

Schuengel, C., Bakermans-Kranenburg, M. J., & van IJzendoorn, M. H. (1999). Attachment and loss: Frightening maternal behavior linking unresolved loss and disorganized infant attachment. *Journal of Consulting and Clinical Psychology, 67*, 54–63.

Segal, H. (1957). Notes on symbol formation. *International Journal of Psycho-Analysis, 38*, 391–97.

Segal, Z. V., Williams, J. M. G., & Teasdale, J. D. (2002). *Mindfulness-based cognitive therapy for depression: A new approach to preventing relapse.* New York: Guilford Press.

Seligman, S. (1991). Conceptual and methodological issues in the study of internal representation: A commentary on Infant Mental Health Journal, volume 10.3. *Infant Mental Health Journal, 12*, 126–29.

Seligman, M. E. (1995). The effectiveness of psychotherapy. *American Psychologist, 50*, 965–74.

Shakespeare, W. (2004). *Macbeth.* New York: W. W. Norton.

Shapiro, D. A., & Shapiro, D. (1982). Meta-analysis of comparative therapy outcome studies: A republication and refinement. *Psychological Bulletin, 92*, 581–604.

Shapiro, S. L., & Schwartz, G. E. R. (1999). Intentional systemic mindfulness: An integrative model for self-regulation and health. *Advances in Mind-Body Medicine, 15*, 128–34.

Shea, M., Widiger, T., & Klein, M. (1992). Comorbidity of personality disorders and depression: Implications for treatment. *Journal of Consulting and Clinical Psychology, 60*, 857–68.

Shea, M. T., Elkin, I., Imber, S. D., Sotsky, S. M., Watkins, J. T., Collins, J. F., Pilkonis, P. A., Beckham, E., Glass, D. R., Dolan, R. T., & Parloff, M. (1992). Course of depressive symptoms over follow-up: Findings from the National Institute of Mental Health Treatment of Depression Collaborative Research Program. *Archives of General Psychiatry, 49*, 782–87.

Shedler, J. (2002). A new language for psychoanalytic diagnosis. *Journal of the American Psychoanalytic Association, 50*, 429–56.

Shedler, J., & Westen, D. (1998). Refining the measurement of Axis II: A Q-sort procedure for assessing personality pathology. *Assessment, 5*, 333–53.

Shill, M. A., & Lumley, M. A. (2002). The Psychological Mindedness Scale: Factor structure, convergent validity and gender in a non-psychiatric sample. *Psychology and Psychotherapy: Theory, Research, and Practice, 75*, 131–50.

Shirk, S. R., & Karver, M. (2003). Prediction of treatment outcome from relationship variables in child and adolescent therapy: A meta-analytic review. *Journal of Consulting and Clinical Psychology, 71*, 452–64.

Sifneos, P. E. (1973). The prevalence of alexithymic characteristics in psychosomatic patients. *Psychotherapy and Psychosomatics, 22*, 255–62.

Silverstein, L. B., Auerbach, C. F., & Levant, R. F. (2006). Using qualitative research to strengthen clinical practice. *Professional Psychology: Research and Practice, 37*, 351–58.

Slade, A. (2005). Parental reflective functioning: An introduction. *Attachment and Human Development, 7*, 269–81.

Slade, A., Bernbach, E., Grienenberger, J., Levy, D., & Locker, A. (2004). *Addendum to Fonagy, Target, Steele, & Steele reflective functioning scoring manual for use with the Parent Development Interview*. Unpublished manuscript, The City College and Graduate Center of the City University of New York.

Slade, A., Grienenberger, J., Bernbach, E., Levy, D., & Locker, A. (2005). Maternal reflective functioning, attachment, and the transmission gap: A preliminary study. *Attachment and Human Development, 7*, 283–98.

Slade, A., Sadler, L. S., & Mayes, L. C. (2005). Minding the baby: Enhancing parental reflective functioning in a nursing/mental health home visiting program. In L. J. Berlin, Y. Ziv, L. Amaya-Jackson, and M. T. Greenberg (Eds.), *Enhancing early attachments: Theory, research, intervention, and policy* (pp. 152–77). New York: Guilford Press.

Smith, M. L., & Glass, G. V. (1977). Meta-analysis of psychotherapy outcome studies. *American Psychologist, 32*, 752–60.

Smith, M. L., Glass, G. V., & Miller, T. I. (1980). *The benefits of psychotherapy*. Baltimore: Johns Hopkins University Press.

Solomon, J., & George, C. (1999). The place of disorganization in attachment theory: Linking classic observations with contemporary findings. In J. Solomon and C. George (Eds.), *Attachment disorganization* (pp. 3–32). New York: Guilford Press.
Solomon, J., George, C., & De Jong, A. (1995). Children classified as controlling at age six: Evidence of disorganized representational strategies and aggression at home and at school. *Development and Psychopathology, 7*, 447–63.
Speca, M., Carlson, L. E., Goodey, E., & Angen, M. (2000). A randomized, wait-list controlled clinical trial: The effect of a mindfulness meditation-based stress reduction program on mood and symptoms of stress in cancer outpatients. *Psychosomatic Medicine, 62*, 613–22.
SPSS® for Windows (2006). Release 15.0.0. Chicago: SPSS Inc.
Steele, H., & Steele, M. (in press). Reflecting on reflective functioning. *Psychoanalytic Inquiry.*
Sterba, R. (1934). The fate of the ego in analytic therapy. *International Journal of Psycho-Analysis, 15*, 117–26.
Stern, D. B. (2006, April). *On having to find what you don't know how to look for*. Paper presented at the meeting of the Psychoanalytic Association of the Westchester Center for the Study of Psychotherapy and Psychoanalysis, Rye, New York.
Stern, D. N., Sander, L. W., Nahum, J. P., Harrison, A. M., Lyons-Ruth, K., Morgan, A. C., Bruschweiler-Stern, N., & Tronick, E. Z. (1998). Non-interpretive mechanisms in psychoanalytic therapy: The "something more" than interpretation. *International Journal of Psycho-Analysis, 79*, 903–21.
Stevens, S. E., Hynan, M. T., & Allen, M. (2000). A meta-analysis of common factor and specific treatment effects across the outcome domains of the phase model of psychotherapy. *Clinical Psychology: Science and Practice, 7*, 273–90.
Stiles, W. B., Shapiro, D. A., & Elliott, R. (1986). Are all psychotherapies equivalent? *American Psychologist, 41*, 165–80.
Strauss, A. L., & Corbin, J. (1998). *Basics of qualitative research: Techniques and procedures for developing grounded theory* (Second ed.). Thousand Oaks, CA: Sage.
Stricker, G., & Gooen-Piels, J. (2004). Projective assessment of object relations. In M. J. Hilsenroth and D. L. Segal (Eds.), *Handbook of psychological assessment: Vol. 2 Personality assessment* (pp. 449–65). Hoboken, NJ: Wiley.
Strupp, H. H. (1988). What is therapeutic change? *Journal of Cognitive Psychotherapy, 2*, 75–82.
Strupp, H. H., & Hadley, S. W. (1979). Specific vs non-specific factors in psychotherapy: A controlled study of outcome. *Archives of General Psychiatry, 36*, 1125–36.
Stuart, G. L., Treat, T. A., & Wade, W. A. (2000). Effectiveness of an empirically based treatment for panic disorder delivered in a service clinic setting: 1-year follow-up. *Journal of Consulting and Clinical Psychology, 68*, 506–12.
Tallman, K., & Bohart, A. (1999). The client as a common factor: Clients as self-healers. In M. Hubble, B. Duncan, and S. Miller (Eds.), *The heart and soul of change: What works in therapy* (pp. 91–131). Washington, DC: American Psychological Association.

Target, M., & Fonagy, P. (1994a). The efficacy of psychoanalysis for children: Developmental considerations. *Journal of the American Academy of Child and Adolescent Psychiatry, 33*, 1134–44.

——. (1994b). The efficacy of psychoanalysis for children with emotional disorders. *Journal of the American Academy of Child and Adolescent Psychiatry, 33*, 361–71.

——. (1996). Playing with reality: II. The development of psychic reality from a theoretical perspective. *International Journal of Psycho-Analysis, 77*, 459–79.

Task Force on Psychological Intervention Guidelines. (1995). *Template for developing guidelines: Interventions for mental disorders and psychosocial aspects of physical disorders.* Washington, DC: American Psychological Association.

Taylor, G. J. (1995). Psychoanalysis and empirical research: The example of patients who lack psychological mindedness. *Journal of the American Academy of Psychoanalysis, 23*, 263–81.

Teasdale, J. D. (1999). Metacognition, mindfulness and the modification of mood disorders. *Clinical Psychology and Psychotherapy, 6*, 146-155.

Teasdale, J. D., Moore, R. G., Hayhurst, H., Pope, M., Williams, S., & Segal, Z. V. (2002). Metacognitive awareness and prevention of relapse in depression: Empirical evidence. *Journal of Consulting and Clinical Psychology, 70*, 275–87.

Teasdale, J. D., Segal, Z. V., & Williams, J. M. G. (1995). How does cognitive therapy prevent depressive relapse and why should attentional control (mindfulness) training help? *Behavior Research and Therapy, 33*, 25–40.

Teasdale, J. D., Segal, Z. V., Williams, J. M. G., Ridgeway, V. A., Soulsby, J. M., & Lau, M. A. (2000). Prevention of relapse/recurrence in major depression by mindfulness-based cognitive therapy. *Journal of Consulting and Clinical Psychology, 68*, 615–23.

Thase, M. E. (2002). Studying new antidepressants: If there were a light at the end of the tunnel, could we see it? *Journal of Clinical Psychiatry, 63* (Suppl. 2), 24–28.

Tolor, A., & Reznikoff, M. (1960). A new approach to insight: A preliminary report. *Journal of Nervous and Mental Disease, 130*, 286–96.

Treurniet, N. (1993). What is psychoanalysis now? *International Journal of Psycho-Analysis, 74*, 873–91.

Tronick, E. Z., Als, H., Adamson, L., Wise, S., & Brazelton, T. B. (1978). The infant's response to entrapment between contradictory messages in face-to-face interaction. *Journal of Child Psychiatry, 17*, 1–13.

Tronick, E. Z., Bruschweiler-Stern, N., Harrison, A. M., Lyons-Ruth, K., Morgan, A. C., Nahum, J. P., Sander, L., & Stern, D. N. (1998). Dyadically expanded states of consciousness and the process of therapeutic change. *Infant Mental Health Journal, 19*, 290–99.

Trudeau, K. J., & Reich, R. (1995). Correlates of psychological mindedness. *Personality and Individual Differences, 19*, 699–704.

Truman, S., Levy, D., & Mayes, L. (in press). Reflective functioning as mediator between drug use, parenting stress, and child behavior. *Attachment and Human Development.*

Tuckett, D. (1993). Some thoughts on the presentation and discussion of the clinical material of psychoanalysis. *International Journal of Psycho-Analysis, 74*, 1175–88.

Tyrrell, C. L., Dozier, M., Teague, G. B., & Fallot, R. D. (1999). Effective treatment relationships for persons with serious psychiatric disorders: The importance of attachment states of mind. *Journal of Consulting and Clinical Psychology, 67*, 725–33.

Valbak, K. (2004). Suitability for psychoanalytic psychotherapy: A review. *Acta Psychiatrica Scandinavica, 109*, 164–78.

van IJzendoorn, M. H. (1995). Adult attachment representations, parental responsiveness, and infant attachment: A meta-analysis on the predictive validity of the Adult Attachment Interview. *Psychological Bulletin, 117*, 387–403.

Vygotsky, L. (1978). *Mind in society: The development of higher psychological processes*. Cambridge, MA: Harvard University Press.

Walach, H., Buchheld, N., Buttenmüller, V., Kleinknecht, N., & Schmidt, S. (2006). Measuring mindfulness—The Freiburg Mindfulness Inventory (FMI). *Personality and Individual Differences, 40*, 1543–55.

Wallerstein, R. S. (1989). The psychotherapy research project of the Menninger Foundation: An overview. *Journal of Consulting and Clinical Psychology, 57*, 195–205.

Wallerstein, R. S., & Robbins, L. L. (1956). The Psychotherapy Research Project of the Menninger Foundation. IV. Concepts. *Bulletin of the Menninger Clinic, 20*, 239–62.

Wampold, B. E. (2001). *The great psychotherapy debate: Models, methods, and findings*. Mahwah, NJ: Erlbaum.

———. (2005). Establishing specificity in psychotherapy scientifically: Design and evidence issues. *Clinical Psychology: Science and Practice, 12*, 194–97.

Wampold, B. E., & Brown, G. S. (2005). Estimating variability in outcomes attributable to therapists: A naturalistic study of outcomes in managed care. *Journal of Consulting and Clinical Psychology, 73*, 914–23.

Wampold, B. E., Mondin, G. W., Moody, M., Stich, F., Benson, K., & Ahn, H. (1997). A meta-analysis of outcome studies comparing bona fide psychotherapies: Empirically, "all must have prizes." *Psychological Bulletin, 122*, 203–15.

Waters, E., & Deane, K. E. (1985). Defining and assessing individual differences in attachment relationships: Q-methodology and the organization of behavior in infancy and early childhood. In I. Bretherton and E. Waters (Eds.), *Growing points in attachment theory and research. Monographs of the Society for Research in Child Development, 50*(1-2, Serial No. 209), 41–65.

Waters, E., Merrick, S., Treboux, D., Crowell, J., & Albersheim, L. (2000). Attachment security in infancy and early adulthood: A twenty-year longitudinal study. *Child Development, 71*, 684–89.

Weinberger, J. (1995). Common factors aren't so common: The common factors dilemma. *Clinical Psychology: Science and Practice, 2*, 45–69.

———. (2002). Short paper, large impact: Rosenzweig's influence on the common factors movement. *Journal of Psychotherapy Integration, 12*, 67–76.

Weinberger, J., & Eig, A. (1999). Expectancies: The ignored common factor in psychotherapy. In I. Kirsch (Ed.), *How expectancies shape experience* (pp. 357–82). Washington, DC: American Psychological Association.

Weinfield, N. S., Sroufe, L. A., Egeland, B., & Carlson, E. A. (1999). The nature of individual differences in infant-caregiver attachment. In J. Cassidy and P. R. Shaver (Eds.), *Handbook of attachment: Theory, research, and clinical applications* (pp. 68–88). New York: Guilford Press.

Wells, A. (1999). A cognitive model of generalized anxiety disorder. *Behavior Modification, 23*, 526–55.

———. (2002). GAD, metacognition, and mindfulness: An information processing analysis. *Clinical Psychology: Science and Practice, 9*, 95–100.

Werman, D. S. (1979). Chance, ambiguity, and psychological mindedness. *Psychoanalytic Quarterly, 48*, 107–15.

Westen, D. (1990). Towards a revised theory of borderline object relations: Contributions of empirical research. *International Journal of Psycho-Analysis, 71*, 661–93.

———. (1991a). Clinical assessment of object relations using the TAT. *Journal of Personality Assessment, 56*, 56–74.

———. (1991b). Social cognition and object relations. *Psychological Bulletin, 109*, 429–55.

———. (1993). *Social cognition and object relations scale: Q-sort and TAT data (SCORS-Q)* (Rev. ed.). Unpublished manuscript, Harvard University Medical School, Cambridge, Massachusetts.

———. (1995). *Social Cognition and Object Relations Scale—Global Ratings (SCORS-G)*. Unpublished manuscript, Harvard University Medical School, Cambridge, Massachusetts.

Westen, D., Nakash, O., Thomas, C., & Bradley, R. (2006). Clinical assessment of attachment patterns and personality disorder in adolescents and adults. *Journal of Consulting and Clinical Psychology, 74*, 1065–85.

Westen, D., Novotny, C. M., & Thompson-Brenner, H. (2004a). The empirical status of empirically supported psychotherapies: Assumptions, findings, and reporting in controlled clinical trials. *Psychological Bulletin, 130*, 631–63.

———. (2004b). The next generation of psychotherapy research: Reply to Ablon and Marci (2004), Goldfried and Eubanks-Carter (2004), and Haaga (2004). *Psychological Bulletin, 130*, 677–83.

Westen, D., & Shedler, J. (1999a). Revising and assessing Axis II: I. Developing a clinically and empirically valid assessment method. *American Journal of Psychiatry, 156*, 258–72.

———. (1999b). Revising and assessing Axis II: II. Toward an empirically based and clinically useful classification of personality disorders. *American Journal of Psychiatry, 156*, 273–85.

———. (2000). A prototype matching approach to personality disorders: Toward DSM-V. *Journal of Personality Disorders, 14*, 109–26.

Whitham, J. C., Gerald, M. S., & Maestripieri, D. (2007). Intended receivers and functional significance of grunt and girney vocalizations in free-ranging female rhesus macaques. *Ethology, 113*, 862–74.

Wilson, G. T. (1999). Rapid response to cognitive behavior therapy. *Clinical Psychology: Science and Practice, 6*, 289–92.

Winnicott, D. W. (1956). On transference. *International Journal of Psycho-Analysis, 37*, 386–88.

———. (1960). The theory of the parent-infant relationship. *International Journal of Psycho-Analysis, 41*, 585–95.

———. (1965). *The maturational processes and the facilitating environment: Studies in the theory of emotional development*. New York: International Universities Press.

Wishy, B. (1968). *The child and the republic: The dawn of modern American child nurture*. Philadelphia: University of Pennsylvania Press.

Wolfson, A., & Sampson, H. (1976). A comparison of process notes and tape recordings: Implications for therapy research. *Archives of General Psychiatry, 33*, 558–63.

Wolitzky, D. L., & Reuben, R. (1974). Psychological-mindedness. *Journal of Clinical Psychology, 30*, 26–30.

Wolpe, J., & Rachman, S. (1960). Psychoanalytic "evidence": A critique based on Freud's case of little Hans. *Journal of Nervous and Mental Disease, 131*, 135–48.

Yalom, I. D., Houts, P. S., Zimerberg, S. M., & Rand, K. H. (1967). Prediction of improvement in group therapy: An exploratory study. *Archives of General Psychiatry, 17*, 159–68.

Yeomans, F. (2007, May). Questions concerning the randomized trial of schema-focused therapy vs. transference-focused psychotherapy [Letter to the editor]. *Archives of General Psychiatry, 64*, 609, 610.

Yeomans, F. E., Clarkin, J. F., & Kernberg, O. F. (2002). *A primer of transference-focused psychotherapy for the borderline patient*. Lanham, MD: Jason Aronson.

Yeomans, F. E., Selzer, M. A., & Clarkin, J. F. (1992). *Treating the borderline patient: A contract-based approach*. New York: Basic Books.

Young, J. E. (1994). *Cognitive therapy for personality disorders: A schema-focused approach* (Rev. ed.). Sarasota, FL: Professional Resource Press.

Young, J. E., Klosko, J., & Weishaar, M. E. (2003). *Schema therapy: A practitioner's guide*. New York: Guilford Press.

Zetzel, E. R. (1956). Current concepts of transference. *International Journal of Psycho-Analysis, 37*, 369–75.

Zimmerman, M., McDermut, W., & Mattia, J. (2000). Frequency of anxiety disorders in psychiatric outpatients with major depressive disorder. *American Journal of Psychiatry, 157*, 1337–40.

Author Index

Subject Index

About the Author

Geoff Goodman, PhD, is associate professor of psychology at Long Island University. He is also a licensed clinical and school psychologist with a private practice in Manhattan and New City and is certified by the American Board of Professional Psychology (ABPP). Goodman earned a PhD in clinical psychology from Northwestern University, and he completed a child clinical psychology internship at Babies Hospital, Columbia-Presbyterian Medical Center, a two-year postdoctoral fellowship in developmental research at Columbia University under Larry Aber, and a two-year postdoctoral fellowship in the research and treatment of borderline personality disorder under Frank Yeomans and Otto Kernberg.

Goodman was instructor of psychology in psychiatry at Cornell University Medical College from 1995 to 1998 and was assistant unit chief of the children's psychiatric inpatient unit. He also holds adjunct faculty positions at Columbia University and Weill Medical College of Cornell University, and he is an advanced candidate in the child and adult programs at the Psychoanalytic Training Institute of the New York Freudian Society. Goodman is the author of over a dozen articles on the development of psychopathology in high-risk infants, children, and adults and of *The Internal World and Attachment* (2002).

www.ingramcontent.com/pod-product-compliance
Ingram Content Group UK Ltd.
Pitfield, Milton Keynes, MK11 3LW, UK
UKHW012035150926
475560UK00001B/24

9 780765 705389